Linguistics

Linguistics
An Introduction

William B. McGregor

continuum

Continuum International Publishing Group

The Tower Building   80 Maiden Lane, Suite 704
11 York Road   New York
London SE1 7NX   NY 10038

British Library Cataloguing-in-Publication Data
A catalogue record for this book is available from the British Library.

ISBN: 978-1-8470-6366-3 (Hardback)
       978-1-8470-6367-0 (Paperback)

Library of Congress Cataloging-in-Publication Data
The Publisher has applied for CIP data.

Typeset by Newgen Imaging Systems Pvt Ltd, Chennai, India
Printed and bound in Great Britain by Antony Rowe, Wiltshire

Contents

Part III LANGUAGE: UNIFORMITY AND DIVERSITY

List of Figures

List of Maps

List of Tables

Preface

My intention in writing this book to provide a basic introduction to modern linguistics that conveys an idea of the scope of the subject, and a feeling for the excitement of doing linguistics – the excitement of finding out about language and languages, including your own. I hope it will stimulate an **understanding** of the subject, rather than rote memorization of facts. I would also like to convey some appreciation of the reasons why linguists do what they do, and for the approaches and methods they adopt in studying languages. The third thing I would like to encourage is the development of your powers of observation, as well as your critical and creative faculties.

There are many excellent introductory textbooks on linguistics. Why another? My motivation lies mainly in dissatisfaction with particular aspects of the existing textbooks. None offers precisely what I desire in terms of manner of presentation, pedagogic philosophy, the range and type of information presented and theoretical stance. As a result of teaching an introductory course in linguistics in 2002, I was convinced of the need to write my own textbook to remedy these dissatisfactions.

Organization and presentation

Manner of presentation

This book employs a clear physical layout of information, presenting the material in brief, clear sentences and sections. Each chapter begins with a short abstract, a detailed table of contents, a list of the main goals of the chapter and a checklist of the major terms and concepts introduced. It concludes with a summary, a guide to further reading and a list of problems and issues for further thought.

The book is accompanied by a website containing additional information and a set of multiple-choice questions designed to test your understanding of the main points of each chapter. Address: http://www.continuumbooks.com/linguistics/mcgregor. Where particularly relevant, you will be directed to this website by the icon in the left or right margin.

This manner of organization should permit the book to be used not just as a textbook for a course in linguistics, but also by an independent reader wanting to find out about linguistics.

Pedagogic philosophy

My two major concerns are first to encourage and facilitate understanding linguistic concepts and how to use them, and secondly to promote observation of language. Thus the work aims to present not just 'facts' but also ways of dealing with them, ways of understanding them in relation to the broad issues of concern to linguistics. To this end, each chapter includes a set of questions for further thought (some quite challenging) and exercises. I believe that it is through attempting to solve simple – and difficult! – problems that students can learn and understand a subject, more so than by reflecting on larger philosophical issues.

You have to *understand* linguistics to do it. But at the same time, you have to *do it* to understand it: you have to get your hands dirty by engaging with data – grappling with data, attempting to understand it and relating it to what you already know (or think you know) about language or a language. Until you begin doing both of these, it is pointless, in my opinion, to dwell on the philosophical issues surrounding the subject, as fascinating as they may be. A part of what is especially attractive about linguistics is that there is still a lot to learn about every one of the roughly 7000 languages spoken in the world today. Even a student new to the subject can, if they are attentive to speech around them, learn something new (or not widely known) about their own language. This I know, having seen some nice examples from students in past courses.

Not only do doing and understanding go together, but a third component is essential, namely the 'facts', the knowledge about language and languages. Notice that I said in the first paragraph of this section that my aim was to present '**not just** "facts"'; I didn't say or suggest that facts are unimportant or uninteresting! To the contrary, the 'facts' are extremely interesting, and to ignore them would be suicidal for a linguist, as it would be for any scientist or researcher. Some chapters rely rather more heavily on facts than others.

Another aspect of understanding linguistics to see it in a historical perspective: part of understanding why linguistics is as it is, and why linguists do things the way they do, requires and appreciation of the intellectual traditions of the subject. The introductory chapter contains a section presenting modern linguistics from a broad historical perspective; it also contains an exercise directing students to find out about particular linguists. The website for the book extends on these by presenting a brief overview of the history of the subject.

Range and type of information

Many textbooks focus almost exclusively on one language, English. This book also uses many examples from English, presuming that anyone who can read it will have sufficient knowledge of the language to permit it to be used as a foundation on which an understanding of concepts and arguments can be constructed. However, numerous examples are given from other languages, many 'exotic' and/or endangered, including languages I have first-hand experience of myself. Partly this is a statement that other languages are as important as English to linguistics, and indeed are crucial to the subject. These examples are also intended to encourage you to try to understand and appreciate the ways other languages do things, which can be very different to the way English does things.

Theoretical framework

Modern introductory textbooks tend either to specifically acknowledge no particular theoretical framework, purporting to be either atheoretical or catholic in orientation, or to adopt the dominant theoretical framework in linguistics, that is, generative grammar (see §1.5). Almost no introductory textbook presents linguistics from any of the many alternative perspectives. For these other perspectives one must go to more advanced textbooks on specific topics. This book is intended to fill the lacuna, and present beginning linguistics from an alternative perspective, specifically one in which meaning and use play absolutely central roles. While I have my own minority theoretical perspective, I do not attempt to present or argue it here; rather I stand back from it, and adopt a more general stance that includes many theories within the so-called functionalist and cognitivist domains. Needless to say, not all practitioners in these theories will agree with everything I say.

There are other reasons why I believe it is unhelpful to adopt a too non-partisan approach in an introductory text. It is important for beginning students to get the feel for working and thinking within one approach. This has the advantage of permitting them to go more deeply into a topic and gain some 'hands-on' experience in doing things according to that approach. On the other hand, presentation of theoretical variety – perhaps chaos – tends to leave students bewildered on the one hand, and on the other, frustrated with the sketchy treatment of topics. The typical unfortunate result is that they acquire no usable skills.

Structure of the book

Aside from Chapter 1, *Introduction*, which sets the scene for the book, this book is divided into three parts. Part I, consisting of Chapters 2–6, focuses on the structure and system of human languages. It presents a number of central notions of modern linguistics that are essential to an understanding of the subject, both in the remainder of the book and in subsequent courses in linguistics. These chapters are fairly demanding on understanding, and you are likely to find them fairly heavy going.

It is perfectly normal for beginning students to feel lost in the first few weeks of their introductory linguistics course: it takes time to get the 'feel' of what linguistics is all about, and to appreciate the unfamiliar ways of thinking about language. Things should start to become clearer in the second month; if not, you should consult your lecturer or the tutor.

Part II, *Language: a human phenomenon*, consists of Chapters 7–10. These chapters look beyond the structure of individual languages, and situate human language and languages in the wider contexts of human life and culture, including other forms of communication and other languages. The remaining three chapters, Chapters 11–13, make up Part III, *Language: uniformity and diversity*. These chapters focus on variation in languages: with the cross-linguistic range of variation in language structures, language change over time and the linguistic diversity of the world. You should find Parts II and III easier going conceptually, though perhaps more taxing on memory.

The Parts II and III are relatively independent, and may be read or taught in either order. Both, however, presume knowledge and understanding of some of the basic notions presented in Part I. In particular, notions of the phoneme and morpheme, are presumed in a number of places. With a little additional introductory material, or explanation of concepts as encountered, it would be possible to present Part II prior to Part I; Part III, however, demands more of the notions developed in Part I, and would be unsatisfactory prior to Part I. I teach, and have placed, Part II after Part I largely for purposes of variety, and as respite from the rather heavy-going Part I.

Guide for the student

This book contains far too much material to be covered in a standard one-semester introductory course on linguistics. Your lecturer will be selective in the range of chapters covered and the material from each chapter that is used. Nevertheless, my advice is to read the entire book, including the chapters not covered in your course, and the material on the accompanying website. You should of course focus more on the chapters covered in your course – but do read the others. They provide valuable additional information and perspectives on the subject.

I advise students to read and attempt to understand each chapter before the lecture on that topic. But don't get too bogged down on details. If you don't understand something after making an honest attempt at it, move on, keep reading. The lectures will present the fundamental ideas of each chapter in a different medium, orally, providing you with another chance to understand the topic.

Your lecturer or tutor can also be consulted on points you have difficulty with. But you should first make a serious attempt to understand and attempt to formulate precise questions. Your lecturer or tutor will be able to answer a specific question, though they will be hard-pushed to help you if you can't formulate a question. It is very hard to help if you can only say you don't understand! I always advise my students to formulate at least one question about each chapter to ask me or the tutor prior to the lecture or tutorial.

Here is my advice on how to attack each chapter. Begin by examining the preliminary materials, which give an idea of the scope, contents, goals and organization of ideas in the chapter; the list of key terms highlights concepts to take particular notice of as you read the body of the chapter. With this background, read the chapter through. I would recommend first reading it rapidly, and then to go back and read it more carefully, focusing in particular on the places where you had difficulties in understanding.

After you finish reading a chapter, go back over the list of key terms, and check that they now make sense to you. If they don't, review that part of the text, and refresh your memory and understanding.

I also advise doing this after the lecture as well: that is, review what you have read. At this point, that is, after the lecture, try to summarize the chapter in a few sentences, in your own words. Compare your summary with the summary included at the end of the chapter.

> Can you answer the basic question: what is the chapter about?

Each chapter, as mentioned above, contains a number of exercises and questions for further thought. There are too many for you to complete each week. You will need to be selective – read each question through, and select the ones that you find most interesting and attempt them first. (Don't just start at the first, and go until you run out of steam or time.) Answers are not provided for these questions – it is just too tempting to look at an answer before thinking a problem through.

> One of the skills that you need to learn at university is how to be selective in what you do and think carefully about, and how to make good choices in your selections. This is a skill that you should attempt to develop over time: don't expect it to come immediately and naturally to you. One of the ways you can develop the skill is by comparing your summary of the chapter with the summary in the book. Have you focused on a minor issue? Have you identified all of the major points identified in the chapter summary?

A set of multiple-choice questions can be found on the website for the book. The idea of these is to test your understanding of the main ideas of each chapter. You should also attempt these each week to keep track of your progress. Feedback is provided at the completion of the test, when you submit your responses. Your overall performance is indicated, and specific comments are provided on each of the questions you got wrong.

What else should you read? Each chapter contains a list of further readings on the topics covered. No one expects you to read all of these things: that would take you much longer than the course. The references are mentioned for your information, for you to follow up if you are especially interested in some topic. (Here again you need to develop your skills in selectivity.)

This could as well be after the course, perhaps even at a later time in your linguistic studies. Glancing over this section of the chapter may also alert you to some issues not dealt with in the text, or only briefly dealt with.

> Sometimes reading another treatment of a topic will assist your understanding of it; but if you have difficulty in understanding something, take the advice given above, rather than attempt to read about it in a dozen different books – as likely as not you will still not understand!

I am certainly not discouraging you from reading. What I do discourage is reading as a replacement to thinking. Reading should be, rather, an enhancement to your thinking. Read as much additional material as you can find the time for, focusing in particular on those issues that most interest you.

I am sometimes asked, 'What do I need to remember?' This is a difficult question to answer. As indicated above, I consider understanding the subject more important than rote memorization of facts. Understanding, however, also involves memory, and if you understand a particular point, you will want to remember the general drift of ideas leading up to it, even if you don't remember every tiny detail. The general patterns are much more important to remember than the details; specific minor details you can find by referring to this or some other book. But think about it! The less you remember, the more you need to rely on finding or re-finding the information. Imagine if every time you added 2 and 3 you had to look up your mathematical tables or work it out from first principles or on your fingers. This would be more than a little impractical when you go shopping.

> My advice is that you should remember the main concepts – i.e. both the terms and their meanings – given at the beginning of each chapter. These are notions that are likely to be used in later chapters, lectures and other courses. If you have to look them up every time you encounter them your understanding will be seriously impaired.

Århus, April 2008

Acknowledgements

For useful comments on draft chapters I thank Peter Bakker, Jan Rijkhoff, Alan Rumsey, Jean-Christophe Verstraete and six anonymous referees; they have provided much useful advice, and prevented me making a number of mistakes. I alone am responsible for any remaining errors of fact or interpretation. I would have liked to include more additional topics and themes that they suggested, but limitations of space precluded doing so. Thanks also to the classes of 2004 (*Grundkursus*), 2005, 2006 and 2007 (*At forstå lingvistik*) at Aarhus University for their helpful input as end-users.

Many people have contributed to this book by providing information on languages they have expert knowledge of, including: Paula Andersson, Peter Bakker, John Bowden, Hilary Chappell, G. Tucker Childs, Ann Elveberg, Nick Enfield, Michael Fortescue, Yoko Fukuda, Gerd Haverling, Birgit Hellwig, Judit Horváth, Tine Larsen, Eva Lindström, Andy Pawley, Alan Rumsey, Johanna Seibt, Paul Sidwell, Tsunoda Tasaku and Hein van der Voort. Many thanks to them all. Aleksandr Kibrik kindly gave permission to use the Archi problem in Chapter 5.

The videos of ASL included on the accompanying website are courtesy of the National Center for Sign Language and Gestrures Resources at Boston University (directors Carol Neidle and Stan Sclaroff). Thanks also to the signer, Lana Cook, for permission to use this video, and Carol Neidle for useful assistance and advice. The phonetic font, DoulosSIL is used courtesy SIL International. Credits for graphical materials are given in the captions.

Thanks also to my editor at Continuum, Gurdeep Mattu, who has consistently and promptly provided helpful advice and assistance, and to Anders K. Madsen for constructing the accompanying website.

Abbreviations and Conventions Used in Examples

I have avoided using abbreviations as far as possible, in most cases restricting them to glosses in example sentences, and occasionally for cited forms of morphemes in the text. Just a few of the technical terms used in the text are abbreviated; these are not included in the list below, but can be found in the *Glossary* at the end of the book.

The following is a list of the main abbreviations used in the example sentences. Where possible they follow the recommendations of the *The Leipzig glossing rules: conventions for interlinear morpheme-by-morpheme glosses*, available online at http://www.eva.mpg.de/lingua/resources/glossing-rules.php. In a few cases an abbreviation has more than one different interpretations; it should be obvious from context which interpretation is intended.

ABS	absolutive (case of object and transitive subject)
ACC	accusative (object case)
ACT	active (case of active participant)
AdjP	adjectival phrase
AdvP	adverbial phrase
APP	applicative ('do with (something)')
AUX	auxiliary
C	clause; consonant
CL	classifier
COMP	complementiser (like *that* in *think that X*)
DAT	dative ('for')
DEC	declarative
DET	determiner
ERG	ergative (case of transitive subject)
FUT	future

GER	gerund
INACT	inactive (case of an inactive participant)
IND	indicative
INTER	interrogative word
IO	indirect object (e.g. recipient)
IRR	irrealis ('didn't or mightn't happen')
MAS	masculine (gender of nouns referring to things classified like male human beings)
N	noun, nominal
NEUT	neuter (gender of nouns referring to things)
NF	non-finite
NOM	nominative (case of transitive and intransitive subjects)
NP	noun phrase
NPST	non-past (present or future)
O	object (grammatical relation)
OBJ	object case form
P	phrase
PART	participial
PFV	perfective
PL	plural ('many')
POSS	possessive
PP	prepositional phrase; postpositional phrase
PROG	progressive
PRF	perfect
PRS	present
PST	past
REL	relative clause marker (e.g. *who* as in *the woman who saw it*)
RPST	recent/past
S	subject (grammatical relation)

SG	singular ('one')
SUB	subject case form
SUBJ	subjunctive ('it is hoped or wished that')
TR	transitive
V	verb; vowel
VOL	volitional ('to want to do something')
VP	verb phrase
1	first person ('I', 'we')
2	second person ('you')
3	third person ('he', 'she', 'it', 'they')
*	ungrammatical or unacceptable sentence in syntax; proto-form in historical linguistics
?	questionable expression
-	morpheme boundary
→	acting on
[ ]	phonetic representation
/ /	phonemic representation
< >	graphemic (written) representation

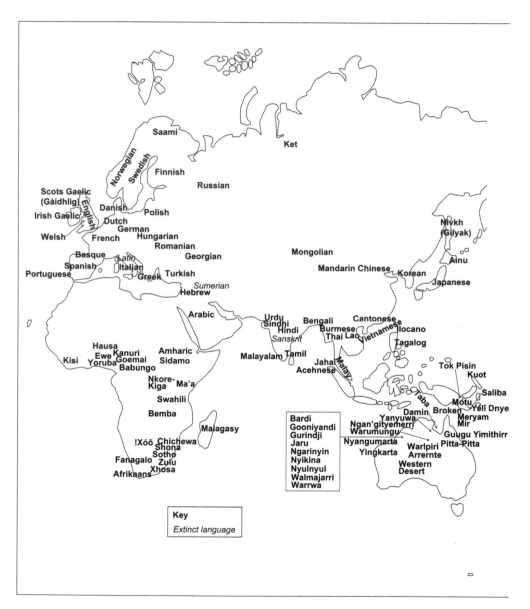

Map 1 Approximate homeland locations of main languages mentioned in this book.

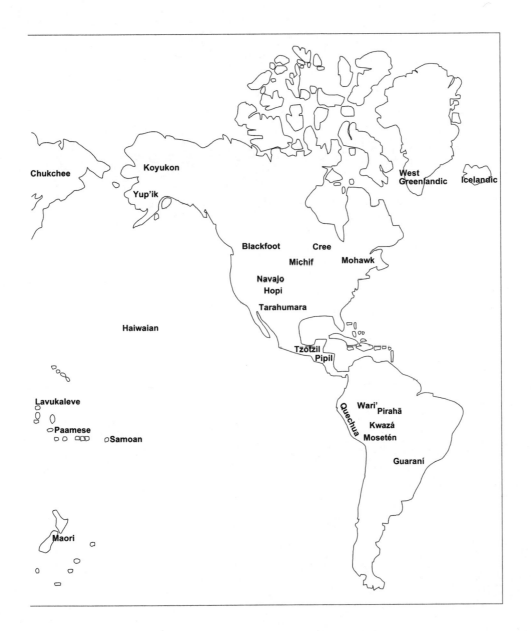

Introduction

1

In this chapter we introduce some fundamental concepts of linguistics, including the notion of the *sign*, and outline the major features of human language. We also present linguistics as a science, and overview its main concerns.

Chapter contents

Goals

The goals of the chapter are to:
- present linguistics as a science and outline the main concerns of the discipline;
- lay out the main orientations of modern linguistics, situating them in a historical perspective;
- introduce some fundamental concepts of modern linguistics;
- overview the main distinguishing features ('design features') of human languages;
- draw a distinction between speech and writing, and show that speech is primary; and
- introduce deaf sign languages as fully fledged human languages.

Key terms

arbitrariness	duality	productivity	speech
cultural transmission	formalism	reflexivity	structuralism
deaf sign languages	functionalism	Saussure	symbol
design features	icon	scientific method	syntagmatic relation
displacement	paradigmatic relation	sign	writing

1.1 What is linguistics?

David Crystal's *Dictionary of Linguistics and Phonetics* begins the entry for linguistics with the words '[t]he scientific study of **language**' (Crystal 1980/2003: 272). He goes on to say that it is also called *linguistic science*, and refers to it as an academic discipline. Ask any linguist what linguistics is and you are likely to be given a similar answer mentioning both its scientific character and its subject matter, language.

Linguistics as a science

What does it mean to say that linguistics is a science or scientific field of study? To begin with, it says something about the approach taken to the subject matter. A scientific approach to the study of language involves a critical and inquiring attitude, and refusal to accept uncritically, on faith, or on authority, ideas or ways of thinking about language. It strives for objectivity, for developing hypotheses and putting them to the test by confronting them with observations. This means that linguistics is empirically grounded: it is based on actual language data, including observations of language use by speakers, and their intuitions about their language.

Linguistics is thus descriptive rather than prescriptive: its primary goal is to describe languages as they are actually spoken, indicating what they are like and how they are used, rather than prescribe how they ought to be spoken. Many people are concerned about how their language ought to be spoken, as a glance in a newspaper is likely to reveal: people often comment on 'wrong' grammar or pronunciation that people (usually others!) use.[1] At school you may have learnt that you should say *That is the child whom the dog bit* and not *That is the child who the dog bit*. But in modern English (Indo-European, England)[2] most people say the latter, and few could use the school rule consistently and properly without consciously thinking about it. Linguistics is concerned with what people actually say, not with what they should say.

A scientific approach is not purely empirical in the sense of merely collecting observations. It involves formulation and testing of hypotheses and generalizations, as well as theory development, development of ways of understanding language. This calls for rigorous and explicit formulation of ideas, as well as rigour in testing them. Linguistics as a scientific endeavour is as much a theoretical enterprise as an empirical one: whatever observations one makes are useful and make sense only in relation to hypotheses and theories.

As a science, linguistics is concerned with developing theories that account for and explain the phenomena of language and language use. Doing linguistics is concerned with theory development and testing, and with making generalizations about language – with uncovering regularities and repeated general characteristics. **Exceptions** play a crucial role: they challenge the generalizations, and force the investigator to rethink matters, and refine or revise their ideas. We will see in this book places where exceptions loom large in scientific thinking about language, and have resulted in significant new developments.

An important skill to develop is the ability to recognize the significance of observed phenomena as exceptional or unexpected. Linguistics is a relatively new science, and it is possible, as mentioned in the Preface, for beginners to observe new things about their language (even as well studied a language as English), including things that challenge existing theories. While reading this book you should be constantly thinking about and observing the language in use around you, and linking your observations to the discussion and generalizations we make.

Linguistics is often regarded as a humanities (or arts) subject, though in many ways it straddles the boundaries between humanities and sciences, with a foot in both camps. Links to humanities include to language history and philosophy, as well as to ancient and modern 'language' subjects taught in universities, such as English, French (Indo-European, France), German (Indo-European, Germany), Ancient Greek (Indo-European, Greece), Sanskrit (Indo-European, India) and so on; links to social sciences include to sociology, psychology, anthropology and archaeology. But there are also links to the 'hard' sciences such as biology, physiology, physics and mathematics, most obviously in the production and perception of speech.

The human side of linguistics is as central as its scientific face. Language is a human artefact, and many types of linguistic research involve interaction between the linguist and other human beings, speakers of languages. Their work thus not infrequently confronts linguists with human considerations, such as provision of professional expertise or services.

The subject matter of linguistics

Being a scientific subject, linguistics is in principle concerned with all aspects of language. This immediately raises the question: What is language? The term has many senses. People talk of the language of bees, the language of the genetic code, the language of science, body language, computer language(s), the English language, the American language and so on. Here we use the term specifically in reference to natural human languages, such as French, Mandarin Chinese (Sino-Tibetan, Mainland China), Basque (Isolate, Spain and France) and Hausa (Afroasiatic, Nigeria). This is of course not a definition of the term; to provide one now would be premature, as it would presuppose much of the content of this book. In §1.3 we make a beginning by discussing some features that characterize human language and distinguish it from other communication systems, including those of other animals. The question is returned to a number of times in subsequent sections of the book, not always explicitly – so keep awake! By the time you have finished reading the book, you should have a clearer notion of what linguists mean by the terms *language* and *languages*, and an appreciation of some of the difficulties.

Perhaps the best way to begin is to shelve the terminological question, and outline the main branches of the subject. If you do a degree in linguistics, you are likely to study many of these branches, some of which will be covered in their own course. Each branch is touched on in this book, sometimes in its own chapter, sometimes in just a section or paragraph or two.

- **Phonetics** and **phonology** deal with the sounds of languages. Phonetics is concerned with the ways speech sounds are made, their nature (the physics of sound waves) and how they are perceived. Phonology is concerned with the ways sounds are patterned in a language, with those characteristics that are significant in the sound system of the language. These two branches are dealt with in Chapter 2.
- **Morphology** deals with the way the words of a language are structured, how they are made up of smaller meaningful parts. For example, *reads* is made up of *read* and the ending *s*, which tells you that the reading is being done by one person (not the speaker or hearer) at the present time or generally. Morphology is treated in Chapters 3 and 4.
- **Syntax** is concerned with the ways words go together to form sentences, and how the words are related to one another. For instance, *The boy reads comics* consists of a subject or doer of the action *the boy*, a verb representing an event *reads* and an object or patient of the action *comics*. Sometimes words go together to make up constructions of intermediate size – larger than words, but smaller than sentences. An example is *the boy* in our previous example. Syntax is the topic of Chapter 5. Syntax and morphology together make up the core of **grammar**.
- **Semantics** and **pragmatics** deal with meaning. Semantics is concerned with the aspects of meaning that are encoded by words and grammar. Pragmatics handles the aspects of meaning of an utterance that come from its use in a particular context. The sentence *Come again!* is made up of two words each of which has a meaning, as does the whole sentence (it is an instruction to the hearer to do something); these matters are the concern of semantics. But you can use this sentence in different ways to mean different things. If said when farewelling a visitor it could be interpreted as an invitation to return at a later time. In other contexts it could be interpreted as an expression of disbelief, or a request that the hearer repeat what they have just said. Such interpretations are the concern of pragmatics. Chapter 6 treats semantics and pragmatics.
- **Psycholinguistics** and **neurolinguistics** are concerned with the processes involved in language production (e.g. speaking and writing), comprehension (e.g. listening and reading) and acquisition. Psycholinguistics investigates the mental processes underlying language processing, while

neurolinguistics is biologically oriented, focusing on the brain's language processing activities. Psycholinguistics tends to adopt methods of psychology, neurolinguistics, medical methods and technology. These topics are treated in Chapters 8 and 9.

- **Typology** and **universals** are concerned with the range and limitations on structural variation among languages. Typology seeks to discover and account for the variation by classifying languages into types according to some structural feature (for instance, the order of subject, verb and object), and classifying linguistic structures according to their similarities and differences (e.g. whether possession is expressed by a 'have' verb, or a verb 'be at'). The study of language universals is concerned with identifying features common to all of the world's languages. These matters are the concern of Chapter 11.

- **Historical linguistics** studies how languages change over time. Languages never remain static for long; indeed they change rapidly. Historical linguistics has methods for working out what changes are likely to have happened over time to a language or group of languages. It is also concerned with establishing genetic relations amongst languages: that is, with showing that certain languages are related by having evolved from the same ancestor language. The comparative method is a technique devised for this purpose. Chapter 12 deals with historical linguistics.

- **Sociolinguistics** is concerned with language in its social context, with the relations between language and society. It explores the variation in languages associated with social phenomena such as the social group to which speakers and/or hearers belong (for instance, differences in speech according to class in Western societies). Other topics of interest in sociolinguistics are multilingualism, language choice (what motivates language choice in multilingual settings), attitudes to languages and language variation, and standard and non-standard varieties of a language. **Anthropological linguistics** has basically the same range of concerns as sociolinguistics, but takes inspiration more from anthropology than sociology, and usually deals with small-scale non-Western cultures. Sociolinguistics is dealt with mainly in Chapter 7.

- **Discourse analysis** examines stretches of language, both spoken and written, larger than the sentence. It attempts to find regularities in the formation of these stretches, and correlations with grammatical, phonological, lexical and semantic phenomena. Among the issues that have attracted interest are: how sentences are connected; how texts are made coherent; and the use of words like *well*, *like* and so on. **Conversation analysis** focuses attention on the properties of everyday conversation, including turn-taking (how conversation partners organize the exchange of speaker and hearer roles), negotiation of interactive expectations and goals, use of discourse markers and conversational coherence. We do not deal with discourse analysis in this book, although a chapter is included on the website for the book.

- **Evolutionary linguistics** is concerned with the origins of language, with how we came to speak. Perhaps the basic question is why are we the only species with language? Is language a part of our genetic make-up as human beings, or does biology merely permit us to speak? Some ideas about language origins and evolution are discussed in §10.3.

1.2 Fundamental concepts

The sign

One of the most important concepts of modern linguistics is the notion of the **sign**, a fundamental unit used in the representation and conveyance of information. The sign

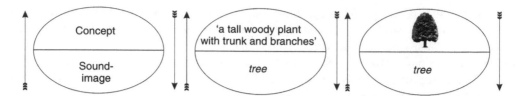

Figure 1.1 Saussure's conceptualization of the linguistic sign. Here 'sound-image' refers to 'form' (the idealized sound-shape of a word, ignoring variations in particular instances of production); 'concept' refers to 'meaning', illustrated here by means of an explanatory definition, and visually (see Saussure 1959/1974: 66–67). © 2009 William B. McGregor and his licensors. All rights reserved.

involves a pairing of a **form** (roughly, something perceivable) and a **meaning** (a mental notion or idea). Some examples of written (or graphic) signs are: ♂, meaning 'male'; €, meaning 'euro'; &, meaning 'and'; and 3 meaning 'three'.[3] A gesture such as the 'thumbs-up' is also a sign, since it pairs the hand-shape with a meaning like 'OK, right, go ahead'. Signs can also involve sound forms, that can be heard rather than seen, as in the case of spoken words, for example, the spoken words *ten* and *tree*.

The fundamental properties of the sign are illustrated in Figure 1.1, which is based on Ferdinand de Saussure's diagram of the word as a linguistic sign (see p. 8), exemplified by the English word *tree*.

Saussure likened the sign to a coin: just as both faces are essential for a coin to count as an object that can be used in economic transactions, so also are form and meaning both essential to the sign as a unit in information exchange. Without a meaning we have no sign: the letter *h* of the Latin alphabet has no meaning in written English words, and so is not a sign: it can no more be used in information conveyance than the image of a head on a coin can be used in a shop. Nor is a disembodied meaning or concept without a form a sign.

Relations between form and meaning in the sign

Depending on how the form and meaning of a sign are related we can talk of iconic signs and symbolic signs. A third type, indexical signs, is identified in §10.1.

Iconic signs

An **iconic sign** or **icon** is a sign that has a form resembling its meaning in some way: the form shows some characteristics of the corresponding concept. Figure 1.2 gives some examples. Notice that the form of an icon is never an exact representation of the meaning; it shows salient features in stylized ways, ignoring other features. Different forms can iconically represent the same concept by selecting different features of the concept. The first two icons, (a) and (b), represent the same concept, 'telephone', although (b) depicts only a single aspect

Figure 1.2 Some iconic signs. The forms of (a) and (b) visually depict silent characteristics of telephones, and thus iconically represent 'telephone'; (c) depicts characteristics of an hour glass in operation, and thus is used to indicate the passage of time as a computer processes data. (Note that (c) does not iconically represent time.)

Figure 1.3 Some symbolic signs. (a), the symbol for the mathematical operation of division in the English-speaking world, shows no likeness to the operation itself, and in Denmark represents instead subtraction. The cross in (b) indicates 'wrong, incorrect' when placed by a teacher next to an answer on a school test. This is a purely conventional link, and is often used in boxes on multiple-choice questions to indicate the correct option. (c) is used in comics to indicate that the words enclosed in it are representations of the thoughts of a character. The link between the graphic form and meaning is not based on any actual resemblance – thoughts do not look like (c) (although one might suggest a link via the notion that thoughts are fluffy things like clouds, to which (c) shows some similarity.)

of the concept, the receiver. Many manual gestures are iconic: holding up a hand with the digits spread out to represent the number 'five' is iconic.

Symbolic signs

A **symbolic sign** or symbol is a sign the form and meaning of which are related purely by convention, being established and acquired through repeated instances of use in communication: the form bears no apparent similarity to the meaning, nor is it naturally associated with it. Figure 1.3 gives some examples.

The line between symbols and icons is not clear-cut, and they are not really different types of sign. What is a symbol to one person might be an icon to another. To someone who knows only mobile phones, the signs in Figure 1.2 might appear completely arbitrary and inexplicable, established purely by convention. Iconic signs always involve some degree of conventionality and arbitrariness in the form–meaning link; they are not connected by necessity, and could be otherwise. Think of the equals sign =, which has a clear iconic basis, and was first used by the English mathematician Robert Recorde (1510–1558) with this in mind. Its orientation on the page is arbitrary, and some mathematicians of Recorde's time used the equally iconic ‖ .

Language as a sign system

The examples discussed in the previous sections illustrate non-linguistic signs. It was one of Saussure's important insights that human language is a system of signs. This means first that human language is made up of signs, and second that the signs interrelate and form a system; they do not exist in isolation from one another.

Nature of signs in human language

Symbolic signs in language

We have already said that the word *tree* is a sign, being constituted in speech by a **phonetic** (sound) form and in writing by an **orthographic** (written) form in association with a meaning. The same goes for the word for 'tree' in other languages: *qoqa* in Aymara (Aymaran, Peru), *icimuti* in Bemba (Niger-Congo, Zambia), *miistsís* in Blackfoot (Algonquian, Canada and USA), *træ* in Danish (Indo-European, Denmark), *tree* in English, *girili* in Gooniyandi (Bunuban, Australia), *fa* in Hungarian (Uralic, Hungary), *arbor* in Latin (Indo-European, Italy), *uhs* in Papago (Uto-Aztecan, USA) and *laau* in Samoan (Austronesian, Samoa). Clearly these word-signs are symbolic. There is no natural connection between the sound or orthographic forms and the meaning; each form is as good as another for expressing the meaning 'tree', none is in any way suggestive of the meaning (if you did not know the language you would not be able to guess the meaning if you heard the form), and there is little similarity among the various forms (except in the case of the two closely related languages Danish and English). Most words in human languages are symbols.

> It is often said that linguistic signs are typically 'arbitrary' (see also §1.3). This is a potentially misleading statement: it does not mean that 'anything goes', that a speaker is free to choose whatever form or meaning they like to associate together in a sign. Humpty Dumpty may have believed that he could: '"When I use a word," Humpty Dumpty said, in a rather scornful tone, "it means just what I choose it to mean – neither more nor less"' (Carroll 1899: 123). Clearly communication would be impossible with such anarchy. Arbitrariness refers to the non-necessary relation between the form and the meaning of a sign.

Iconic signs in language

There are exceptions. Some words are iconic. The phonetic forms of words like *woof-woof, cock-a-doodle-do, baa-baa, meow, ding-dong, pop* and *ping* are quite suggestive of the meanings, which are sounds, the sound made by dogs, roosters, sheep and so on. The spoken form is somewhat similar to the sound it represents; such words are **onomatopoeic**. (The written forms of these words, however, do not resemble the meanings.)

Many languages have onomatopoeic words for the characteristic calls of animals. These need not be exactly the same in different languages – remember that icons also involve conventional associations of form and meaning – though they are often similar. The noise made by a cat is *miau* in Hungarian (pronounced almost exactly as in English), *mjá* in Icelandic (Indo-European, Iceland), *nyao* in Japanese (Japanese, Japan), *miook* in Bulu (Niger-Congo, Cameroon), *mya:u(:)* in Hindi (Indo-European, India), *meu-meu* in Bengali (Indo-European, Bangladesh), *niaou* in Greek (Indo-European, Greece) and *ngeong* in Indonesian (Austronesian, Indonesia). No one would mistake these for the noise of a dog or horse. But we sometimes find no phonetic similarity in onomatopoeic forms: both *woof-woof* and *bow-wow* are onomatopoeic of the noise of a dog; they represent different sounds made by the same animal.

Young children often call a dog a *bow-wow*, and a sheep a *baa-baa*. In fact, in many languages we find words for at least a few animals (especially birds) that are identical with or similar to an onomatopoeic sign for their characteristic call. In Gooniyandi *minyawoo* is the word for 'cat'; the word for 'peewee, peewit, mudlark' is *diyadiya*, for 'galah' is *gilinygiliny* and for 'brolga' is *goorrarlga*. Anyone who has heard these birds will recognize the similarity to a characteristic call. We can regard these word-signs as iconic (they are not onomatopoeic since they denote animals not sounds).

A more complex example of iconicity in words is drawing out the pronunciation of the word *long* to *loooong* or *big* to *biiiig*. The increased length of the word represents increased size – that the thing is very long or big. Other languages allow similar things: in Gooniyandi you can lengthen *girabingarri* 'long' to *giraaabingarri* to mean 'very long' and *nyamani* 'big' to *nyaaamani* 'very big'. It is not the phonetic form of the words *loooong* or *giraaabingarri* that iconically represents the meaning 'long'. That meaning is associated with the word-forms *long* and *girabingarri* themselves. The iconicity comes in at a different level: the phonetic **difference** between *long* and *loooong* represents the meaning **difference** between 'long' and 'very long'. Here we have a sign with the form 'extra length word-form' and meaning 'very word-meaning'. This is why *teeny* can be lengthened to *teeeeeeny* in English, and *jiginya* 'small' to *jigiiiinya* 'really small'; the lengthened words obviously do not convey a sense of 'larger in size'.

Relations between linguistic signs

This brings us to the second aspect of language as a sign system, the notion of system: the notion that the signs of any human language interrelate to form a coherent whole. This happens on two dimensions, **syntagmatic** and **paradigmatic**.

Syntagmatic

In everyday speech and writing, linguistic signs occur in combination with other signs. Human beings often put together many signs to convey complex meanings; they are not restricted to producing single-sign utterances like one-year-old children and most animals. In speech, word-signs follow one another in order, even though the boundaries between them are fuzzy; in writing, they follow one another in a conventional spatial sequence (in the writing traditions of Europe, from left to right, top to bottom).

This dimension is called **syntagmatic**. The signs that go together to make up an utterance are not put together randomly, but are related in specific ways to one another. In *I will never forget that terrible day* the order of signs plays an important function. The fact that *I* precedes *will* tells us that the utterance is a statement. If these two words had occurred in the reverse order, we would have a question, *Will I never forget that terrible day?*

Relations between signs that appear in the presence of one another are **syntagmatic relations**. For example, *terrible* describes *day*, and is dependent on it (you can omit it, but you can't omit the following word *day*). The words *never* and *forget* are also syntagmatically related; but the relation is different: *never* does not describe *forget* in the way *terrible* indicates a quality of the day in question. The term **syntagm** refers to any coherent grouping of signs that form a unit together. Thus *I will never forget that terrible day* is a syntagm; so also is *that terrible day*: these three words belong together and function as a single unit (they cannot be split up or separated) in a way that *never forget that* does not.

Paradigmatic

Not only do speakers put signs together in strings, but they choose the signs that go in the sequence from a number of possible alternative signs that could have been used instead. This gives us the **paradigmatic** dimension, the notion that each sign invokes a contrast with other signs that might have been used instead; signs so related are in a **paradigmatic relation**.[4] Signs in paradigmatic relation form a **paradigm**.

The paradigmatic dimension is important because the set of signs in paradigmatic relation with a particular sign in a syntagm is restricted. In our example sentence *I will never forget that terrible day*, *I* contrasts with *you, he, she, my brother, John, John's older brother*, and many other signs, simple and complex. But it does not contrast with *hit, and, not, up, won't* and so on. The existence of such restrictions is evidence that the signs in the syntagm are genuinely syntagmatically related, that there is structure on the syntagmatic dimension, and that the signs are not arbitrarily placed in sequence one after the other.

If we examine the signs in paradigmatic alternation with *I* in our example sentence, it is clear that they relate in different ways to one another. *I, you, he* and *she* are more closely related to one another than any is to *John* or *John's older brother*. Imagine a game in which I say a word, and you respond with as many words as come to mind in 30 seconds. Most likely, if I say *I*, you would respond with *you, he, she, we*; responses *John, John's older brother* and *hit* would be less likely. If I were to say *brother*, the chances are that you would respond with words like *sister, father, mother, son*, rather than *we, you, atom* or *star*. The signs in the groups of likely responses have similar meanings. For *brother* and *sister* the difference is in terms of the sex of the relative; for *brother* and *father* it is in terms of the genetic relation. These dimensions of contrast recur throughout the paradigm.

The meaning of a sign in a language is dependent in part on the other signs in close paradigmatic relationship with it. In English *we* means 'me and someone else'; it contrasts with *I* in terms of the number of persons specified. Gumbaynggirr (Pama-Nyungan, Australia) has

four words for 'we', *ngalii*, *ngiyaa*, *ngaligay* and *ngiyagay*, as well as *ngaya* 'I'. The first two words, *ngalii* and *ngiyaa*, are used if the group includes the hearer; the second pair, *ngaligay* and *ngiyagay*, if it does not. The first word of each pair is used if there are just two persons in the 'we' group, the second, if there are more. The Gumbaynggirr word *ngalii* does not mean the same thing as English *we* partly because of the other words in paradigmatic contrast to it.

> The meaning of a stretch of language depends both on the signs present in it and on the signs absent from it. The same goes for its grammatical structure. The two dimensions, paradigmatic and syntagmatic, are important both to meaning and to form; just as the meaning and form of a sign are inseparable, so also are the paradigmatic and syntagmatic dimensions.

1.3 Design features of human language

Many animals use signs to communicate with other members of their species. Some species of bees, for instance, use dances to indicate the location of a source of nectar (see §10.1). Human beings, however, are obsessed with signs, and can't help seeing them everywhere. Dress is a sign system; so also are the Hindu/Arabic numerals (1, 2, 3, . . .) and traffic lights. Human language occupies a privileged place among sign systems. It is a particularly elaborate sign system that has properties not manifested, or weakly manifested, in other sign systems.

What might these features be? The American linguist Charles Hockett proposed a set of **design features** of human language, a set of features satisfied by all human languages that distinguishes them from other sign systems. This set has undergone modifications and additions since it was first proposed in Hockett (1960). Below we discuss six of the most important features. Some of these will be taken up again in our discussion of animal communication in Chapter 10.

Arbitrariness

We have already mentioned **arbitrariness** as a property of word-signs in human languages, and explained that it is to be understood in the sense that the form and meaning of a word-sign are not connected by necessity. Arbitrariness is a matter of degree, and ranges from highly iconic and motivated (though never bereft of some conventionalization), to purely symbolic.

In the animal world, too, most signs show some degree of conventionalization. In some cases the signs are quite iconic – the dance of some bee species iconically represents the direction to a nectar source by one of the axes of their figure-eight dance. But the forms for this meaning could easily have been otherwise. Mating and territorial calls and dances of animals are generally even more conventionalized.

Displacement

People often talk about things that are not present. They speak about events and things from distant times and places – about things that happened years ago in far-away places. Indeed, these may be entirely imaginary, like unicorns and time travel. This book would not have been possible otherwise, if language could only be used to describe what is actually physically present in the writer's environment. This is called **displacement**.

Animal communication systems sometimes allow limited displacement, for signalling things that aren't physically present and perceivable. The bees dance can signal presence of nectar at a distance of some kilometres from the hive. Some studies have shown that chimpanzees can sign about items that are not visible. In one study it was shown that the chimpanzee Panzee, using a system of signs on a monitor, could call attention to items of food it observed hidden by a trainer, sometimes days previously. But the displacement revealed in these examples is limited: what is communicated about is something that is relevant to the present circumstances. Thus the invisible food Panzee indicated seems to have always been the last item of hidden food, and the communication was concerned with its retrieval. Displacement is a matter of degree rather than an all-or-nothing thing.

> Displacement is not always a good thing to have in a sign system. The system of alarm calls of vervet monkeys (see §10.1) would be compromised if it permitted displacement. It would then no longer be a system of alarm calls, but of calls sometimes used as alarms calling for immediate evasive action, and sometimes referring to the presence of a predator from a different occasion. Similarly, the system of sirens used on emergency vehicles would be of little use if it allowed displacement!

Cultural transmission

Children learn to speak the language or languages used in the environment in which they are reared; they do not inherit their language via parental genes, in the way they inherit hair and skin colour. Languages are passed on by **cultural transmission**. Many of the world's languages are endangered due partly to interruptions in transmission across the generations.

Animal communication systems by contrast are largely instinctive. The communicative noises produced by domestic cats appear to be the same regardless of whether the cat lives in Europe or New Zealand, and regardless of whether it was reared by humans in the virtual absence of other cats.

Some birds do require exposure to the songs of other members of their species. Lacking this, they still instinctively produce songs, but these will be abnormal in some way. This is like some types of body behaviour in human beings such as laughing, smiling and crying: though universal, they admit cultural modifications and elaborations.

Although the language a person speaks is culturally transmitted, the ability to speak is a genetic predisposition. The extent of this predisposition – what aspects of language are genetically encoded – is a controversial issue on which linguists take conflicting positions.

Duality

Utterances in human languages are patterned simultaneously on two levels, the level of form and the level of meaning. This is called **duality**. The Warrwa (Nyulnyulan, Australia) word *yila* 'dog' is made up of sounds that are meaningless in themselves, but when put together in a certain way make up the sign-form. Put together in a different way, for instance as *layi*, and we get a different word, meaning 'alone, singly'. Put together in yet other ways, for example, *iayl*, we get forms that are not possible words in the language. Duality of patterning permits a large number of different words to be made up from a small number of meaningless elements that are put together in various ways.

Duality of patterning is not found in animal communication systems. Their sign-forms are simple in the sense that they cannot be analysed into components that are re-used in other signs; there is an absence of patterning in the forms and the meanings. Each form is completely different from every other form, and does not involve components that are reused to make other forms. The various calls your cat produces are separate whole units, and cannot be divided into parts that can be reused to make other calls with other meanings – *miaou* is not divided into separate sounds like *m* and *i* (*ee*) that could be used in different orders, to produce different calls, say *im*.

Productivity

Productivity or creativity is the characteristic whereby speakers can make new meanings by producing new expressions and utterances. Linguistic signs can be put together to form sequences that may never have been produced before; and even if they are not entirely novel, they may be innovative in that they are not drawn from memory. Not only do we effortlessly create such utterances, but hearers have little difficulty understanding them.

A good deal of what we say is not new: we use formulaic greetings and farewells many times in the average day. We express meanings that have been expressed, with perhaps slight variations in wording, innumerable times before, as in the case of poetry, jokes, oral traditions and urban myths, for instance.

Another aspect of the productivity of language is that speakers can invent new words to express new ideas and new objects and events that they encounter. No living human language has a rigidly closed class of words, that admits no new members. Think of the number of new English words that have been invented in recent years to facilitate talking about computers and the internet. Some of the main ways that new words are incorporated into a language are discussed in §4.2.

The communication systems of non-human animals, by contrast, are typically non-productive, and do not admit new combinations of signs or the invention of new signs for new meanings. The systems allow for the expression of a small set of possible meanings. The honeybees' dance that indicates the location of a nectar source (see §10.1) is restricted to the horizontal dimension, and bees are incapable of communicating information about the location of a nectar source vertically above the hive.

Reflexivity

This book is about human language, and is written in a human language. Your lectures on linguistics are about language and are spoken in a human language. All human languages can be, and often are, used in this way, for conveying information about themselves. This need not be abstruse linguistic information; it could be something as simple as 'that word is not nice to use in polite company'. This property is **reflexivity**.

No known animal communication system allows reflexivity. Likewise, many sign systems human beings employ cannot be used to convey information about themselves. Traffic lights do not allow for messages about themselves, and nor do gestures or facial expressions.

1.4 Speech, writing and signing

The primacy of speech

Speech is the primary medium for language. With the exception of sign languages (which we will talk about soon) and some dead languages, most natural human languages are spoken most of the time. A good number of the world's languages have no tradition of writing, and are exclusively (or almost exclusively) spoken. Even for languages with longish traditions of writing (e.g. Chinese, French, Japanese) most people produce and hear more words in speech than in writing, and spend more time talking than reading or writing. In fact, writing is a recent invention. If you were able to travel back in time just 7,000 years you would find all languages were exclusively spoken – as they had been for tens of millennia previously.

Writing is a system of representing the words of a language visually; certain visual forms and combinations of forms represent words. Writing must be distinguished from other systems of visual representation (like paintings, carvings, notches on sticks and so on) which do not represent words of a language. All systems of writing represent, at least sometimes, aspects of the sound of the spoken word. How consistently and accurately they do this differs from system to system.

Languages written with **alphabetic** scripts ideally represent words by their sounds. Some do this reasonably well, and you can make a good guess at the pronunciation of a word from its written form, if you know the correspondences between letters and sounds. This is the case for Spanish (Indo-European, Spain) and Hungarian. Other languages, including English, French and Danish, have notoriously poor representations of the spoken forms of words.

Some languages employ **logographic** writing systems, in which each symbol or character represents, at least ideally, a word or meaningful unit. The Mandarin Chinese writing system is a logographic system. Over 90 per cent of the modern characters are combinations of components indicating something about the meaning and pronunciation of the word. The characters shown in (1-1) all represent words concerning cooking and associated notions of burning and heating; all involve the 'fire' radical 火 *huǒ*. Those shown in (1-2) all involve the same phonetic element, 堯, *yáo*; this gives a rough guide to the pronunciation of the word: that the word rhymes with *ao*, roughly as in the vowel sound in word English *loud*.[5]

(1-1)

燒	灰	灶	炕	煤	燃
shāo	huī	zào	kàng	méi	rán
'cook, burn'	'ash'	'oven'	'heated brick bed'	'coal'	'ignite'

(1-2)

饒	澆	燒	曉
ráo	jiāo	shāo	xiǎo
'forgive'	'pour'	'cook, burn'	'dawn'

Writing is derivative from speech, and secondary to it. Speech is historically prior, and is represented in some form or another in all true writing systems. Human beings are born to speak; the normal child cannot help mastering in a matter of a few years or so the language spoken around it. We are not born to write; writing is usually explicitly taught, and few children acquire it through mere exposure.

Linguists are generally more interested in speech than in writing, although both are appropriate topics for linguists to study.

It is important not to confuse speech and writing. Beginning students frequently make this mistake, and are apt to be misled by features of the way their language is written. For instance, many beginners believe that English has five vowels because five vowel letters are used in writing the language *a, e, i, o, u*. In fact, as we will see in Chapter 2, most dialects of English have around a dozen vowels, as well as a number of diphthongs (double vowel sounds such as in the pronunciation of the word *I*).

The term *letter* should be reserved for talking about writing. It is misleading to speak of the letters of spoken language; instead, the terms *phone* or *sound* should be used.

Sign languages

Not all human languages employ the spoken mode. Languages of deaf communities in many parts of the world today use the medium of **signing**, visible bodily movements made mainly by the hands, face and head. These systems of signs, called **sign languages**, are natural languages that developed spontaneously in deaf communities, and are not the same thing as invented systems based on spoken languages (such as the British Two Handed Finger Spelling Alphabet). Nor should they to be confused with auxiliary gestures that might be employed by speaking people when communicating with deaf people. They are genuine

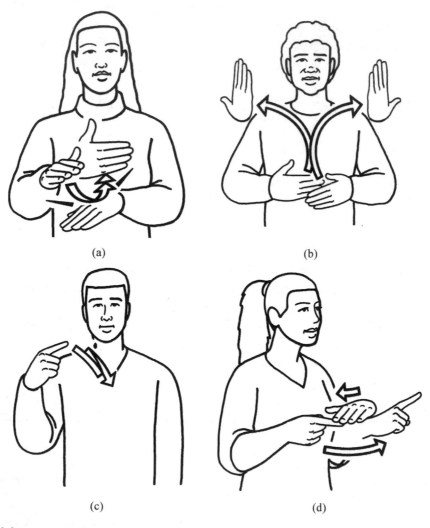

(a)   (b)

(c)   (d)

Figure 1.4 Four signs of Auslan. Can you guess their meanings? If you are told that they mean 'day', 'go out', 'cat' and 'white', can you guess which sign represents which meaning? (Source: Johnson and Schembri 2003. Reproduced with permission from the authors.) Answers at end of chapter.

human languages with vocabularies comparable in size to those of spoken languages, and intricate grammatical systems; they satisfy Hockett's design features (§1.3), and have communities of mother-tongue users.

Ethnologue (a listing of the languages of the world – see §13.1) lists 119 deaf sign languages, including American Sign Language (the sign language used in the deaf community in the USA), British Sign Language, Danish Sign Language, Hungarian Sign Language and Nicaraguan Sign Language. These are distinct languages, unintelligible to signers of the others: monolingual signers of American Sign Language and British Sign Language cannot understand one another. In fact, the two languages arose independently, probably around the beginning of the nineteenth century. Nicaraguan Sign Language arose even more recently, after the demise of the Somoza regime in 1979.

The signs of sign languages often show some degree of iconicity, generally to a greater extent than spoken languages. However, the relation between the form and meaning of the sign remains conventional, and in most cases it is impossible to predict the meaning of a sign from its form. In Figure 1.4 the first sign is highly iconic, and it is not difficult to guess the meaning. But the second is much less iconic, and the meaning is more difficult to guess.

The manual signs of sign languages are analysable as combinations of meaningless features of hand-shape, location and movement. Grammatical information is sometimes expressed by modifications of these manual signs, sometimes by separate manual signs, sometimes by the order of signs, and sometimes by simultaneous gestures of the face or head. Figure 1.5 shows how a question is expressed in Finnish Sign Language.

Lowered brows
Head tilt

Paper   Where   Palm-up

'Where is the paper?'

Figure 1.5 Questions in Finnish Sign Language. The PALM-UP sign indicates a question. Note the accompanying facial and head movements; the horizontal lines indicate the extent of the utterance over which they applied. (Source: Zeshan 2004: 33. Reprinted from *Language* 80 (2004), p. 33, by permission of the Linguistic Society of America. Thanks to Ulrike Zeshan for the digital images.)

1.5 Outline of modern linguistics from a historical perspective

People everywhere talk about language: they have ideas about its nature, uses, origins, acquisition, structure and so on – recall reflexivity (p. 14). Some of these notions are enshrined in mythology (e.g. the Tower of Babel story). In some sense the things people say and believe about language could qualify as linguistics, perhaps folk linguistics. But, as we are using it, the term *linguistics* refers to a scientific system of knowledge. Before we go deeper into the subject, it is useful to overview the main trends, situating them in a broad historical perspective.

The earliest certain evidence of discourse about language dates to about 4,000 years ago, when scribes in ancient Mesopotamia listed forms of Sumerian nouns and verbs on clay tablets. They did this because Sumerian, the language of religion and the law, was no longer in everyday use, and it had to be taught as a foreign language. For similar reasons, traditions of linguistics also emerged in ancient India, Greece and Rome.

The study of linguistics intensified in the Middle Ages. Subsequently, with the advent of European colonialism in the fifteenth century, Europeans came into contact with an unexpected diversity of languages and peoples. From information gathered by travellers, missionaries and others, it became apparent that some languages are related to one another. Procedures for establishing these relationships were gradually honed, until the late nineteenth century, by which time the comparative method (see §13.2) had been largely perfected.

Modern linguistics emerged soon after, with a change of focus from historical concerns to the notion of language as a system, the basis of structuralism, which still permeates the subject. The Swiss linguist Ferdinand de Saussure (1857–1913) was a key figure in this refocusing of interest, and is regarded as the founding father of modern linguistics. His *Cours de linguistique générale* [Course in general linguistics] was published posthumously in 1916, reconstructed from his students' lecture notes.

As we have already noted, modern linguistics is an empirical endeavour, concerned with describing and accounting for patterns of speech and language, and that to account for the patterns means to explain them, and for this theory is essential. As in other social sciences, there is considerable theoretical diversity. However, theories tend to cluster into two main types, **formal** and **functional**, according to whether the primary emphasis is on language as an algebraic system of symbols put together according to rules, or on language as a system that has developed in particular ways in order to serve functions in human life. We discuss these two approaches in the following subsections.

Formal linguistics

In America, from the 1930s onwards, mainstream structuralism became increasingly algebraic in orientation and focused increasingly on syntax. In 1957 it suffered a major blow with the publication of Noam Chomsky's (1928–) *Syntactic structures*. Influenced by developments in mathematical logic, Chomsky's program explicitly rejected some of the dominant pre-occupations of American structuralism, including its empiricist philosophy (that knowledge derives from sense experiences). Instead, Chomsky advocated a rationalist philosophy (that knowledge is based on reason).

Chomsky's thought quickly became dominant, not just in America but also in Europe and elsewhere; it has effectively defined mainstream linguistics ever since. Grammar is considered as a formal system making explicit the mechanisms – first in terms of rules, later by other means – by which the grammatical sentences of a language can be generated; and for this reason the tradition is called Generative Grammar.

Generative theory developed rapidly, and mainstream Chomskian generative grammar has undergone numerous substantial changes and renovations. Alternative generative theories were also developed by others.

Functional linguistics

The late 1950s also saw new developments in linguistics in Europe, that took off in functional directions, stressing both the meaning side of the Saussurean sign and the idea that language developed the way it did because of the uses it is put to. Key figures were André Martinet (1908–1999) and Michael Halliday (1925–). The schools they initiated continue to this day as minor but significant forces on the linguistic landscape.

Later, other functionally oriented schools emerged, mainly in opposition to generative linguistics. One was Functional Grammar, developed from the late 1960s by the Dutch linguist Simon Dik (1940–1995). A rather amorphous tradition arose in the USA around the same time, West Coast Functional Grammar. Prominent in this tradition was the idea that grammatical categories are functional, that they arose to serve a purpose. More recently, two more coherent schools arose in the USA largely replacing West Coast Functional Grammar, Cognitive Grammar (associated with Ronald Langacker (1942–)) and Construction Grammar (Charles Fillmore (1929–) and associates). Both assign a prominent place to the Saussurean sign.

Scope of modern linguistics

Contemporary linguistics is a richly diversified field, with so many specializations that no scholar can cover them all. Many branches acquired their separate identities and methodologies in the second half of the twentieth century, although most had been investigated previously. Generative Grammar remains a major force determining the orientations and goals of most branches, although other theories have had some impact.

The majority of the almost 7,000 languages spoken in the world today and in the recent past have yet to be adequately documented and described. Many linguists are engaged in gathering data on the poorly documented languages, normally by doing fieldwork in remote locations, and describing them by writing grammars and compiling dictionaries and collections of texts. Missionary linguists, many working under the umbrella of SIL International, a missionary organization established in the USA in 1934, continue to play a prominent role. Over 1,000 languages are currently under investigation by SIL linguists. Speakers of poorly documented languages are increasingly playing prominent roles, both as gatekeepers determining access to speech communities and controlling the direction of research and its applications, and in describing and documenting their languages.

The need for this descriptive work is underlined by the fact that many of the world's languages are endangered, and unlikely to survive into the next century (see §7.4). Despite the political rhetoric, this field does not occupy a prominent position in linguistics, or on the agenda of many research funding bodies, and a relatively small proportion of linguists are active in it.

Like other sciences, linguistics has applications, including to language learning, literacy and translation. In fact many branches of linguistics have contributed to applied linguistics, the field concerned with the applications of linguistics, for example: descriptive linguistics to maintaining and strengthening endangered languages; psycholinguistics to assisting individuals with language difficulties (e.g. resulting from strokes); pragmatics and conversation analysis to cross-cultural communication; and sociolinguistics to the educational field. Recent years have seen linguists increasingly called on for expert advice in the legal domain, including speaker identification and land-rights for indigenous peoples. Another major area of application is in the computational field, including to machine generation and recognition of speech, automatic parsing of texts, translation, and building and maintaining large corpora (collections of texts).

Summing up

Linguistics, the **scientific study of language**, has its roots in our everyday knowledge of, thinking about, and talking about language. This everyday thought is often prescriptive. By contrast, modern linguistics has a **descriptive** orientation: it is an empirical endeavour, concerned with describing and accounting for patterns in speech and language. To do this theory is essential; modern linguistics is dominated by two opposing theoretical orientations, **formal** and **functional**.

One of the most fundamental notions of modern linguistics is the **sign**, a unit made up of a **form** paired with a **meaning**. Most linguistic signs are arbitrary, the connection between the form and the meaning being established purely by convention. Such signs are **symbols**. Some linguistic signs, however, display likeness between their form and meaning: these are **icons**.

The signs of a language form a **system**, a primary characteristic of which is the relationships amongst the signs, which are either **paradigmatic** or **syntagmatic**.

To distinguish language from other systems of communication, Hockett proposed a set of **design features** of human language, including: arbitrariness, displacement, cultural transmission, duality, productivity and reflexivity.

Speech is the primary medium of human languages. It is historically prior to writing, which is a recent invention, dating back only a few thousand years. Most languages are virtually exclusively spoken; many writing systems have emerged only in the last century, and many are used quite irregularly. An alternative medium for the representation of languages is gesture, and in many deaf communities **sign languages** are used in which words are represented by gestures. These are full languages satisfying Hockett's design features, and are lexically and grammatically distinct from the surrounding spoken languages.

Guide to further reading

Of the enormous range of introductory textbooks on linguistics, my recommendations are: Bolinger (1975); Fromkin and Rodman (1974), which has subsequently appeared in many editions (e.g. Fromkin et al. 2005); Hudson (2000); and Yule (2006). Four other introductory books, not intended as textbooks, make excellent reading: Hudson (1984); Matthews (2003); Parkvall (2006); and Trask (1999).

It is advisable to have a good dictionary of linguistics, such as Crystal (1980/2003); Matthews (2007); or Trask (1998). Encyclopaedias such as Frawley (2003); and Crystal (1987) are also worth digging into. Aronoff and Rees-Miller's *The Handbook of Linguistics* (2001) contains 32 articles covering most fields of modern linguistics.

Design features of human language were first proposed by Charles Hockett (1960); the list has been subsequently modified and expanded. On writing systems, see Daniels (2001) and Coulmas (1996, 2003). On deaf sign languages see Sandler and Lillo-Martin (2001). Kaplan (2002) gives an indication of the scope of applied linguistics, while Oaks (2001) is an excellent collection of articles illustrating the applications of linguistics to education, law, medicine, the film industry, business, etc.

On the nature of science and the scientific method, see Chalmers (1976); Riggs (1992); and Godffrey-Smith (2003). Horgan (1996) contains interviews with leading scientists on the limitations of science, and gives insights into the lives and work of scientists. The best introduction to the history of linguistics is Robins (1984); for a brief overview see the website for this book.

Issues for further thought and exercises

1. Depicted below are the forms of various signs in everyday use. What are their meanings? Is the sign an icon or a symbol? Justify your answers.

   ⌘ ☺ ☠ 👁 ♿ ⚥ 🚭

2. Traffic lights form a sign system. Describe the system of traffic lights in use in your country. To do this you should identify the range of signs belonging to the system, specifying their forms and meanings. Answer also the following questions. What combinations of signs are permitted? How would you describe their syntagmatic relations? Which of Hockett's design features are satisfied, and to what extent?

   (Continued)

Issues for further thought and exercises—Cont'd

3. If you were to ask me for the loan of a book, I might reply with a simple *No!* If I had replied in a very loud voice, **No!** this would probably be understood as an emphatic and unequivocal refusal. What meaning would you say loudness conveys, and do you consider loudness to be iconic of this meaning? Can you think of other iconic ways of expressing similar meanings?

4. Here's a chance to do your first piece of research: find out about a linguist. See what you can learn about one of the following linguists: Leonard Bloomfield, Frans Boas, Dwight Bolinger, Joan Bresnan, William Bright, Arthur Capell, Yuan Ren Chao, Noam Chomsky, Bernard Comrie, Simon Dik, J. R. Firth, Joseph Greenberg, Mary Haas, William Haas, Michael Halliday, Louis Hjelmslev, Charles Hockett, Otto Jespersen, Daniel Jones, Ronald Langacker, John Lotz, Johanna Nichols, Kenneth Pike, Edward Sapir, Nikolai Trubetzkoy and Benjamin L. Whorf. Put together a brief biography of the person (When and where were they born and educated? Where did they work? What other interests did they have?) and the type of linguistics they did (What were their main interests in linguistics? What are their major publications, and what are they best known for?)

5. Collect comments on 'incorrect' or 'sloppy' English (or another language spoken in your community) from the media and everyday speech. What aspects do they target (e.g. pronunciation, meaning, grammar)? What is the basis for the claim (are arguments produced, and if so, what are they)? What do they reveal about the author of the comment?

6. The male Australian lyre bird's mating song is made up of sequences of songs from other bird species, in various selections (depending on the range of other birds it has heard) and coming in orders that differ from bird to bird. Does this illustrate duality of patterning? Explain your answer.

7. Does English writing show duality of patterning? What about Chinese writing? Explain. If your answer to both questions is 'yes', is the duality manifested in the same or different ways in the two types of writing?

8. We discussed six design features of human languages. Others have been proposed. Find out what they are, and think about their usefulness and the extent to which they distinguish human language from traffic lights or another system of signs used by humans or animals. (Begin with the website http://www.ling.ohio-state.edu/~swinters/371/designfeatures.html. Web-addresses change frequently, and you may need to search with Google or another search-engine.)

9. We said that both speech and writing are suitable subjects for linguistic investigation. Is a good piece of writing also a good piece of speech if it is read aloud? What differences would you expect to find between speech and writing in the ways that things are expressed? What grammatical differences would you expect?

10. Writing does not only influence the way that people think about their language, but can also influence speech. What are some of the ways your language (and opinions about it) has been influenced by the way it is written?

11. What is a syllabary? What are some languages that employ syllabaries in writing? See what you can find out about the nature and development of one syllabary. Answer the following questions: When was it invented? By who? How many symbols does it use? What do they represent? Do you think a syllabary would be a good system for writing English? Explain your reasons.

12. What is Signed English or Manually Coded English? Find out about this system of manual signs, and write a brief description (about a page). Mention where the hand-signs come from, and the relation of the system to English – is the system similar to anything discussed in this chapter? Who uses this system, and where? Comment also on any advantages or disadvantages of this system in relation to deaf sign languages such as ASL (American Sign Language) and BSL (British Sign Language).

13. We have mentioned a number of branches of linguistics in this chapter. The list was selective, and there are many more named branches. Here are some: forensic linguistics, philosophical linguistics, corpus linguistics, dialectology, computational linguistics, onomastics, stylistics, mathematical linguistics, philology, contrastive linguistics, lexicography and narratology. Look one or more of these terms up in an encyclopaedia or dictionary of linguistics, and/or on the web, and write a paragraph description in your own words explaining what the branch studies.

Answers to question in Figure 1.4

The answers are (a) 'cat'; (b) 'day'; (c) 'white'; and (d) 'go out'. Clearly the signs are to a large extent 'arbitrary'. Do you agree that two are at least partly iconic?

Notes

1. A perhaps apocryphal story has it that Winston Churchill, the British Prime Minister during World War II, once received a minute from a civil servant who objected to his ending a sentence with a preposition in an official document. Churchill pencilled in the margin *This is the sort of pedantry up with which I will not put.*

2. We adopt the convention of indicating in brackets following the language name, on its first mention in the text, the name of the family to which it belongs (see Chapter 13) and its main country of origin. See Map 1 (pp. xxii–xxiii) for the locations of the main languages mentioned in the book.

3. The concepts of form and meaning are both difficult to define. Form does not refer to the actual physical properties of a particular instance of a sign. Any instance of a sign will always be slightly different from other instances, if you examine it closely enough; for example, minor variations in the paper will mean that the examples of the sign ∞ in each copy of this book are slightly different. (The actual physical instance is sometimes referred to as the *substance*.) The notion of form is an abstraction from the instances, ignoring variations that make no difference – which are perceived or regarded as the same by users, who can't tell them apart. In a way, the form is the sign-user's concept of its shape. Meaning is also an abstraction from the specific meaning of an instance of use of a sign; for instance, in Saussure's example, the concept 'tree' ignores the variation amongst different trees and types of tree.

4. Sometimes the paradigmatic dimension is described as vertical, in contrast with the syntagmatic dimension which is horizontal. Thus we could represent some of the syntagmatic and paradigmatic relations in our example sentence as follows (where the braces enclose items in paradigmatic relations):

I	will			that	terrible	day
He	won't		forget	this	amazing	night
She	might		remember	a	splendid	afternoon
John	mightn't	never	recall	the	nasty	year
My brother	shall	ever	describe	one	remarkable	winter

Notice that not all of the sentences predicted from this display are acceptable: choice of one word can have implications on the selection of another. For instance, if you choose *will* or *might*, the following choice needs to be *never*, but if you choose *won't* or *mightn't*, it will be *ever*.

5. The second line gives the standard Pinyin spelling of each word. The diacritics (marks) over the vowels indicate different tones (see §2.5).

Part I
Language: System and Structure

Sounds of Language: Phonetics and Phonology 2

This chapter deals with spoken language, and sets up the basic framework for describing speech sounds. The bulk of the chapter deals with the ways speech sounds are produced. It also explores the ways speech sounds pattern in the sound-systems of languages, which leads us to the notion of distinctive sounds or phonemes.

Chapter contents

Goals

The goals of the chapter are to:
- describe the basic structure of the speech organs or vocal tract;
- explain how speech sounds are produced;
- identify the main types of speech sounds and how they are classified;
- present the essentials of the main system for representing speech sounds, the IPA;
- outline the basic prosodic properties of speech (pitch, tone, intonation, and stress) and how they are used in different languages;
- explain the notions of phoneme and allophone;
- show how to determine the phonemes of a language; and
- describe the major methods of transcribing speech.

Key terms

acoustic phonetics	diphthong	manner of articulation	suspicious pair
allophone	ejective	minimal pair	syllable
articulatory phonetics	free variation	phone	tone
auditory phonetics	glottalic airstream	phoneme	velaric airstream
click	implosive	pitch	vocal tract
complementary distribution	International Phonetic Alphabet	place of articulation	voicing
consonant	intonation	pulmonic airstream	voice onset time
		stress	vowel

2.1 Fundamental properties of speech sounds

The speech chain

A simple and influential model of speech communication, the so-called speech chain model (presented in Denes and Pinson 1973), identifies the following steps in conveying a message from speaker to hearer.

- A thought emerges in the brain of the speaker and is encoded in language.
- Messages are sent through nerves from the brain to the vocal apparatus – the various muscles and organs that act together to produce speech sounds.

- The muscles and organs are positioned and set into motion.
- As a result, sounds are produced that travel through the air.
- These sounds reach the ears of the hearer, which 'process' the sounds, converting them into electrical signals.
- These electrical signals travel along the auditory nerves to the hearer's brain.
- The brain of the hearer decodes these impulses, arriving at a thought (which is hopefully similar to the thought that started in the speaker's brain).
- The last three steps also apply to the speaker, in a feedback loop: the sound reaches the speaker's ear, is converted to electrical signals that travel to the brain, which decodes them and compares the spoken utterance with the intended utterance.

The three processes in the middle of this list, marked by the vertical bars, are the main concerns of phonetics, and give us the three primary divisions of the subject: **articulatory phonetics** (concerning the production of the sounds), **acoustic phonetics** (concerning the physical properties of the sound waves) and **auditory phonetics** (concerning the perception of speech sounds). We deal mainly with articulatory phonetics in this chapter.

Phones

Most readers of this book will be familiar with the idea that a stretch of speech such as the spoken version of *The farmer kills the duckling* can be divided up into a sequence of **phones** or sounds coming one after another. First there is the sound written *th* and pronounced in the same way as in ***they*** and ***them***; this is followed by another sound written *e* and pronounced like the *a* in *sofa*. Then comes the *f* sound (as in *frog*), an *a* sound as is also found in *father*, and so on.

But the reality is not so simple. Figure 2.1 shows the sound wave for my production of this short sentence. What you can see immediately is that the sound is a continuous stream: it is not made up of separate blocks of sound separated by pauses. There is no precise point where you could say that the sound written *th* ends, and the one written *e* begins – the best we can say is that the *e* sound begins at around 0.04 second. Nor is there a clear division between the words, and the *f* sound runs on directly from the *e* sound at around 0.11 seconds, and is followed immediately by the *a* sound, at around 0.22 seconds. There is no interruption in the sound-stream throughout the word *farmer*. Between about 0.55 and 0.57 seconds there is a significant reduction in the sound wave. But this is not between *farmer* and *kills*, but within the *k* sound! Similar remarks apply to the remainder of the utterance. In particular, the two other apparent breaks in the sound wave occur within the *d* and *k* of *duckling*, and not between sounds.

The same goes for the pronunciation of the sentence. The parts of the mouth involved in producing the sounds are in continuous motion; they do not move in a series of jerks from one fixed position to another. You do not first put your tongue in the position to make

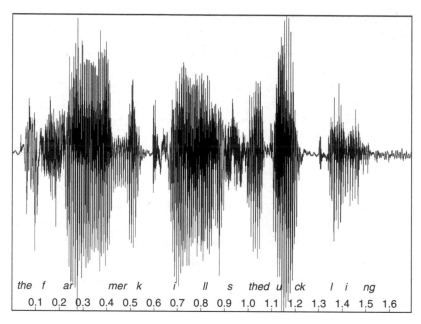

Figure 2.1 Sound wave of the author's production of *The farmer kills the duckling*.

the *th* sound, then shift it instantaneously to the position to produce the *e* sound, then immediately put your lower lip against the upper teeth to make the *f* sound and so on.

Even if you cannot draw an exact boundary between each of the phones in the way that you can between the letters making up the words of the printed sentence (an ordinary handwritten version would raise the same difficulties of division), it does seem that the stream is made up of stretches of different types of sound. Corresponding to the utterance of the word *the*, we can see in the figure two types of sound according to the general shape of the wave, which follow one after the other (but are not precisely separated); similarly for the remainder of the sentence.

The idea that you can divide stretches of speech into phones is a reasonable approximation. As linguists we often need to represent phones in writing. For this purpose we use the **International Phonetic Alphabet** (IPA), a set of symbols based primarily on the Latin alphabet, and extensive and flexible enough to accommodate the sounds of any language. Table 2.1 shows the main symbols from the latest version of the IPA.

2.2 The vocal tract

The organs involved in producing the sounds of speech are referred to collectively as the **vocal tract**. These are the lungs, the larynx, the oral cavity and the nasal cavity; see Figure 2.2.

Table 2.1 Main symbols of the IPA

Consonants (pulmonic)

		Bilabial	Labiodental	Dental	Alveolar	Alveo-palatal	Retroflex	Palatal	Velar	Uvular	Pharyngeal	Glottal
Stop	voiceless	p			t		ʈ	c	k	q		ʔ
	voiced	b			d			ɟ	g	ɢ		
Nasal		m	ɱ		n		ɳ	ɲ	ŋ	ɴ		
Fricative	voiceless	ɸ	f	θ	s	ʃ	ʂ	ç	x	χ	ħ	h
	voiced	ß	v	ð	z	ʒ	ʐ	ʝ	ɣ	ʁ	ʕ	ɦ
Affricate	voiceless				ts	tʃ						
	voiced				dz	dʒ						
Lateral	voiceless				ɬ							
	voiced				l		ɭ	ʎ	ʟ			
Rhotic	tap, trill				ɾ, r		ɽ			ʀ		
	approximant				ɹ		ɻ					
Glides		w*						j	ɰ			

*w is a voiced labio-velar glide.

Consonants (non-pulmonic)

Clicks		Voiced implosives		Ejectives	
ʘ	Bilabial	ɓ	Bilabial	'	Examples:
ǀ	Dental	ɗ	Dental-alveolar	p'	Bilabal
ǃ	Retroflex	ʄ	Palatal	t'	Dental-alveolar
ǂ	Alveo-palatal	ɠ	Velar	k'	Velar
ǁ	Lateral	ʛ	Uvular	s'	Alveolar fricative

Diacritics

n̥ d̥	Voiceless	b̤	Breathy voiced	ɫ	Velarized
tʰ dʰ	Aspirated	b̰	Creaky voiced	d̪ n̪	Dental
u̟	Advanced	tʷ	Labialized	ẽ	Nasalized
u̠	Retracted	n̩	Syllabic	d̚	Unreleased
ˈ	Primary stress	ˌ	Secondary stress	ː	Long
ˑ	Half long	.	Syllable boundary	k͡p	Coarticulated

Vowels

	Front	Central	Back
High	i y	ɨ ʉ	ɯ u
	ɪ		ʊ
High Mid	e ø		ɤ o
		ə	
Low Mid	ɛ œ	ɜ	ʌ ɔ
	æ	ɐ	ɑ ɒ
Low	a		ɑ ɒ

Where symbols are paired, the first symbol indicates the unrounded vowel, the second, the corresponding rounded vowel.

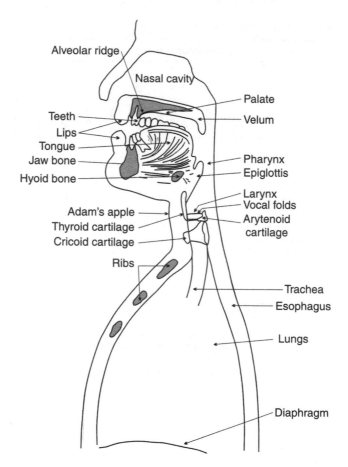

Figure 2.2 The human vocal tract.

The lungs

Most speech sounds are produced on a stream of air forced out from the lungs, through the trachea or wind-pipe, and then through the upper vocal tract, where the airstream is modified in various ways to produce different sounds. This stream of air is called an **egressive pulmonic airstream**. Speech in English and most other languages is usually produced on egressive pulmonic air.

It is also possible to produce speech sounds on air drawn into the lungs, on an **ingressive** pulmonic airstream. This is like speaking while breathing in. Although not as often used as egressive pulmonic air, in some languages it is used to convey certain emotional effects. For instance, in Danish and other Scandinavian languages, words – particularly *ja* 'yes' – are sometimes produced on an ingressive airstream to indicate sympathy or commiseration. Other airstream mechanisms used in human languages will be discussed in §2.4.

The larynx

In the larynx the airstream passes between a pair of muscular flaps called the **vocal folds** or **cords**, which can be drawn together to interrupt the airstream, or left open.

If you bring the vocal folds together closely but not too tightly, forcing air between them will cause them to vibrate regularly. This is how you produce the sound *aaa* after the first sip of a long-awaited drink, or when lying down for a well-needed nap. These vibrations of the vocal folds, called **voicing**, can be felt by holding your thumb and first finger against your Adam's apple. Now say *ssss*, the sound of a deflating tyre. You will notice that the vibrations are not present while you produce this sound.

Sounds like *aaa* that are produced with voicing are called **voiced** phones, while those produced without it, like *ssss* are called **voiceless**. Compare *the* and *thin*. You will notice that the first phone of one of them is voiced, the other voiceless. Which is which?

In producing voiced speech sounds the vocal folds vibrate regularly, usually at between 80 and 400 cycles per second or **hertz** (Hz). This means that they move from the closed position to the open position and back again to the closed position between 80 and 400 times in a second, with each complete cycle taking about the same time.

While you are producing an *aaa* sound tighten your vocal folds further until the airstream is blocked off completely. Release it, continuing with the *aaa* sound. What you got in the middle is called a glottal stop, written ʔ in IPA. This sound can be heard in some English words, for example, the interjection written *uh-oh*.

From now on, we will use the IPA to represent phones, and enclose them in square brackets – thus [ʔ] is the glottal stop.

The oral cavity

After travelling through the larynx, the airstream passes through the **oral cavity** (mouth) and/or **nasal cavity** (nose), and then to the outside air. In the oral cavity the airstream can be modified in many different ways to produce different sounds. The main organs used to make these modifications are the tongue and lips; the jaw is also involved, though in more subtle ways.

The phones [b] and [z] are produced on the same physical input, a voiced egressive airstream. But they sound quite different, and are formed differently. [b] is produced by first completely blocking airstream through the oral cavity at the lips, allowing no air can escape to the outside; then the air behind the closure is released. [z] is produced by partially blocking the airstream at the alveolar ridge. These two phones differ in both the way they are produced and where they are produced.

The nasal cavity

At the back of the roof of the mouth is the **velum** or soft palate, which can be raised or lowered. When lowered, the airstream can enter the nasal cavity; when fully raised, the airstream is channelled into the oral cavity. In uttering the word *bad* [bæd] the velum remains closed throughout, and the air passes entirely through the oral cavity; all of these phones are **oral**. To produce the word *man* the only difference is that the velum is lowered so that the airstream enters into the nasal cavity; unless you speak very carefully, the velum will remain lowered throughout the word, including on the vowel, giving [mæ̃n]. (In the IPA, a ˜ over a symbol indicates that the sound is nasalized.) Phones like[m], [æ], and [n] are called **nasals**.

2.3 Types of phones

Speech sounds are divided into two main types, consonants and vowels. **Consonants** involve a constriction in the vocal tract, obstructing the flow of air; the airstream is impeded or interrupted somewhere along the way from the lungs to the outside. **Vowels** are produced with no significant obstruction to the passage of air through the oral cavity, and the air exits unimpeded through the oral cavity (and perhaps the nasal cavity as well). Vowels are the most resonant phones, those that resound or re-echo the most, like the chime of Big Ben. Consonants are either non-resonant (like [d] and [f]), or are somewhat resonant (like [m] and [l]), though less resonant than a vowel (compare these phones with [i] or [a]).

Consonants

Consonants are described in relation to the point where the airstream is impeded, and how it is impeded. These two properties are called the **place of articulation** and the **manner of articulation**. By convention, the places of articulation are shown across the top row of the IPA chart, the manners of articulation down the first column.

Places of articulation

The main places of articulation are illustrated schematically in Figure 2.3. Below we make a few remarks on each of them.

Labial

Labial sounds are made with the lips. If both lips are used, the phone is called a **bilabial**. The initial sounds of *bad* [bæd] and *mad* [mæd] are bilabials: they are made by bringing the upper and lower lips together; so also is the initial sound of *pad* [pʰæd].

Instead of bringing both lips together, you can bring the lower lip into contact with the upper teeth to form a **labiodental**. The phones [f] and [v], as in the beginning of the English words *fix* [fɪks] and *Vicks* [vɪks], are produced in this way.

Dental

Dental sounds are formed with the tongue and the upper teeth. Usually the tip of the tongue is used, and touches the upper teeth, as in English [θ] and [ð], the initial phones of *three* and *this*, respectively. In some dialects of English, including Californian English, the tip of the tongue actually protrudes between the upper and lower teeth for these consonants, which are

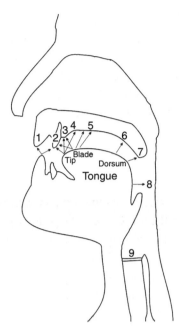

Figure 2.3 The upper vocal tract showing main places of articulation of consonants: 1, labial; 2, dental; 3, alveolar; 4, post-alveolar; 5, palatal; 6, velar; 7, uvula; 8, pharyngeal; 9, glottal. Arrows emanate from the main active parts (articulators) and point towards typical targets (passive articulators). More precise descriptions of places of articulation can be given by first specifying active articulator, then the passive one, thus: apico-alveolar; lamino-palatal, dorso-velar, and so on. (The tongue tip gives apico-; the blade gives lamino-; and the dorsum gives dorso-.)

called **interdentals**. The [n] and [d] phones in French are made with the tip of the tongue touching the upper teeth; this can be indicated in the IPA by the tooth symbol under the letter, as in [d̪]. (In English the contact is slightly further back, at the alveolar ridge.)

In some languages dental sounds are made not with the tip of the tongue against the teeth, but the blade of the tongue, the part behind the tip. Many Australian languages have such phones. The Yindjibarndi (Pama-Nyungan, Australia) word *thugu* 'young boy', begins with this type of phone, as does *nhuurga* 'ankle'. (In Yindjibarndi spelling, the *h* indicates that it is the blade of the tongue that makes contact with the upper teeth.)

Alveolar

Sounds made with the front part of the tongue – usually the tip, sometimes the blade – touching or almost touching the alveolar ridge (the ridge on the roof of the mouth just behind the upper teeth) are called **alveolars**. The initial phones of the English words *top*, *dog*, *log*, *nag*, *rag*, and *sag* are all alveolars.

If the tip of the tongue makes contact just behind the alveolar ridge, the sound is some-times called **post-alveolar** or **retroflex**.[1] Post-alveolar phones occur in the Yindjibarndi words *marda* 'blood' (the *rd* indicates that the *d*-sound is made further back than ordinary [d]) and *thurla* 'eye'.

Palatal

The palate or hard palate is the large region of the roof of the mouth extending from a little behind the alveolar ridge to the soft palate or velum. Sounds made with contact (or approximation) between the tongue and the palate are called **palatals**. If this is in the front part of the palate, immediately behind the alveolar ridge, the sound is an **alveo-palatal**. The English words *shingle*, *jungle* and *child* begin with alveo-palatals. For the first phones of the Hungarian words *nyak* 'neck' and *gyufa* 'match' (represented in spelling by *ny* and *gy*) the contact is further back, and these phones are palatals.

Velar

Behind the hard palate lies a soft area called the soft palate or velum. Consonants made with the back of the tongue touching the velum are called **velar** sounds. (Although it is physically possible to touch the velum with the tip of the tongue, it is not easy, and no language is known to employ this combination.) Velar sounds begin the English words *cull*, *kill*, *car*, *go*, *grip* and *give*. (The first three words have the sound written [k] in IPA, despite the different spellings.) The nasal sound at the end of the English word *sing* is also a velar (IPA [ŋ]).

Uvular

The uvula is the appendage hanging down at the back of the velum. The relatively few phones made with the back of the tongue and the uvula are **uvulars**. The *r*-sound of Parisian French, many dialects of Dutch (Indo-European, Europe) and German, and a few dialects of English (spoken in the north-east of England) are uvular trills (IPA [ʀ]), made with rapid vibration of the uvula (see p. 39).

Pharyngeal

The pharynx is the chamber behind the back of the tongue, above the larynx, and roughly at right angles to the oral cavity. **Pharyngeal** consonants are made by pulling the root of the tongue back to narrow the pharynx so that the air passes through noisily. Pharyngeals are not found in English; Arabic (Afroasiatic, Arabian peninsula and north Africa), however, has them. So does Danish, in the *r*-sound of words like *råd* 'council'.

Glottal

Glottal consonants involve a constriction of the glottis or opening between the vocal folds. We have already encountered one segment made at this place, namely the glottal stop (see §2.2), which is produced by holding the vocal folds together and then releasing them. The initial phones of the English words *hot* [hɒt] and *hill* [hɪɫ] are also glottal.

Manners of articulation

Seven main manners of articulation are used in human languages: stops, nasals, fricatives, affricates, laterals, rhotics and glides.

Stops

A phone that has complete closure or blockage of the airstream is a **stop** or **plosive**. Stops can be made at (almost) any place of articulation, from the glottis ([ʔ]) to the lips (e.g. [p], [b]).

At the beginning of a word such as *bed* or *pet*, the bilabial phone involves complete blockage of the airstream, followed by an abrupt release of the pent-up air behind the blockage. When an English speaker says *bed*, the vocal folds are vibrating during the production of the initial stop. But for *pet* the vocal folds do not begin to vibrate until a short time after the first stop has been released. Stops like [b] are voiced; those like [p] are voiceless.

The period of time (measured in milliseconds or thousandths of a second) between the release of a stop and the onset of vibration of the vocal folds is called **voice onset time** (VOT). For the English [b] this is usually a negative number, as voicing begins before the release of the stop. For the English [p], at the beginning of a word, voice onset time is usually a little under 50 milliseconds (ms). For Danish, the voice onset times of stops are slightly longer, while in Spanish they are shorter.

When the VOT of a stop is rather long, as in the case of English and Danish voiceless stops, a puff of air follows the release of the stop, before the regular voicing of a following vowel begins. This is called **aspiration**, and indicated in IPA by a small raised ^{h}, as in [pʰ]. You can observe this puff of air if you hold a small piece of paper loosely in front of your mouth when you say *pin*. Now say *spin*. What do you notice?

The stops at the end of the English words *bed* and *pet* are voiced and voiceless respectively. Voicing extends into the closure of the alveolar stop in *bed*, but not (or more accurately, only a little way) into the closure of the alveolar stop in *pet*. The stop at the end of both words can be either **released** or **unreleased**: that is, you can either release or not release the pent-up air behind the alveolar blockage, resulting in a noise. If you say *my pet dog Rover*, it is likely that you will not release the [t] of *pet*; but if you say this phrase very carefully, separating *pet* from *dog*, you might release the [t] before forming the following [d]. Unreleased stops are indicated in the IPA by a raised angle ⌐. So the English word *pet* could be pronounced as either [pʰɛt] or [pʰɛt̚].

Nasals

Nasals have already been described (§2.2) as phones produced by lowering the velum to permit air to flow through the nose. Nasal consonants are like stops in having a complete blockage of the airstream through the oral cavity; but they allow the air to flow freely through the nasal cavity. Thus for [m] there is a complete closure of the oral cavity at the lips, as in [b] and [p]; but the velum is lowered, and the air travels out through the nose.

Nasals are normally voiced. Burmese (Sino-Tibetan, Myanmar), however, has voiceless bilabial, dental, palatal and velar nasals.

Fricatives

Fricatives are produced with incomplete closure at the place of articulation. A narrow passage is left open through which the airstream is forced, giving rise to a 'noisy' sound a bit like the sound you get by rubbing your hands on your clothing, or scratching your head.

Fricatives are found in many, though not all languages, and can be produced at any place of articulation, from the lips to the glottis. English has both voiced and voiceless fricatives. There is a voiced labiodental fricative, [v] as in *vale*, and a voiceless fricative at the same point of articulation, [f] as in *fail*. Other fricatives in English are dental [θ] and [ð], alveolar [s] and [z], alveopalatal [ʃ] and [ʒ], and glottal [h]. Ewe (Niger-Congo, Ghana) has both voiceless and voiced bilabial fricatives [ɸ] and [β], as well as labiodental fricatives [f] and [v]. Velar fricatives are found in German (as in *Buch* [buːx] 'book'), and many other languages.

Affricates

Phones produced by combining a stop and a fricative are called **affricates**. English has two affricates, both alveopalatal: voiceless [tʃ] (the first sound of *church*) and voiced [dʒ] (the first phone in *jungle*). The alveopalatal region is the most common place of articulation for affricates, though other places are possible. For instance, Mandarin Chinese has both aspirated and unaspirated alveolar and retroflex affricates, and Beembe (Niger-Congo, Democratic Republic of Congo) has labiodental affricates, again both aspirated and unaspirated.

Laterals

Phones like the initial [l] of English *laugh* are called **laterals** because the sides of the tongue are lowered at the point of articulation, allowing air to pass on both sides of a central closure.

The most common place of articulation of laterals is at the alveolar ridge. Dental and post-alveolar or retroflex laterals are also possible. A fair number of languages have palatal laterals, produced by contact between the blade of the tongue and the hard palate, with the sides open. This sound is found in Castilian Spanish *llave* 'key'. Velar laterals are also possible, though rare. In my dialect of English (Australian) words such as *milk* involve a velar lateral; the tip of the tongue is not used in this sound. The Papuan language Melpa (Papuan, New Guinea) also has a velar lateral.

In many dialects of English the back of the tongue is raised in the production of the lateral, especially when it occurs at the end of a word, as in *ball* or *school*; this lateral has a 'dark' quality. The IPA symbol for this sound is [ɫ]. In Australian English the alveolar lateral is usually dark, even at the beginning of a word. By contrast, the lateral of Danish and French is always 'clear', that is, is produced without the velar quality.

Like nasals, laterals are normally voiced; just a few languages have voiceless laterals. Burmese and Welsh (Indo-European, Wales) both have the voiceless alveolar lateral [ɬ].

Rhotics

The term **rhotic** is used for *r*-like sounds, which are represented in IPA by some variant of the Latin letter *r*. Rhotics come in a wide variety of shapes and forms, the main ones being taps, trills and approximants.

Taps (or flaps) involve a single rapid short closure (shorter than for a stop), usually between the tip of the tongue and the teeth or alveolar ridge, as in the Spanish words *caro* [kaɾɔ] 'expensive' and *pero* [peɾɔ] 'but'. This is the usual rhotic of Scottish English.

Trills are phones consisting of two or more rapid taps one after another. Usually trills are produced with the tip of the tongue, as in Spanish *perro* [perɔ] 'dog'. They can also be produced by vibrating the uvula rapidly, as in Parisian French, Standard German and some varieties of Southern Swedish and Dutch. Bilabial trills – like the disrespectful 'raspberry' in English – are found in a few languages, for instance in Kele (Papuan, New Guinea).

Rhotic approximants involve proximity, rather than contact, at the place of articulation. The *r*-sound of most dialects of English is an approximant. However, it differs considerably between dialects. In Australian English and Estuary English (London) it is an apical approximant, in which the tip of the tongue points towards the alveolar ridge, but does not make contact with it. Uvular approximants are found in Northumberland English (the uvula trill is sometimes also used in this dialect), and sometimes in German and French.

Glides

Glides or semivowels are the most vowel-like of the consonants, having the least constriction at the point of articulation. They are characterized by movement of one articulator, which travels towards but does not reach the other.

The *y*-sound of English, IPA [j], is a glide in which the blade of the tongue moves towards the palate. The blade of the tongue can also move towards the teeth. Bunuba (Bunuban, Australia) and Unggumi (Worrorran, Australia) have such glides (as well as the palatal glide); the so-called 'soft-*d*' of Danish (as in *mad* 'food') is a dental approximant.

English has a second glide, the labiovelar [w], which is produced by moving the back of the tongue towards the velum and at the same time rounding the lips. This phone occurs in about three-quarters of the world's languages (the palatal glide is found in a slightly higher fraction of the languages, about 85 per cent). A few languages have a plain velar glide [ɰ], unaccompanied by lip rounding, and even fewer have a bilabial or labiodental glide without an accompanying velarization.

Vowels

Vowels are speech sounds produced without interruption to the passage of air through the vocal tract. The vocal tract is used as a resonating chamber for an airstream vibrating from the action of the vocal folds; and as this suggests, vowels are normally voiced in all languages.

The cavities above the glottis act rather like an organ pipe or the chamber of a wind instrument, except that it has a characteristic right-angled bend between the vertical pharynx and the horizontal oral cavity. The shape of the cavities can be modified by positioning and shaping the tongue in different ways, which has an effect comparable to directing the airstream in an organ into different sized pipes.

The position of the high point of the tongue during the production of a vowel effectively defines the size and shape of the two resonating chambers, and thus the quality of the vowel. If the high point is high up and towards the front of the mouth, you get vowel sounds like the one usually written *ee* in English, as in *beet* [biːt], or the one written *i* in *bit* [bɪt]. These vowels are called **high front** vowels. If instead the high point of the tongue is high up, and towards the back of the oral cavity, you get a vowel like the one written *u* in *put* [pʰʊt]. These are **high back** vowels. For high vowels the body of the tongue is raised above its neutral or rest position.

If the body of the tongue rests at a relatively neutral height, as for the vowel of *bed* [bɛd] we have a **mid** vowel; lowering the body of the tongue results in a **low** vowel, such as the vowel of *fat* [fæt].

The front-to-back dimension is also usually divided into three: **front**, with the high point relatively front; **back**, with the high point towards the back; and **central**, with the high point in between, in the central region.

Table 2.2 shows the vowels of BBC English, the variety used by national newscasters, with the IPA symbols and illustrative examples.

Other dialects of English have slightly different ranges of vowels. General American English, for instance, the variety used by many national broadcasters in the USA, lacks the low back unrounded vowel [ɒ], and has [ɚ] in place of [ɜː]. There are also minor differences in the quality of the vowels, due partly to differences in the positioning of the high point of the tongue.

New Zealand English has the high central [ɨ] instead of the [ɪ] of other dialects. This vowel, though not common, is found in other languages, including Amharic (Afro-Asiatic, Ethiopia) and Nimboran (Papuan, West Papua).

Table 2.2 Chart of vowels of BBC English showing IPA representation and examples (based on Ladefoged 2001: 27–28)

	Front	Central	Back
High	iː *bead* ɪ *bit*		uː *boot* ʊ *put*
Mid	ɛ *bed*	ə *the* (as normally spoken) ɜː *bird*	ʌ *cut*; ɔː *ought*
Low	æ *at*		ɒ *cot*; ɑː *bard*

High and mid back vowels are usually accompanied by lip-rounding, and so are called **rounded vowels**. High- and mid-front vowels are usually produced with spreading of the lips, while low vowels are usually produced with the lips in a neutral position.

These correlations are imperfect. Some languages have high- and/or mid-front rounded vowels. Danish has three rounded front vowels: high front rounded [y]; mid-high front rounded [ø]; and mid-low front rounded [œ]. These have the same tongue positions as the three non-low front vowels [i], [e], and [ɛ],[2] respectively. Fewer languages have high- and/or mid-back unrounded vowels. But Vietnamese (Mon-Khmer, Vietnam) has three unrounded back vowels, [ɯ], [ɤ] and [ʌ], which have the same heights as the rounded [u], [o] and [ɔ].

The velum can be lowered during a vowel, allowing air to pass through the nasal cavity. This gives a **nasal vowel**. We have already seen that vowels in English can be nasal before a nasal consonant, as in *man* [mæ̃n]. French has nasal vowels, as in *lent* [lã] 'slow'.

2.4 Some additional features

The previous section presented an overview of the basic types of speech sounds found in the world's languages. In this section we mention a few additional features of the phonetics of human languages.

Airstream mechanisms

In addition to the pulmonic airstream, two other airstreams are used for the articulation of speech sounds: glottalic and velaric.

Glottalic

A number of languages of Africa, India and the Americas employ a **glottalic airstream** in the production of some (never all) phones. This airstream is created by closing the vocal folds and raising or lowering the larynx, while a closure – usually complete – is made somewhere in the oral cavity.

Ejectives are produced on egressive (outgoing) glottalic airstream, formed by raising the larynx so as to compress the air behind the oral closure; this closure is released while the glottal closure remains, resulting in a popping sound. About a fifth of the world's languages have ejectives. Quechua (Quechuan, Peru) has three, with alveopalatal, velar and uvular places of articulation: [ʧ'aka] 'hoarse', [k'ujui] 'to twist', and [q'aʎu] 'tomato sauce'.

Implosives are produced by pulling the larynx downwards during oral closure, and releasing the oral closure, resulting in an audible inrush of air. Only about 10 per cent of the world's languages have implosives. Sindhi (Indo-European, India) has bilabial (as in [ɓəni] 'field'), retroflex (as in [ɗɪnu] 'festival'), palatal (as in [ʄətu] 'illiterate'), and velar (as in [ɠənu] 'handle') implosives (as well as ejectives).

Velaric

The 'tutting' sound written *tsk tsk* in English involves an **ingressive velaric airstream**. It is produced by forming closures between the tip of the tongue and the alveolar ridge and the back of the tongue and the velum, keeping these closures in place while the body of the tongue is drawn downwards, rarefying the enclosed air. Then the contact between the tip of the tongue and the alveolar ridge is released, with the result that air is drawn into the mouth. The kissing sound is made in the same manner, except that front closure is at the lips. These sounds are called **clicks**.

Khoisan languages and some neighbouring Bantu languages of southeast Africa employ the velaric airstream in speech sounds. !Xóõ (Khoisan, Namibia) has bilabial, dental, alveolar, lateral and palatal clicks, along with various accompanying velar onsets. These are illustrated in [ʘʔôo] 'get stuck', [k|ʔâa] 'die', [k!ʔàã] 'be seated', [k‖ʔàa] 'not to be', and [k‡ʔãa] 'shoot you'.

Coarticulation

It was mentioned above that the *w*-sound of English is produced with simultaneous movement of the lips and of the back of the tongue towards the velum. Such sounds, with simultaneous constriction at two places of articulation involve **coarticulation** or **double articulation**.

Stops and nasals can also be coarticulated. The most common are bilabial-velar combinations. Various languages of West Africa have such phones. Idoma (Niger-Congo, Nigeria) has coarticulated voiceless and voiced stops, and a coarticulated nasal: [àk͡pà] 'bridge', [àg͡bà̰] 'jaw', and [aŋ͡màa] 'body painting'. Other combinations are rarer. Yélî Dnye (Papuan, Rossel Island) also has bilabial-alveolar coarticulated stops and nasals, in addition to labio-velars, as in [t͡pɛnɛ] 'lung' and [n͡mo] 'bird'. Perhaps the most unusual coarticulated phone is found in Wari' (Chapacura-Wanham, Brazil): a voiceless dental stop coarticulated with a voiceless bilabial trill, [t͡ʙ̥].

Diphthongs

Vowels are produced with the tongue in a relatively steady state throughout its articulation. A **diphthong** is produced when instead the tongue is in constant motion throughout, travelling from one vowel position to another. English dialects generally have a fair number of diphthongs, as can be seen in Table 2.3. (There are further minor differences that are not shown.)

Syllables

Phones combine into larger units called **syllables**. These are surprisingly difficult to characterize precisely, and there is disagreement amongst phoneticians concerning their defining criteria. Nevertheless, syllables have more psychological reality for speakers than do phones, and native speakers of any language will usually be able to divide spoken utterances into syllables without difficulty.[3] For instance, the word *phonetics* has three syllables (the boundaries of

Table 2.3 Diphthongs of three dialects of English (based on Ladefoged 2001: 27–28)

BBC English	Australian English	General American English	Examples
[aʊ]	[æʊ]	[aʊ]	bowed, loud
[əʊ]	[oʊ]	[oʊ]	grow, owe
[ɔɪ]	[ɔɪ]	[ɔɪ]	boy, quoit
[eɪ]	[eɪ]	[eɪ]	day, say
[aɪ]	[aɪ]	[aɪ]	my, dry
[ɪə]	[ɪə]		beer, leer
[eə]	[ɛə]		hair, lair
[ʊə]	[ʊə]		poor, boor
[aə]			hire, pyre

which are indicated by dots), [fə.nɛ.tɪks]. Even if you are not a native speaker of a language it is not normally too difficult to guess what the syllable division of a word is. The Gooniyandi word *girili* 'tree' has three syllables, and you can probably guess what they are.[4]

Syllables generally consist of a vowel surrounded by one or more consonants, usually before the vowel, sometimes after it. Some languages allow syllables consisting of just a vowel; some allow syllables consisting of a consonant, generally a nasal or lateral. English has syllables of both of these types: consider *about* [ə.bæʊt] and *medal* [mɛd.ɫ]; these words also illustrate syllables with a consonant before and after the vowel, that is, CVC syllables (where C stands for consonant, and V for vowel). English has a considerable number of syllable types (including CV, CVC, V, VC, CCV and C), and thousands of possible syllables.

Languages differ considerably in terms of the syllable types they allow. In Gooniyandi all syllables must contain a vowel; usually it is preceded by a consonant, giving the most common form of the syllable CV; syllables can however also end in consonants. CV syllables are the most common syllables in human languages, and are the most frequent in most languages.

2.5 Prosodies

Vowels and consonants are segments, that come one after another in speech (although the boundaries between them are generally not precisely delimited, as we have seen). Some phonetic properties are spread over sequences of phones. These are called **prosodies** or **suprasegmentals**. Two prosodies are discussed in this section, pitch and stress. Others include loudness, tempo, length and rhythm.

Pitch

Pitch refers to the frequency of vibration of the vocal folds. When you speak the pitch varies from moment to moment. Variations in pitch are used in two main ways in languages: to distinguish between words; and to convey different inflections on the meaning of an utterance. In the former case, we speak of **tone**; in the latter, of **intonation**.

Tone

Many languages use different patterns of pitch to distinguish words; these pitch differences are called **tones**. Languages that use tones are called tone languages. Cantonese (Sino-Tibetan, China) is, like many nearby languages, a tone language. Differences in the pitch on the syllable [si] give six different words: with high falling tone, it is the word 'poem'; with mid-level, 'to try'; with low level, 'matter'; with extra low, 'time'; with high rising, 'to cause'; and with mid-rising, 'city'.[5] In fact, Cantonese has three more tones, nine in total.

Intonation

All languages use variation in pitch over an utterance to convey modulations of the meaning expressed by the words. If you say *I'll see you tomorrow* as a plain statement, you will probably say it with fall of pitch at the end. If you want to ask your friend whether they will be coming into the university on the following day, you would utter it with a rise in pitch on the final word. Produced with a rising-falling intonation contour on *tomorrow*, the utterance would convey a degree of insistence. Pitch variations also convey other kinds of information, including information about grammatical structure and the speaker's emotional state, for example whether they are angry, happy or sad.

The variations of meaning that are expressed by different intonation patterns are difficult to specify exactly, and differ somewhat amongst dialects of English – as well as between languages.

Stress

Syllables can be produced with different degrees of forcefulness or lung energy, which is normally accompanied by differences in the tension of the vocal folds. Increasing the energy gives greater intensity, loudness and usually higher pitch. Syllables with greater energy are **stressed** syllables, indicated in the IPA by a ' before the syllable. Other phonetic differences sometimes correlate with stress. For instance, in English the vowel of an unstressed syllable is typically schwa, as in the usual unstressed utterance of words such as *the* ([ðə]) and *a* ([ə]), and the second syllable of *farmer* (['fɑːmə]).

In some languages stress always falls on a particular syllable of a word. In most Australian languages the first syllable of a word is always stressed. The following examples from Walmajarri (Pama-Nyungan, Australia) illustrate this: *ngarpu* ['ŋaɻbu] 'father', *kurrapa* ['kuɾapa] 'hand', and *martuwarra* ['maʈuˌwaɾa] 'river'. (As the last example shows, the third syllable of a word with four syllables is also stressed.) Stress in Hungarian also goes to the first syllable of a word. In Swahili (Niger-Congo, Democratic Republic of Congo) and Polish (Indo-European, Poland), by contrast, it is the second-last syllable of a word that normally gets stress.

In English, stress goes on different syllables, depending on the word. Compare the placement in the three trisyllabic words (where the stressed syllable is bolded): **pho**tograph, di**plo**ma and disa**gree**. There are a fair number of pairs of nouns and verbs that are distinguished by placement of stress. Stress goes on the first syllable of the noun, as in *an **im**port*, *a **con**vict* and *an **in**sult*, but on the second syllable of the corresponding verb: *to im**port**, to con**vict*** and *to in**sult***.

2.6 Phonology

How many phones does English have? Every time you utter a word or sentence there will be slight differences in the precise configuration of your vocal tract and the surrounding air (it's a bit like not being able to step into the same river twice!). With sufficiently accurate instruments you could find minor differences in the shape of the vocal tract, and in the sound wave. In this sense you might say that English effectively has unlimited number of phones. Many of the differences are too small to be perceived. Some differences are perceptible in principle – that is, are not beyond the distinguishing capabilities of the human ear – but are ignored by speakers. **Phonology** investigates the sound differences that are linguistically relevant in a language, and how the sounds pattern as a system.

Phonemes and allophones

The bilabial stops in the three words *ban*, *pan* and *span* are all phonetically different: [b], [pʰ] and [p]. However, to native speakers of English the [pʰ] and [p] of the second and third words are the 'same' sound, while the [b] of the first word is perceived as a different sound. To a native speaker of Nyulnyul (Nyulnyulan, Australia) with no knowledge of English all three would sound the same, and they would experience difficulty in telling them apart. On the other hand, in the simple CV syllables [ba], [pʰa] and [pa], native speakers of Thai (Tai-Kadai, Thailand) would have no trouble hearing all three bilabial stops as different. This is not because Nyulnyul speakers have worse ears than us, and Thai speaker have better ears than we do. Rather, it is because none of the differences are important in Nyulnyul, but all are important in Thai.

How can this be? For the speaker of English [pʰ] and [p] of *pin* and *spin* are both instances of the voiceless bilabial stop. You cannot get a different word by replacing one of the phones by the other – at worst, you will get a weird-sounding production of the same word. If you said [spʰɪn] instead of [spɪn] no one would think this was a new word of English; they would still interpret it as *spin*. Similarly, at the end of a word such as *sip* you could produce either [pʰ] or [pˀ], and no difference would result.

But you do get a difference if you replace the [pʰ] at the beginning of *pin* with a [b]: you have another word, *bin*, with a completely different and unrelated meaning.

In Thai, replacing [p] by either [b] or [pʰ] makes a difference. The word [pâː] means 'aunt'; if you were to replace the first phone by a [b] you would get [bâː] 'crazy', and if you replace it by [pʰ] you get [pʰâː] 'cloth'. These are three completely different words in Thai, no more related than English *pin* and *bin*.

The phones [p], [pʰ] and [pˀ] do not contrast with one another in English; the difference between them is said to be **non-contrastive**. It is not used in the language to distinguish between words. These phones are said to be **allophones** (the *allo-* comes from Greek *allos* 'other' – literally, 'other sounds').

The difference between [pʰ] and [p] is significant in English; [pʰ] and [b] contrast, and the difference between them is **contrastive**. These phones are not allophones in English, but represent distinct **phonemes**. In Thai, [b], [p], and [pʰ] all contrast, and so represent three distinct phonemes. In Nyulnyul none of the three contrast, and so they are all allophones of a single phoneme. English, Thai, and Nyulnyul organize the phonetic 'reality' in three different ways.

Phonemes are distinguished from phones in writing by putting them in slanted brackets, //. Thus /p/ indicates the voiceless bilabial stop phoneme that has (in English) allophones [pʰ], [p] and [p˺], and is different from the phoneme /b/.

Non-contrastiveness of allophones

By definition, allophones do not contrast with one another: no allophone can be used in place of another to make a different word in a language. This can be for one of two reasons. First, the phones might be able to occur in the same phonetic context, without having any effect on meaning; in this case the phones are in **free variation**. Second, the phones might be unable to occur in the same phonetic environment; if this is so, we speak of **complementary distribution**.

> Do you understand why phones in either free variation or complementary distribution cannot contrast? Think carefully about it – this is a crucial point to understand!

Free variation

Free variation can be illustrated by the stop phones at the end of words in English, which may be either released or unreleased.[6] The word *slab* can be produced with either a final released [b] or an unreleased [b˺]. In Gooniyandi the phones [ʎ] and [l̪] (a lateral made with the blade of the tongue touching the back of the upper teeth) are in free variation at the end of a syllable and after a low vowel. So the word *galyba* 'soft' can be pronounced as either [kaʎbɐ] or [kal̪bɐ]. At the end of a word in the Gooniyandi the tap/trill [r] and flap [ɾ] are in free variation.

We also speak of free variation across speakers or dialects when some speakers use one phone, others another. For instance, the English rhotic is produced in a variety of different ways in different dialects, including [ɹ], [ɾ], [r], and [ʀ].

Complementary distribution

The phones [pʰ] and [p] in English are in complementary distribution. Unaspirated [p] occurs after [s], and within a word before an unstressed vowel. Aspirated [pʰ] occurs elsewhere: at the beginning of a word, and within a word before a stressed vowel; it never follows [s]. Where [p] occurs, [pʰ] does not, and vice versa.[7] The two vowel phones [ɪ] and [ĩ] are also in complementary distribution in English. The oral vowel occurs in words like *sip* and *pill*; the nasal vowel occurs in words like *sin* and *sing*. More precisely, the nasal vowel occurs before a nasal consonant in the same syllable; the oral vowel occurs elsewhere.

Rules of realization

The allophones of a phoneme are its phonetic realizations, the phonetic substances that as it were make up the abstract phonemic unit. Below are a few phonemes of English together with their allophonic realizations. (This list is incomplete: there are other phonemes in English, and those shown have other allophones.)

/p/	[p], [pʰ], [p˥]	/b/	[b], [b˥]
/t/	[t], [tʰ], [t˥], [tʷ], [t̪], [ɾ], [ʔ]	/d/	[d], [d˥], [d̪]
/k/	[k], [kʰ], [k˥], [kʷ], [k̟], [k̟ʰ]	/g/	[g], [g˥], [g̟]
/m/	[m], [ɱ]	/n/	[n], [n̥], [n̪], [ŋ]
/l/	[l], [ɫ], [l̪], [ʟ], [l̥]	/s/	[s]
/θ/	[θ], [θ̬]	/ð/	[ð], [ð̥]
/ɪ/	[ɪ], [ɪ̃], [ɨ]	/i/	[iː], [ĩː]
/ʊ/	[ʊ], [ʊ̃]	/ɛ/	[ɛ], [ɛː], [ɛ̃]

Some of the allophones shown are in free variation. Some allophones are **conditioned** by the surrounding phonetic context: that is, the allophone is chosen in a particular instance because of the phones in the neighbourhood, or because of a prosodic feature such as stress or length. Thus the [ɱ] allophone of /m/ occurs only before a labiodental fricative, as in *bumf*; it is conditioned by the following sound. We can express this as a rule:

- /m/ is realized as labiodental [ɱ] before a labiodental fricative; otherwise it is bilabial

To give a more complex example, we can express some of the allophonic variation of the voiced velar stop in English as follows:

- /g/ is realized by the voiced velar stop [g], except when:

  (i) it is followed by a high front vowel, in which case it is advanced towards the back of the palatal region, [g̟];

  (ii) it is followed by the high back vowel [u] or the labio-velar glide [w], in which case it is labialized, [gʷ]; and

  (iii) before another stop or nasal, and optionally at the end of a word, it is unreleased [g˥].

It is sometimes useful to express realization rules more formally, to give a clearer and more succinct statement. The above two rules can be written as follows:

$$/m/ \quad \rightarrow \quad \begin{cases} [ɱ] & / \quad \_\!\_\ \{[f], [v]\} \\ [m] & / \quad \text{otherwise} \end{cases}$$

(Continued)

—Cont'd

$$
/g/ \quad \rightarrow \quad
\begin{cases}
[g] & / & \_\_ \{[i], [ɪ]\} \\
[g^w] & / & \_\_ \{[u], [w]\} \\
[g^ˀ] & / & \_\_ \text{ stop consonant} \\
[g^ˀ] & / & \_\_ \# \text{ (optional)}
\end{cases}
$$

In these rules the arrow → indicates 'is realized as'; the slash / is to be read 'in the environment; the underline _ indicates where the segment occurs; # marks a word boundary; and braces (either a single one, or a pair) { } indicate alternatives. Other standard symbols not used in this rule include: round brackets () for optional items, and $ for a syllable boundary.

2.7 How to establish the phonemes of a language

All human languages distinguish a limited number of phonemes, between ten for Pirahã (Mura, Brazil) and just over a hundred for some Khoisan languages of southern Africa. English is a relatively typical language with some 38 (some dialects of American English) or 39 (British English, Australian English) phonemes.

How does one go about determining the phonemes of a language? This section outlines the procedure and reasoning. This may perhaps give the misleading impression that it is a mechanical process, which it certainly is not, when you are confronted with a real language. But it is important to explain the basic steps since beginning students often experience difficulties in putting the considerations outlined in §2.6 into practice.

The two basic steps can be summarized as follows. First, look for **suspicious pairs** of phones, phones that are phonetically similar enough to count as possible allophones of a single phoneme. Next, examine their distribution to see if they are in complementary distribution, free variation or contrastive variation (i.e. occur in the same environment). Let's put this to work.

Example

Gooniyandi has stop phones [d] and [ḍ], both made with the tip of the tongue in roughly the same region: the alveolar ridge, and just behind it. They are illustrated in the following short but representative list:

[ɟʊdu]	'straight'	[larɡaḍi]	'boab tree'
[ŋaḷʊdu]	'three'	[lambaḍi]	'little'
[waḍa]	'star'	[bɪḍi]	'thigh'
[lambadi]	'father-in-law'	[maːdi]	'cold'
[ɟʊḍu]	'dust'	[ṭaɻdi]	'heavy'
[bɪdi]	'they'	[lawadi]	'shoulder'

The phones [d] and [ɖ] are phonetically similar, suspicious pairs, and we must determine whether they are allophones of a single phoneme (like their counterparts in some dialects of English) or separate phonemes. Before reading on, examine the list carefully yourself, and see if you can come to a conclusion.

We begin by looking for **minimal pairs**, pairs of words that differ only in that one has the phone [d] and the other has [ɖ]. This is because if we can find such pairs of words, we know that the two phones occur in the same phonetic environment, and therefore contrast. The list has three minimal pairs: [ɟʊdu] 'straight' and [ɟʊɖu] 'dust'; [lambadi] 'father-in-law' and [lambaɖi] 'little'; and [bɪdi] 'they' and [bɪɖi] 'thigh'. The pairs differ only in that the where there is a [d] in the first member of each pair there is a [ɖ] in the second. We have to conclude that [d] and [ɖ] contrast, and cannot be allophones of a single phoneme. They must represent two separate phonemes, which we naturally write /d/ and /ɖ/.

Although the existence of minimal pairs is evidence for a phonemic contrast, their absence does not prove allophone status. This is an important point to appreciate, because minimal pairs are rare in some languages. Lacking minimal pairs, one sometimes has to be satisfied with near minimal pairs. That is, with pairs of words that differ not just in the targeted segment but in others as well. Examples of near minimal pairs for [d] and [ɖ] in the list above are [lawɑdi] 'shoulder' and [larɡaɖi] 'boab tree', and [taɹɪdi] 'heavy' and [bɪɖi] 'thigh'. The first pair shows that both [d] and [ɖ] can occur between a low vowel and a high vowel, while the second shows they can occur between high vowels. Nothing in the wider phonetic environment is likely to guarantee the occurrence of one or the other of these phones, and we can conclude that they belong to separate phonemes.

There are two other suspicious pairs in the above list, [i] and [ɪ], and [u] and [ʊ]. In this case there are no minimal pairs for either contrast. Examination of the list reveals that the first member of each pair, the higher vowel phone, occurs exclusively at the end of a word, while the second member, the lower phone, occurs within words. They are in complementary distribution. If this data is representative, we are justified in identifying two separate phonemes, /i/ and /u/, each with two allophones.

Beginning students sometimes wonder which of the allophone symbols should be chosen as the label for the phoneme. The answer is that it doesn't matter. We could equally have chosen to call the two phonemes just discussed /ɪ/ and /ʊ/ – or even /£/ and /ɯ/. Practicality is the main guiding principle: it makes sense to use familiar symbols that are easiest to type. It is also more sensible to use the symbol representing a widespread allophone than one that occurs in just one narrow phonetic environment.

Why focus on suspicious pairs?

In deciding on the phonemes of a language it is sensible to focus on phonetically similar phones, suspicious pairs. Phones that are phonetically very different are unlikely to be allophones of a single phoneme in a language: if they are very different it is unlikely that they will be treated as 'the same', and speakers are unlikely to regard them as variants.

This is so even if the phones are in complementary distribution. The phones [h] and [ŋ] are in complementary distribution in English: [h] can only occur at the beginning of a syllable, and [ŋ] only at the end. But they are phonetically very different from one another, and are not normally regarded as allophones. And consistent with this, native speakers of English do not feel that they are in any sense the same sound.

Or consider [p] and [kʰ], which are in complementary distribution in English. No one would regard them as allophones, when [p] is clearly each much more similar to [pʰ].

This is why we begin by looking for suspicious pairs. You do not need to slavishly go through every pair of phones and decide whether or not they contrast. Nevertheless, you do need to be awake to the possibility that phones that initially seem phonetically different to you might be allophones in the language. For instance, [r] and [l] probably sound very different to you; but they are allophones of a single phoneme in Japanese.

2.8 Transcription

The process of accurately representing speech in writing is called **transcription**. Three types of transcription are: **phonemic**, **broad phonetic** and **narrow phonetic**.

Phonemic transcription represents the spoken word phonemically, and by convention is enclosed in slashes, //. A phonemic transcription can be useful for many purposes. For instance, in a dictionary, accompanying the standard orthographic representation of a word the phonemic representation might provide information not predictable from the spelling. With knowledge of the rules of realization (such as outlined in §2.6) and dialectal variation, a user could pronounce the word accurately. It is more economical for the dictionary maker to use phonemic representations than to try and represent the range of phonetic variation of each word.

Phonetic transcription represents the phonetic substance of speech, and by convention is enclosed in square brackets, []. The IPA is generally used for phonetic transcription. Phonetic transcription can never be absolutely and completely precise, and the two types, broad and narrow, refer to extremes of accuracy in representation.

Broad phonetic transcription is the least accurate, and ignores many of the precise phonetic details, especially those predictable by general rules. Thus, in a broad transcription of English aspiration of voiceless stops is likely to be ignored, since it is predictable. Generally speaking the use of diacritics in broad transcription is kept to a minimum.

> Broad transcription is quite similar to phonemic transcription. However, they are **not** the same thing, since the units represented are completely different! It is quite possible, for example, to make a broad transcription of utterances in a language you do not know, and have not analysed. This would not be a phonemic transcription, which presumes an analysis of the sound system of the language.

In narrow transcription one represents as much phonetic detail as is possible, given the circumstances. This means that you should not represent more than can be perceived by ear, eye and/or instrumental means; to do so would misrepresent rather than improve the accuracy of the transcription. In a narrow transcription of English one would indicate such things as the aspiration of voiceless stops, velar quality of the lateral and so forth.

Broad and narrow phonetic transcriptions differ in degree, in the accuracy of representation. It is perfectly reasonable to combine them, representing some things narrowly, others broadly. In a phonetic study of stop consonants in a language it would make sense to represent vowels and other consonants fairly broadly (especially those not in the immediate environment of the targeted phones), and the stops narrowly.

Below are three transcriptions of a simple English sentence to illustrate the three types of transcription. Notice that in this case the phonemic and broad phonetic transcriptions are the same, though what is represented in each is different: phonemes in the first case, phones in the second. The narrow transcription represents a spoken version of the sentence in Standard Australian English, which can be found on the website for this book; it is not as narrow as it could be: for instance, stress and intonation are not represented. (As an exercise, you could try to improve its accuracy by marking in these features.)

Orthographic representation	*The farmer kills the duckling*
Phonemic transcription	/ðə fɑːmə kɪlz ðə dʌklɪŋ/
Broad phonetic transcription	[ðə fɑːmə kɪlz ðə dʌklɪŋ]
Narrow phonetic transcription	[ðə fã̠ːmə kʰɪɫz ðə dʌkɫĩŋ]

Summing up

The scientific study of speech sounds is **phonetics**, and is divided into three main branches: **articulatory**, **acoustic** and **auditory**.

Speech sounds are produced by continuous movement of the speech organs. This continuous stream can be divided into discrete segments called **phones**. Phones are produced by movement of air through the vocal tract. This air normally comes from the lungs, and is pushed through the vocal tract and out of the mouth and/or nose. This is the egressive pulmonic **airstream mechanism**. Speech sounds can also be produced on an ingressive pulmonic airstream. Some languages use **velaric** (giving clicks) or **glottalic** (giving ejectives and implosives) airstreams.

Two main classes of phones are consonants and vowels. **Consonants** involve a constriction at some point in the vocal tract. They are defined by **place** and **manner of articulation**. The vocal folds may be drawn together to vibrate regularly, giving **voicing**, or held apart, giving **voiceless** phones. For stops, **voice onset time** is relevant. Some phones involve two simultaneous places or manners of articulation; this is called **coarticulation**.

Vowels do not involve a constriction in the vocal tract. They are resonant sounds, characterized by the position of the highest point of the tongue, and the shape of the lips. Vowels are almost always voiced, and are normally oral; nasal vowels do occur in some languages. **Diphthongs** are vocalic phones characterized by movement of the tongue throughout.

Consonants and vowels combine together to form **syllables**. **Length**, **pitch**, **loudness** and **stress** are **prosodic** features. These apply over phones, syllables or larger stretches of speech.

Phonology is concerned with the sound system of a language. The most important concept is the **phoneme**, realized as a set of **allophones**.

To establish the phonemes of a language one first looks for **suspicious pairs** of phones. Next one looks for **minimal** (or near minimal) **pairs**. If these can be found, the phones must represent distinct phonemes. If the phones are in either **complementary distribution** or **free variation** they are allophones. Phonological rules describe where the different allophones occur.

Transcription is the systematic representation of the sounds of a stretch of speech, usually using the **International Phonetic Alphabet**. The main modes of transcription are **phonetic** (either broad or narrow), and **phonemic**. Phonetic transcriptions are enclosed in square brackets, []; phonemic transcriptions, between slashes, //.

Guide to further reading

Most introductory textbooks discuss the basics of phonetics and phonology (see the list at the end of Chapter 1). Collins and Mees (2003) gives a good overview of English phonetics and phonology; Hughes et al. (2005) provides detailed information on phonetic and phonological differences among British dialects.

An excellent introductory textbook on phonetics is Ladefoged (2005); Laver (2001) is a useful synopsis of the subject; Ladefoged and Maddieson (1996) surveys the phonetics of the world's languages; and Denes and Pinson (1993) is a comprehensible account of all three major branches of phonetics. *The Handbook of the International Phonetic Association* (1999) is a necessary reference work for the serious student of phonetics. Samples of phones in most of the languages illustrated in this handbook can be accessed at the website of the International Phonetic Association, http://www2.arts.gla.ac.uk/IPA/ipa.html.

This chapter touches on the very basics of phonology, the identification of phonemes. Modern phonology has a more theoretical agenda, and is concerned with identification of distinctive patterns of sound in human languages, and how these are best captured, represented and accounted for. A succinct account is Cohn (2001); introductory textbooks include Clark and Yallop (1990); Carr (1993); and Gussenhoven and Jacobs (1998/2003).

Two useful introductory courses on CD-ROMs are Handke (2000) (phonetics and phonology) and Reid (1999) (phonetics). Both include numerous illustrations of sounds of the world's languages.

Issues for further thought and exercises

1. Transcribe the following English words and expressions, pronounced as in your dialect, in broad phonetic, narrow phonetic and phonemic transcriptions:

butter	*mutton*	*tarry*	*really*	*blur*	*phew*
singer	*ginger*	*lymph*	*rouge*	*catches*	*brr* (for 'it's cold')
antiques	*ask*	*button*	*canyon*	*atom*	*Adam*

2. Transcribe the following English sentences, pronounced as in your dialect, in broad phonetic, narrow phonetic, and phonemic transcriptions:

Would you please stop that racket?
I haven't seen my brother for ages.
Did you talk to her about it yesterday?
'Seems like we'll have to wait for another killing,' Bony said calmly.
I haven't got the faintest idea where you put it.

3. Below are some words written in a broad phonetic transcription. Identify the words, and write them in ordinary English orthography and in phonemic transcription. The transcription represents the author's pronunciation of the words (in his dialect of Australian English), and may differ from yours. If there are differences, retranscribe the word in the IPA according to your pronunciation.

[səbmɪt]	[θɪðə]	[hjɯːmn̩]	[sɪgnɫ]	[fĩŋgõneɪɫ]
[kʰɜːɫi]	[meɹi]	[əbɹʌpˈtʰ]	[stɹɒŋ̍ti]	[ʤɛ̃nəsaɪd]

4. Divide the following English words into syllables and indicate stress:

hesitate	*influence*	*influenza*	*habitual*	*habit*
sentential	*essence*	*essential*	*sentence*	*raspberry*
supermarket	*bookcase*	*notebook*	*economy*	*economics*

5. Pronounce the following phones (if necessary, practise making the phone, adding in a vowel where necessary) and explain in as much detail as you can their articulatory features:

[ə̃]	[ɲ]	[ɳ]	[ɾ]	[ʌ]	[ɴ]	[ʙ]	[ɣ]	[ʃ]	[ɭ]
[æ]	[ø]	[ʊ]	[ɒ]	[ɔ]	[ʔ]	[ʤ]	[i]	[ŋ]	[ǃ]

6. Give one minimal pair for each of the following contrasting phonemes in English:

/s/, /z/	/s/, /ʃ/	/z/, /ʒ/	/θ/, /ð/
/l/, /r/	/n/, /ŋ/	/tʃ/, /dʒ/	/f/, /v/
/ɛ/, /æ/	/ɒ/, /ɔ/	/ɔ/, /ʊ/	/ʊ/, /u/

(Continued)

Issues for further thought and exercises

7. Based on the data below, say whether the placement of stress predictable in Taba (Austronesian, Halmahera). If it is, state the rule.

['plaŋ]	'fly'	[ka.'tʃu.paŋ]	'grasshopper'
['po.jo]	'head'	[ˌpa.ra.'di.du]	'run-away child'
['bub]	'hornet'	['lu.ri]	'rosella'
[ma.'ni.tap]	'work'	[ˌma.nu.'si.a]	'people'
[su.'sa.ra]	'twins'	[ˌku.pat.'ba.waŋ]	'small woven rice basket'
[ˌsa.ko.'a.mo]	'to insert'	[kam.ˌkum.pa.'ppi.do]	'large woven rice basket'

8. We gave a number of allophones for English /t/ and /n/ in §2.6. List as many examples as you can of words with these allophones. What factors motivate the choice of allophone? Can you write a rule to explain some or all of the allophonic distribution?

9. Gooniyandi has velar nasal phones [ŋ] and [ŋ̠] that differ in terms of how far back the point of contact between the tongue and velum is. Based on the following data, are they allophones of a single phoneme, or do they contrast? Justify your answer.

[ɲi:di]	'we'	[ŋela]	'east'
[jiɲi]	'name'	[maɲu]	'Mangu' (a place name)
[juʊŋgu]	'scrub'	[ɲumbaɲɟ]	'husband'
[ŋɑːbu]	'father'	[bɪraɲi̥]	'their'
[ŋɑːŋgi]	'your'	[ɲaḷʊdu]	'three'

10. Based on the following data, what are the distributions of the bilabial stop phones [b], [p], [pʰ], and [ɓ] in Goemai (Afroasiatic, Nigeria)? Pay attention to the positions of the phones in the words, and specify whether they are in contrastive distribution, free variation or complementary distribution in the specified positions? How many phonemes do they represent? How would you describe what happens at the end of words?

[baŋ]	'gourd'	[mʉep]	'they'
[gəba]	'one who returned'	[pen]	'remove'
[paŋ]	'stone'	[gəɓaːr]	'one who saluted someone'
[bukʰ]	'return'	[reːp]	'girl'
[pʰaŋ]	'snake'	[mʉepʰ]	'they'
[pʰaːtʰ]	'five'	[gəpaːr]	'one who sent something'
[ɓaŋ]	'red'	[bi]	'thing'
[petʰ]	'exist'	[ba]	'return'
[poːtʰ]	'narrow'	[tʰebul]	'table'
[kaɓan]	'face down'	[ɓetʰ]	'belly'
[ɓoːtʰ]	'able'	[pʰe]	'place'
[gəpʰaːr]	'one who jumped'	[pʰepʰe]	'cover'
[reːpʰ]	'girl'	[ɓakʰ]	'here'

11. It has been suggested that *ghoti* is a possible way of spelling the word *fish* (i.e. [fɪʃ]) in English orthography. It is possible to find words in which *gh* represents [f], *o* represents [ɪ], and *ti* represents [ʃ]. See if you can find examples, and then see if you can argue that in fact *ghoti* is not a possible spelling of *fish* after all.

12. Based on the following words, say what types of syllable are found in Kuot (Papuan, New Ireland) – that is, indicate what shapes of syllable are found in terms of the sequences of consonants and vowels. Syllable boundaries have been marked in words of more than one syllable. What rules of syllabification have been observed?

[dʊs]	'stand'	[dʊ.ri]	'sleep'
[u.waʊ]	'cloud'	[nʊ.nə.map˥]	'life'
[ɛs.pan]	'sun'	[u.de.bʊn]	'banana plant'
[sə.gər]	'egg'	[ʊt˥]	'be full'
[lɛj.lom]	'dolphin'	[lə.kə.bwon]	'stick of firewood'
[pa.ku.ɔ]	'taro leaf'	[fa.nu.ɔ]	'short side of house'
[lə.le.u.ma]	'termite'	[mwa.ba.ri]	'sun'
[na.bwaj.ma]	'ant species'	[mus.gju]	'bird species'
[kejn]	'type of basket'	[si:ge:]	'spoon'
[dan.wot]	'river'	[a.fa.ji]	'raintree'

Notes

1. Strictly speaking there is a difference between post-alveolar and retroflex sounds, though often the terms are used interchangeably. Both are made with the tongue behind the alveolar ridge, but with retroflex sounds the tip is turned back. Many languages of the Indian subcontinent (e.g. Hindi-Urdu (Indo-European), Tamil (Dravidian) and Telugu (Dravidian)) have retroflex consonants.

2. In the phonetic alphabet used specifically for Danish (e.g. in dictionaries), the last of these vowels is represented by the symbol [æ], which in the IPA represents a rather lower front vowel.

3. Speakers of languages which, like English, have orthographies that represent sounds poorly are apt to identify syllables from the written forms of words rather than from their spoken form. You should be careful not to do this, and always work from the pronunciation.

4. Did you correctly guess *gi.ri.li* [gɪ.ɹɪ.li]?

5. It is important to understand that it is **not** that these six different tones give different meanings of the word *si* in Cantonese, as is sometimes said. There is no word *si* in the language, but rather six different words, each with a different form and meaning.

6. Absolutely free variation is rare. Usually there are reasons for it, perhaps the speaker's dialect, perhaps the emphasis the speaker wants to put on the word. Free variation is 'free' in that it never results in a different word.

7. Sometimes a pair of phones is in partial complementary distribution in a language – there are some circumstances in which one of the phones occurs but the other does not, although this is not across the board. This can be illustrated by the unreleased [p˥] and the released and aspirated [pʰ] in English. They are not in complementary distribution because both can occur at the end of a word. But within words they share no environment of occurrence: [p˥] occurs only before another stop consonant or a nasal (as in *apt* and *one-upmanship*), while [pʰ] cannot occur in this environment.

3 Structure of Words: Morphology

In this chapter we turn attention to what is perhaps the most salient unit in the grammar of human languages, and also to speakers: the word. The boundaries of words in spoken utterances are not overtly marked, so we need criteria for their identification. We introduce the widely used notion of the word as a minimal free form. We also examine the internal structure of words, that is, how they can be divided into smaller meaningful units. The scientific investigation of this domain is called morphology.

Chapter contents

Goals

The goals of the chapter are to:
- explain the concept of word as a minimal free form;
- introduce and explain the key concepts in the study of the structure of words, including morpheme and allomorph;

- distinguish and classify the main types of morpheme according to their behaviour;
- exemplify the main methods and techniques of identifying morphemes and allomorphs;
- show how the structure of words in a language can be described; and
- raise the question of the psychological reality of morphological analysis.

Key terms

allomorph	infix	morphophonemic rule	suffix
bound morpheme	inflection	noun	suppletion
case	inflectional morpheme	number	tense
clitic	lexeme	person	verb
derivational morpheme	morph	prefix	word
enclitic	morpheme	root	zero morpheme
free morpheme	morphophonemic form	stem	

3.1 Words

Notion of the word

Speakers generally have some notion of words in their language, and all languages probably have a word for 'word' – that is, a word that can translate *word* in some context. (The same does not hold for most of the other terms used in grammatical description, including many of the terms we encountered in the previous chapter, such as *phone*, *phoneme*, *syllable* and so on.)

Speakers of English generally have a good feel for how an utterance can be divided into words. This may seem trivial: surely words are the things that are separated by largish white spaces in writing. But this does not always work smoothly. *Bookcase* and *bookshelf* would be words by this criterion, and this probably agrees with your intuitions. On the other hand there is no apparent motivation for writing *church mouse* as two words, *churchman* as one. And of course, you could not use this criterion at all for an unwritten language.

In speech we find no corresponding pauses between the words – recall Figure 2.1, the sound wave for *The farmer kills the duckling*. Nevertheless, no speaker of English would have any doubt that there are five words in this sentence, *the*, *farmer*, *kills*, *the* (again) and *duckling*. No one would say that there is a word boundary between *farm* ([fɑːm]) and *erkills* ([əkʰɪɫz]), or between *kill* ([kʰɪɫ]) and *s* ([z]).

Although no pauses occur between the words, you could potentially pause at any of the word boundaries in uttering the sentence, or put an *um* or *er* in between the words, as you might do in hesitating while trying to think of the right word. You could say, for instance, *The farmer . . . kills the duckling* (where . . . represents a pause), or *The um: farmer kills um the duckling*. But you can't put pauses within the words: you wouldn't say *Th. . .e* ([ð. . .ə]) *farmer kills the duckling* or *The farm. . .er kills the duckling* or *The farmer kills the duck-um-ling*. In the last case, you would, rather, say *duck um duckling*, saying the full form rather than part of it.

We can extend this observation. First, notice that each word in the example sentence can be separated from its neighbour by another word: *The **hairy** farmer **always** kills **all** the **little** ducklings*. Second, each word can stand alone as an utterance. For instance, if a non-native speaker of English had said *De farmer kills de duckling*, a native speaker might possibly correct them by saying just *the* ([ðə]); the same can be done for the other words. But only full words would be corrected in this way: no native speaker would correct *The farmer kills the duckring* with just *ling* or *l* – they would repeat the whole word, *duckling* (with perhaps extra stress on the final syllable).

Words are thus **minimal free forms**: they have a degree of independence from other words in the sentence in the sense that they can be separated from them (this gives us the 'free' bit), and no smaller part of them has such freedom (giving the 'minimal' bit).[1]

> Returning to our earlier problem examples, *church mouse* and *churchman*, can you now decide whether they are each single words or two words?

The structure of words

We begin by drawing a distinction between **simple words** like *farm*, *kill* and *duck* that have no internal structure, and **complex words** like *farmer*, *kills* and *duckling* that do have internal structure. Complex words can be divided into smaller meaningful pieces: *farmer* into *farm* and *-er*; *kills* into *kill* and *-s*; and *duckling* into *duck* and *-ling*. By contrast the simple words *farm*, *kill* and *duck* can't be divided up further into meaningful pieces: no smaller part of these words has a meaning. Nor can we divide *-er*, *-s*, or *-ling* into smaller meaningful pieces.

The 'pieces' we have been talking about are minimal linguistic signs: they have a form and a meaning, and cannot be divided into smaller linguistic signs. Such pieces are **morphemes**. Morphemes are in a sense atomic signs: they can't be split up further. Simple words consist of a single morpheme; complex words of more than one morpheme.

Languages differ vastly in terms of the word-complexity they permit. English words are generally made up of relatively few morphemes. By comparison, words in Yup'ik (Eskimo-Aleut, Alaska) tend to be more complex, and often correspond to full sentences in English.

Thus the single word *kaipiallrulliniuk* means 'the two of them were apparently really hungry', and is made up of six morphemes:

(3-1) kai-   -pia-   -llru-   -llini-   -u-   -k
      be:hungry- -really-   -past-   -apparently-   -statement-   -they:two

We return to the issue of the relative morphological complexity of languages in Chapter 11.

Morphemes are linguistic signs, not mere phonological forms. The word *duct* /dʌkt/ (referring to a type of tube) contains the phoneme string /dʌk/ found at the beginning of *duckling*, which we separated off as a morpheme, as well as /t/, which is found in /fɪnɪʃt/ and means 'past time'. But *duct* is a simple, not complex, word and does not mean anything like 'a duck in the past', or 'a onetime duck'.[2] To identify a morpheme requires that we identify a repeated form–meaning correlation, not just a repeated form (or meaning).

3.2 Morphemes, allomorphs and morphs

Morphemes sometimes come in different phonological shapes. For instance, we identified a morpheme with the shape /z/ in *kills*, which indicates that a single person (not the speaker or hearer) is doing the event now. For *pat* the corresponding form ends instead in /s/, and for *touches*, it ends in /əz/. These variant forms are called **allomorphs**. Other allomorphs in English are /t/, /d/, and /əd/, which are variant forms of the morpheme that attach to verbs and indicate past time, as illustrated by *kissed* /kɪst/, *killed* /kɪld/ and *batted* [bætəd], respectively.

In Yingkarta (Pama-Nyungan, Australia) future time is indicated in some verbs by adding *-ku*, in others by adding *-wu*, and in others by *-lku*: *karnkaya-ku* 'will call out', *nyina-wu* 'will sit' and *kampa-lku* 'will cook'. The three forms *-ku*, *-wu* and *-lku*, are allomorphs of the future morpheme.

Allomorphs, like allophones, may be in either complementary distribution or free variation. The allomorphs /ə/ and /æn/ of the English indefinite article (these are not the only allomorphs) – written *a* and *an* respectively – are in complementary distribution: the former occurs when the following word begins with a consonant, the latter when it begins with a vowel. Free variation is illustrated by alternative realizations of the word *exit* as /ɛgzɪt/ and /ɛksɪt/, and *off* as /ɔːf/ and /ɒf/. Both forms of each pair are found in the speech of many speakers of English, and are phonemically distinct: elsewhere [gz] and [ks] (*exist* and *excel* are near minimal pairs), and [ɔː] and [ɒ] contrast phonemically.

The term **morph** is sometimes (albeit infrequently) used on analogy with phone in phonetics to refer to any meaningful form in a language. Thus some morphs are grouped together as allomorphs of a morpheme. In English we have two morphs with the same phonological form /z/, one going on nouns and specifying plural ('more than one'), as in *dogs* /dɔgz/, the other going on verbs, and indicating 'he, she or it is doing something'. There are also two morphs with the phonological shape /s/, and two with the shape /əz/ (in my dialect, Australian English). This gives six morphs altogether, forming two sets of allomorphs of two morphemes.

3.3 Main types of morphemes

Types according to occurrence

Free morphemes

Words, as we have already seen, are free forms. A simple word consists of a single morpheme, and so is a **free morpheme**, a morpheme with the potential for independent occurrence. In *The farmer kills the duckling* the free morphemes are *the*, *farm*, *kill* and *duck*. It is important to notice here that (in this sentence) not all of these free morphemes are words in the sense of minimal free forms – *farm* and *duck* are cases in point.

Bound morphemes

Bound morphemes, by contrast, require the presence of another morpheme to make up a word; they can't occur independently. The morphs *-er*, *-s* and *-ling* in our example sentence are bound morphemes; all the other morphemes are free. Yingkarta *-ku*, *-wu* and *-lku* (see §3.2) are also bound morphemes.

Bound morphemes which, like those discussed in the previous paragraph, go onto the ends of words, are called **suffixes**. Another type of bound morpheme is a **prefix**, which precedes the morpheme to which it is attached. The bound morphemes *un-* and *re-* in English are prefixes, as in *un-happy* and *re-constitute*. A third type of bound morpheme is an **infix**, that goes inside another morpheme, as in Tagalog (Austronesian, Philippines) *-in-* 'past' in *ib-in-igay* 'gave', which occurs within the morpheme *ibigay* 'give'. Collectively, suffixes, prefixes and infixes are called **affixes**.

> It is important to stress that infixes are affixes that occur within other morphemes, and not between them. Thus *-er* (/ə/) is **not** an infix in *farmers*, where it occurs between the two morphemes *farm* and *-s*, not within either of them; *-er* remains a suffix. The closest thing to infixation in English is the incorporation of expletives into words, as in *abso-bloody-lutely* and *fan-fucking-tastic*.

The distinction between bound and free morphemes is not always completely clear cut. A morpheme can have both free and bound allomorphs. For example, *not* in English has a free form /nɒt/, and a bound form /nt/: *he is not going* has the free form, while *he isn't going* has the bound form. There are also words like *deride* (/dəˈɹaid/) that have a different bound form, /dəˈɹɪʒ/, as in *derision*.

Types of morpheme according to function or use

A different classification can be arrived at if we consider the usage of a morpheme, including the type of meaning it conveys, instead of its distributional possibilities. This is the basis for the distinction between lexical and grammatical morphemes.

Lexical morphemes

Lexical morphemes are those like *farm, kill, happy, constitute, book* in English and *ibigay* 'give' in Tagalog, that convey the major 'content' of a message, specifying the things, qualities and events spoken about. The lexical morphemes of a language form a large set, which allows new members – new lexical items are constantly being introduced into languages in response to the changing worlds in which speakers live (see Chapter 4). Lexical morphemes, that is, form an open set.

Farm, kill, happy, constitute, book are free lexical morphemes, or free **roots**, which may serve as bases to which bound morphemes can be attached. Lexical morphemes can also be bound; there are **bound lexical roots** and **derivational affixes**.

Bound roots

Recall that some lexical roots have bound and free allomorphs. Sometimes lexical roots are bound in all of their manifestations. Nyulnyul has around 50 bound roots, mainly terms for parts of the body, that must take a prefix indicating the owner of the part. There is no free lexical morpheme 'hand'. The root is the bound form -*marl* that has to have a prefix, as in *nga-marl* 'my hand', *nyi-marl* 'your hand', *ni-marl* 'his or her hand', *irr-marl* 'their hand', and so on. Nyulnyul has in addition, some hundreds of other bound roots, including -*jid* 'go', -*m* 'put', -*j* 'do, say'.

Derivational affixes

These are affixes that attach to a lexical root and result in a new word, a complex lexeme called a **stem**. The suffix -*er* /ə/ in English is a derivational suffix: adding it to a lexical root gives a stem with a related meaning. Attaching this suffix to *bake* gives *baker*, to *boil* gives *boiler* and so on. Other derivational suffixes in English include -*ish* as in *childish*, -*ic* as in *alcoholic*, -*ful* as in *tearful* and -*ly* as in *precisely*, among others. Notice that these suffixes do not only change the meaning of the morpheme they are attached to, they also change its part-of-speech (see §4.1). Thus from nouns like *child*, *alcohol* and *tear*, we get adjectives like *childish*, *alcoholic* and *tearful*.

Not all derivational morphemes change the part-of-speech of a root. For example, *-hood* normally attaches to a noun, giving another noun: *childhood*, *priesthood* and *sisterhood*. Most derivational prefixes in English are like this.

Nyulnyul has a derivational morpheme *-id* – with a meaning similar to English *-er* – that can be attached to a lexeme of virtually any type to give a noun (so it may or may not change a morpheme's part-of-speech): *yaward-id* (horse-er) 'horseman', *-alm-id* (head-er) 'hat', *majanbin-id* (to:jump-er) 'jumper' and *junk-id* (run-er) 'runner'.

Stems can often be further derived to give yet more complex stems. For instance, from the root *help* we can derive *helpful*, which can be further derived to *unhelpful*; this new word can be further derived by suffixing *-ness*, *unhelpfulness*, or *-ly*, *unhelpfully*.

Grammatical morphemes

Whereas lexical morphemes give the major meaning content of an utterance, **grammatical morphemes** mainly give information about the grammatical structure of the utterance, about how to put the content together to form a coherent whole. Grammatical morphemes are generally demanded by the grammar, and contribute relatively abstract schematic meanings concerning the functions of the lexical items. For this reason they are sometimes called **function morphemes**. Like lexical morphemes, they can be either free or bound.

Free grammatical morphemes

Free grammatical morphemes in English include words like *and*, *but*, *by*, *in*, *on*, *not*, *the*, *a*, *that*, *it*, *me* and so forth. Languages only rarely acquire new grammatical morphemes, and the grammatical morphemes in a language can be regarded as effectively forming a closed class.

The most frequent words in English are free grammatical morphemes. An investigation I made of three corpora – totalling just over two million words from both speech and writing – revealed the following as the ten most frequent words (in order of frequency):[3] *the*, *be*, *of*, *and*, *a ~ an*,[4] *to*, *in*, *he*, *have* and *that*. With the possible exception for *have*, these are grammatical morphemes; *have* arguably has both lexical uses (e.g. in *She has two kittens*) and grammatical uses (e.g. in *She has stolen two kittens*). In fact, almost all of the 40 most frequent words in these corpora are grammatical words. The three or four that are not all have grammatical uses as well as lexical uses.

Bound grammatical morphemes

Inflectional affixes   **Inflectional affixes** are bound morphemes that give grammatical information relevant to the interpretation of a sentence. They do not give rise to new lexical words, but to different forms of a single lexical word, different forms that are appropriate for the use of the lexical word in the sentence.

Consider the following Latin sentence:

(3-2)   *serv-ī*   *cōnsul-em*   *audi-unt*
        slave-PL:SUB   consul-SG:OBJ   hear-they:PRS
        'The slaves hear the consul.'

This example shows the standard way of laying out example sentences, and should be followed. The first line shows the words in the language, divided into morphemes separated by hyphens; this line is given in italics. Below is a line giving a gloss (simple translation), for each morpheme. For grammatical morphemes the gloss is usually given as an abbreviation in capitals: in the above example, PL stands for 'plural', PRS for 'present' (i.e. an event going on now), OBJ for 'object', SG for 'singular' and SUB for 'subject'. When more than one word is used in the gloss for a single morpheme in the language line, the words are separated by a colon (:). The third line shows a free translation, a translation that indicates the meaning of the entire sentence. This is enclosed in single quotation marks. For fuller details of recommended conventions see *The Leipzig glossing rules: conventions for interlinear morpheme-by-morpheme glosses*, available at http://www.eva.mpg.de/lingua/resources/glossing-rules.php.

The suffix -*ī* on *serv* 'slave' indicates that this word is the subject of the sentence, and that more than one slave is involved, that is, that the word is plural in number; the -*em* suffix on the second word indicates that *cōnsul* 'consul' is the object and is singular in number. (See §5.4 on of the notions of subject and object.) The suffixes -*ī* and -*em* are inflectional suffixes that give information about how the words they are attached to are incorporated into the grammar of the sentence. Attaching them to the roots *serv* 'slave' and *cōnsul* 'consul' does not give rise to new words, but to forms of the same words that are appropriate to particular grammatical environments. If instead the sentence was to express the meaning that the consul heard the slaves, the word *cōnsul* 'consul' would be used as is, and the suffix -*ōs* would be attached to *serv* 'slave'.

The suffix -*unt* added to *audi* 'hear' is also an inflectional suffix, giving a form of this word that should be used when the subject is plural. If the subject was singular, the suffix -*t* would have been used instead. The suffix also indicates that the event is going on at the present time. The lexical words *serv* 'slave', *cōnsul* 'consul', and *audi* 'hear' come in different forms according to the grammatical features of the sentence they occur in. Thus compare (3-2) with (3-3).

(3-3) *cōnsul* *serv-ōs* *audi-t*
       consul:SG:SUB slave-PL:OBJ hear-he:PRS
       'The consul hears the slaves.'

Inflections on nouns indicating the grammatical role of the noun in the sentence are called **cases**. It is usual to call the subject case (as in Latin) the **nominative** (abbreviated NOM), and the object case **accusative** (abbreviated ACC). The inflections on the verb are called **agreement** inflections: they agree with the subject in terms of whether it is 'I', 'we', 'you', 'they' and so on.

English also has inflectional suffixes, including a regular plural suffix with allomorphs /s/ ~ /z/ ~ /əz/ as in *magistrates*, *slaves* and *churches*, respectively. (Some nouns have irregular plurals, for example, the plural of *mouse* is *mice*, and of *ox* is *oxen*.) The suffix /z/ on *hears* and *kills* is also an inflectional suffix, giving the form of these words appropriate to sentences with a singular subject excluding the speaker or hearer (i.e. 'he', 'she' or 'it') and present time reference.

Clitics

Not all bound grammatical morphemes are inflectional affixes. The bound form of *have*, written *'ve*, is an example. *Have* is a free grammatical morpheme in *They have broken in again*: it indicates that the event happened in the past but is relevant to the present time; it does not express possession, the lexical meaning of *have*. In *They've broken in* the word *they've* is not a distinct form of *they* chosen because of the grammar. Nor is it a new lexeme. Bound grammatical morphemes like this, which behave grammatically as separate words, but are phonologically part of the preceding word, are called **enclitics**. If they are part of a following word, they are called **proclitics**; the term **clitic** is a generic term covering both types.

Not all clitics have corresponding free form words like *'ve* and *have*. The English possessive morpheme written *'s* – with allomorphs /s/, /z/ and /əz/ – is an example. This morpheme does not give a variant form of the morpheme to which it is attached, a form that is appropriate to a particular grammatical environment. This is because it is attached not to the end of a word, but to the end of a phrase, a group of words that go together (§5.3) as a single unit. Although in *the king's crown* it might appear that the *'s* gives a form of the noun when it is a possessor, this is not always the case. In *the king of England's crown* it is still the king who is the possessor, not England; similarly he remains the possessor in examples such as *the king who beheaded him's palace*, *the king we saw's palace* and *the king they knocked the crown from's palace*. There is no free allomorph of *'s*.

Differences between derivational affixes, inflectional affixes and clitics

Three main types of bound morphemes were introduced in the previous sections, derivational affixes, inflectional affixes and clitics. Derivational affixes give rise to new lexical words, while inflectional affixes give different forms of the word to which they are attached, forms that are appropriate to the grammatical context of the sentence.

There are several other differences between derivational and inflectional affixes, that are tendencies rather than absolute differences.

- **Concept distinctiveness**. Attaching a derivational affix to a word generally gives a new concept, that could in principle be expressed by a simple lexical root; attaching an inflectional affix does not give a new concept. In Warrwa the derived word *burr-kurru* 'a thing associated with a brumming noise' means 'car'; the alternative form *mudika* (borrowed from English) is a root expressing the same meaning.
- **Degree of abstraction**. Derivational affixes tend to have more concrete meanings than inflectional affixes: their meaning is more like that of a lexical word, while inflectional affixes have meanings

more like grammatical words. For example, the English derivational suffix -*ess* has a quite concrete, lexical like meaning, 'female'.

- **Relevance**. The meaning of a derivational affix is usually relevant to the meaning of the root; the meaning of an inflectional affix may not be very relevant to the meaning of the word.
- **Replaceability**. A word with a derivational affix attached to it can usually be replaced by a single simple word; this is not normally possible for a word with an inflectional affix, which will usually have to be replaced by another inflected form.
- **Regularity**. Derived words often have irregular or not entirely predictable meanings; the meanings of inflected words are normally completely regular and predictable. The lack of regularity in meanings of derived words can be illustrated by the derivational suffix -*ize*, which has rather different effects in *publicize* 'draw to public attention, make well known', *romanticize* 'portray in a romantic fashion', *vaporize* 'to cause something to become a vapour', and *winterize* 'prepare something for use in winter'.
- **Productivity**. Derivational affixes usually have limited applicability; inflectional affixes usually apply to all words of a particular part-of-speech (with perhaps a small class of irregularities). The English has a derivational suffix -*ess* occurs on *heiress*, *authoress*, *lioness*, *goddess* and so on. But there are arbitrary restrictions on the suffix: joking aside, we do not say *elephantess* for 'female elephant', *maness* for 'woman', *workeress* for 'female worker' or *professoress* for 'female professor'.

Clitics do not give a new form of the word to which they are attached, and nor do they result in new lexical words. The forms *I've* and *they've* are not inflected forms of *I* and *they*, and nor are they separate lexical items that need to be listed individually in a dictionary.

Differences between clitics and affixes include the following, which are again tendencies rather than absolute differences.

- **Freedom of position**. Clitics often (though not always) have a degree of freedom of movement in a sentence, a feature not shared by affixes. Gooniyandi has a question clitic -*mi* that can go on any word of a sentence. No affix has this degree of freedom.
- **Selectivity**. Clitics tend to be relatively free in terms of the range of lexical items they can be attached to (as we saw for English 's); affixes are generally more selective in the company they keep.
- **Allomorphic variation**. Clitics generally show few allomorphs, and any they do can usually be explained by the phonological environment, as is the case for the allomorphs of the possessive 's. Allomorphs of affixes can have peculiarities that are not explicable phonologically (as in the case of the Latin inflections discussed on pp. 62–63).
- **Predictability of meaning**. There are rarely semantic idiosyncrasies in clitics. Regardless of what word they happen to be attached to, the meaning is generally predictable.
- **Prosodic integration**. Clitics are often not prosodically integrated into the words they are attached to, whereas affixes tend to be integrated. In some languages inflected or derived words are stressed like roots; words and their clitics are often not stressed like roots.

Figure 3.1 attempts to bring out by analogy the difference between the three types of bound morphemes.

If bound morphemes of all three types can be attached to a given word, it is derivational affixes that normally go next to the root, giving a stem; then come inflectional affixes, and

(1)

(2)

(3)

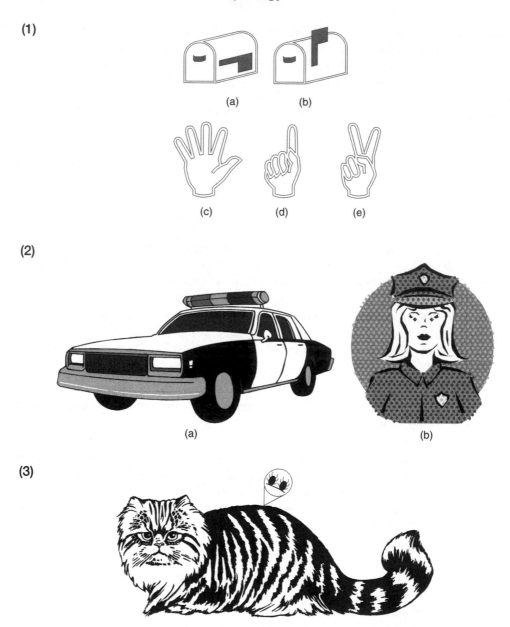

Figure 3.1 A conceptual representation of the differences between the three main types of bound morpheme. (1) **Inflection** gives different forms of a single item. For example, (a) and (b) are different forms a letterbox can be found in; (c), (d), and (e) are different shapes a hand can take. (2) **Derivation** gives rise to something new, an item different from the one it derives from, and not a different form of it. The distinctive markings on the car in (a) mark it as a police vehicle, and give rise to vehicle used in particular ways. Similarly, wearing a uniform in (b) specifies the individual as discharging a specific social role. (3) **Clitics** are items that lean on or depend on other items, like ticks on a cat. The thing that they depend on is their host; the clitic is lke a parasite. the presence of a tick does not give rise to a new form of a cat, nor does it derive a new animal type from it. © 2009 William B. McGregor and his licensors. All rights reserved.

finally clitics, at the greatest distance from the root. Thus in English the plural inflection of nouns follows derivational affixes such as -er: teach-er-s, farm-er-s and so on. Similarly in energ-is-ed the derivational affix is next to the root, and is followed by the inflection. And in the robot we energ-is-ed-'s co-processor the possessive enclitic -'s comes finally.

Summary of morpheme types

We can summarize the classification of morphemes given in this section as shown in Table 3.1.

Table 3.1 Summary of major morpheme types

	Free	**Bound**
Lexical	Lexical words English: *man, dog, big, love, run*	Bound lexical roots and stems Nyulnyul: -*alm* 'head', -*marl* 'hand' (must have a prefix) Derivational morphemes English: -*er*, -*ion*
Grammatical	Grammatical words English: *of, the, not, we, be*	Clitics English: *'s, 've* Inflectional morphemes English: -*ed* (past), -*s* (on noun, singular)

3.4 Allomorphs and allomorph conditioning

We have now introduced the main morphological units found in languages, and their types. In this section we will look at the relations between allomorphs: how allomorphs of a morpheme resemble one another phonologically; and the factors that condition the choice between them.

Types of allomorph

So far the morphemes we have discussed have allomorphs that are phonologically similar. The three English plural and possessive allomorphs /s/ ~ /z/ ~ /əz/ are obviously very similar phonologically. They are called **phonological allomorphs**.

But allomorphs can be quite different phonologically. The derived comparative and superlative forms of *good* are *better* and *best*, with the regular derivational suffixes -*er* and -*(e)st*. However these suffixes are not attached to *good* to give *gooder* and *goodest* (although these can be found in the speech of children, and in jocular, playful, or foreigner speech of adults). The derivational morphemes are instead attached to *bet-* and *be-* (which are phonological allomorphs), allomorphs of *good* that are not phonologically related to it. Variants like *good* and *bet-* ~ *be-* are said to be **suppletive allomorphs**.

Goemai (Afro-Asiatic, Nigeria) has a fair amount of suppletion in its lexicon. Compare *f'yer* and *nan* the singular and plural verbs 'become big', and *mat* and *sharap* the singular and plural forms of the noun 'woman'.

Suppletion can also be found in grammatical morphemes. For instance, in Yawuru (Nyulnyulan, Australia) verbs take prefixes indicating whether the subject is 'I', 'we', 'you', 'he', 'they' and so on. The form of the prefix for subject 'you (one individual)' is usually /mi/, as in /minaɲanda/ 'you caught it' and /miɲɟurkuɲ/ 'you were cutting hair'. In reference to a future event, however, the form is instead usually /wal/: /walaɲa/ 'you will catch it', and /walɟurku/ 'you will cut hair'. But for a few verbs it is /ŋa/, as in /ŋaɟali/ 'you will return'. The three forms /mi/, /wal/ and /ŋa/ are suppletive allomorphs of the second person singular subject prefix.

Types of conditioning factors

Conditioning factors are the factors that determine which allomorph of a morpheme you use. In **phonological conditioning** different allomorphs are selected according to the phonological environment. The choice between the allomorphs /ə/ and /æn/ of the English indefinite article is phonologically conditioned by the following phoneme, whether it is a vowel or a consonant. The three possessive allomorphs /s/ ~ /z/ ~ /əz/ are also phonologically conditioned, though in this instance by the preceding phoneme.

Sometimes allomorphs show **lexical conditioning**. That is, the choice of allomorph depends on the particular word the morpheme is attached to. A specific case of this is the plural suffix /n/ found on the irregular noun *ox*. So also is the choice between *-en* (phonological form /n/) and *-ed* (/t/ ~ /d/ ~ /əd/) in the past participle, the form of the verb used after *have* and *had*. Thus we have on the one hand *(have) given*, *(have) eaten*, *(have) broken* and on the other *(have) finished*, *(have) grabbed* and *(have) wanted*.

A third possibility is **morphological conditioning**. Here it is the grammatical rather than lexical morphemes that condition the presence of the allomorph. We saw an example in the previous section, with the distribution of the suppletive allomorphs of the 'you subject' prefix in Yawuru (which depend in part on whether the event is in the future or not).

All three types of conditioning factor can be relevant to the choice amongst allomorphs of inflectional and derivational affixes, including combinations of factors. For allomorphs of clitics, conditioning is almost always phonological.

Morphological rules

In §2.6 we saw that phonemes are abstract forms that are realized by phones, and a phoneme can be regarded as a set of phones. Likewise, in morphology it can be descriptively and conceptually useful to identify abstract forms for morphemes that are realized by different phonological allomorphs. Thus the regular past suffix in English has three phonological allomorphs, /d/ ~ /t/ ~ /əd/, which are in complementary distribution. We could presume that they are alternative realizations of a more abstract form of the morpheme: the phonemes would thus relate to the abstract form in the same way as phones relate to phonemes. Such abstract forms are sometimes called **morphophonemes**; the specification of a morpheme in terms of these units is its **morphophonemic** (or underlying) form.

Rules are needed to get from the morphophonemic form of a morpheme to its phonological forms, its allomorphs (and then rules to get from that to the phonetic form). We could presume that the regular allomorphs of the past suffix in English have the underlying form {d}, using braces in order to maintain a distinction from phonemic and phonetic levels. The three allomorphs could be accounted for by two rules:

1. Insert a schwa (/ə/) following a verb stem ending in an alveolar stop.
2. {d} is realized by: (a) /t/ when the preceding segment is voiceless; otherwise (b) it is realized by /d/

Thus, the past of the regular verb *wish* is /wɪʃt/, which can be derived from {wɪʃ-d} by rule 2a; the regular form of *kill* is /kɪld/, which derives from /kɪl-d/ by 2b (which indicates to do nothing). What about verbs ending in an alveolar stop, like *debate*? This can be accounted for by first applying rule 1 (of schwa insertion), giving /dəbeɪt/ then rule 2b, giving /dəbeɪt-əd/. Notice that the rules must be applied in this order. Otherwise, you would get the incorrect form /dəbeɪtət/, by first realising the {d} as /t/ and then inserting the schwa after the first /t/. You should verify these rules for a selection of regular verbs (e.g. *love, bow, hoe, pitch, wish, want, raid, grab*) to ensure they give the correct result.

There are more formal ways of writing morphophonemic rules, allowing for more succinct statements of the rules. These follow basically the same conventions as phonemic rules (see box on pp. 47–48), with the addition of the hyphen for a morpheme boundary. Thus, for example, the above rule for the realization of the English regular past morpheme could be expressed as follows:

1. insert /ə/   /   alveolar stop - _

2. {d}   → $\begin{cases} /t/ \ / \text{ voiceless segment - \_} \\ /d/ \text{ otherwise} \end{cases}$

3.5 Morphological description

To describe the morphology of a language requires:

a. identification of the grammatical morphemes, their allomorphs and conditioning factors; and
b. specification of the possible shape of words as combinations of morphemes of various types.

We give below some illustrations of how aspects of the morphology of a language can be described in these terms.

Case morphology in Warumungu

As in Latin, cases in Warumungu (Pama-Nyungan, Australia) are marked by inflectional suffixes to nouns. The basic shape of a noun is stem (a root, or a root plus derivational suffix) plus an optional case suffix. Here we ignore the complexities of Warumungu case marking morphology, and deal with just five case suffixes, and their forms on roots of two syllables. They are dative (roughly 'for'), allative (roughly 'towards'), locative ('at'), ablative ('from') and adversative ('lest').

The ablative and adversative each have a single allomorph, /ŋaɹa/ and /kaːɟi/ respectively. Some examples illustrating the ablative are /kaʈiŋaɹa/ 'from the man', /ŋapaŋaɹa/ 'from water' and /manuŋaɹa/ 'from the country'.

The other three case-marking inflections each have three allomorphs: /ki/, /ka/ and /ku/ for the dative; /kina/, /kana/ and /kuna/ for the allative; and /ŋki/, /ŋka/ and /ŋku/ for the locative. The three allomorphs are chosen in the same way:

- If the root ends in /i/, use /ki/, /kina/ or /ŋki/, as in /kaʈiki/ 'for the man'.
- If the root ends in /a/, use /ka/, /kana/ or /ŋka/, as in /ŋapaŋka/ 'in the water'.
- If the root ends in /u/, use /ku/, /kuna/ or /ŋku/, as in /manukuna/ 'to the country'

These allomorphs are phonological and phonologically conditioned.

Underlying forms can be suggested for the three morphemes: {ki}, {kina} and {ŋki}, together with a rule whereby the first {i} is realized as /a/ when the preceding vowel (the final vowel of the stem) is /a/, and /u/ when it is /u/. (The fact that the first vowel of the ablative and adversative, /a/ remains unchanged suggests that the first vowel can't in the dative, allative and locative be /a/. It could of course equally be /u/ as /i/, and there is no way of making an informed decision on the basis of the little evidence we have; to avoid making a decision, you might suggest instead that the underlying form is V_H, for 'high vowel'.

Morphology of locative case marking in Turkish

Case marking in Turkish (Altaic, Turkey) is also by means of suffixes to nouns. The suffixes follow the plural inflectional suffix /ler/ ~ /lar/, if present.

The locative suffix has four allomorphs: /da/, /de/, /ta/, /te/. They are chosen as follows, where IPA symbols are used, rather than Turkish orthography:

- /da/ is used when following a voiced segment, and the vowel immediately preceding it is a non-front vowel. Examples are: /binada/ 'in the building', /kapɨda/ 'at the door' and /pulda/ 'on the stamp'.
- /de/ is used following a voiced phone, and when the vowel immediately before it is front. Examples are /evde/ 'in the house', /evlerde/ 'at the houses' and /kedide/ 'at the cat'.
- /ta/ is used following a voiceless consonant, and when the immediately previous vowel is non-front: /kitapta/ 'on the book', /tarafta/ 'on the side' and /balɨkta/ 'on the fish'.
- /te/ occurs when the previous phone is voiceless, and the vowel immediately before is front: /køpekte/ 'on the dog', /gyneʃte/ 'on/in the sun'.

The locative case allomorphs are phonological, and are phonologically conditioned. As an exercise, suggest underlying forms for the locative, and suggest a rule that would give the occurring forms.

Locative case in Meryam Mir

Case in Meryam Mir (Papuan, Murray Island) is indicated by suffixes attached to noun roots and stems. The locative suffix has five allomorphs, /e/, /ge/, /ɟdoge/, /doge/ and /idoge/, which are chosen as follows:

- /e/ is used on ordinary nouns ending in a velar stop: /mayke/ 'with/at the widow'.
- /ge/ is used on other ordinary nouns, not ending in a velar stop: /metage/ 'at the house', /utebge/ 'at the place' and /kimyarge/ 'at/with the married man'.
- /ɟdoge/ is used on names of persons and places when the name ends in a vowel: /eydyanaɟdoge/ 'at Eidiana's place'.
- /doge/ is used on names of persons and places which end in a /ɟ/: /pomoɟdoge/ 'at Pomoy's place'.
- /idoge/ is used on other names of persons and places: /lezidoge/ 'at Les' place', /opnoridoge/ 'at/on the Barrier Reef'.

The allomorphs fall into two sets of phonological allomorphs: /ge/, /e/; and /idoge/, /ɟdoge/, /doge/. The factors conditioning choice among the members of the two sets are phonological, concerning the final segment of the word to which they are attached. The conditioning factors for the choice between the two sets are lexical, depending on whether the word is a proper name or not. How are the members of the two sets related? Notice that the three members of the second set each involve the first allomorph of the first set attached to a connecting form, whose shape is phonologically conditioned. It seems that the locative forms of proper names require a perhaps meaningless connecting form before the ordinary locative suffix is added.

3.6 Morphological analysis

Sample morphological analysis: Hungarian verbs

Listed below are a small selection of verb forms in Hungarian, given in phonemic representation using IPA symbols. Before reading further, you should attempt to identify the morphemes, their allomorphs and the order they occur in.

/futok/	'I am running'	/holɔdott/	'he/she/it moved forward'
/ugɔtott/	'it barked'	/ɔd/	'he/she is giving'
/futott/	'he/she ran'	/vaːr/	'he/she is waiting'
/ɔdok/	'I give'	/vaːrok/	'I am waiting'
/futottɔm/	'I ran'	/mɔrott/	'he/she/it remained'
/laːtok/	'I see'	/olvɔʃok/	'I am reading'

/laːt/	'he/she sees'	/mɔrɔdok/	'I remain'
/olvɔʃtɔm/	'I read (before)'	/ugɔt/	'it barks'
/olvɔʃ/	'he/she is reading'	/hɔlodok/	'I move forward'
/ɔdott/	'he/she gave'	/mɔrɔd/	'he remains'
/fut/	'he/she is running'	/hɔlɔd/	'he/she/it is moving forward'

Grammatical morphemes

From the list, it is easy to see that the phoneme sequences /ok/ and /ɔm/ are always associated with the subject 'I', that is, with first person singular subject. These are suppletive allomorphs. Examining their contexts of occurrence reveals that /ok/ occurs when the verb refers to an event going on right now, and /ɔm/ to one that happened previously. The allomorphs are morphologically conditioned by the time of occurrence of the event.

It will also be noticed that where the 'I' form has /ok/ or /ɔm/, there is nothing in the corresponding form for subjects 'he', 'she' or 'it' – that is, for third person singular subjects.

When the verb describes an event in past time there is always either a /t/ or an /ott/; this is absent when the event is happening now. These are allomorphs of a morpheme that specifies that the event happened before, 'past time'. The allomorph /ott/ is found following an alveolar consonant, /t/, /r/, /d/ or /l/; following /ʃ/ we find the allomorph /t/. The conditioning is thus phonological: the first allomorph follows an alveolar segment, the second, a palatal.

A grammatical morpheme that specifies the time of occurrence of an event is called a **tense** marker. The basic tenses are **present**, for events happening now; **past** for events that happened before; and **future** for events expected to happen later (not present in the Hungarian data).

Lexical morphemes

Looking at the list we find that there are the following invariant phonological segments associated with the lexical meanings indicated:

/fut/	'run'	/ugɔt/	'bark'
/ɔd/	'give'	/vaːr/	'wait'
/hɔlɔd/	'move forward'	/mɔrɔd/	'remain'
/laːt/	'see'	/olvɔʃ/	'read'

These are identical with the forms for third person singular subject and present tense; the other forms can be considered to be based on them.

Structure of the verb

As a first attempt, we could give the following description of the structure of the above Hungarian verbs (recall that the round brackets indicate optional material):

(3-4)   Lexical verb root + (Tense suffix) + (Subject suffix)

The tense suffix is there if the verb is in the past, but absent if in the present; the subject suffix is there for first person singular subject, but absent for a third person singular subject.

The absence of anything in the place where the past tense suffix goes tells us that it is present tense; the absence of anything in the place where the first person singular subject suffix goes tells us that it is third person singular.

An alternative way of describing the structure is possible if we identify not two grammatical morphemes, but four:

first person singular subject	/ok/ ~ /ɔm/
third person singular subject	ø
past	/t/ ~ /ott/
present	ø

Here ø represents a zero form – that is, the morpheme expressing the particular meaning has no phonological form. Such morphemes, lacking phonological form, but having a meaning, are called **zero morphemes**. The usefulness of zero morphemes is firstly that it allows us to say that for both tenses, and both types of subject, there is a grammatical morpheme indicating that category. And secondly, it allows us to state the structure of the verb as follows:

(3-5)   Lexical verb root + Tense suffix + Subject suffix

This formula provides a characterization of the Hungarian verb that is in some ways preferable to the previous formula. There are no options in the structure, and we have a more general way of speaking about tense and subject marking. Furthermore, it implies that a form such as /fut/ can be interpreted as to either of two things: the plain verb root *fut* 'run', or the inflected form of this verb, *fut-ø-ø* 'he/she is running'. These forms are phonologically identical, but morphologically different.

> Zero morphemes are somewhat controversial in linguistics, and not all linguists are happy with them. It is always necessary to have reasons for identifying them. Generally, absence of phonological form should be interpreted as absence of morphemes. You need no reason to make this presumption, that nothing in the phonological form corresponds to nothing in the morphology. (As William Haas 1957: 53 aptly observed, 'If some men in civilian clothes are soldiers, this is no reason for suggesting that they wear zero-uniforms.') But you **do need** good reasons to suppose that there is a zero morpheme in the absence of a phonological form!

Morphological analysis by speakers

There is reason to believe that it is not only linguists who engage in morphological analysis, but also language learners and speakers.

The child learning her first language begins with words or larger units as unanalysed wholes. Each word is a separate sign in itself, bearing no perceived relation to any other word. But by four years of age, the normal child has heard many millions of words in the speech of those around it, and has a vocabulary of signs that amounts to over a thousand words.

By this time the number of signs has become so large that it is impractical for them to be all treated as separate, isolated entities. The child must engage in analysis of the units; she must treat them no longer as separate and unrelated items, but divide them into smaller meaningful, morpheme-sized components. This is reflected in the fact that the child begins to over-use regular morphemes, extending them to irregular words. Thus whereas at an early age the child acquiring English has both *foot* and *feet*, *see* and *saw*, and *go* and *went*, morphologically irregular forms, at around the age of about four, most likely she will begin using regular forms like *foots*, *seed* and *goed*. (See further §9.1.) These are unlikely to have been learnt from the speech of those communicating with the child. This indicates that the child has separated out and identified morphemes like the regular plural -*s* and the regular past tense -*ed* – forms that were probably previously not separately identified, being seen as unanalysed parts of lexical forms.

Speakers continue to apply morphological analysis into adulthood, extracting apparently meaningful parts from words, sometimes even extracting meaningless parts and imbuing them with meaning. An example is provided by the bound morpheme -*gate* which indicates 'a political scandal associated with a place'. This has nothing to do with the free word *gate*, as in an entrance in a fence. Rather, its source is *Watergate* – the name of a building in which certain now infamous events occurred – from which has been extracted *gate* and treated as though a meaningful unit. Now this form can be attached quite productively to placenames, as in *Iran-gate* and the recent *planet-gate* and *fornigate*. (If you haven't encountered these words, look them up on the internet to see how they fit with meaning given above.)

Many languages are morphologically much more complex than English, to the extent that it is unlikely that every form of every lexical item could be stored as a separate item in the speaker's mind. There are languages in which each verb has many hundreds of distinct inflectional forms. The more frequent forms of high frequency verbs may well be stored in the mind as separate items. But many forms are liable to be very infrequent, and likely to be created on the spur of the moment, using allomorph shapes and descriptions of word shapes such as given in the previous section. The verb form meaning 'I'll hit you' is likely to be of the first type since (like it or not) it describes a common threat in real life in most (if not all) societies, while the form meaning 'they two could have interrogated us all' is less likely to stored as a whole.

Summing up

A word is a **minimal free form**. Some words are structurally complex, and are made up of smaller meaningful atoms, **morphemes**. There are regularities in the way morphemes combine together in a language, and **morphology** studies these regularities.

The words of a language can be described as sequences of morphemes. Usually there are restrictions on the ordering of morphemes in a word, so that it is possible to give a general description of the morphological shape of words of particular types, such as the nouns of English. Languages differ considerably in their morphological structures and complexity; English is morphologically rather simple.

Morphemes may be **free** or **bound**, and **lexical** or **grammatical**. The main types of bound morphemes are **affixes** (**suffixes**, **prefixes** and **infixes**) and **clitics** (**enclitics** and **proclitics**).

Lexical morphemes include **roots** and **derivational** affixes, which create new **stems** from roots. Grammatical morphemes include inflectional affixes, which convey information about the grammatical function or category of the lexical morpheme to which they are attached; examples are **case** and **number** inflections on nouns and/or pronouns, and **tense** inflections on verbs. Grammatical morphemes can also be free words.

Like phonemes, morphemes often come in different phonological forms, called **allomorphs**. Allomorphs that resemble one another in form are **phonological allomorphs**; otherwise they are **suppletive allomorphs**. The circumstances governing the choice of allomorphs are **conditioning factors**, which may be **phonological**, **lexical** or **morphological**.

One way of providing a more general account of phonological allomorphs is to identify a single abstract **morphophonemic** representation of the morpheme, plus rules that derive phonological representations from it.

Speakers and language learners also engage in morphological analysis, and show awareness of the components of complex words. While irregular forms of frequent words are learnt early by the child, around the age of four children begin to construct regular forms. This suggests that the child has learnt and internalized the regular morphological patterns of the language, and is not merely repeating forms they have heard. Adults also sometimes analyse out meaningless parts of words and interpret them as though they were morphemes, as in the case of the emergent morpheme *-gate*.

Guide to further reading

Most introductions to linguistics (see the list at the end of Chapter 1) treat the basic notions of morphology, and include sample problems in morphological analysis. For a comprehensive description of English morphology see Bauer (1983).

This chapter adopts an approach to morphology focusing on the syntagmatic dimension (recall §1.2), the 'item-arrangement' approach (Hockett 1954), that deals with items (morphemes) and their arrangements into strings. Most morphologists today favour a 'word-paradigm' approach, which takes the word as the central concept and adopts a paradigmatic orientation. Robins (1959) is the classic paper arguing in favour of the word paradigm approach.

Spencer (2001) presents a good overview of the field, and identifies a range of problems in morphological theory and description. Bauer (2004) provides clear explanations of the essential terminology of morphology. For more advanced textbook treatments see Bauer (2003); Carstairs-McCarthy (1992); Haspelmath (2002); and Matthews (1972, 1974). Spencer and Zwicky (1998/2001) contains papers on a range of topics in, and approaches to, morphology; it is, however, quite technical and is most useful to advanced students.

The field that compiles and investigates language corpora (see p. 62) is corpus linguistics. Good introductions are Kennedy (1998) and Biber et al. (1998). Numerous corpora of English and other languages are accessible via the internet. *Gateway to Corpus Linguistics on the Internet*, at http://www.corpus-linguistics.de/, lists numerous electronic corpora. Most require permission and/or a fee for access.

Issues for further thought and exercises

1. Divide the following passage into morphs, list the morphs, and label each according to whether it is free or bound, lexical or grammatical. You should encounter some problems in identifying morphs: dubious cases where the status of a form as a meaningful element is not entirely certain, and where it is difficult to decide precisely where the morpheme division occurs. Identify and discuss these difficulties.

   The city wasn't pretty. Most of its builders had gone in for gaudiness. Maybe they had been successful at first. Since then the smelters whose brick stacks stuck up tall against a gloomy mountain to the south had yellow-smoked everything into uniform dinginess. The result was an ugly city of forty thousand people set in an ugly notch between two ugly mountains that had been all dirtied up by mining. Spread over this was a grimy sky that looked as if it had come out of the smelters' stacks. (Hammett 1929/2003: 1–2)

2. What are the conditioning factors for the three allomorphs of the possessive enclitic in English? Are they identical with the conditioning factors for the regular plural morpheme? What grammatical differences can you find between the two morphemes? (Use the properties of the various morpheme types mentioned in the text to help you find differences. You could also think about their ordering.) What happens when the enclitic is attached to plural nouns (regular and irregular)?

3. The past tense suffix for regular verbs in English has three allomorphs that are similar in form to the plural noun suffix and the possessive enclitic. What are they? Are they phonological allomorphs? Are the conditioning factors for the past tense allomorphs the same as the conditioning factors for the plural noun suffix and possessive clitic? If not, can you identify anything common between them?

4. Based on the following data from Gumbaynggirr, what are the allomorphs of the lexical and grammatical (case) morphemes? (Note that ergative is the name for the case that marks the subject of a transitive clause (like *John sees Mary*) but not intransitive (like *John ran*).) Are they phonological or suppletive allomorphs? What are their conditioning factors? For the phonological allomorphs can you suggest a morphophonemic representation, and rules of phonological realization?

	Ergative	Locative	Dative	Ablative
'man'	/niːgadu/	/niːgada/	/niːgargu/	/niːgana/
'small'	/ɟunuɟɟu/	/ɟunuɟɟa/	/ɟunuɟgu/	/ɟunuɟnar/
'father'	/baːbagu/	/baːbaɲumbala/	/baːbaɲu/	/baːbaɲumbajɲa/
'flood'	/duːlgambu/	/duːlgamba/	/duːlgamgu/	/duːlgamɲar/
'tail'	/ɟuːndu/	/ɟuːnda/	/ɟuːngu/	/ɟuːɲɲar/
'pademelon'	/gulɟuːdu/	/gulɟuːda/	/gulɟuːgu/	/gulɟuːɲar/
'mother'	/miːmigu/	/miːmiɲumbala/	/miːmiɲu/	/miːmiɲumbajɲa/
'mosquito'	/guɹaːdu/	/guɹaːda/	/guɹaːgu/	/guɹaːɲar/
'brother-in-law'	/ɲaɟiːgu/	/ɲaɟiːɲumbala/	/ɲaɟiːɲu/	/ɲaɟiːɲumbajɲa/
'cattle'	/bulangu/	/bulanga/	/bulangu/	/bulaɲnar/
'brother'	/gagugu/	/gaguɲumbala/	/gaguɲu/	/gaguɲumbajɲa/
'magpie'	/ŋaːmbulu/	/ŋaːmbula/	/ŋaːmbulgu/	/ŋaːmbulɲar/
'whiting'	/ɟuruwiɲɟu/	/ɟuruwiɲɟa/	/ɟuruwiɲgu/	/ɟuruwiɲnar/

5. Below are some verb forms in Saliba (Austronesian, Sariba and Rogeia Islands). Describe the morphology of the verb, and identify the lexical and grammatical morphemes; suggest a meaning for each morpheme.

/selaoko/	'they went already'	/yeseseko/	'it is already swollen'
/yelaoma/	'he came this way'	/sekeno/	'they slept'
/sedeuli/	'they washed it'	/yalaowako/	'I already went away'
/yeligadi/	'she cooked them'	/yeligako/	'she cooked it already'
/yadeuli/	'I washed it'	/yakitadiko/	'I saw them already'
/yeheloiwa/	'he ran away'	/selageko/	'they arrived already'
/sekitagau/	'they saw me'	/sepesama/	'they came out here'

6. It was mentioned that English *have* has, according to some linguists, both grammatical and lexical uses. Do you think it is preferable to consider these to represent different uses of a single lexical word, or two homophonous words, one lexical, one grammatical? Explain your reasoning.

7. Examine the following sentences in Northern Sotho, written phonemically. Identify the morphemes, stating their phonological form and their meanings, as revealed by these examples. Describe the morphological structure of words.

    a. /mpʃa elomilɛ ŋwana/   'The dog bit a child'
    b. /basadi barɛka diaparɔ/   'The women buy clothes'
    c. /bana batla/   'The children come'
    d. /mosadi orɛkilɛ nama/   'The woman bought meat'
    e. /dimpʃa dilomilɛ bana/   'The dogs bit the children'
    f. /monaŋ olomilɛ mmutla/   'The mosquito bit a hare'
    g. /ŋkwe ebɔna dintlo/   'The leopard sees the huts'
    h. /ŋwana otlilɛ/   'The child came'
    i. /banna barɔbilɛ selɛpɛ ntlɔŋ/   'The men broke an axe by the hut'
    j. /monna obona setimɛla/   'The man sees a train'

8. English nouns mark plural regularly by the morpheme /s/ ~ /z/ ~ /əz/, and irregularly by a variety of means. The singular never has any phonological marking. Is there sufficient evidence to suppose that there is a zero suffix marking the singular? Discuss the pros and cons of identifying a zero morpheme. (In answering this question, consider the consequences of this analysis for nouns like *fish* and *sheep*.)

9. Analyse the following Warrwa verb forms and identify the morphemes that correspond to the English pronouns; what are the allomorphs and their conditioning factors? How is information about the time of the event expressed? (Note that there is no direct representation of 'it' as object.) How would you describe the structure of the verb?

	'looked'	'pierced (it)'	'was cooking (it)'	
a.	/ŋamuɹuŋuɲ/	/ŋanaɹaɲ/	/ŋanamaɹana/	'I'
b.	/mimuɹuŋuɲ/	/minaɹaɲ/	/minamaɹana/	'you'
c.	/yamuɹuŋuɲ/	/yanaɹaɲ/	/yanamaɹana/	'we two (me and you)'
d.	/muɹuŋuɲ/	/naɹaɲ/	/namaɹana/	'he'
e.	/yarmuɹuŋuɲ/	/yaraɹaɲ/	/yaramaɹana/	'we all'
f.	/gurmuɹuŋuɲ/	/guraɹaɲ/	/guramaɹana/	'you plural'
g.	/ɲimuɹuŋuɲ/	/ɲiraɹaɲ/	/ɲiramaɹana/	'they'

10. Compare the root and progressive (indicating that the event is in progress) forms of Babungo verbs below. How is the progressive formed? (Tone is not shown.)

    a. /faʔ/   'work'   /fìfaʔ/   'be working'
    b. /tɔə/   'dig'   /tìtɔə/   'be digging'

(Continued)

Issues for further thought and exercises—Cont'd

c. /baj/	'be red'	/bɨbaj/	'be becoming red'
d. /zasə/	'sick'	/zɨzasə/	'be sick'
e. /fesə/	'frighten'	/fɨfesə/	'be frightening'
f. /bʷəj/	'live'	/bɨbʷəj/	'be living'
g. /kuːnə/	'return'	/kɨkuːnə/	'be returning'

11. Examine the following noun forms in Kuot, which inflect regularly for number, which can be singular or non-singular (one or more than one) for inanimates, or singular, non-singular and dual (for animates and some inanimates). Describe number formation and identify the number markers; account for the distribution of allomorphs.

singular	non-singular	dual (2)	
a. /ie/	/iep/		'knife'
b. /ŋof/	/ŋofup/		'nostril'
c. /alaŋ/	/alaŋip/	/alaŋipien/	'road'
d. /nur/	/nurup/		'coconut'
e. /kuala/	/kualap/	/kualapien/	'wife'
f. /kobeŋ/	/kobeŋip/	/kobeŋipien/	'bird'
g. /iakur/	/iakurup/	/iakurupien/	'vine'
h. /nəp/	/nəpup/		'part'
i. /pas/	/pasip/		'stick'
j. /kakok/	/kakokup/		'snake'

Not all nouns in Kuot form numbers in this way. How are the following inflected forms constructed? How would you account for the two different patterns?

a. /irəma/	/irəp/	/irəpien/	'eye'
b. /dədema/	/dədep/	/dədepien/	'word'
c. /karaima/	/karaip/		'nail, claw'
d. /muana/	/muap/	/muapien/	'reason'
e. /tabuna/	/tabup/		'door'

Notes

1. Note that we are restricting ourselves to the particular sentence. *Farmer* is a minimal free form, since here *farm* cannot be separated from it; in other sentences (e.g. *The farm is the site of numerous killings of ducklings*) *farm* is a minimal free form.

2. However, there is a word *ducked* (as in *He ducked to avoid the javelin*) that is phonologically identical with *duct* and which can be divided into two morphemes, /dʌk/ 'move rapidly downwards to evade something' and /t/ 'past time'. This example also illustrates that two distinct morphemes *duck* (the bird) and *duck* (the movement) can share the same phonological form. Such words are called homophones (see §6.2).

3. The three corpora were: *Australian Corpus of English* (written), *The Lancaster-Oslo/Bergen Corpus of British English* (written) and *The Machine-Readable Corpus of Spoken English* (spoken). The counts were made for lexical items in their various forms (so *be* includes *was, were* and so on). If instead the counts are made over free morphs, one gets slightly different results. The ten most frequent morphs are all grammatical: *the, of, and, to, a, in, is, that, was* and *for*.

4. The tilde ~ is conventionally used to separate alternating allomorphs.

4 Lexicon

In the previous chapter we discussed the notion of the word, and explored how words can be analysed into smaller meaningful components; we also distinguished lexical words and morphemes from grammatical ones. In this chapter we focus on lexical items. We begin by discussing how they can be grouped together into types on the basis of shared grammatical behaviour; this gives the notion of parts-of-speech or word classes. We then turn to some of the means available in languages for making new lexemes. We conclude with a brief discussion of two other topics: fixed expressions involving lexemes, and the attitudinal values of words.

Chapter contents

Goals

The goals of the chapter are to:
- introduce two primary concepts, the lexicon and parts-of-speech;
- outline criteria for distinguishing parts-of-speech, and identify the main types found in human languages;
- identify and exemplify some of the main ways of creating new words;
- touch briefly on idioms as more or less fixed strings of words forming single lexemes; and
- show that not all words are neutral, but can evoke emotional responses in speakers of a language and be used to soften or make harsher unpleasant realities

Key terms

acronyming	clipping	extension of meaning	postposition
adjective	coinage	idiom	preposition
adverb	collocations	interjection	pronoun
auxiliary	compounding	lexicon	reduplication
backformation	conjunctions	narrowing of meaning	taboo word
blending	derivation	noun	verb
borrowing	dysphemism	part-of-speech	
calquing	euphemism	phonaesthesia	

4.1 The lexicon

Nature of the lexicon

As a literate speaker of English, you doubtless expect that the words of a language can be listed in a dictionary. You perhaps imagine this as an alphabetical list of entries that tells you how to pronounce each word, and gives a description of its meaning; you might also expect information about the type of word it is, whether it is a noun, verb or whatever. This information is crucial if you want to use an unknown word correctly. It seems reasonable to believe also that speakers of a language have internalized mental dictionaries, from which they make selections in constructing utterances. Experimental evidence shows that these are not organized in the same way as standard dictionaries, as alphabetical lists. Rather, they are much more structured, with links both between the phonological forms and the meanings of the items: they are more like web-documents than printed ones. Instead of the everyday term *dictionary*, linguists use the technical term **lexicon** for such a list.

Let us leave aside for now the question of how the lexicon is structured, and enquire into what should go into it. To begin with, we have assumed that it contains the words of a language. It would have to include all of the root morphemes; it must also contain the derived stems, since (as seen in the previous chapter) their meaning is normally not entirely predictable, and must be recorded. For English the lexicon will have *farmer* as well as *farm*. On the other hand, forms like *farmers* and *farmer's* need not be listed, since knowledge of the morphology of English is sufficient to permit full understanding of these words from the meaning of the component morphemes. That is provided that the bound morphemes are also listed, including inflectional and derivational affixes as well as clitics.

Other things you would expect to find in a lexicon are irregular inflectional forms of words, such as the irregular forms of *be*, *are* and *is*, since these can't be predicted from the morphology (although their meaning can be). Morphologically complex words like *blackboard, strawberry, penknife* and so on (see §4.3) will also need to be in the list. You will probably agree that a comprehensive lexicon should also list longer expressions such as *kick the bucket, know by heart, grasp the nettle, chew your heart out, kill time* and so on. Expressions like these, the meaning of which can't be guessed from the meanings of the component words and the grammar, are called **idioms** (see §4.4).

In short, the lexicon of a language should contain all signs whose meaning is not predictable, whether they are single morphemes, words or combinations of words. Anything that has a predictable meaning – like an ordinary non-idiomatic sentence such as *John kicked the bucket down the street* – does not need to be included.

Beware of a potential confusion in terminology! In classifying morphemes the term lexical is used in contrast with grammatical to indicate morphemes that convey content meaning. But the lexicon of a language, as it is usually conceived, includes all morphemes, regardless of whether they are lexical or grammatical.

Openness

The lexicon of a language is not fixed; it does not remain constant forever. Indeed, lexicons change quite rapidly. You are doubtless aware of changes that have happened during your own lifetime, as new words come into use, and old ones lose popularity, and are eventually forgotten. Some changes are due to social and technological changes: new terms are required for new items, and old words are forgotten as the items go out of use. But other factors can be relevant, including multilingualism (ability to speak more than one language) and tabooing of words (see §4.5). In sections 4.2 and 4.3 we examine some ways languages add to their lexicons.

Even the grammatical morphemes of a language change over time, although they are more stable than lexical morphemes. Over long periods of time new grammatical morphemes are created, often out of existing lexical items, and old ones wear out, so to say, and disappear from use. When we said (p. 62) that grammatical morphemes form closed classes, this is meant in a relative sense: they are not absolutely closed, but much less likely to be added to or taken from than lexical morphemes.

Parts-of-speech

Main categories

The notion of **parts-of-speech** or **word classes** is the idea that the words in the lexicon of a language can be put into different classes. Traditionally, these classes were defined intuitively, in terms of the type of meaning expressed. But in modern linguistics grammatical behaviour is the primary consideration, although meaning does play a role, and serves as the basis for labelling the classes. The idea is, on the one hand, that not all words show the same grammatical behaviour, and, on the other, there are sufficient commonalities among some groups of words to allow us to make generalizations about them. It is not the case that each word behaves in an idiosyncratic manner.

Below is a list of some of the main parts-of-speech found in the world's languages, with some brief remarks indicating the typical semantic content of the members of each class, and some characteristics of the part-of-speech in English. (Different criteria will be required for most other languages.)

- **Nouns** are words that typically specify things or entities (people, animals, objects, places, abstract ideas).[1] Grammatical characteristics of English nouns include the ability to inflect for number (except for a small set of irregular nouns), and that they can be preceded by modifiers such as *the*, *a* and adjectives. In many languages nouns distinguish inflectional categories of number (§3.3), case (§3.3) and gender (see §7.2).
- **Adjectives** indicate qualities or properties of things, such as age, colour, size, speed and shape. In English adjectives usually go before nouns; they can usually be preceded by an intensifier like *very* or *too*; they can often be negated by the prefix *un-*; and they can be used in making comparisons by adding the suffix *-er* or the word *more*. They also admit the superlative suffix *-st*.
- **Pronouns** are words like *I*, *me*, *you* and *they* that are used instead of nouns to refer to persons and things, especially known and identifiable ones. Pronouns are grammatical morphemes, and form closed classes that can't normally be added to. Pronouns in English make case-distinctions (see §3.3) that are not made for nouns.
- **Verbs** generally designate events (actions, states, processes, happenings, mental and bodily activities). In English, verbs can be distinguished by the fact that they make past tense forms regularly by the suffix *-ed* (and irregularly by other means, including suppletion); many take the agentive derivational suffix *-er* to form nouns (*thinker*, *walker*, *caller*, *lover*). Verbs in many languages inflect for tense, and person and number of the subject.

- **Auxiliaries** are verbs that express grammatical rather than lexical information, and are used along with lexical verbs denoting events. Auxiliaries in English include *do*, *be* and *have*, as in *Does the duckling love the farmer?*, *The duckling is quacking* and *The farmer has killed the duckling*.
- **Adverbs** indicate qualities and properties of events (e.g. like *quickly*, *happily*, specifying the manner of performance), or indicate intensity of a quality (like *very* in *a very slow train*). In English, as in many other languages, adverbs do not take inflections, and many (though not all) show the derivational affix *-ly*.
- **Prepositions** are grammatical words like *at*, *in*, *to*, *by* and *from*, that go with nouns to specify how they are related to the rest of the sentence (e.g. by locating the event in space or time). Some languages have **postpositions**, which are words that do the same work as prepositions, but follow the noun rather than precede it. The closest thing to a postposition in English is the possessive clitic *'s*.
- **Conjunctions** are grammatical words like *and*, *or*, *but*, *if* and the like, that join words or groups of words together. In English they admit no morphological modification, and usually occur in front of the last item of the list of words joined together (*salt and pepper*; *Tom, Dick and Harry*).
- **Interjections** are words like *hey!*, *yuk!*, *strewth!*, *erk!* which mostly express the speaker's emotional attitude, or call for attention. Important characteristics of these words are that they can stand alone as full utterances, and do not allow any morphological modification.

Criteria

As mentioned above, in modern linguistics parts-of-speech are defined by grammatical behaviour, not meaning. Thus a word such as *seem* can hardly be interpreted as denoting an event, although its grammatical behaviour in English groups it with verbs: it takes the regular past tense suffix *-ed* (here /d/), and third person singular present *-s* (here /z/) and occurs in the same position in English sentences as event-denoting verbs like *hit*, *walk* and so on.

The grammatical features characterising the parts-of-speech vary from language to language. In some languages it is relatively easy to set up nouns and verbs as distinct parts-of-speech by morphological behaviour. Thus in Pitta-Pitta (Pama-Nyungan, Australia) nouns take case marking suffixes, and verbs tense suffixes. This criterion works very well, giving distinct, almost disjoint, classes – just two words can take both sets of suffixes.

But in many languages things are more complex: simple morphological criteria like the ability to take certain morphemes lead to parts-of-speech with considerable overlapping of members. This is the case in English.

Linguists have different opinions as to what to do in such cases. Some are not bothered by massive overlapping; others look for ways to reduce overlap. There are also differences of opinion on at least two other points. One is whether we should be satisfied with defining parts-of-speech in a language-specific way, or whether we should be seeking universally valid criteria. The other is whether to use morphological criteria (as in Pitta-Pitta), or syntactic criteria – that is, to assign words to parts-of-speech according to the way they are used in sentences – or a mixture of both.

Parts-of-speech across languages

Not all languages distinguish all of the parts-of-speech listed above. A fair number of languages do not recognize a distinct class of adjectives. This is so in many Australian languages, where words translating as adjectives in English belong together with nouns in a single part-of-speech. Nor is Mandarin Chinese usually believed to distinguish adjectives; instead, words translating into English as adjectives belong with verbs.

Probably the majority of languages distinguish at least the two major lexical parts-of-speech, nouns and verbs. But even this distinction is perhaps not universal. Some languages of Native North America – including many Salishan languages – have been claimed to lack this distinction. (There are differences of opinion among specialists.) Samoan is another such language. It seems that in principle any word can behave either like a noun or like a verb; English translation equivalents of a single word can be either a noun or a verb, as illustrated by *lā* 'sun', 'suns, be sunny' in (4-1) and (4-2).[2] There is thus, it has been argued (e.g. by Hengeveld et al. 2004), no reason to distinguish nouns from verbs as different parts-of-speech.

(4-1)	*'Ua*	*mālosi*	*le*	*lā*	Samoan
	perfective	strong	article	sun	

'The sun is strong.' More literally, 'the sun strongs'.

(4-2)	*'Ua*	*lā*	*le*	*aso*	Samoan
	perfective	sun	article	day	

'The day is sunny.' More literally, 'the day suns.'

While some of the parts-of-speech listed above may not exist in a language, additional categories are not infrequently distinguished. In many northern Australian languages words corresponding to verbs in English belong to two different parts-of-speech: members of one group are morphologically complex, and take inflectional affixes; members of the other group are morphologically simple, and admit no inflection and just a little derivation. The first group is a closed set with between about ten and two hundred members, while the second group is open, with many hundreds of members. In the following Warrwa sentence, -*wani*- 'be' belongs to the class of morphologically complex verbs, and takes the prefix *ngirr*- which indicates subject 'they', the suffix -*n* indicating present time, and the suffix -*bili* indicating that the persons are two in number. (These glosses are rough, and the morpheme analysis is incomplete.) The word *nganka* is a member of the second part-of-speech; the suffix -*ngkaya*, indicating ongoing or continuous action, is the only bound morpheme that can be attached to it.

(4-3)	*kujarra*	*nganka-ngkaya*	*ngirr-wani-n-bili*	Warrwa
	two	talk-continuous	they-be-present-two	

'The two of them are speaking together.'

Grouping words together into parts-of-speech categories does not imply that every word in each class patterns in precisely the same way. Rather, they are sufficiently similar to make it reasonable to group them together. Sometimes one can identify subclasses of major parts-of-speech because of shared minor differences. On the other hand, in some languages one finds a small number of lexical items that have their own unique patterning, and show no substantial similarities with any other words.

4.2 Ways of making new words

Limitations on formation of new words

In this section and the next we look at some of the ways in which languages expand their lexicons; we will be concerned with lexical morphemes, and ignore grammatical morphemes and idioms. This section discusses ways of expanding the lexicon by making new word forms, sometimes to express new meanings, sometimes to express existing meanings. The following section identifies ways in which existing forms can be used to make new lexical signs expressing new meanings.

The formation of new words is constrained in many ways. New forms must normally satisfy the phonological system of the language; thus a new word with final /ŋ/ would be possible in English, though one with initial /ŋ/ would be impossible. There are also meaning constraints: the meaning must be a one that speakers are likely to want to make. The meaning 'quark' is useful only in a language spoken in a scientifically oriented society. The lexical item *quark* entered the English language in the twentieth century, when the meaning was needed, not in 1063!

Aside from these constraints, human inventiveness is not unlimited, and it is unusual for a new lexeme to be totally original in both form and meaning. More usually, we put together bits and pieces of old forms and meanings according to relatively well established patterns (sometimes grammatical, sometimes not), to come up with new lexemes.

Etymology is the study of origin of words. It is often difficult to be sure how and when a word entered a language. This is particularly true of languages which, like most human languages, are unwritten or just recently written. At least for a language with a long tradition of writing old records may be preserved, permitting one to conclude that a certain word was in use by a particular time. However, it doesn't follow that the earliest written record remaining is the first use of the word – relevant written documents may well not have survived, and it is likely that the word was used in speech before it was ever written. (Writing is generally more conservative than speech.) Moreover, the basis on which the word was formed may not be apparent, or there may be two or three quite different though equally likely explanations.

Dictionary makers these days keep a careful eye – and ear – open for new words entering the major European languages like English, French, German and Spanish. But for the vast majority of languages there are no written dictionaries, let alone sufficient human and financial resources to monitor the acquisition of new words.

Clipping

Clipping is the shortening of an existing word of more than one syllable, generally to a single syllable. Common examples are *pub* (from *public house*), *fan* (in one sense from *fantastic*, in another from *fanatic*), *fax* (from *facsimile*), *ad* (from *advertisement*), *condo* (from *condominium*) and *flu* (from *influenza*). Personal names are often clipped in English – *Mike*, *Ron*, *Rob*, *Sue* and *Liz*.

Over time, clippings may become more frequent than the longer forms. This has happened with *pub*, *pram* and *fan* (in the 'devoted follower' sense), for which links with the source-words are not recognized by many speakers. Sometimes the long and short forms take on different senses, or become associated with different contexts of use (e.g. formal vs. casual speech). This is the case for short and long forms of names in English, where short forms tend to be used in more informal and intimate contexts, long forms in formal contexts. In the case of *fax* and *facsimile* the former has come to apply specifically to a document sent via the telephone system, while *facsimile* is restricted to an exact replica of a document, preserving its original written or printed form.

A variant on clipping that is common in Australian English is **hypocorism**. This involves first clipping a word down to a closed monosyllable. Next the suffix *-y ~ -ie* (/i/) is attached to the clipped form. Some examples are *Aussie* 'Australian', *brekky* 'breakfast', *bickie* 'biscuit', *barbie* 'barbeque' and *telly* 'television'. The same suffix can be added to clipped personal names (e.g. *Mickey*, *Robby*, *Lizzie*); but there is no suffix-less *brek* or *bick* corresponding to *brekky* and *bickie*.

Acronyming

Acronyms are words formed from the first letters of a string of words. There are two types: word acronyms and spelling acronyms.

Word acronyms are pronounced as single words, following the spelling to pronunciation rules. Examples are *RAM* (*random access memory*), *ROM* (*read only memory*), *NASA* (*National Aeronautics and Space Administration*), *UNESCO* (*United Nations Educational, Scientific, and Cultural Organization*) and *AIDS* (*Acquired Immune-Deficiency Syndrome*). Acronyms are often written with capital letters, giving away their status; but many well established acronyms are written as ordinary words: *laser* (*light amplification by stimulated emission of radiation*), *scuba* (*self-contained underwater breathing apparatus*), and *radar* (*radio detecting and ranging*). Few people realize that these words are acronyms. Famous is *snafu*, an acronym dating from the Second World War, that stands for *situation normal all fucked* (or *fouled*) *up*.

Spelling acronyms are pronounced as sequences of the names of the letters used, rather than as words (often because the sequences of letters are unpronounceable). Examples are *EU* (*European Union*), *PR* (*public relations*), *VCR* (*video cassette recorder*), and *CD* (*compact disk*). The widespread *OK*, which has been borrowed into many languages as an expression meaning 'all right, satisfactory, acceptable', began life as a jocular acronym for *orl korrect*, coined in 1839.

Acronyming is a popular way of forming new terms in modern English and many other European languages, especially names for organizations. They are often chosen so as to be evocative of the function of the organization, as in Ian Fleming's *SPECTRE* (*Special Executive for Counterintelligence, Terrorism, Revenge and Extortion*), *WAR* (*women against rape*), *NOW* (*National Organization for Women*), and *MADD* (*mothers against drunk driving*).

Acronyming is restricted to languages with established traditions of alphabetic writing and widespread literacy. It is not universally employed, and is dependent on the visual medium. To the best of my knowledge, speakers of no languages construct words from the initial phonemes of strings of words.

Blending

Blends involve the combination of parts of two separate words to form a single word. Usually it is the first part (often syllable) of one word together with the second part of the other word (either syllable or single final consonant), which occur in that sequence. The word *motel* is a blending of *motor* and *hotel*; *smog* is a blending of *smoke* and *fog*; and *bit* is a blending of *binary* and *digit*. Other examples are *Chunnel* (the tunnel under the channel between England and France) from *channel* and *tunnel*, *refolution* 'a peaceful revolution' from *reform* and *revolution*, and names for various mixes of languages such as *Franglais*, which blends *français* (French) and *anglais* (English), and *Japlish* a blend of *Japanese* and *English*. While speakers undoubtedly realize the status of some of these words as blends, others are not so obvious.

Occasionally it is the first part of both words that are combined together, as in *modem*, a blend of *modulator* and *demodulator*.

Borrowing

Major features of word borrowing

Borrowing, the process of incorporating into one language words from another, is perhaps the most common source of new words. Words that have been borrowed are called **loanwords**.

Loanwords are normally adapted to the phonological (and phonetic) patterns of the language they are borrowed into, although if the source (or loaning) language is well known to most speakers of the borrowing language, this adaptation does not always occur. An example is the word *kangaroo*, a borrowing from Guugu Yimithirr (Pama-Nyungan, Australia). The Guugu Yimithirr word is /gaɲuru/, with stress on the first syllable. But this is not a possible word in English, and it has been regularized to follow the phonemic patterns of the borrowing language: the velar nasal beginning the second syllable has been replaced by the nasal-stop cluster /ŋg/ (which is a possible sequence), and the /r/ – a tap or trill [r] (phonemically distinct from the continuant [ɹ] in Guugu Yimithirr) – has been replaced by the English rhotic ([ɹ] in most dialects). In addition, stress has shifted to the third syllable, and the vowel of the second syllable has been reduced from /u/ to /ə/. The other two vowels also show different qualities.

This example illustrates another characteristic of loanwords: their meaning need not be identical with the meaning of the word in the source language. The Guugu Yimithirr word refers to a particular type of macropod, not to kangaroos in general. According to one story, speakers of the language did not recognize the word as one of their own when pronounced in the English fashion because the English speaker was pointing to the wrong type of macropod!

Sometimes borrowed words are misidentified. A number of borrowings from Arabic include along with the lexical item also the definite article *al*, or a part of it. For example, *lute* comes from Arabic *al ūd*, the morpheme boundary being wrongly placed after the initial vowel; *algebra* (from *al jabr* 'the reunion of broken parts') and *algorithm* (from *al Khwārizmī*, 'the man from *Khwārizm* (Khiva)'), on the other hand, preserve the entire definite article as a part of the root.

Loan translations or **calques** are a special type of borrowing in which the morphemes composing the source word are translated item by item. Examples are English *power politics* from German *Machtpolitik* and Chinese *nan pengyu* (male friend) from English *boyfriend*. Similar to calques are loanblends, in which one of the morphemes, the main lexical morpheme, is borrowed, and the other is native, as in Pennsylvanian German *bassig* 'bossy', with borrowed stem and native suffix, *-ig* a German morpheme corresponding to the English *-y* suffix.

Some borrowings into English

Over the last millennium or so English has borrowed a vast number of words. Indeed, it has been estimated that over 60 per cent of the vocabulary of the average text in the modern language has been borrowed since 500 AD (Williams 1975). Knowledge of the time and place of these borrowings gives something of a picture of the history of the language and its speakers. Below is an outline of some of the major sources of borrowings.

Some centuries after the invasion of Britain by west Germanic tribes in the fifth century there occurred another invasion of Germanic tribes from Denmark. Around 900–1000 AD numerous Danish words were borrowed into English; many remain, including a number of very basic words, among them *sky*, *sister*, *egg*, *both* and *thing*.

The Norman invasion of England in 1066 resulted in French becoming the second language of many inhabitants. Numerous French loanwords date from this period, including many terms relating to the political and economic sphere such as *duke*, *cost*, *labour*, *rent* and *calendar*, as well as some everyday lexemes such as *uncle*, *aunt* and *easy*.

From about the tenth to the sixteenth centuries English borrowed a considerable number of Latin and Greek words. The loanwords dating from those times are mainly from the scientific and philosophical domains: these developing intellectual pursuits required terminologies, and Latin and Greek were good sources because they were known by the educated elite. Examples include *solar*, *gravity*, *telescope*, *history* and *legal*.

Following the colonization of America, numerous words were borrowed into English – as well as the other major colonial languages Spanish, French and Portuguese (Romance, Portugal) – from Native American languages. Many were words for places (e.g. *Michigan, Chicago, Texas*), and for plants (*maize, tomato, tobacco*) and animals (*moose, skunk, caribou*) that were unfamiliar to the European invaders. A number were subsequently borrowed into other European languages.

The post-1788 colonization of Australia brought another rash of loanwords, again primarily lexemes for places, plants and animals. Some 200 words have been borrowed from Australian languages into Australian English, and subsequently into other dialects. These include *kangaroo* (see pp. 88–89), *boobook* 'an owl type' and *dingo* 'wild dog' (from the language of Port Jackson), and *koala* (from the language of the Sydney area). Some of these words, including *kangaroo, emu* and *boomerang*, have since been borrowed into other languages (including other Australian Aboriginal languages).

Some borrowings from English

English has also contributed loans to numerous languages, especially in the colonial and post-colonial periods. Thus the languages of North America and Australia borrowed numerous words from English, again often words for previously unknown objects (e.g. cattle, sheep, horses, guns and later cars) and activities (e.g. branding, mustering and working).

With the increasing globalization of English during recent decades, and its status as the international language of business, science and technology, many languages have borrowed, and continue to borrow, considerable numbers of English specialized terms from these domains. Danish has borrowed numerous terms from the technological domain including *computer, video, radio, internet, harddisk, rom, pc* and *cd*. For logging off my server I go to the button labelled *log af*, a loanblend from *log off*. When I've finished working on the computer, I click *luk computeren* (literally 'close the computer'), at which point have the choice of going to *standby* (a straight borrowing from English), *luk* 'shut down' (indigenous Danish), or *genstart* (literally 'again-start' a loanblend from *restart*). Examples of calques in Danish are *fjernsyn* (*fjern* 'distant' and *syn* 'sight') 'television' and *fjernstyring* (*fjern* 'distant' and *styring* 'control') 'remote control'.

Coinage

Very rarely, a word is completely novel, an entirely creative invention; such words are called **coinages**. Coinages are always restricted to the limits imposed by the phonology of the language. Possible examples in English are *nerd, chunder* ('to vomit', primarily in Australian English), *barf* ('to vomit', mainly in American English), *naff* 'unfashionable, worthless, faulty', *razoo* ('imaginary coin' in Australian and New Zealand English), and brand names, like *Kodak, xerox, Vegemite* and *Exxon*.

More usually the degree of creativity of a new word is limited, and speakers exploit existing words and word patterns. Thus, according to *The New Shorter Oxford English Dictionary* the word *rayon*, which refers to fabric made from fibres and filaments of a certain type, is an invented word, that could be suggestive of the now rare *rayon* 'ray of light', and/or the noun *ray* with ending *on* (which is not a morpheme) motivated by *cotton*. Other invented words like *nylon* and *teflon* might further exploit this meaningless ending.

We have already remarked (§1.2) on the iconicity of some words, in particular of onomatopoeic words that represent the sound characteristic of some object, animal or event. A fair number of Australian languages have an invented onomatopoeic word for 'cat': *minyawoo* in Gooniyandi, *minyawu* in Warrwa and *mijawu* in Nyulnyul.

Sometimes certain phonemes or combinations of phonemes are felt by speakers to be evocative of certain meanings. For instance, in many languages the high front vowel [i] conveys a suggestion of smallness or closeness in contrast with [a] or [u]. Compare, for instance English *ding* and *dong* – which of these do you feel best describes the noise of a large bell?[3] If I was a betting man I would bet you chose *dong*, and that you would go for *ding* for the sound of a small bell. Interestingly, in Australian English a small dent on the body of a car is referred to as a *ding*. And in English (among other languages) the lateral *l* has a tendency to suggest liquids and fluid or uncontrolled movements.

A related phenomenon is **phonaesthesia**, where certain phones tend to be associated in the lexicon of a language with certain meanings, often on a partially iconic basis. For instance, many English words with initial *gl-* have to do with brightness, as in *glisten, gleam, glitter*; and many beginning with *sl-* tend to be associated with uncontrolled, liquid-like movements, as in *slip, slide* and *slither*. Phonaesthesia can be exploited at least to some extent by speakers in coining new words. Indeed, coinages that display some degree of phonaesthesia are perhaps more likely to gain acceptance than those that are totally arbitrary.

A special type of coinage is that of **nonsense words**, forms that could be words in the language, but are not. Lewis Carroll was a master inventor of nonsense words, which he used in many poems in Carroll (1899). These poems (sometimes called nonsense verse) use the usual grammatical morphemes of English, but replace some of the lexical words by nonsense words, sometimes with stunning effect. Here is the first verse of Carroll's poem *Jabberwocky* (Carroll 1899: 28):

> 'Twas brillig, and the slithy toves
>   Did gyre and gimble in the wabe;
> All mimsy were the borogoves,
>   And the mome raths outgrabe.

Carroll also went on to explain, in a dialogue between Humpty Dumpty and Alice, the meanings of the nonsense words, and their motivations. It is worth repeating the explanation of the first two lines here not just because of its sheer brilliance, but also because it alludes to some of the processes we have identified.

(Continued)

—Cont'd

'"*Brillig*" means four o'clock in the afternoon – the time when you begin *broiling* things for dinner.'

'That'll do very well,' said Alice: 'and "*slithy*"?'

'Well, "*slithy*" means "lithe and slimy". "Lithe" is the same as "active". You see it's a portmanteau – there are two meanings packed up into one word.'

'I see it now,' Alice remarked thoughtfully: 'and what are "*toves*"?'

'Well, "*toves*" are something like badgers – they're something like lizards – and they're something like corkscrews.'

'They must be very curious-looking creatures.'

'They are that,' said Humpty Dumpty; 'also they make their nests under sun-dials – also they live on cheese.'

'And what's to "*gyre*" and to "*gimble*"?'

'To "*gyre*" is to go round and round like a gyroscope. To "*gimble*" is to make holes like a gimlet.'

'And "*the wabe*" is the grass-plot around a sun-dial, I suppose?' said Alice, surprised at her own ingenuity.

'Of course it is. It's called "*wabe*" you know, because it goes a long way before it, and a long way behind it–'

'And a long way beyond it on each side,' Alice added.

Carroll 1899: 125–127

4.3 Ways of using old forms to get new meanings

In this section we focus attention on new meanings instead of new forms. Of course, there is overlap with the strategies for making new forms discussed in §4.2, most of which give rise to new meanings. Conversely, many of the processes we discuss here result in new forms; but, in contrast to the processes discussed in the previous section, these new forms are more systematically related to existing forms.

Derivation

Derivation is the process of forming new words by use of derivational morphemes, morphemes that create new lexical stems (see §3.3). Derivation is commonly used in English to form new words in science, medicine and technology. Linguistics is typical, and numerous derived forms can be found in this book. Dating from the mid-twentieth century are *deverbal*, *denominal* and *deadjectival*, referring to derivational processes by which verbs, nouns and adjectives loose their original part-of-speech membership.

Compounding

Two separate words are sometimes joined together to form a single word, a new word with a new meaning of its own, a meaning that is not entirely predictable from the component words. This process is called **compounding**. An example is *loanword*, a single word made up of two independent words *loan* and *word*. Notice that although a loanword is a type of word, one that has been borrowed into one language from another, the meaning of *loanword* is not entirely predictable from the meaning of the individual words making it up. Why is this? There are two main reasons. First, a loanword is not borrowed in the way that things are usually borrowed – the word *loan* suggests a temporary change of possession (otherwise it is surely a gift), which does not apply in this case: the word remains in both donor language and borrowing language. (I would be happy to loan you any amount of money if I knew that I would keep the same amount in my possession!) Second, as described earlier, the word applies to the specific case in which the word is incorporated into the lexicon of another language, which usually means that it adapts to the phonological structure of the borrowing language. A loanword is not just any word of Danish that I as a native speaker of English living in Denmark might insert into my spoken English, although nothing in the meaning of the words making up the compound precludes words of this type.

Compounding is quite heavily used in English, German, Dutch and Danish as a means of forming new words. Kiowa (Kiowa Tanoan, USA) also makes extensive use of compounding: *t'ɔ́á* (ear-stick) 'earring', *mɔ́n-kʰɔ́y* (hand-cloth) 'glove', *mɔ́n-sɔ́ꞏdè* (hand-hook:on) 'bracelet' and *mɔ́n-pà-tò* (hand-against-hold) 'weapon'. It is less frequent in Romance languages such as French, Spanish and Romanian, and almost non-existent in Mosetén (Mosetenan, Bolivia).

Reduplication

Many languages form new words by repeating an existing word either in full or in part. This is called **reduplication**. Oceanic languages usually make a good deal of use of reduplication as a means of making new words. For example, in Saliba (Oceanic, Papua New Guinea) nouns can be formed from verbs by reduplication, as in *kuya-kuya* (sweep-sweep) 'broom', and *lau-lau* (go-go) 'way, method'. A verb can also be reduplicated to form a word expressing a quality: *dou-dou* (cry-cry) 'crying (person)'. If the word has more than two syllables, reduplication is partial, the first two syllables only being repeated, and attached to the front of the word, as in *tago-tagodu* (break-break) 'broken (thing)' and *hede-hedede* (talk-talk) 'word, talking'.

Reduplication is often iconic. Reduplication of verbs generally conveys the idea of a frequent and repeated event, or one that is habitual or characteristic of something, as in the Saliba examples just cited. Reduplication of a noun often indicates numerosity or multiplicity, or intensity. In many Australian languages reduplication of nouns results in a new noun indicating a multiplicity of things; this is illustrated by the Jaru (Pama-Nyungan) reduplications *maluga-maluga* (old:man-old:man) 'many old men', *manga-manga* (girl-girl) 'many girls', and *guju-guju* (baby:animal-baby:animal) 'many baby animals'. Reduplication of nouns in Chichewa (Niger-Congo, Malawi) indicates intensification: *m-kází-kazi* (*m*-woman-woman)[4] 'cute and cultured woman' and *munthu-múnthu* (person-person) 'a real (i.e. humane) person'.

Reduplication is often considered marginal in English, although this is questionable: over 2,000 words are formed by this process according to Burridge (2004: 47). Sometimes the whole stem is repeated, as in *fifty-fifty*, *hush-hush* and *never-never*; more often there is a slight phonological change in the repeated element, as in *helter-skelter*, *dilly-dally*, *higgeldy-piggeldy*, *teeny-weeny*, *hanky-panky* and *shilly-shally*.

Backformation

In **backformation** a shorter word is created from a longer one by removing a part that is wrongly taken to be an existing morpheme. From the noun *television* the verb *televize* was backformed on analogy with other pairs such as *revise ~ revision*, and *incise ~ incision*, that involve the nominal derivational suffix *-ion* (*-ɜn̩*). Another example is *burger*, which, as most speakers of English know, comes from *hamburger*. But the term was originally *Hamburg-er*, with the derivational suffix *-er* attached to *Hamburg*, the name of a city in northern Germany. Speakers reanalysed the word as *ham-burger*, doubtless interpreting the *ham* as the word for a type of meat. By analogy with pairs like *ham sandwich ~ sandwich*, the pair *hamburger ~ burger* is expected. Other examples are the verbs *edit* from *editor*, *emote* from *emotion* and *babysit* from *babysitter*.

Meaning extension

Our final two processes of word formation do not involve changes to word forms. The first is **meaning extension**, which is the process of extending the meaning of an existing word, broadening it to embrace new senses. This is a quite common way of forming new words – new words because the meaning associated with the old form is a new one, and not fully predictable from the old sense. This can be exemplified by the word for 'policeman' in many Australian languages: in Walmajarri it is *limpa* 'a type of biting fly that swoops down on person'; in Bardi (Nyulnyulan) it is *liinyj* 'sour'. On the opposite side of the continent, Dhurga (Pama-Nyungan) has extended the word *jungga* 'octopus' (the eight arms of the law!), while Djabugay (Pama-Nyungan) has extended *jun.gi* 'freshwater crayfish type'. Money, in Australian languages (a non-traditional artefact), is often designated by the word for 'rock, stone', an extension based on the resemblance of coins to stones; these days the term shows, in many languages, a further extension to include paper money as well.

Examples of meaning extensions are not difficult to find in English either. The word *holiday*, for instance, comes from the compound *holy-day*, a day on which one did not work. It has extended to cover any day designated as work-free (as in *today is a holiday*, which happens to have been true at the time I first composed this sentence), and thence to the travel and other enjoyable activities one might perform on a work-free day (as in *I will go for a holiday next month*). A number of product brand-names have extended their meaning to embrace any artefact of their type. An example is *hoover*; indeed, this word has extended further to the activity one typically performs with the instrument, namely vacuum-cleaning the floor.

Meaning narrowing

Meaning narrowing is the reverse of meaning extension: a word's sense becomes restricted. For example, *doctor* in everyday spoken English shows narrowing from 'person holding a doctorate degree' to 'person holding a doctorate in medicine'. To express the former meaning one would normally use a more specific expression such as *doctor of philosophy*, *doctor of science* or *PhD*. (*Doctor* has subsequently extended meaning its to 'qualified medical practitioner', relaxing the requirement of having a doctorate in medicine.)

The word *doctor* has perhaps narrowed due to the lack of a suitable term for the professional in the medical field: *medical practitioner* has a formal air, while terms like *physician* and *surgeon* have more specific senses. Not all narrowings are motivated by lack of a suitable term. In seventeenth century English *meat* meant 'food', and *flesh* meant 'meat'. The meaning of *meat* has since narrowed to one particular type of food, that derived from animals; *flesh* has at the same time shifted its meaning to refer to part of an animal's or person's body, regardless of whether or not it is to be eaten. And *food* took the place left by *meat*.

4.4 Fixed expressions

Idioms

Recall that idioms are more or less fixed expressions like *kick the bucket* 'die', the meanings of which are not predictable from the component words or grammar (see p. 82), and which need to be listed in the lexicon.

Some idioms are virtually unchangeable, like the Australian English *Don't come the raw prawn with me*, meaning 'don't try putting that behaviour over me' (also idiomatic). You can't change this to the positive form *Come the raw prawn with me*, or into a statement in past time *He didn't come the raw prawn with me*, or with different persons *I won't come the raw prawn with you*. Nor can you replace *raw prawn* by *cooked prawn*, *raw meat*, *raw lobster* or any other such expression.

Most idioms are not so fixed, and allow at least some grammatical modifications. For example, *give (someone) a piece of your mind* can be modified in various ways, according to time, purpose of the utterance and the persons involved: *She gave me a piece of her mind*, *(Don't) give her a piece of your mind* and so on. Although you can modify the structure of this idiom somewhat (even to a limited extent rephrasing it, for example, *A piece of my mind is what I intend to give her*), you can't do so as freely as for an ordinary non-idiomatic sentence like *She gave the postman the wrongly addressed letter*. Whereas you can rephrase the latter sentence as *The wrongly addressed letter was given to the postman*, you can't rephrase the idiom as *A piece of your mind was given to her*, or *She was given a piece of your mind*. (The latter sentences invoke the non-idiomatic readings that something was handed over.)

More interestingly, perhaps, idioms can often be exaggerated by either the addition of elaborating material, or replacement of a salient word, injecting life back into tired and worn-out expressions. Examples are *take with a generous pinch of salt*, *take with a ton of salt*, *I'll eat my hat . . . and shoes as well!* and *up shit creek in a barbed-wire canoe without a paddle* – as if being up shit creek wasn't bad enough! Even the invariant *Don't come the raw prawn with me* can be modified by lexical replacement to *Don't come the uncooked crustacean with me!* Similarly, *Hold your horses!* can appear as *Hold your ponies!* Like grammars – as Edward Sapir famously observed – idioms leak.

Although the meaning of an idiom is not predictable from the words that make it up, in many cases it is possible to guess some motivation for it. Idioms like *don't look a gift horse in the mouth*, *throw your weight around*, *I'll eat my hat*, *hold your horses*, *get it off your chest* and *get off your high horse* are not entirely arbitrary. Thus, you can imagine if you examine too carefully a horse given to you that you might find something wrong with it, and this idea is obviously behind the idiom. To be sure, some remain puzzling, if not downright inexplicable, like *don't come the raw prawn with me*, and *kick the bucket*. (Don't ask me to explain these!)

Presumably all languages have idioms. One domain where idioms are frequently found is in the expression of emotions. These are often constructed as idiomatic expressions involving reference to parts of the human body, as in the following examples:

(4-4) *ngiya-mad-ju*   *barij*   *wi*   Ngarinyin (Worrorran, Australia)
my-kidney-to   rise   it:is
'I'm happy.' (Literally, 'My kidney is rising.')

(4-5) *tôi*   *đau*   *lòng*   Vietnamese
I   sick   intestines
'I'm broken-hearted.' (Literally, 'I'm sick in the belly.')

(4-6) *ti-n*   *mīs*   Paamese (Austronesian, Vanuatu)
intestines-he   he:cries
'He/she feels sorry.' (Literally, 'His intestines cry.')

(4-7) *ti-n*   *tīsa*   Paamese
intestines-he   he:is:bad
'He/she is angry.' (Literally, 'His intestines are bad.')

To wind up this section consider (4-8), a common idiomatic expression in Romanian. With a little thought you should be able to understand its motivation.

(4-8) *m-ai*   *lovit*   *în*   *pălărie*   Romanian
me-have:you   hit   in   hat
'What you are saying (or doing) is so stupid that you fail to hit the target.'
(Literally: 'You hit me in the hat.')

Collocations

Some fixed expressions have meanings that are fully predictable from the component words. Examples are so-called **binomials**, such as *salt and pepper, pen and paper, up and down, cup and saucer*. The words of binomials come in a relatively fixed order; thus you normally say *Pass the salt and pepper*, not *Pass the pepper and salt*. Of course, you can say *Pass the pepper and salt*, but that is not the way speakers of English normally phrase the request.

Binomials are examples of **collocations**, habitual combinations of words. Words are somewhat fussy about the company they keep; there is often some degree of predictability of one word given another: *salt* is statistically more likely to be followed (within two words) by *pepper* than by *sauce, cardboard* or *brontosaurus. Coffee* collocates with *strong, weak, sweet* and *hot*, but not with *heavy, hard* or *cloying*. You would use the former adjectives to describe a cup of coffee, in preference to the latter: *a cup of strong coffee* or *a strong cup of coffee* rather than ?*a cup of hard/heavy coffee*, or ?*heavy/hard a cup of coffee*, and *sweet coffee* rather than ?*cloying coffee*. You might not expect separate entries in speakers' mental lexicons for collocations such as the above, their meanings being predictable. However, knowledge of the collocations of a word is certainly crucial to their usage, and the collocations themselves are not predictable: there is no particular reason why *strong* rather than *hard* should go with *coffee* – *hard* collocates with other words for drinks: a strong alcoholic drink is *hard liquor*. Another illustration of this point is that *the* collocates with *radio* in *I heard it on the radio* (where *the* is unlikely to be left out), but not with *television* or *TV* in *I saw it on TV* (where *the* is less likely to be used). This difference seems to be idiosyncratic. It is reasonable to expect the entry for a word in a speaker's mental lexicon to contain information about the words it collocates with.

An enormous variety of collocations is found in English, and doubtless other languages. They vary from collocations of the type we have been discussing with predictable meanings, to idiomatic collocations such as *spick and span, livelong day* and *eke out*, in which the first word is not used outside of the collocation, and so completely predicts the following words. It is difficult to draw the line between idioms and collocations. Many words in idioms collocate quite strongly with one another: *green* collocates with *envy* (*you'll be green with envy*); other colour words do not.

4.5 What's in a word?

Word taboos

'A rose by any other name would smell as sweet', said Juliet. True this may be, but not all words smell equally sweet, at least to speakers of a language. Words are not neutral; they carry emotional overtones. Whether you use the word *policeman, cop, bobby, fuzz, the filth, (a) John* or *pig* you may be referring to an officer of the law; whether you say *strike breaker, blackleg* or *scab* you may be referring to someone who takes the place of workers on strike.

But these words have different overtones, and your choice among them clearly conveys your attitude.

For the words we've just discussed, the overtones are associated with the words in particular uses: *scab* doesn't have such overtones when used to describe the hard dried blood of a sore. But some words have particularly strong affective values; for example, *shit*, *fuck* and *cunt* are among the most highly-charged words in English. They are often called 'dirty' words or 'filthy' words, although there is nothing intrinsically dirty (or for that matter, clean) about them, and there is nothing at all unpleasant about them phonetically or phonologically. (*Fuck* surely sounds no better or worse than *duck*, *luck*, *fun* or *fuddle*.)

Nevertheless, these three words are felt to be in some sense 'bad' by speakers of English, who tend to avoid their use in 'polite company', and, for instance, when speaking to their mother, to a prospective employer or on a televised quiz-show. Indeed, in the USA it was not until 1926 that *fuck* was first printed openly; its use in printed sources has increased considerably in recent years. (As a foreigner in Denmark I have often been surprised by seeing *fuck* written in places where its use would be considered offensive in Australia or Britain.) Words like *fuck* are called **taboo** words – *taboo* is a borrowing from Tongan (Austronesian, Tonga) *tabu*, which refers to actions or things that are prohibited by social or religious convention.

In English and other European languages many words relating to sexual activity, the genitals and some bodily functions and exuviae (urine, faeces, menstrual blood) are taboo. In English, of course, there are more acceptable words for these activities and body parts and products. Interestingly, it is the words inherited from Anglo-Saxon that are taboo; those borrowed from Latin (like *faeces* and *vagina*) tend to be accepted as 'clean' terms. Certain words with religious connotations are also tabooed in many cultures when used outside of the appropriate religious context. This is the case for words like *God*, and *Christ* – as a child I was often told 'Don't take the lord's name in vain'.

There are other quite different types of word taboos. Terms for game animals are often taboo to hunters. In many societies in New Guinea and Australia, there is a taboo on uttering the name of a recently dead person. In many Australian languages this taboo extends to a word that sounds like the name of the deceased. Thus, when a man named Djäyila died at Yirrkala (North-East Arnhem Land, Australia) in 1975 the verb *djäl-* 'to want' was tabooed, and replaced by *duktuk-*; after a few years *djäl-* started reappearing.

Euphemisms

Euphemisms are indirect or evasive expressions used to avoid direct mention of unpleasant or taboo ideas; euphemisms provide ways of avoiding being offensive by being evasive. A few examples are: *pass away* and *go to sleep* for 'die'; *bathroom* (American English) and *loo* (Australian English) for 'toilet, lavatory'; *smalls* and *unmentionables* for 'underclothing'; and *girl*, *working girl*, and *woman of the street* for 'prostitute'. The word *undertaker*, which originally meant 'odd-job man', was used as a euphemism for someone whose job is to bury the dead. Its meaning narrowed to this sense alone, as often happens with euphemisms. Now a new euphemism is now replacing it, *funeral director*.

The unpleasantness of touchy events or things is felt to be lessened by use of an indirect term, because it reminds one of something more pleasant. Euphemisms are commonly found in the domains around which taboos are often found, including sexual activity, sex organs, bodily functions and products, death and killing. But they are not restricted to these domains, and can be found for any sort of unpleasant reality: for example, *honorariums* instead of *bribes*, *campaign contributions* instead of *graft*, *make redundant* instead of *sack* and *tactical withdrawal* instead of *retreat*.

Dysphemisms

Dysphemisms are the inverse of euphemisms: a euphemistic or neutral expression is replaced by a particularly direct or harsh term, with offensive overtones, often a taboo term. Examples of dysphemisms include: *shithouse* and *boghouse* for *toilet* (compare the euphemisms *bathroom* and *loo*); use of tabooed terms like *fuckwit*, *cunt* and *shithead* and terms for animals such as *pig*, *slut*, *monkey* and *bitch* in insults.

A slightly different illustration of dysphemism is the use in many languages of terms like 'rubbish' and 'worthless' for the most sacred or important ideas or items – in this circumstance without offensive overtones. In Nyulnyul the word *riib* 'rubbish, no good' can be used dysphemistically in reference to the most sacred objects. It is as though by using this term the powerful and potentially dangerous is trivialized or neutralized, thereby losing some of its harmful potential. In this example the effect is more like the effect of a euphemism, while the form is dysphemistic.

> Words and expressions are not necessarily inherently euphemistic or dysphemistic. It can depend on the context in which they are uttered. Some of the words that are most dysphemistic in ordinary usage can, in certain contexts, lose their offensiveness and be used as terms of intimacy and endearment. This is the case in the institution of mateship among Australian males, where the stronger the term of abuse the greater the intimacy expressed.

Summing up

The **lexicon** of a language is a listing of its unpredictable signs, including **idioms**. This listing ideally provides information about the form and meaning of each, as well as (for a word) its classification and the words it **collocates** with. Speakers of a language have **mental lexicons** in which these types of information are stored.

Words and morphemes are classified into **parts-of-speech** according to their grammatical behaviour, which varies from language to language. Widely found parts-of-speech include nouns, verbs, pronouns, adjectives, adverbs, prepositions, postpositions, conjunctions and interjections. Not all of these categories are found in all languages; indeed, it is not certain that any are universal.

The lexicon of a living language is **open**, and new words are regularly added while old words may be lost. New lexemes can be constructed by inventing novel forms via processes such as **clipping**, **acronyming**, **blending**, **borrowing** and **coinage**. They can also be constructed by re-using old forms and processes, including **derivation**, **compounding**, **reduplication** and **backformation**. New lexical items can also be formed by **extension** and **narrowing** of the meanings of existing words.

Words may be attitudinally charged. Some are prohibited in particular circumstances; these are **taboo words**. Other illustrations of the affective values of words come from **euphemisms** and **dysphemisms**.

Guide to further reading

Parts-of-speech systems are dealt with in most introductions to linguistics, and in grammars of particular languages. For more detailed discussion see Evans (2000); Hengeveld et al. (2004); Rijkhoff (2007); and Schachter and Shopen (2007).

Numerous books treat word formation in English. Among them Bauer (1983), and Marchand (1969) are recommended. On the history of English, see Bragg (2003); Pyle and Algeo (1993); Williams (1975). Burridge (2004) is an accessible and entertaining book dealing with all of the topics mentioned in this chapter in relation to English.

I recommend Wescott (1980) for a fascinating discussion of phonaesthesia and a variety of unusual and often ignored linguistic phenomena, albeit mainly in English. Although sound symbolism is relatively marginal in mainstream linguistics, many distinguished linguists have studied it, including Edward Sapir (1929) and Roman Jakobson (1978; Jakobson and Waugh 1979). Hinton et al. (1994) contains articles on sound symbolism in a variety of languages.

A good treatment of idioms is Fernando (1996). The reader is also referred to dictionaries of English idioms such as Kirkpatrick and Schwarz (1995); Speake (2002); and Spears (1990).

Allan and Burridge (1991, 2006) are recommended as detailed but accessible accounts of euphemisms and dysphemisms. Bolinger (1980) also deals with euphemisms and dysphemisms, among other things, and is well worth reading. Sheidlower (1995) provides much information on one English taboo word, and words based on it.

Issues for further thought and exercises

1. What word-formation processes are illustrated by the following English words (classify them according to the schemes of §4.2 and §4.3)? Try making an educated guess first, then look up the word in a good dictionary.

typo	boatel	wordsmith	brolga
teens	AC/DC	galoot	Darwinian
porn	carpeteria	peddle	alcohol
asap	gargantuan	doodad	la-di-da
Reagonomics	sandwich	karaoke	Frigidaire

2. Find out about the meaning and origin of the word *googol*. What sort of word formation process does it illustrate? Why do you think this word caught on? How would you account for *googolplex*?

3. A number of English words for large numbers are constructed with the ending of *-llion*. What is the basis of these formations? Find as many such words as you can, and state their meanings. Are there any additional motivations for any of these terms?

4. It was mentioned in §4.3 that the word for 'policeman' in Walmajarri is *limba*, the word for a particular type of fly. In the local dialect of Aboriginal English this same fly is referred to as a *bolijman blai* (policeman fly). What sort of word-formation processes does this illustrate?

5. List some idioms in a language you know, along with their meanings; determine what modifications (including exaggerations) they allow. Try to account for the idiom.

6. Make a list of as many binomial expressions as you can. Can you see any patterns in the ordering of the words, in which word goes first? Can you find any trinomials?

7. Find a newspaper or magazine article reporting on a war. List the expressions referring to events involving the killing of people; classify the expressions as euphemisms, dysphemisms or neutral expressions. Are there any differences in the expressions – or their frequency – that are used for killing of people on different sides? If there are differences, what do they reveal? What other euphemistic or dysphemistic expressions can you find in the article?

8. *Slang* is a somewhat imprecise term used for colloquial, informal or non-standard language. What are some examples of slang terms used by people in your generation? See what you can find about the slang of your parents' generation. What similarities and differences do you find? How would you classify the expressions you collected in terms of the processes discussed in §4.2 and §4.3 above?

9. What word-initial phonemes or phoneme sequences do you think are phonaesthesic in English? What meaning do you intuitively feel is associated with them? Make up a list of words beginning with the sequences that support your intuitions.

10. Here are a few apparently relatively new technical lexemes culled from recent issues of *Scientific American*. Can you guess their meanings? What processes of word formation do they exemplify? To what extent is their meaning arbitrary or motivated?

exoplanet	wiki
D-GPS	ADDL
zeptoliter	pre-bang universe
geolocation	picokelvin

11. Recent years have seen a spate of words ending in *-aholic ~ -oholic*, as in *workaholic*. Find as many of these words as you can (look on the internet). What sort of word-formation process is involved? What does *-aholic ~ -oholic* mean, and where does it come from?

Notes

1. It must be emphasized that the semantic characteristics mentioned here are not decisive in the part-of-speech classification of a word. Rather, it is the grammatical characteristics – which will be different in different languages – that

are criterial. The semantic characteristics indicate tendencies among words of the particular part-of-speech, which motivate the label.

2. The meanings of the glosses for the grammatical morphemes may be disregarded here as they do not affect the point being made.

3. The reader is reminded that in talking of associations such as these, which have some iconic basis, there is no claim of necessity of connection. It is easy to find words in English which do not show the associations. The point is merely that some association exists as something that speakers of a language experience. If given the choice between *feeny* and *mung* as words to describe two objects, one a small pointed star like object, the other a larger roundish glob-like object, most speakers would feel that *feeny* is more appropriate to the former object. There is experimental evidence supporting this claim.

4. The *m* is a prefix indicating the noun is human; it is irrelevant here.

Structure of Sentences: Syntax

5

In the previous two chapters we examined the internal make-up of words and their classification into parts-of-speech. We turn now to the ways words can be put together to form sentences, and examine the structures and types of these units. Sentence structure in all human languages is complex, and (like morphology) varies considerably from language to language. However, in all languages two things are recurrent: the existence of units intermediate in size between words and sentences, and of grammatical relations between them. Differences in these units and relations permit us to distinguish different sentence types within and across languages.

Chapter contents

Goals

The goals of the chapter are to:
- introduce and explain three key concepts of syntax: openness, grammaticality and hierarchical structure;
- present the fundamental syntactic units, and give criteria for their identification;
- show how the syntactic structures of sentences can be represented in tree diagrams;
- explain the need to identify syntactic relations;
- identify some of the major types of syntactic relation;
- illustrate by example some differences in the structure of sentences of the world's languages; and
- remark on similarities and differences between morphology and syntax.

Key terms

Actor	Event	Object	textural role
adjectival phrase	grammaticality	openness of syntax	Theme
clause	grammatical relation	postpositional phrase	Undergoer
constituent analysis	hierarchical structure	prepositional phrase	verbal phrase
embedding	interpersonal role	sentence	
experiential role	nominal phrase	Subject	

5.1 What is syntax?

Openness

In all human languages words can be put together in sequences to express meanings for which no separate words exist: the range of complexities and nuances of meanings that a speaker might want to express – and distinguish from other possible meanings – is much larger than can be expressed by the lexical and morphological resources of any language. For instance, no human language would have a single word to express a meaning like that expressed by the previous sentence. Words and morphology alone are insufficient to make all the complex meanings and meaning distinctions people regularly need to make in thought and communication.

Syntax is concerned with the means available in languages for putting words together in sequences. Sometimes the term *grammar* is used instead of *syntax*, though more usually grammar is considered to cover not just syntax but also morphology, and often phonology and semantics as well. The way we are using the terms, syntax is grammar above the word.

It should be clear from the previous two chapters that morphology and lexicon are not completely closed systems: languages can acquire new lexemes, even new grammatical morphemes (see §12.5). But these resources are somewhat limited, even in languages that are morphologically much more complex than English, such as Yup'ik, in which single words can express meanings that require full sentences in English, as in example (3-1), repeated as (5-1). Not all English sentences, however, can be expressed as single words in Yup'ik: as (5-2) shows, sentences in this language sometimes consist of more than one word (the glosses have been simplified somewhat).

(5-1) *kai-*   *-pia-*   *-llru-*   *-llini-*   *-u-*   *-k*   Yup'ik
       be:hungry- -really-   -past-   -apparently- -statement-   -they:two
       'The two of them were apparently really hungry.'

(5-2) *tauku-t*   *atsa-t*   *tegu-k-ai*   Yup'ik
       that-PL   fruit-PL   take:in:hand-PART-he→them
       'He took those pears.'

Syntax provides additional means of 'opening' the grammatical system for the expression of new meanings, nuances of meanings, precision in meaning and links between ideas; it provides means for speakers to go beyond the limitations of the morphology and lexicon. Syntax enhances the creativity of expression in language. In this respect the difference between syntax and the other domains is one of degree rather than kind. Openness is a characteristic of all grammatical systems, phonological, lexical, morphological and syntactic; it is most salient in syntax.

The notion of sentence

The sentence, as it is usually conceived in linguistics, is the largest linguistic unit showing grammatical structure, the largest unit over which grammatical rules or patterns apply; it is at the opposite end of the scale of grammatical items from the morpheme, the smallest grammatical unit. This understanding of the sentence goes back to the American linguist Leonard Bloomfield (1887–1949) who proposed that a sentence is a string of words not included in any larger linguistic form by virtue of grammatical structure. According to this criterion, (5-3) consists of two sentences, since the two components, (5-4) and (5-5), and are grammatically independent of one another.

(5-3) *The fisherman hung the net on the fence. I saw him.*

(5-4) *The fisherman hung the net on the fence.*

(5-5) *I saw him.*

To be sure, there are relations between the parts of the sentences: *him* in (5-3) is naturally interpreted as referring to the same person as *the farmer*. But this is not by grammatical rule, and the second sentence could as well have been *I saw it*, or even *I saw the poor guy* (still referring to the fisherman, although it could also refer to someone else). Notice the difference from the situation for (5-6), where the grammatical form of the material following the comma is dependent on the preceding string of words: it can be only *didn't he*, or *did he*. Thus you can't use a different verb, such as *isn't*, *saw*, or *hung*, and preserve the structure, as you can in the case of separate sentences, as in (5-3).

(5-6)   *The fisherman hung the net on the fence, didn't he?*

Nor can *he* in (5-6) refer to anyone bar the fisherman, whereas *him* in *I saw him* can, given the right context, be interpreted as referring to someone other than the fisherman.

The openness of syntax referred to in the previous subsection can now be understood as the openness of the set of sentences of any language. The syntax of a language provides a ready-made system of principles for the construction (production by a speaker) and interpretation (understanding or interpretation by a hearer) of novel sentences – sentences that have never previously been uttered in the language, sentences that express new meanings and sentences that express old meanings in new ways. This can be referred to as creativity in sentence formation – a somewhat restricted sense of the term, to be sure. Of course, not every sentence is novel; but speakers do fairly often produce novel sentences which hearers find quite unremarkable. The invention of new words is a much less common phenomenon, and is more likely to strike hearers as unusual, humorous or smart.

Grammaticality

Not all possible strings of words in a language form grammatically acceptable sentences. While *The fisherman hung the net on the fence* does represent a grammatical sentence, the same words in a different order, for example, *The the hung fisherman fence net on the* is clearly not grammatical. It does not follow the grammar of English, and a speaker could not make much sense of it. Such strings of words are ungrammatical. It is standard practice to put a star before ungrammatical strings of words: *The the hung fisherman fence net on the.

The notion of grammaticality should not be confused with meaningfulness or interpretability. Noam Chomsky's famous *Colourless green ideas sleep furiously* is a fully grammatical sentence of English, although it makes little sense, and can hardly designate any ongoing situation in the real world.[1] And Lewis Carroll's *Jabberwocky* (§4.2) consists of fully grammatical sentences, though it is 'nonsense verse'. By contrast, *Fisherman hanged net on fence* is not a grammatical sentence, although no speaker of English would have the slightest difficulty understanding it.

The notion of ungrammatical sentences is useful for revealing things about the syntax of a language. What is grammatical needs to be seen in the context of what is not, if one is to produce a revealing and complete description of the syntax of a language. As we find elsewhere in linguistics (indeed in science generally) paying attention to where things go wrong can reveal insights about the situation in which they go right, insights that might not be perceived through exclusive focus on the normal situation.

Caution must be observed in using ungrammatical sentences to make syntactic arguments. The borderline between what is grammatical and what is ungrammatical is not always clear cut, and especially if the linguist is relying exclusively their own intuitions they are liable to be misled by their own presuppositions, or by failure to properly interpret a string of words. Here is an example from personal experience. Standard accounts of English grammar say that tag questions can be added to statements (as in *The fisherman hung the net on the fence, didn't he?*) and commands (as in *Hang the net on the fence, will you?*). One infers from this that tags can't be added to questions (if it is not said, then it is not true); indeed, some linguists have explicitly claimed that such sentences are ungrammatical, and starred sentences like *Are you going now, are you?* In the early 1990s I began to notice examples of this type in Australian English, and over the next few years collected some hundreds of instances. Clearly these sentences were grammatical, and not errors. Some grammarians responded 'not in my dialect': this was a peculiarity of Australian English, they said, that did not occur in British English. Nevertheless, BBC television programmes such as *The Bill* revealed examples in British English.

5.2 Hierarchical structure in sentences

Grouping

We have now three types of grammatical unit at our disposal for describing the syntactic structure of a language, sentences, words and morphemes. Are they sufficient? Can we provide a complete account of the syntax of sentences as strings of words and/or morphemes coming one after the other?

Evidence suggests not, that we need to recognize other units intermediate in size. Consider the English sentence (5-7).

(5-7)   *The train chugged along the line through the mountains.*

Some morphemes and/or words seem to belong together: for instance, the first *the* is naturally interpreted as belonging with *train* rather than with *chugged* or *along*. At minimum, it seems reasonable to identify three groups of words or morphemes in (5-7): *the train*, *chugged* and *along the line through the mountains*. Within the third group another group can be recognized, *the line through the mountains*, within which in turn *through the mountains* forms yet another word group.

Such descriptions in everyday English quickly become cumbersome and difficult to understand, and it is useful to represent groupings of morphemes/words in diagrammatic form. Example (5-8) shows one form of representation. In such figures the groups are indicated by sets of vertical lines that are connected by a horizontal line.

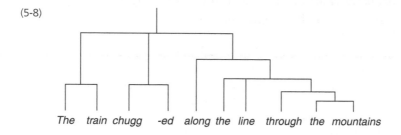

(5-8)

The   train chugg   -ed   along the line   through the mountains

Other styles of figure are also used. Example (5-9) illustrates the most frequently used type, that represents the groups by connecting them together with slanting lines, thus ∧ instead of ⊓. In this case, just two branches meet at any node; this means that more word groups are recognized than in (5-8), and the structure is more hierarchical. You can of course always redraw (5-8) to represent the same hierarchical structure as (5-9), and vice-versa – try it!

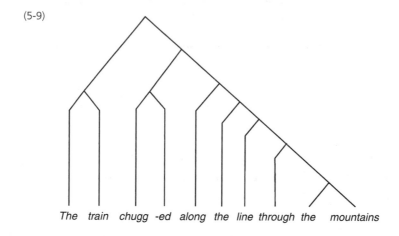

(5-9)

The   train   chugg -ed   along   the   line through the   mountains

Representations like (5-8) and (5-9) are called **tree diagrams**, or simply **trees**. Tree diagrams enjoy a prominent place in syntax. Figures like (5-9), using mainly two-way branches, were popular in American linguistics during the 1930s–1950s, and are associated with an approach called Immediate Constituent Analysis (or IC Analysis). Modified versions still enjoy considerable popularity, especially within formal syntax (see §1.5). Trees like (5-8), with more rake-like (less hierarchical) structures, tend to be used in functional grammars; they are sometimes said to represent string constituent analysis. As we will see later in the chapter, there are reasons to prefer the string constituent type analysis.

Evidence for groupings of words

Grammarians are not satisfied with grouping words together on intuitive grounds. They demand evidence from the language. Three main considerations – three main tests – provide evidence for groupings: movability, contractibility and structural ambiguity. We deal with these in turn.

Movability

The idea behind **movability** is that if certain words always move about together in a sentence they constitute a single group: since they can't be split apart, they presumably belong together. That is, if we compare a sentence with similar-meaning sentences involving the same lexical items in different orders, and find that certain words always cluster together in the same way, this suggests that they form a word-group. Returning to (5-4), repeated as (5-10), compare the following sentences:

(5-10)   *The fisherman hung the net on the fence*

(5-11)   *On the fence the fisherman hung the net*

(5-12)   *It was on the fence that the fisherman hung the net*

(5-13)   *The net was hung on the fence by the fisherman*

(5-14)   *It was the fisherman who hung the net on the fence*

(5-15)   *It was the net that was hung on the fence by the fisherman*

Examples (5-11) and (5-12) show that *on the fence* behaves as a single unit; (5-13)–(5-15) show that *the fisherman* and *the net* each separately forms a single grouping of words. The words *the* and *fisherman* always go together; they can't be shifted around independently of one another, and separated by other words from the same sentence.

This criterion is a good, though imperfect guide to word groupings; grammatical criteria (or tests) are rarely perfect. Sometimes word-groups can be split up, as illustrated by (5-16), which shows that *on* can be separated from *the fence*.

(5-16)   *It was the fence that the fisherman hung the net on*

What you don't find, however, is that words that do not form a group together always move around in concert. For instance, the three words *the net on* does not behave in this way, as revealed by the unacceptability of the following:

(5-17)   **The net on was hung the fence by the fisherman*

(5-18)   **It was the net on that was hung the fence by the fisherman*

Contractibility

Contractibility is the potential for a string of words to be replaced by a single word. In (5-10) we can replace *the fisherman* by *he*, *the net* by *it*, and *on the fence* by *out* or *up*: *He hung it out*.

The idea behind this is that if the string can be replaced by a single word it behaves as a single word, which we know is a grammatical element. Thus the string behaves like a single grammatical item, and so the component words form a single syntactic group.

Again this criterion is imperfect: in (5-7) it is not clear that a single word could replace *through the mountains*, or indeed *the line through the mountains* (*it* perhaps works marginally – *The train chugged along it*). Nevertheless, replacement of non-groupings of words is not possible. You can't replace *chugged along the* by a single word.

Meaning differences

A single stretch of speech or writing sometimes has two or more distinct meanings – like *bank* 'side of a watercourse' and *bank* 'a financial institution'. This is called **ambiguity**. In some cases a string of words admits various interpretations that can be explained by different groupings of the morphemes or words. For example, we could explain the different interpretations of *The policeman shot the man with a rifle* in this way. In one interpretation *the man with a rifle* forms a single word-group, specifying a man carrying a rifle. In another interpretation the rifle was used to shoot the man, in which case *the man with a rifle* is not a single word-group, but two. (5-19) and (5-20) show tree diagrams for the two different analyses, respectively.

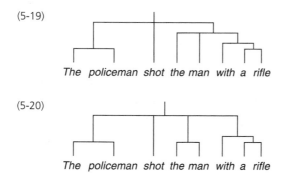

(5-19)

The policeman shot the man with a rifle

(5-20)

The policeman shot the man with a rifle

5.3 Syntactic units

Syntactic units are grammatical items showing unified behaviour, that behave as indivisible wholes. Words, morphemes and sentences are syntactic units. So are the intermediate word-groups discussed in the previous section. In this section we say a bit more about these intermediate units, distinguishing types according to their size. Units of two intermediate sizes exist between words and sentences: phrases and clauses. This gives us a hierarchy of units according to increasing size: morpheme, word, phrase, clause and sentence.

Clauses

Sentences come in a variety of types ranging from the utmost simplicity of single morphemes (for instance, interjections such as *hey!* and *yuck!*) to complex syntactic configurations.

Sentences like (5-7) and (5-10) above are what could be called **simple sentences**; they contain just one verb, and specify a single event. Simple sentences can be joined together to form **complex sentences** like (5-21) and (5-22), which refer to combinations of events; often, as in these examples, words like *when* and *and* are used to connect the two parts.

(5-21)   *The car skidded when it hit the oil slick.*

(5-22)   *The fisherman hung the net on the fence, and the farmer pulled the plough into the shed.*

Sometimes the simple sentences that are put together to form a complex sentence need to be modified in some way. We can for instance combine (5-10) with (5-23) to give (5-24), but adjustments are necessary to (5-23): *the fisherman* must be replaced by *he*, *the fence* should be omitted, and *that* used as a connector.

(5-23)   *The fisherman made the fence last year.*

(5-24)   *The fisherman hung the net on the fence that he made last year.*

A string of words that is either a simple sentence, or a modified form of a simple sentence is called a **clause**. In many languages, clauses come in two main types. First, we have a simple single-morpheme type, consisting of a word used as an interjection (see p. 84); such clauses, sometimes called **minor clauses**, have the simplest structure – effectively none. The second type has (when complete, and nothing is omitted) a verb and accompanying nouns, and refers to an event in the real world, or some imaginary world. These latter, which can be called **major clauses**, are either independent (i.e. they can stand alone as independent sentences), or dependent (can't stand alone as independent sentences, but correspond to clauses that can). In some ways the clause is the most fundamental unit of grammar, and displays the most interesting syntactic properties; we examine its structure in §5.4 below.

Phrases

Nature of phrases

In §5.2 we argued for what can now be seen as units intermediate in size between words and clauses. Such intermediate units are called **phrases**. They are groupings of words that do not normally constitute complete clauses, just parts of clauses. In (5-25) the phrase-sized units we identified in example (5-7) are labelled by Ps, the clause by C.

(5-25)

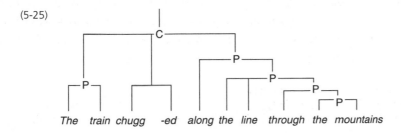

Consider now the following example:

(5-26) *The trains chugged slowly along the line through the mountains.*

The tree structure for this example is shown in (5-27). Comparing this with (5-25), it seems reasonable to suggest that the single word *chugged* in the latter is actually a reduced phrase, in the same way *train* is both a morpheme and a word. Putting things around the other way, we can say that single words can be recognized as phrases provided that there is evidence that they can be expanded into larger units made up of more than one word. Doing this permits some useful syntactic generalizations that we could not otherwise make. In particular, clauses are made up of phrases, that are in turn made up of one or more words.

(5-27)

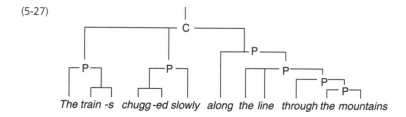

Types of phrase

Phrases can be grouped together into different types according to their internal structure. In the next two subsections we deal with two important phrase types that are found in many languages, noun phrases and verb phrases. Then we briefly mention a few other phrase types that are less widespread across languages. Given that nouns and verbs are not separate parts-of-speech in all languages it is possible that noun phrases and verb phrases might not be distinct in all languages. We do not address this issue here, contenting ourselves with those languages that do draw the distinction.

Noun phrases

These are phrases like *the train, the line through the mountains, the farmer,* and so on. These are made up of a noun, which is usually the most important word in the phrase, possibly together with one or more other words or morphemes. A noun phrase – henceforth NP – refers to some entity, concrete (like a person, animal, tree) or abstract (perhaps an emotion or idea), in a real or imaginary world.

NP structure in English, Swedish, Mandarin Chinese or any language, is usually far from simple, and it would be impossible in an introductory book such as this to provide a comprehensive description of the complexities in any language. Nevertheless, let us look at a few simple examples in Maori (Austronesian, New Zealand), and see how they can be described as sequences of words of particular parts-of-speech. Here are the examples:

(5-28) *wahine pai nei*   'this good woman'   Maori
        te tuuru roa   'the tall chair'

tooku tuuru pai na	'that good chair of mine'
tooku wahine nei	'this woman of mine'
te wahine pai	'the good woman'

Based on these few examples (the reality is not so simple!), it appears that an NP in Maori can consist of up to four words, including a noun (*wahine* 'woman' and *tuuru* 'chair'). The noun can be preceded by a determiner (*te* 'the') or possessive pronoun (*tooku* 'my'), and can be followed by either an adjective (*pai* 'good' or *roa* 'tall'), or a demonstrative (*nei* 'this' and *na* 'that'). A full NP would look like one or the other of the following structures:

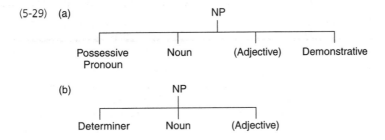

(5-29) (a)

(b)

Verb phrases

Verb phrases (VPs) are groups of words and morphemes like *chugged, was chugging, might chug* and so on. VPs contain a lexical verb, which conveys the most important lexical information, usually along with other morphemes, grammatical and/or lexical, bound and/or free. Whereas NPs refer to entities, VPs refer to the events these entities are involved in; these are specified by the central item, the lexical verb.

Again we illustrate how VP syntax can be described by examining a small fragment of Northern Sotho (Niger-Congo, South Africa). Below are the examples:

(5-30)	*o-rêk-ilê*	'she bought it (e.g. meat)'	Northern Sotho
	o-tlô-rêk-a	'she will buy it'	
	o-bê a-rêk-a	'she was buying it'	
	o-rêk-a	'she buys it'	
	o-tlô-ba a-rêk-a	'she will be buying it'	
	o-bê a-rêk-ilê	'she had bought it'	
	o-tlô-ba a-rêk-ilê	'she will have bought it'	

It can be seen (assuming *rêk* 'buy' is a typical verb) that VPs in plain tenses are simple inflected verbs, involving a prefix indicating the gender of the subject,[2] in this case the buyer, and an affix indicating tense – a prefix and suffix for the future, a suffix for present and past. The two morphological structures can be specified as GEN-V-PRS/PST and GEN-FUT-V-PRS, where GEN stands for gender-agreement prefix for the subject. The verbs expressing the more complex relative tenses – where the time of the event is specified in relation to a reference point of time other than the time of speaking, either in the past or future – involve another word that inflects rather like the verb 'buy': it takes a gender prefix, the future prefix, but has apparently irregular root forms in the past and future. It is presumably an auxiliary verb. Assuming that the *a-* prefix on the main verb *rêk* 'buy' is an allomorph of the gender prefix (e.g. selected by the presence of the auxiliary), an approximate description of the VP would be:

(5-31) (GEN-(FUT)-AUX) GEN-(FUT)-V-PRS/PST

This formula is imprecise: impossible combinations such as of the FUT prefix and PST suffix are not excluded. Nevertheless, it shows a syntactic pattern that all acceptable VPs in our data follow. (As an exercise, try to devise a formula that does exclude the non-occurring forms.)

> The reader should be aware that in many theories of syntax, especially formal theories (see §1.5), VPs include not just the verb and its closely associated auxiliaries and the like, but also many of the accompanying NPs – often everything bar the subject. According to this type of analysis, *hung the net on the fence* would be a VP in (5-10), rather than just *hung*. This analytical difference is reflected in the different types of tree diagrams employed, whether string types like (5-8), or IC type trees like (5-9). The arguments are too complex to deal with in an introductory text. Suffice it to say that in favour of the string constituent analysis adopted here is the observation that a meaningful grammatical role can be associated with the VP in examples such as (5-7) and (5-10) – it specifies an event (see further p. 120). No such meaningful role is associated with the larger VP containing everything other than the subject. (A possible contender for a role for this VP would be the role Predicate; however, it is not easy to understand this as anything but a purely formal role.)

Other phrase types

In example (5-7) we have one VP (*chugged*) and three NPs (what are they?). There remain two phrases that are neither NPs nor VPs, *along the line through the mountains* and the included *through the mountains*. Both are clearly made up of a preposition and an NP. Phrases like this are called prepositional phrases, abbreviated PPs. Not all languages have PPs, for the simple reason that not all languages have prepositions. Some languages (e.g. Hungarian, Japanese and Ngarinyin) have postpositions instead, in which case we can speak of postpositional phrases. Some languages have both prepositional and postpositional phrases, while others have neither part-of-speech, so neither phrase type.

Two other types of phrase found in some languages are adjectival phrases (AdjPs) and adverbial phrases (AdvPs). AdjPs in English have an adjective and a modifier indicating degree or intensity as in *very tall*, *quite rich* and *somewhat stupid*. AdvPs have an adverb and a modifier again indicating degree, as in *very badly*, and *excessively well*.

Complications

NPs and VPs sometimes have more complex structures than accounted for in the preceding discussion. For example, our PP *along the line through the mountains* involves a PP within a larger PP. This is called **embedding**: the PP *through the mountains* is **embedded** in the larger PP. Embedding of phrases within other phrases is quite common in English and many other languages. In English, if a PP is embedded in an NP or PP it usually comes at the end of the phrase, as in *the house on the hill, the man on the moon, the end of the universe* and so on. An NP indicating a possessor can also be embedded in another NP, as in: *the old woman's three cats, the new film's boring ending, the new president's flight to the arctic* and so on. Example (5-32) shows the structure of the last example. (Note that here PP indicates both postpositional phrase – recall that the possessive – *'s* of English is a phrasal enclitic, thus effectively a bound postposition – and prepositional phrase.)

(5-32)

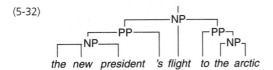

A second complication is that phrases can be **conjoined** by conjunctions such as *and* and *or* to form more complex structures, as in *a word and a number, an instruction booklet and the necessary cables* and *from the cities and from the towns*. Within phrases words can also be conjoined, as in *boys and girls, salt and pepper, big and little people, swam and played* and *might have been tarring and feathering*. Example (5-33) shows two possible structures of *old men and women*, according to the two possible interpretations, depending on whether NPs are conjoined (as in (a), where *women* forms a full NP that could be filled out with, for example, *young*) or whether words are conjoined (as in (b)). In the former case *old* applies only to *men*; in the latter, *old* applies to both nouns *men* and *women*.

(5-33)   (a)   (b)

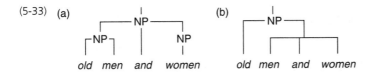

5.4 The structure of clauses

Fundamentals

Description of the clause in terms of phrases
The grammatical notions developed in the previous section permits us to describe clauses as sequences of phrases of various types, in a similar way to our descriptions of NPs and VPs as sequences of words. In this way we can capture similarities among a range of different clauses. Thus the tree diagram in (5-34) captures the structure of both (5-7) and (5-26).

(5-34)

It also characterizes innumerable other sentences, depending on the choice of NP, VP and PP. For example:

(5-35)   *The dog ran towards the child*

(5-36)   *The little child squealed with joy*

(5-37)   *The train goes in the morning*

(5-38)   *The door squeaked on its hinges*

(5-39)   *The little child listened carefully to the story*

Not every English clause, of course, satisfies (5-34). Here are just a few additional patterns, with a single example of each (it is left to you to draw the tree diagrams):

- VP NP PP
  (5-40)   *Is the locomotive in the shed?*

- PP VP NP
  (5-41)   *On the corner stands a statue*

- NP VP NP
  (5-42)   *Marlowe slugged his assailant*

- VP NP NP
  (5-43)   *Is the president Bill Clinton?*

- NP VP NP NP
  (5-44)   *The teacher will give his wife a gift of considerable value*

- INTER VP NP (where INTER stands for interrogative or WH-word, e.g. *what, who*)
  (5-45)   *What is that thing?*

- INTER VP NP PP
  (5-46)   *When was the locomotive on the line through the mountains?*

This is a very small selection from the range of patterns available in English – for instance, one or more additional PPs can be added to many of the above, and we have not yet brought AdjPs or AdvPs into the picture. Think of some additional patterns yourself, give examples and draw tree diagrams.

Problems

It is not difficult to find clauses that don't lend themselves so readily to descriptions of this type. How, for instance, would you give a general description of the syntactic patterns shown by the following very simple clauses?

(5-47)   *Should we go tomorrow?*

(5-48)   *Does the teacher like strong chilli?*

(5-49)   *Will the teacher give his wife a valuable gift?*

(5-50)   *When did the train travel on the line through the mountains?*

If you try this exercise you will notice that you need to look into the structure of some of the phrases. It is impossible to account for clause patterns in English entirely by reference to phrase-sized units, ignoring their internal composition. Specifically, the auxiliary verb in each is separated from the main verb by an NP. The additional clause patterns can be easily listed: AUX NP V PP, AUX NP V NP, AUX NP V NP NP and INTER AUX NP V PP. This fails, of course, to show that the AUX and V belong together as part of the same VP. One could indicate this by labelled brackets, as in: $[AUX]_{VP}$ NP $[V]_{VP}$ PP.

It should be obvious by now that this approach will result in a very long list of different structures. It is also obvious that important generalizations will be missed if the types are merely listed. Thus, the examples so far show that when a clause begins with an INTER, the first NP always follows the first word of the VP, which will be either the main verb or an auxiliary. Recognition of this as a **grammatical rule** would lead us to predict that some patterns – for example, INTER NP VP – are impossible. We can then search for examples to test whether or not this is so, giving us a more powerful method of investigation than searching randomly for new patterns. (Can you find grammatical clauses satisfying this pattern predicted to be ungrammatical?)

One way of thinking about clause structure is to imagine the trees as three dimensional objects like real trees, rather than two dimensional ones; to remain closer to figures like (5-34), they can be thought of as mobiles such as are sometimes found in children's rooms. Units like NPs and VPs can be imagined to be rods of a mobile, together with strings and attached objects. The grammatical rules can then be regarded as ways of projecting the three dimensional mobile to a two dimensional representation – as rules taking the abstract units and putting the elements (the words) in the correct sequence. (Pursuing our analogy, this can be likened to shining a light from a particular position to get a shadow on the wall; shining it from different positions will give different shadows.) This allows us to operate with a more general, though slightly weakened, criterion of movability than the one given in §5.2: the bits must move around in concert, although they need not necessarily stick together in the projection to word sequences.

Grammatical relations

A more serious problem with the type of description outlined in the previous subsection is that, although it captures generalizations about the possible forms of clauses, it fails to reveal anything about their meanings: it leaves completely out of account the systematic similarities and differences in meaning among the clauses. The syntactic patterns in that mode of description are no more than specifications of possible formal shapes, related only by virtue of the fact that they involve similar component units. By recognizing grammatical roles or functions associated with the formal elements it is possible not just to account for differences of meaning expressed by formally related sentences, but also to describe clausal syntax in a way that goes beyond a mere listing of alternatives. In what follows we identify three different types of grammatical functions, which express fundamentally different types of meaning.

Experiential roles

Consider clauses (5-51)–(5-53). These exhibit three different syntactic patterns in terms of units and their combinations: each has the same three types of unit (an NP, a VP and a PP), but in different orders.

(5-51)   *The train is leaving from platform two*

(5-52)   *Is the train leaving from platform two?*

(5-53)   *On platform two the train is leaving*

Notice that each clause describes an ongoing situation, and the NP specifies the thing that is engaged in it, the thing that is moving or about to move. By contrast, in (5-54) and (5-55) – which are identical with (5-51) and (5-52) in terms of their patterns of phrases – the NP refers to something that is acted on, rather than something that does or performs an activity.

(5-54)   *The train was shunted from platform two*

(5-55)   *Was the train shunted from platform two?*

We can account for these similarities and differences with the idea that the NPs serve in two different **grammatical relations** or **roles** in the two sets of sentences. In (5-51)–(5-53) the NPs are **Actors**: their function in the clause is to indicate the doer of the event. In (5-54) and (5-55) they are **Undergoers**: they designate the patient or sufferer of the event, what the event happened to or impinged on.

The terms Actor and Undergoer are not just intuitively meaningful labels; they are labels for grammatical roles – genuine elements of the grammatical structure of English clauses. The terms are given with initial capitals for this reason, to make it clear that we are dealing with grammatical phenomena, not merely with intuitively identified meanings. You can't just call an NP an Actor or Undergoer by inspection of isolated examples. For instance, in *the famous linguist died* intuition suggests that the linguist (the person, not the phrase!) was more of an undergoer than an actor. But in the grammar of English *the famous linguist* (now the phrase) serves in the same role as it does in *the famous linguist climbed the mountain.* The actual meanings of the grammatical roles Actor and Undergoer are not to be confused with the meanings of the corresponding lexical items *actor* and *undergoer.* They are to be found by studying clauses with the roles, not dictionary meanings of the terms.

Perhaps this all appears very abstract, even based on fancy: the grammatical role is not something you can tell by inspection of the linguistic form, and its meaning is difficult to pin down precisely. But even if we don't have direct indication of the roles, there is indirect evidence for them. We have identified them using an argument reminiscent of the ambiguity of meaning test for units (§5.2), where the idea was that a single ambiguous string of words might allow different divisions into units – different structures. Here the same style of argument is being used, but at the level of phrase patterns: the same pattern of phrases has different meanings – indeed meanings that differ systematically – and therefore reflects different structures. The structural difference cannot be in terms of division into units (they are precisely the same); it has to be something else: the functions of those units in the clause.

In some languages the situation is clearer, and the roles are **overt** rather than covert. In Acehnese (Austronesian, Sumatra) the roles of Actor and Undergoer are distinguished morphologically, and their meanings are closer to the senses suggested by the labels. Actors are distinguished by an agreeing prefix to the verb, as shown by (5-56); Undergoers optionally have an agreeing suffix, as shown by (5-57).

(5-56)	*gopnyan*	*gɘu-mat*	*lôn*	Acehnese
	(s)he	(s)he-hold	me	
	'(S)he holds me.'			

(5-57)	*gopnyan*	*geu-mat-lôn*	Acehnese
	(s)he	(s)he-hold-me	
	'(S)he holds me.'		

A clause describing controlled movement has an Actor, as in (5-58); if the movement is uncontrolled, it has an Undergoer, as in (5-59).

(5-58)	*geu-jak*	*gopnyan*	Acehnese
	(s)he-go	(s)he	
	'(S)he goes.'		

(5-59)	*lôn*	*rhët(-lön)*	Acehnese
	me	fall(-me)	
	'I fall.'		

The two grammatical roles Actor and Undergoer are fundamental in many languages, perhaps even universal. In most languages the majority of clauses have at least one of them: that is, at least one is obligatory.[3] Also obligatory is a VP. In clauses like most discussed above, this refers to an event; associated with the VP is the grammatical role **Event**. These three roles then give us a handle on the clause in terms of the way our world of experience is interpreted and construed. The clause is structured so as to express this general type of meaning, called **experiential** or **representational** meaning. Roles like Actor, Undergoer and Event are accordingly experiential roles.

Subject and object

It is unlikely that just these three grammatical relations, Actor, Undergoer and Event, are sufficient to describe the syntax of any language, let alone all languages. At least in some languages – for instance many languages of Europe – Subject, and perhaps also Object, are also required. Comparing (5-60) and (5-61) we see that *the tourist* is Undergoer in each clause. But *the tourist* in (5-61) also shares some grammatical behaviour with the Actor NP *the sniper* in (5-60). First, they occur in first place in the clause, immediately preceding the verb. Second, the verb in each sentence agrees, to a limited extent at least, with this NP. Third, both NPs could be replaced by nominative pronouns: *he* or *she* rather than *him* or *her*. And finally, if a tag is added, its pronoun picks out these NPs – we could add *didn't she?* to (5-60) and *wasn't he?* to (5-61). These commonalities in behaviour motivate identifying Subject as a grammatical relation in English, distinct from Actor.

(5-60)   *The sniper shot the tourist*

(5-61)   *The tourist was shot by the sniper*

There has been much debate in linguistics about the need for, and nature of, Subject as a grammatical relation. Some deny its universality, while accepting its existence in certain languages; some deny it for all languages. Many grammarians consider Subject as a purely formal grammatical role associated with an NP in a particular structural position in the clause. Others suggest that, like Actor and Undergoer, Subject is also a meaningful grammatical relation.

A number of related notions have been suggested in recent decades that begin to make sense of Subject as a meaningful grammatical relation. Simon Dik has suggested (1989: 212ff.) that it provides the perspective from which the clause is presented, the vantage point from which it is viewed. Thus (5-60) presents things from the perspective of the sniper, while (5-61) presents it from the perspective of the tourist. Michael Halliday suggests (1985: 76) that the Subject represents the thing in reference to which the truth of the proposition can be affirmed or denied. Thus one would argue about or evaluate (5-60) in relation to the sniper, (5-61) in relation to the tourist. Ronald Langacker has suggested (1991: 304–329) that Subject relates to cognitive prominence; he has refined this idea in more recent work (1999) to the notion of event profiling: the event is profiled from the perspective of the subject. Other similar suggestions have been made.

It is more difficult to appreciate Object – the role of *the tourist* in (5-60) – as a meaningful grammatical relation. Nevertheless, both Dik (1989) and Langacker (1990: 225) suggest that the Object represents a secondary vantage point from which the clause is perspectivized. Thus the difference between *The teacher will give the pupil a gift* and *The teacher will give a gift to the pupil* concerns whether the pupil or the gift is taken as the secondary vantage point.

According to these views, Subject and Object have nothing to do with the construal of the world of experience, with experiential meaning. They are concerned with the selection of positions for perspectivizing the situation: with the angle from which the speaker chooses to view it and present it to the hearer. This sets the stage for the hearer to adopt the same angle, the same viewpoint. Meaning of this type is **interpersonal** (the term comes from Halliday, who was the first to suggest Subject expresses this type of meaning): it is concerned with the interactive dimension of language, with the establishment of a shared perspective.

Theme

In many languages the initial NP or PP of a clause appears to serve an important role. Consider the following German examples:

(5-62) *Der*   *Priester*   *traf*   *den*   *Bischof*
the:MAS:NOM   priest   meet:PST   the:MAS:ACC   bishop
in   *Hamburg*   *am*   *nächsten*   *Tag.*
in   Hamburg   on:the:MAS:DAT   next   day
'The priest met the bishop in Hamburg the following day.'

(5-63) *Den Bischof traf der Priester in Hamburg am nächsten Tag.*
'The bishop the priest met (him) in Hamburg the following day.'

(5-64) *Am nächsten Tag traf der Priester den Bischof in Hamburg.*
'The following day the priest met the bishop in Hamburg.'

(5-65) *In Hamburg traf der Priester den Bischof am nächsten Tag.*
'In Hamburg the priest met the bishop the following day.'

These clauses all describe the same situation, with *traf* as Event, *der Priester* as Actor, and *den Bischof* as Undergoer. They also present it from the same perspectives (as per the previous section), *der Priester* is Subject and primary perspective in each, and perhaps *den Bischof* as Object and secondary perspective. Thus the four clauses express the same experiential and interpersonal meanings, and are made up of the same NPs serving in the same experiential and interpersonal roles. Nevertheless, the clauses differ subtly in meaning. Example (5-62) ostensibly presents a message about the priest, saying what he did; (5-63) by contrast seems to be about the bishop, presenting information about him. The first NP specifies what the clause is about; it serves in the grammatical role **Theme**, sometimes called **Topic**.

If the first NP is the Theme, the Themes of (5-64) and (5-65) should be *am nächsten Tag* 'on the following day' and *in Hamburg* 'in Hamburg' respectively. But it seems somewhat implausible to say that these clauses are saying something about a time (the following day) and a place (Hamburg), respectively. In these cases the initial PP manifestly establishes a setting (temporal or spatial) within which the event occurred. (Note that this accounts for only a part of the meaning difference between the four examples; we cannot go into other differences here.)

So a Theme can either be what the clause is about, or establish a setting for it. There is something common to both: the Theme anchors the message down, providing a fixed point from which the message can be expanded. The type of meaning conveyed by the Theme is **textural**: it serves to give texture to the clause, distinguishing it from an arbitrary string of words.

> Constructing a clause is a bit like putting an Ikea bookshelf together. You start with a particular piece, and build up from it. The first piece is like the Theme: the other pieces are anchored to it. Although the instruction kit gives a sequence of putting the bits together, it is not the only way – though it might be in some sense the best, or most natural. Likewise in syntax, one choice of Theme is often the most natural: in the case of our German examples, it is the choice in (5-62). Other choices are less natural, and less common in language use.

Morphology and syntax

Both morphology and syntax deal with arrangements of grammatical items. But there are differences that underline the need to distinguish them. To begin with, only some of morphology is conveniently viewed in arrangement terms. Some aspects (especially of inflectional morphology in highly inflecting languages) are better viewed in word-paradigm rather than item-arrangement terms (see p. 75) – that is, in terms of paradigmatic contrasts among words, rather than as morphemes in sequence. In syntax item-arrangement description always works, even though (as we have seen) it may demand recognition of other things (grammatical rules, grammatical relations) in addition.

Another difference is that in morphology the arrangements of the items are usually quite fixed. Little variation in order is permitted. A single structural formula specifying the ordering of the morphemes can normally be given accounts for the morphological shape of nouns and verbs. Certainly the complex situation we encountered for English clauses in §5.4 does not arise.

Lastly, while units serve grammatical relations in syntax, in morphology they do not. We can describe morphology without bringing roles of morphemes into consideration; description in terms of form is adequate. As we have seen, the same NP *the farmer* occurs in the two clauses *the farmer kills the duckling* and *the duckling kills the farmer*, though it serves a different grammatical role. This situation does not arise in morphology. Although the same phonological form /z/ is found in /kɪl-z/ and /bɛd-z/, we do not have one morpheme /z/ in different roles; rather we recognize two distinct morphemes that happen to share the same phonological shape.

Summing up

The lexical and morphological resources of a language are insufficient to allow the expression of the range of meanings people need to make; to get around this limitation, words are combined together into larger units. These units are structured according to patterns that differ from language to language, and define the **syntax** of a language; this is the most open grammatical system of a language.

Fundamental to syntax is the **sentence**, the largest unit in a language that shows grammatical patterning. A sentence made up of a string of words that observe the syntactic patterns of a language is **grammatical**; otherwise it is an **ungrammatical** string. Study of ungrammatical strings, and comparison with grammatical sentences, can yield insights into the syntax of a language.

The structure of sentences is **hierarchical**. Words in a sentence go together to form groups of intermediate sizes – **clauses** and **phrases** – identified by criteria of movability, contractability and ambiguity. Clauses are effectively simple sentences, that can be combined together to form complex sentences. Clauses are constituted by phrases, which fall into different types, corresponding to the main parts-of-speech of a language.

The hierarchical structure of sentences into clauses, phrases, words and morphemes can be represented in **tree diagrams**, the nodes of which are labelled according to the type of unit.

Sentences cannot be adequately described in terms as strings of units of various sizes and types. It is necessary to also recognize the **grammatical relations** or **roles** borne by the component units. These are characterized in terms of both form (e.g. verbal agreement, case-marking affixes or adpositions) and meaning. Grammatical roles fall into three general types according to the type of meaning they express. **Experiential** roles express meanings concerning the construal the world of experience, and include **Actor**, **Undergoer** and **Event**. **Interpersonal** roles are concerned with meanings relating to the interactive dimension of language, including perspective taking. **Subject**, and perhaps also **Object**, is, according to some linguists, an interpersonal role. **Textural** roles are concerned with giving texture to syntactic units, with providing the glue that binds sentences together. **Theme** is a textural role.

Guide to further reading

Almost all introductory textbooks adopt a more formal approach to syntax than adopted in this chapter. An exception is Finch (2003), which devotes one section of the syntax chapter (Chapter 4) to each of formal and functional approaches. Van Valin (2001a) gives a brief, but fair overview of functional theories. The two volume set Butler (2003a, 2003b) provides a more detailed discussion and comparison of three major functional theories, Van Valin's Role and Reference Grammar, Systemic Functional Grammar and Functional Grammar. Lockwood (2002) is a good textbook on functional syntax, and includes numerous examples and exercises from diverse languages. Van Valin (2001b) is one of the best non-partisan introductory textbooks on syntax; although functionally oriented, its final chapter discusses mainstream formal theories.

The leading figure in mainstream formal syntax since the late 1950s is Noam Chomsky, whose ideas have had an enormous impact on the almost every branch of linguistics. In syntax they have spawned not only an array of formal theories – which generally go under the umbrella term generative grammar – but also several functional theories. Those interested in finding out more about generative grammar could begin with Baker (2001) and Wasow (2001).

Anyone serious about syntax should read not just about syntactic theories, but about the syntax of particular languages. Among the myriad grammars of English, Huddleston (1984) is recommended for its careful argumentation and insights. More comprehensive is Huddleston and Pullum (2002); Huddleston and Pullum (2005) is a shortened student's introduction. Grammars of English based on large corpora include Greenbaum (1996), Greenbaum and Quirk (1990) and Sinclair (1990). More or less detailed treatments of the syntax of other languages can be found in reference grammars listed in the references at the end of this book, and in grammars appearing in series such as the Mouton Grammar Library, Lingua Descriptive Studies/Croom Helm Descriptive Grammars/Routledge Descriptive Grammars, Pacific Linguistics and Cambridge Grammatical Descriptions.

Issues for further thought and exercises

1. Below is a tree analysis of (5-10) showing structure down to the level of the word, ignoring the division of words into morphemes; the nodes are labelled according to the category of unit. (DET stands for determiner.)

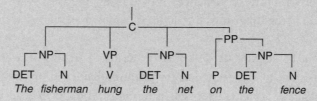

Draw similar tree diagrams for the English clauses below. In some cases the clauses are ambiguous; give separate diagrams appropriate to the different interpretations. Can you justify each of your groupings? Comment on any cases where you have difficulty deciding on the appropriate analysis.

a. *The farmer will kill the duckling in the shed.*
b. *Why is the farmer in the shed?*
c. *Who is the man in the shed?*
d. *They followed his dripping blood until nightfall.*
e. *The old men and women are on holidays in the Alps.*
f. *The hungry mountaineer ate the tiny mouse raw.*
g. *The hungry mountaineer didn't eat the tiny mouse raw.*
h. *The slithy toves did gyre and gimble in the wabe.*
i. *What are slithy toves?*
j. *What gyred and gimbled in the wabe?*
k. *Mary gave John the recipe for Thai curry.*

2. Draw tree diagrams for the two complex sentence examples (5-21) and (5-22) in §5.3. Suggest a tree diagram for *The fisherman who hung the net on the fence saw the farmer.*

3. Examples (5-54), (5-55) and (5-61) illustrate the passive voice in English, and correspond to active voice forms in which the Undergoer serves as Object, and the *by* PP (if there is one) corresponds to the Actor (also Subject) of the active – compare (5-61) with (5-60). What are the passive voice forms of the following:

   a. *The farmer killed the duckling.*
   b. *The hungry mountaineer ate the tiny mouse.*
   c. *They will follow his dripping blood until nightfall.*
   d. *The fisherman may have been hanging the net on the fence.*
   e. *Marlowe could have slugged the assassin.*

   Answer the following two questions. (i) Does inclusion of a *by* PP seem equally good in all examples, or is it awkward in some cases? If some examples seem awkward, can you specify in which conditions? (To answer this you should construct further examples of passive constructions yourself.) (ii) How would you describe the structure of the passive in terms of syntactic units and their arrangement? What formal features indicate the passive voice?

4. Below are some examples of acceptable and unacceptable English NPs. (Check that you agree with my intuitions!) List the acceptable and unacceptable NP structures that these examples reveal. What do you conclude from the distribution of units of different types? (Three hints: (a) it may be useful to think of other examples in answering this question; (b) review §5.4; and (c) what conclusions can we draw from complementary distribution?)

   a. *the hairy fisherman*   **the fisherman hairy*
   b. *the fisherman who is hairy*   **the who is hairy fisherman*
   c. *the bird on the fence*   **the on the fence bird*
   d. *the bird hanging on the tree*   **the hanging on the tree bird*
   e. *the tove with no ears*   **the with no ears tove*
   f. *the earless tove*   *the tove earless
   g. *the distant star*   *the star distant
   h. *the star in the distance*   **the in the distance star*

5. Below are some NPs in Saliba with word and morpheme divisions indicated. List each morpheme, and give it an English gloss, and tentative part-of-speech classification; for the grammatical morphemes also explain their function. Comment on any uncertainties. Describe the structure of NPs as sequences of morphemes of various types.

   a. *tenem nogi-ne hauhau-na-ne*   'that new grass skirt'
   b. *tobwa leiyaha*   'pandanus leaf basket'
   c. *tenem tobwa-ne hauhau-na-ne*   'that new basket'
   d. *mwauyope buina-na*   'a ripe pawpaw'
   e. *numa gagili*   'a toilet'
   f. *tenem numa-ne*   'that house'
   g. *mwaedo gagili-na*   'a small eel'
   h. *mwaedo gagili-di*   'small eels'
   i. *mwauyope yo baela buina-di*   'ripe pawpaws and bananas'

6. The examples below illustrate some simple NPs in Indonesian. List the morphemes and give them glosses. How would you describe the words *orang, buah, ékor, seorang, sebuah,* and *seékor* – when do you use them, and how do you choose between them? Give a description of the structure of NPs according to this data.

   a. *guru ini*   'this teacher'
   b. *tujuh orang guru*   'seven teachers'

(Continued)

Issues for further thought and exercises—Cont'd

c.	*lima orang guru ini*	'these five teachers'
d.	*bayi itu*	'that baby'
e.	*tiga orang bayi*	'three babies'
f.	*enam orang bayi ini*	'these six babies'
g.	*buku*	'a book'
h.	*dua buah buku*	'two books'
i.	*sebuah buku*	'one book'
j.	*prahoto ini*	'this truck'
k.	*sebuah prahoto*	'one truck'
l.	*tiga buah prahoto*	'three trucks'
m.	*lima ékor kucing*	'eight cats'
n.	*seékor kucing*	'one cat'
o.	*kera ini*	'this monkey'
p.	*tiga ékor kera ini*	'these three monkeys'

7. The following sentences allow different interpretations, though not all are ambiguous. What are the different interpretations each allows? Which are ambiguous, and what type of ambiguity do they involve (i.e. lexical or structural – see p. 110)? Comment on any cases where you think that the different interpretations would or could be resolved in speech by different prosodies.

a. *Be careful of my glasses.*
b. *Criminal lawyers can be dangerous.*
c. *They'll hang the prisoner in the yard.*
d. *Helen hates her husband.*
e. *The pen has fallen down.*
f. *The kangaroo is ready to eat.*
g. *Don't lie around here.*
h. *You can see the man in the park with binoculars.*
i. *Smoking pipes will not be tolerated in this office.*
j. *His photograph appears on page two.*

8. Below are some simple Malagasy (Austronesian, Madagascar) clauses with free translations into English. Identify each lexical word with its English gloss, and identify as many morphemes as you can. Describe the sentences first in item-arrangement terms, and then in terms of experiential roles (Actor, Undergoer and Event).

a.	*Namaky boky zaza*	'A child read a book'
b.	*Nahita boky amboa*	'A dog saw a book'
c.	*Nisasa zaza vehivavy*	'A woman washed a child'
d.	*Nankany anjaridaina amboa*	'A dog went to the park'
e.	*Nankany antrano vehivavy*	'A woman went to a house'
f.	*Nahita trano zaza*	'A child saw a house'
g.	*Natory amboa*	'A dog slept'

9. Below are some simple clauses in Warao (language isolate, Suriname), with English translations. List the words and give each an English gloss; identify any grammatical morphemes you can. Describe the structure of the clauses in item-arrangement terms, and in terms of experiential roles.

a.	*Noboto nakae*	'The child fell'
b.	*Tira wabae*	'The woman died'

c. *Tira hube abuae* — 'A snake bit the woman'
d. *Hube anibak ahikomo tate* — 'The young girl might hit a snake'
e. *Noboto wabakomo tate* — 'The child might die'
f. *Ma noboto ahiae* — 'The child hit me'
g. *Anibak nakaera* — 'Did the young girl fall?'
h. *Sina nakaera* — 'Who fell?'
i. *Kasikaha noboto abuaera* — 'What bit the child?'
j. *Sina ma ahiaera* — 'Who hit me?'

10. Below are some sentences in Archi (North Caucasian, Daghestan). Identify as many morphemes as you can, and give each a suitable gloss and explanation of its use in the case of grammatical morphemes. Comment on any for which your are uncertain, and explain why. Give descriptions of the syntax of Archi in terms of items and their arrangements and grammatical roles.

a. *diya verkurshi vi* — 'The father is falling down'
b. *holn h'oti irkkurshi bi* — 'The cow is seeking the grass'
c. *boshor baba dirkkurshi vi* — 'The man is seeking the aunt'
d. *shusha erkurshi i* — 'The bottle is falling down'
e. *holn borcirshi bi* — 'The cow is standing'
f. *diyamu buva dark'arshi di* — 'The mother is left by the father'
g. *buvamu dogi birkkurshi bi* — 'The donkey is sought by the mother'
h. *dadamu h'oti irkkurshi i* — 'The grass is sought by the uncle'
i. *lo orcirshi i* — 'The child is standing'

Notes

1. At least this is the standard claim. It has been disputed: there is a poem that uses this sentence as a line to show that it can be interpreted.

2. Actually, it indicates a human, not feminine subject, but this need not concern us here.

3. By obligatory I do not mean that the role must be realized by an NP actually present in the clause. The role might be present but the NP omitted because it is predictable. For instance, in *What did you do yesterday? – Worked all day* the final clause has no NP denoting the speaker, *I*. The NP has been omitted because it is clear from the circumstances; yet the role remains there in the grammatical structure.

6 Meaning

Running throughout the previous chapters, suffusing our discussions at every turn, is the notion of meaning. Yet we have said virtually nothing about it. It is high time we remedied this situation, and explicitly discussed meaning. In this chapter we set up basic frameworks for investigating meaning. First we deal with meanings encoded by words and sentences, meanings that belong to the language system. Second we discuss meanings that speakers intend their utterances to express in particular instances of speech, and/or that hearers infer from them.

Chapter contents

Goals

The goals of the chapter are to:

- distinguish among different types of meaning, including between literal and non-literal (figurative) meanings;
- explain the difference between sentence meaning and utterance meaning;

- introduce the study of lexical semantics through discussion of the main semantic relations between words;
- convey some feeling for the considerable differences in lexical semantics among different languages;
- demonstrate one way of specifying lexical semantics;
- introduce four key pragmatic concepts: speech acts, reference, presuppositions and the cooperative principle; and
- reveal the role of context in utterance meaning.

Key terms

componential analysis	figurative meaning	non-literal meaning	sense
compositionality	Gricean Maxims	performatives	speech act
connotation	homophony	polysemy	synonymy
contextual meaning	illocutionary force	pragmatics	vagueness
cooperative principle	intension	presupposition	
deictic expressions	literal meaning	reference	
felicity conditions	metaphor	semantics	

6.1 What is meaning?

The notion of meaning in linguistics concerns that which is expressed by sentences, utterances and their components. Meaning is the content conveyed in communication by language, the message or thought in the mind of a speaker that is encoded in language and sent to a hearer who decodes it. This is admittedly an imprecise and simplistic characterization. But rather than attempt to give a precise definition of meaning, it seems preferable to proceed indirectly, and draw some distinctions that will hopefully clarify the concept.

Reference and sense

In saying *My computer crashed* I am talking about something that happened to an object in the real world, an object that sits on my desk. The NP *my computer* **refers** to this material artefact, and the relationship between the NP and this object is called **reference**. Reference is more general than this, however, and covers the relationship between an NP and imaginary and intangible 'things' existing in possible worlds of human imagination. Thus we speak of reference in relation to *my dream*, *Archimedes* and *Sherlock Holmes*.

Reference is a different thing to the 'meaning' or 'concept' component of the Saussurean sign (see Figure 1.1). On the one hand, words like *hello*, *eh*, *in* and *and* can't be used to refer to anything at all, although they are certainly not meaningless. Signs always have sense, though some are never used in reference. On the other hand, *the Morning Star* and *the Evening Star* both refer to the same material object, Venus (observed in different circumstances), though the NPs surely have different meanings. The term **sense** is sometimes used for this type of meaning.

The sense of a linguistic sign derives in part from its relations to other signs in the language. The sense of the lexeme *hand* is defined in part by the existence of the lexeme *arm*. But Indonesian and Savosavo (Papuan, Solomon Islands) have a single term corresponding to both of the English words *hand* and *arm*. On the other hand, Jahai (Austro-Asiatic, Malaysian peninsular) has three terms, *bling* 'upper arm', *prbér* 'lower arm', and *cjas* 'hand'. The sense of each of the terms in Indonesian, Savosavo and Jahai is different to that of the English terms. The same point can be made for grammatical categories. As Saussure observed, whereas French has a singular vs. plural contrast for nouns, Sanskrit had a three-way contrast between singular, dual and plural. The sense of the plural is different in French and Sanskrit. This aspect of sense – the part derived from the contrasts with other members of the language system – is what Saussure called **value**.

But there is more to sense than just value. For most signs the 'meaning' aspect can also be understood in terms of defining properties that must be satisfied in any application of a linguistic item. Technically, this is referred to as the **intension** of the sign. For instance, the intension of *sheep* will include properties such as 'animal', 'mammal', 'feeds by grazing', 'ruminant', 'has hooves', 'quadruped' and so on.

> Not all linguists agree that intensional definitions are necessary or useful. Nevertheless, few linguists would be happy with value alone, that it is just paradigmatic contrasts with other lexical items that define the sense of a lexical item. Thus it has been suggested by some scholars that value be augmented by something other than defining properties. According to prototype theory, meanings are identified by characteristic instances of the categories of objects, events or whatever, denoted by a word. Thus we usually think of carrots and potatoes as having more of the central characteristics of vegetables than say eggplants, Brussel sprouts and cabbages. A carrot or potato would be the prototype, or a prototypical instance, of a vegetable; eggplants would be peripheral instances. According to this theory, the meaning of *vegetable* will be specified (at least to a large extent) by its prototypes: carrots and potatoes, and other things that share some of their characteristics, that are more or less like them.

Sense and connotations

Words often have **connotations**, unstable meaning associations such as emotional overtones (see §4.5). Unlike the sense of a word, which is an essential part of it, connotations are not always present. Connotations can differ according to a person's attitudes. For example, the word *mathematical* might have quite different connotations depending on a speaker's experience with the subject at school; *that's a very mathematical way of looking at it* could express either a positive or a negative evaluation. Connotations also differ according to the linguistic or speech context. For example, if I used the term *mathematical* of someone's approach to life or social relations a negative evaluation would probably be attached; but it could express a positive rating in a description of a piece of baroque music or of Esher's art.

Connotations can be important in language acquisition and change; over time a connation can become so firmly attached to a sign that it becomes a part of its sense, in the process perhaps replacing aspects of the earlier sense. For instance, for many speakers of English the word *dork* has just the sense 'stupid or contemptible person', with an implicit negative appraisal. The word first appeared as a slang term for 'penis'; the attitudinal component was a connotation that came to stick, ousting the original meaning.

Literal and figurative meaning

We do not always use an expression in its **literal** sense, the sense actually encoded by its component lexical and grammatical signs. Clear illustration is provided by idioms (§4.4) such as *He kicked the bucket* which can mean either 'he hit the bucket with his foot' or 'he died'. The first interpretation is the literal meaning, the second, a **non-literal** or **figurative** meaning. The figurative meaning can be considered to be an extension of the literal meaning (see §4.3). Traditional rhetoric distinguishes a number of different processes of meaning extension; three kinds most relevant to linguistics are:

Metaphor – in which the sense of an expression is extended to another concept on the basis of a resemblance. For instance, in *Belgian drivers are cowboys* the noun *cowboy* is not used in its literal sense 'person who tends cattle', but rather invokes the notion 'person who behaves like a cowboy' (it is up to the hearer to figure out the basis on which the comparison is made).

Metonymy – here the sense is extended to another concept via a typical or habitual association. The literal sense of *university* is to 'educational institution'; in *I'll go to the university tomorrow* the word is used in the sense of 'building in which the educational institution is housed'. In *He's fond of the bottle, the bottle* is used metonymically to refer to the alcoholic beverage typically contained in bottles. Governments are commonly referred to by the city in which they are located, as in *London, Washington, Paris, Kremlin.*

Synecdoche – where the sense is extended via a part–whole relation. For instance, the term *wheels* is often used to refer to one's car. And in the speech of hospital staff, patients are sometimes referred to by their problematic body part. Thus *the kidney* acquires the sense 'person suffering from some kidney complaint'.

It can be difficult to draw a line between literal and figurative senses, and some linguists reject the distinction. Cognitive Linguistics, associated with George Lakoff, Ronald Langacker, Eve Sweetser and others, tends to take this view. According to this approach, metaphor plays a central role in language and thought, and is pervasive in ordinary language. Metaphor is not seen as figurative use of language, but rather as a cognitive strategy allowing people to understand one experiential domain (the 'target domain') in terms of another (the 'source domain'). Thus many domains of experience are understood in terms of space, and are expressed linguistically via spatial relations. In some languages, for example Russian, the target domain of possession is understood in terms of the source domain of space; 'I have a cat' is expressed as '(a) cat (is) at me'.

Sentence and utterance meaning

Consider the simple sentence *The car broke down yesterday*. This describes a situation, the failure of a car. You can easily picture the event and invoke a conceptualization of it in your mind.

How do we get this meaning? According to the (admittedly fragmentary) grammar developed in the previous chapters, the sentence is made up of signs, including morphemes, words, phrases and grammatical relations. These signs all have meanings, concepts associated with their forms. Supposing we know all of these meanings, we could expect that putting them together will give a good indication of the meaning of the whole sentence. We get a good way towards this goal by putting the meaning of *the car* together with the meaning of the grammatical role Actor (see §5.4), the meaning of *break down* with that of Event, and of *yesterday* with the meaning of the grammatical role it serves, let's say Temporal Location. We also need to bring into the picture the meaning of the inflected past tense form *broke* of the lexical root *break*. This gives the meaning of the sentence in the abstract, that is, as an expression in the English language.

Our sentence can be uttered in many different circumstances. Let's consider just two.

(6-1)   Carol: *What's been happening while I've been away?*
        Barry: *The car broke down yesterday.*

(6-2)   Carol: *Do you feel like going out tonight?*
        Barry: *The car broke down yesterday.*

The meaning actually expressed by the sentence remains constant: the same conceptual event is construed. But, depending on context, different meanings are conveyed by uttering the sentence; the meanings of the **utterances** differ. Example (6-1) could from a conversation between friends who have not seen one another for some time due to Carol's absence abroad. Barry is making a plain statement of fact, giving a direct answer to Carol's question. Example (6-2) might also occur in a conversation between friends, but here what Carol says could be an invitation to Barry to go out with her. Barry's response could constitute a refusal. It might alternatively express willingness, simultaneously requesting that Carol pick him up. The **sentence meaning** is invariant, though the **utterance meaning** changes.

The investigation of sentence meaning – and the meanings of the various signs making up sentences – is called **semantics**. Semantics deals with the meaning of expressions taken in isolation, with the meaning they have within the system of the language.

The study of utterance meaning is called **pragmatics**. Pragmatics deals with the specific meaning of actual instances of language use, that is, with the meaning conveyed by a linguistic expression in a particular context of speech. It is concerned with the uses made of signs belonging to the language system in interactions among human beings. There is a system to these uses – they are not arbitrary, but follow regular patterns, though patterns that do not belong to grammar or lexicon as such. Pragmatics is about meaning in relation to speakers and hearers in context, and thus belongs to the system of speech (to be interpreted generally to include writing and signing) rather than of language.

> The distinction between sentence and utterance can be understood in terms of the logical notions of **type** and **token**, where a type is a general category, and a token is a specific instance of the category. Thus in *boys will be boys* there are four word tokens, but just three types: one type, *boys*, occurs in two tokens. A sentence is a linguistic type; an utterance is a token. Semantics is concerned with the meaning of linguistic types, pragmatics with token meaning.

Overview of types of meaning in language

Figure 6.1 puts the distinctions made in the previous sections together in a single diagram to show the sorts of meaning that are linguistically relevant.

This all may seem quite cut and dried. But, as usual in linguistics, things are somewhat fuzzy in practice. It is not always obvious where the line between pragmatics and semantics falls, and linguists disagree about the location of the border. Some linguists, such as Charles Fillmore, Michael Halliday, Ronald Langacker and Peter Matthews are dubious about, or even reject, the division of labour into semantics and pragmatics. However, aside from the fact that it seems conceptually useful to make the distinction, there are clear-cut cases as in (6-1) and (6-2). The line we take in this book is that the two types of meaning are in principle (though not necessarily in practice) distinguishable. Nor are they unrelated; indeed, semantics and pragmatics go hand in hand, to the extent that neither can be investigated in the absence of the other. They also go together in language change and acquisition.

6.2 Semantics

The bulk of this section discusses the semantics of lexical items, items that (regardless of size) need to be listed separately in the lexicon of a language. These are of course signs, and our focus is on their senses. Three key issues in lexical semantics concern: (a) pinning down and

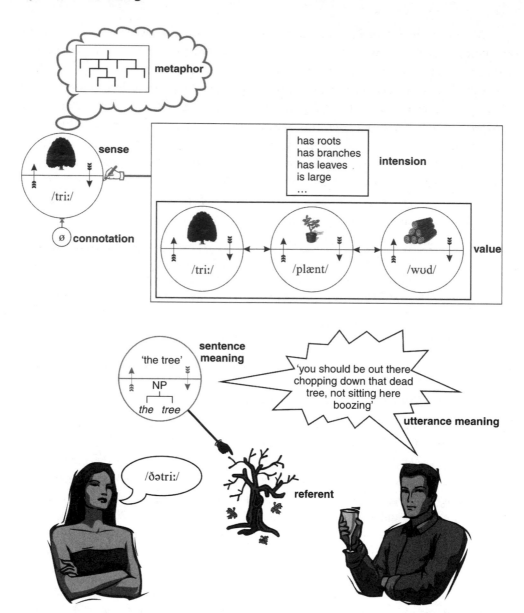

Figure 6.1 Aspects of linguistic meaning. In the meaning system, value and extension are the main components defining the sense of the sign. The sign has a non-literal, metaphoric, meaning (not invoked in this particular instance). Sentence meaning is very roughly represented as the sense of a complex combination of lexical and syntactic signs (the structure of which is not shown). This complex signifying construction points to the referent, the dead tree. This utterance conveys a pragmatic meaning: the hearer is being reprimanded for relaxing when there is an important job to do. © 2009 William B. McGregor and his licensors. All rights reserved.

identifying the meanings of lexical items; (b) the relationships amongst the meanings of lexical items in a language; and (c) the specification of the meanings of items. These concerns are clearly interrelated. Before you represent the sense of an item you have to identify it; you also need to know how it relates to other items in the language, as the value of a sign is determined by the contrasts with other items in the language system.

Homophony, polysemy and vagueness

Two different lexemes sometimes accidentally share the same phonological form; this is called **homophony** or **homonymy**, and the words are said to be **homophones**. Some homophones in English are: *boy* (as in *he is only a boy*) and *buoy* (as in *they marked the place with a buoy*); *port* (as in *I don't usually drink port*), *port* (i.e. 'suitcase', as in *I put the luggage in my port*), and *port* (as in *Århus has a port*); and *bank* (as in *I have no money in the bank*) and *bank* (as in *the fisherman is asleep on the bank of the river*). Word forms such as /bɔɪ/ and /pɔːt/ are ambiguous since they can be interpreted as instances of more than one lexeme.

Sometimes lexemes are partial homophones in the sense that some of their forms share the same phonological shapes. For example, the verb *bear* (as in *she agreed to bear the costs*) and the noun *bear* (as in *the bear attacked the tourist*) share the same phonological shapes in some inflected forms (e.g. both have inflectional forms /bɛː/ and /bɛːz/), but only the verb has /bɔː/ (a phonological form that is incidentally also shared with the verb *bore*).

Homophony is sometimes exploited for humorous effect:

(6-3) *'How is bread made?'*
'I know that!' Alice cried eagerly. 'You take some flour–'
'Where do you pick the flower?' the White Queen asked: 'In a garden or in the hedges?'
'Well, it isn't picked at all,' Alice explained: 'it's ground–'
'How many acres of ground?' said the White Queen. 'You mustn't leave out so many things.'
(Carroll 1899: 184–185)

Polysemy is where identical forms have related meanings. For example, the meanings associated with *ear* in the following sentences seem related:

(6-4) a. *I put cottonwool in my ear.*
   b. *He listened to their difficulties with an impatient ear.*
   c. *That phonetician has a good ear for tone.*
   d. *I tried to get her ear.*

These examples reveal the following clearly related senses (there are others): (a) 'organ of hearing of humans and animals', (b) 'attention to what is being said or to sounds', (c) 'ability at discriminating sounds', and (d) 'favourable attention directed to a person'.

Most dictionaries recognize the distinction between homophony and polysemy by giving separate entries for the former and including the latter under the same entry. But the distinction is not always easy to draw, because of the fuzziness of the distinction between different and related meanings. It is easy to see that the above senses of *ear* are related. Most dictionaries consider the word *ear* as illustrated by *The **ear** withered on the corn plant* to be a homophone of the lexeme *ear* of (6-4). Nevertheless, many speakers do see a connection, and imagine the ear of corn to resemble in some way an ear of a person. In fact, lexicographers do not take just meaning into account in their decisions, but also the history of words. In this case, the words come from two different sources: *ear* (as in the body part) comes from Old English *ēare*, whereas *ear* (as in the plant-part) comes from Old English *ēar*.

Few speakers of English see any semantic relation between the two senses of *bank* mentioned in the first paragraph of this section, and dictionary makers tend to agree, putting them under different head-words. But both, in fact, can be traced back ultimately to proto-Germanic **bangk-* 'ridge, mound, bordering slope'. You can appreciate the connection through the following chains of plausible meaning extensions: (a) ridge > bench > moneylender's counter > moneylender's shop > financial institution; and (b) ridge > slope > side of watercourse. Speakers do not perceive the connection between the two extreme concepts because the other senses barely survive in association with *bank*. Speakers perceive, quite reasonably, a closer semantic connection between the body-part and plant-part senses of *ear* (also supported by many other such connections, as in, for example, *head of cabbage*) than the geographical and institution senses of *bank*.

Homophony and polysemy must also be distinguished from **vagueness** or **generality**, that is, lack of specificity of meaning. Earlier we identified four quite general specifications of the senses of *ear* that are involved in (6-4). Sense (a) 'organ of hearing of humans and animals' covers not just (6-4)a, but also use of *ear* in the two sentences in (6-5).

> (6-5) a. *The teacher pulled the boy along by the ear.*
>   b. *The dog scratched its ear.*

But notice that the 'meanings' in the three cases – the mental concepts invoked in the mind of the speaker and hearer – are quite different: in (6-4a) we think of an orifice at the side of the human head; in (6-5a), of an appendage at the side of the human head; and in (6-5b), of an appendage at the side of a dog's head (which does not look very much like the one on the side of the human head).

We don't usually think of these three meanings as polysemies of *ear* because the meanings are so closely related that they fall under a single general specification, something like '(part of the) organ of hearing of humans and animals'. Similarly for the meanings associated with *wrong* in *It is wrong to speak with your mouth full*, *It was wrong to take Aboriginal children from their mothers*, and *It is wrong to attribute that quote to Saussure*. The first invokes the sense 'improper', the second 'immoral', while the third just 'incorrect'; it is not difficult to see that a single general sense covers each. The sentential context, our knowledge of the world and our knowledge of the speaker's beliefs, can be brought into account to narrow down to the specific meaning invoked.

The meanings that a word acquires from its contexts of use are called **contextual meanings**. As distinct from the sense of a lexeme, which remains invariant, contextual meanings are not fixed. Thus, *It was wrong to take Aboriginal children from their mothers* does not necessarily invoke a moral comment. For instance, a policeman involved in removing Aboriginal children might have seen his actions as fully moral, and 'wrong' only in the sense 'mistaken': the intended results were not achieved.

Like the other distinctions we have discussed, the line between vagueness and polysemy can be difficult to draw. Some linguists, the present author included, believe that lexemes have much vaguer senses than usually thought, and that polysemy is comparatively rare.

Lexical semantic relations

The lexemes of a language relate to one another semantically in various ways, and form a highly structured system, the lexicon. As mentioned in §4.1, this is better thought of as a huge network of interrelated items rather than a mere listing, such as is provided by a dictionary. We discuss four types of semantic relation that give structure to the lexicon, synonymy, antonymy, hyponymy and meronymy.

Synonymy

Synonymy is the relation of sameness or close similarity of meaning; lexemes related in this way are **synonyms**. Some examples of synonyms are: *hide* and *conceal*, *small* and *little*, *rich* and *wealthy*, *mother* and *mum*, *car* and *automobile*, *truck* and *lorry* and *dear* and *expensive*.

You will notice that the members of these pairs are not exact synonyms; indeed, exact identity of meaning is quite rare. Synonyms often belong to different registers or styles (see §7.3) of language such as formal, literary or colloquial. *I concealed the automobile under a tarpaulin* is more formal than *I hid the car under the tarp*. Synonyms sometimes belong to different dialects: *togs*, *swimmers*, *cossies* and *trunks* are words in different dialects of Australian English for the item of clothing worn when swimming. (What are they called in your dialect?)

Synonyms may also differ in the lexical company they keep, in the collocations (§4.4) they enter into. *Strong* and *powerful* are partial synonyms, and share some contexts: *he has strong arms* and *he has powerful arms*. But we speak of *the strong arm of the law* not **the powerful arm of the law*, and *a strong head for alcohol* not **a powerful head for alcohol*. *Strong* enters into many more compounds than *powerful*.

Antonymy

Antonymy is the relation of opposite in meaning, and examples of antonyms include *big* and *small*, *long* and *short*, *up* and *down*, *dead* and *alive* and so on. Several different types of antonymy are usually identified.

Gradable antonyms allow intermediate degrees between the two opposite extremes, like *big* and *small*, *fast* and *slow* and *rich* and *poor*. Gradable antonyms can thus be used in comparative constructions, like *richer than* and *poorer than*. And for gradable antonyms, the negative of one does not necessarily imply the positive of the other: *not fast* does not necessarily mean *slow*.

Non-gradable antonyms are polar opposites, and allow no intermediate degrees. Examples are *dead* and *alive*, *pass* and *fail*, *male* and *female*, and *true* and *false*. For these, the negative of one does imply the positive of the other: *not true* implies *false, not dead* implies *alive.* Non-gradable antonyms do not normally enter into the comparative construction.

Pairs like *push* and *pull, come* and *go,* and *rise* and *fall,* which contrast in direction of movement, can also be interpreted as being opposite in meaning. These are called **reverses,** as also are pairs like *tie* and *untie, pack* and *unpack,* and *inflate* and *deflate* where there is a reversal of the action sequence.

Converses describe the same relation from contrasting viewpoints, as in *own* and *belong to* (*he owns it, it belongs to him*), *like* and *please* (*I like it, it pleases me*), *give* and *receive* (*I gave money to the beggar, the beggar received money from me*), and *above* and *below* (*the red block is above the blue block, the blue block is below the red block*).

Hyponymy

In **hyponymy** the meaning of one lexeme includes the meaning of another. A **hyponym** includes the meaning of a more general word. *Hammer, saw, chisel, screwdriver* all include the meaning of *tool* – they all denote types of tool – and are hyponyms of *tool*; the four terms are **co-hyponyms.** The general term is called the **superordinate** (sometimes the terms **hypernym** or **hyperonym** are used instead). *Dog* and *cat* are co-hyponyms of *animal*; *slap* and *punch* are co-hyponyms of *hit*; and *carrot* is a hyponym of *vegetable*.

Hyponymy is a 'kind of' relation: hyponyms are 'kinds of' the superordinate category, which in turn indicates the general type of the hyponym. Thus, relations of hyponymy associate meanings on taxonomic hierarchies. Certain semantic domains lend themselves well to this sort of analysis, including colour terms, kinship terms and terms for animals and plants. Figure 6.2 shows a very partial network for plant terms in English.

Meronymy

Meronymy is the part–whole relation. *Door* and *window* are meronyms of *room*; *wheel, handlebar* and *pedal* are meronyms of *bicycle*; and *hand* and *face* are meronyms of *clock*. Meronymic relations in the lexicon can be represented in hierarchies similar to taxonomies, as shown in Figure 6.3 for body-part terms in Huastec (Mayan, Veracruz).

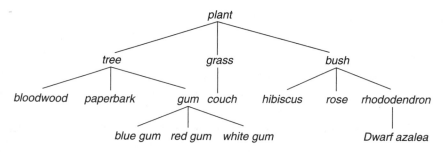

Figure 6.2 A small portion of a taxonomic hierarchy for *plant* in English.

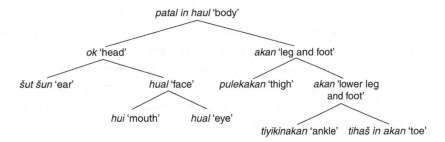

Figure 6.3 Partial meronymic hierarchy for Huastec body-part terms, adapted from Brown et al. (1976). Notice that both *hual* and *akan* appear in more than one place on the hierarchy, indicating that the terms are ambiguous rather than vague.

There is an important difference between the relations of hyponymy and meronymy: the property of transitivity. *Alsatian* is a hyponym of *dog*, which is a hyponym of *animal*; *Alsatian* is also a hyponym of *animal*. This often does not apply in meronymy. For example, *nostril* is a meronym of *nose*, but not of *face*: we do not say that one's nostril is a part of one's face! Hyponymy is a transitive relation, but meronymy is not.

It must be stressed that networks of both hyponymy and meronymy are lexical networks, not networks of relations among real world entities. There are many conceptually different ways the animal kingdom can be taxonomized (the Linnean system of classification into species is just one of many possibilities), and the human body divided into parts. It seems reasonable to believe that the lexical relations of hyponymy and meronymy reflect speakers' conceptual categorizations of the world. 'Folk' conceptualizations – and thus hyponymic and meronymic relations among lexemes – can be at variance with scientific conceptualizations. For instance, *whale* can't be presumed to be a hyponym of *mammal* in English (or all varieties of English) simply because whales are mammals in the Linnean taxonomy.

Specifying lexical meanings

How would you explain the meaning of *mother*? Perhaps the first thing you think of is a biological explanation, and you may think of using semantically related words such as *woman*, *female*, *father*, *child*, *parent* and so on. If you have taken on board the discussion of this section, you will try to think of other senses, and look for sentences using the word, such as *The earth is mother of us all*, *She is my mother by adoption* and *The Stamp Act is the mother of all mischiefs*. You will need to decide whether the different meanings belong to different lexical items sharing the same form, are polysemies, or are separate contextual meanings. These considerations are important in pinning down the sense of the word, and essential to giving an adequate description of its sense.

There is no consensus among semanticists as to how explanations of the meaning of lexical items are best expressed. Some adopt the technique of **componential analysis**, in which the semantic meaning of a lexeme is decomposed into small components, or atoms of meaning.

The standard componential approach identifies semantic features that differentiate words from one another. Consider the following a small set of nouns: *bull, cow, calf, woman, boy, girl, chair, man*. Except for *chair* these words all have in common the concept 'animate'. We could identify [animate] as a semantic feature with a value of either + for animate nouns, or − for inanimate nouns. (It is conventional to put semantic features in square brackets.) Continuing the comparison of the terms, we could also identify features [human], [male] and [adult]. Our eight words could be specified as follows:

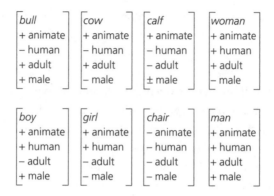

A feature value is given as ± if the word is not specific on that feature: *calf* is [±male] for this reason. Inanimates are given the value −, not ±, for the features [adult] and [male] because they can't be either adult or male.

There are also dependencies among the features. If a word is specified as [−animate], it must simultaneously be [−human], [−adult], and [−male]; if a word is [+human] it is also [+animate]. If a word is specified as [+adult], [+male] or [±male] it must also be [+animate]. (Notice that this conclusion does not follow from [−male], though it does from [±male].) There is no need to specify the predictable feature values, which can be simply left out from the matrix specification. Thus we could economize in the above specifications, representing the meanings as follows:

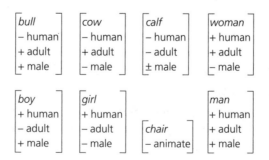

It is important to realize that a dependency among a pair of features is not the same thing as a ± value for a feature. A ± value means either + or − is possible. But leaving out the specification

[+animate] for, for example, *boy* does not mean that either value is possible! Rather, it means that the + value is predictable. (In other cases, a – value is predictable.)

The four features are sufficient to distinguish the eight words, and give at least a partial specification of their senses. Adding more features would allow them to be distinguished from other nouns (e.g. *dog, table, river, whale* etc.), and permit more precise specifications of their meanings. For instance, we could add in [bovine], [canine], [feline] and so on.

This approach can be – and has been – criticized on many grounds. For instance, it adopts an intensional view of semantics, and thus is criticized on this basis by prototype semantics (see box on p. 130), which rejects intensional definitions. A perhaps more telling criticism is that the component features used to characterize the meanings of the terms above are more technical than the terms they describe: it appears that the simple is being defined in terms of the complex. Nevertheless componential analysis has been applied to a range of semantic domains in a number of languages. It seems most useful for the description of words belonging to relatively closed lexical sets such as terminologies for kinship, plants, animals and so on; it is also useful for the description of grammatical morphemes and words (e.g. pronouns and adpositions), which constitute the most closed classes in a language.

Sentence semantics

The meaning of a sentence depends on the meanings of the component words and how they are syntactically combined; sentence semantics is largely **compositional**. The meaning of the sentence *The fisherman hung the net on the fence* is determined by putting together the meaning of the component words, their groupings into phrases and the grammatical relations such as Actor, Undergoer, Subject and Theme. (Of course, a more comprehensive syntactic description than that developed in Chapter 5 is needed to provide a full description of the sentence semantics.)

Idioms aside, can sentence meaning be fully accounted for compositionally? Some linguists have said (or presumed) so: that giving a complete description of lexical semantics and grammar would provide a complete description of a sentence's meaning. Others disagree. Construction Grammar takes the view that grammatical constructions also carry elements of unpredictable meanings, which means that the lexicon of a language contains not just morphemes, words and idioms, but also grammatical constructions. Sentence semantics can still be partly compositional, but an extra grammatical dimension also contributes meaning. I side with Construction Grammar on this issue.

6.3 Pragmatics: the meaning of utterances

In the previous section we dealt with the sense of lexical items and larger linguistic units, that is, the meaning that is actually encoded by linguistic forms. As has already been mentioned, this accounts for only part of the meaning of a stretch of speech. It is as though speakers specify just the bare outlines of the meaning they intend to convey, leaving it to the hearer to reconstruct the details in their full richness. This is something we human beings are good at doing. When you look at the figure below it is difficult not to see a white triangle laid over three black circles. But all that is actually depicted are three circle-segments arranged in a particular configuration; your mind fills in the lines that are not perceived by the sense organs.

In this section we deal first with two types of meaning that speakers and hearers fill in: (a) what the speaker intends to do with the utterance – why they spoke in the first place – and how the hearer infers these intentions; and (b) reference or referential meaning (see p. 129), in particular, of NPs in utterances. Lastly, we discuss a general principle that guides the inferences we draw.

Speech acts

Speech is fundamentally about purposefully doing things with words; it is a social act of doing. Even now as I sit alone in my room typing these words – not an especially social environment – I am engaged in purposeful acts of using language. I want to inform you, the reader, about linguistics, to sway you to my way of thinking about the subject, and to convince you that it is a fascinating thing to do.

Speech acts are the actions speakers perform in uttering sentences, including informing, promising, requesting, questioning, commanding, warning, preaching, congratulating, laying bets, swearing and exclaiming. The type of action performed by the speaker in making an utterance is referred to as its **illocutionary force**.

Performatives

English has (presumably in common with all languages) a number of speech act verbs, verbs like *inform*, *promise*, *request*, *baptize* and so on, that give labels to particular types of speech act. Most can be used in sentences like the following, where they make explicit the speech act the speaker intends to perform:

(6-6)   *I bet you any money you like that we'll win on Saturday*

(6-7)   *I resign*

(6-8)   *I apologize*

(6-9)   *I double dare you to hit me*

(6-10)   *I pronounce you man and wife*

(6-11)   *I order you to leave the premises*

Sentences like the above that make explicit their illocutionary force by a speech act verb are called **performative sentences**, or **performatives**.

Direct and indirect speech acts

Most utterances, however, do not wear their illocutionary force on their sleeve. To the contrary, as examples (6-1) and (6-2) show, a sentence like *The car broke down yesterday* can be used with different illocutionary forces: in the former context it has the force of a statement; in the latter, it may be either a refusal or request.

As a speaker of English you will doubtless feel that there are 'natural' associations between certain syntactic forms of sentences and particular illocutionary forces. Table 6.1 shows these typical associations. The second column gives the technical label for grammatical form of the sentence shown in the first column. Although we did not deal with this aspect of syntax in Chapter 5, it should be clear that the four sentences are syntactically different types. Before reading further, you should attempt to describe each example in item-arrangement terms (as per pp. 115–117); this will give you an idea how the four syntactic forms are defined. The third column of the table indicates the typical illocutionary force associated with sentences of each syntactic type.

If I were to say *Can you pass the salt?* to my neighbour at the table, I would not normally be asking them a question about their ability to pass me the salt, and a purely linguistic response like *Yes* would be judged inappropriate and inadequate. The interrogative form is being used here with the illocutionary form of a command or request. Examples like this, where a syntactic form is used with an illocutionary force other than the one typically associated with it, are called **indirect speech acts**; when the association is the typical or natural one, we speak of **direct speech acts**. Performatives also count as direct speech acts, the difference being that they are specified lexically rather than grammatically.

We often use indirect speech acts to be polite. The difference in politeness between *Can you pass the salt?* and direct speech acts such as *Pass the salt!*, *Give me the salt!* or *I am ordering*

Table 6.1 Syntactic forms and their typical illocutionary forces in English

	Syntactic form	Illocutionary force
You are energetic this evening.	Declarative	Statement
Are you energetic this evening?	Interrogative	Question
Be energetic this evening!	Imperative	Command
How energetic you are this evening!	Exclamative	Exclamation

you to pass the salt, is obvious. Speakers often phrase questions and commands in the declarative for similar reasons. Let us suppose we were sitting in the lunchroom at work on a warm day and you open the window for some cool air. Perhaps this has the undesirable consequence that street noise becomes very loud, so at some point I want you to shut the window again. A polite way of issuing the request would be with a declarative, for example, *It's very noisy in here.* To say *Shut the window!* would be impolite. It also risks the possibility of being ignored, or worse, flatly refused – *Shut it yourself.* Even to say *Please shut the window* would sound somewhat insistent, and suggests that I am presuming authority over you.

Felicity conditions

For a speech act to achieve its intended purpose, its illocutionary force, certain conditions must be satisfied; these are called **felicity conditions**. For instance, a performative such as *I pronounce you man and wife* will only succeed in marrying a couple if the speaker is an authorized marriage celebrant, and only if it is uttered in a particular place in the context of a marriage ceremony. Failing these conditions, the speech act cannot achieve its intended ends, and it is **infelicitous**.

Similarly for non-performative speech acts: more than just an appropriate grammatical form is a requirement for the successful achievement of their purposes. Thus, a question such as *Where are my glasses?* will have as felicity conditions that the speaker doesn't know where his/her glasses are, that he/she wants to know this information, and that he/she believes the hearer may know this information. A request such as *Please give me my glasses* would have as its felicity conditions that the speaker does not have their glasses, but believes that the addressee does, that they are capable of handing the glasses over to the speaker, and that the speaker wants them.

Reference

As already indicated, reference is different from sense in that it is not what is inherently associated with linguistic forms such as morphemes and words. Words as such do not refer; rather speakers use them to refer. The claim on p. 112 that NPs refer is to be interpreted in this way: that it is the specific instance of use of the NP by the speaker – the NP token (see box on p. 133) – that refers.

How are these acts of reference achieved? All languages have words or morphemes that are used to help pin down the reference of a stretch of speech (including writing and signing), that facilitate the hearer's identification of the intended referent. For instance, we can use proper nouns (e.g. for animals and people *Nim Chimpsky, Ferdinand de Saussure, Charles Darwin*; and places *Sydney, Uluru*), and, in languages like English and many other languages of Europe, articles (*the man on the moon, a puppy, the government*). In most cases these expressions do not identify unique individuals, except when used in particular contexts.

For example, *the moon* might be used in a lecture or article on astronomy in reference to one of the moons of Jupiter.

There is a particular class of words or morphemes that are used to assist identifying referents by linking them specifically to the context of the speech act; these are known as **deictic expressions**. Deictic expressions identify things by relating them to the social, linguistic, spatial or temporal context of an utterance, and include pronouns, demonstratives and adverbs of space and time. The reference of these items varies with each context in which they are used.

Personal pronouns such as *I, me, you, we, our* are deictic expressions since their interpretation is always dependent on the speech context: their interpretation depends on knowledge of who is the speaker and who is the hearer. As soon as the speaker changes, the interpretation of *I* and *you* changes. Third person pronouns are generally also deictic: they effectively point to someone or something other than the speaker or hearer. (There are exceptions, including use of *it* in *It is clear that you are not listening to me*.)

Demonstratives such as *this* and *that* are also deictics, effectively specifying referents by indicating whether they are close to the speaker, or distant from the speaker. Thus you might say *this book* to refer to the book you hold in your hands; changing speaker roles, I might then refer to the same book as *that book*. Languages differ in the number of demonstratives they have; for instance in some languages there are three (occasionally more) rather than two. In Tongan, for instance, there are three demonstratives, *eni* 'close to the speaker', *ena* 'close to the hearer', and *ito* 'distant from both speaker and hearer'.

Demonstratives employ spatial deixis. Other spatial deictic elements are the adverbs *here* and *there*. Expressions of temporal deixis include words such as *today, tomorrow, now, then, last week* and so on, which situate the time with respect to the time of speaking, and change their interpretation with changes in the speech context.

It is important to note that the deictic expressions discussed in this section have senses, for instance, for pronouns relating to person, number, gender and case. Their full meaning however is only acquired when they are used in a particular context.

The cooperative principle

Speakers and hearers generally communicate successfully: the utterance meaning intended by the speaker on any particular occasion usually corresponds well with the utterance meaning inferred by the hearer. Of course mismatches do occur; a hearer may take offense when none was intended, or fail to take offense when it was intended. But things normally work relatively smoothly. For this to happen, the speaker and hearer must share some procedures of interpretation, of drawing the appropriate inferences from what is actually encoded.

The philosopher Paul Grice proposed that such an interpretative procedure was the **cooperative principle**. This he explained in the following way: 'Make your contribution such as is required, at the stage at which it occurs, by the accepted purpose or direction of the talk exchange in which you are engaged' (Grice 1989: 26). According to Grice, the cooperative principle is constituted by four component **maxims**:

- **Maxim of Quantity**: Make your contribution as informative as required, but no more (or less) informative than required.
- **Maxim of Quality**: Try to make your contribution true; do not say that which you believe false or for which you lack adequate evidence.
- **Maxim of Relevance**: Be relevant.
- **Maxim of Manner**: Be perspicuous – avoid ambiguity, prolixity, disorderliness and obscurity.

These maxims are principles governing the inferences conversational partners draw; they are not rules that you have to follow to produce interactively or socially acceptable or correct utterances. Thus people often lie, and are not above formulating their utterances in obscure ways, intentionally or unintentionally. However, speakers flout the maxims for reasons, such as to achieve particular effects – for example, apart from pathological liars, people usually lie for a reason, to achieve some end. In this respect the maxims are unlike grammatical rules such as 'an adjective must agree in gender and number with the noun it modifies'; if a language has this grammatical rule, speakers will consistently observe it (excluding speech errors). Speakers don't decide to disobey a grammatical rule in order to achieve some effect. (There are a few exceptions, for instance, when a speaker produces an ungrammatical form to, say, mimic (and perhaps insult) a non-native speaker.)

To illustrate how the Gricean maxims can be used to understand the pragmatic meanings of an utterance, consider the following (invented) conversational fragment involving Carol and Barry again:

(6-12)   Carol: *Did you see the new Spielberg movie on TV last night?*
         Barry: *Is the Pope a Catholic?*

Carol has used asked Barry a yes/no question, using an interrogative clause; but Barry does not reply with either *Yes* or *No* – or anything in between, like *Maybe* or *Some of it*. Nevertheless Carol (and you) will immediately interpret Barry's response as a resounding 'yes', even though it is in the form of an interrogative, which normally has the speech function of a question.

The Gricean maxims can be used to explain how this meaning is inferred. By the Maxim of Relevance, Barry's response, whatever it might be, is interpreted as being relevant to Carol's question. How could the religious affiliation of the Pope be relevant to the question of whether Barry saw the movie? Well, everyone (including Barry) knows that the Pope is a Catholic, so by the Maxim of Manner, Barry cannot be seriously asking for information. Moreover, to be orderly and relevant, Barry must be interpreted as answering Carol's question – his 'question' must really be an answer, and the only way this can be so is for the blatantly obvious answer to Barry's question to be that answer. Hence the inference that Barry did see the movie. But it can also be inferred that Barry means more than this – otherwise he would have just said *Yes*, the briefest and clearest expression of affirmation. The particular roundabout response that he chose implies that things couldn't have been otherwise: 'yes, there was never a question of my not seeing it'.

In applying the Gricean Maxims to (6-12) we had to appeal to background knowledge shared by the conversational participants, in this case information known generally to members of the speech community. In some cases the shared information is specific to the conversation. We also had to appeal to syntactic structure, specifically to the status of Barry's response as an interrogative.

Presuppositions

A **presupposition** is something that must be assumed to be true in order for a sentence to be appropriately uttered. In each of the following examples, the a. sentence presupposes the b. sentence:

(6-13) a. *The bus driver managed to stop in time.*
       b. *The bus driver tried to stop in time.*

(6-14) a. *The baby has stopped crying.*
       b. *The baby was crying previously.*

(6-15) a. *I regretted giving them the donation.*
       b. *I gave them the donation.*

(6-16) a. *He realized that he had been tricked.*
       b. *He was tricked.*

If the driver didn't try to stop, it would not be appropriate to utter (6-13a), that they managed to stop; if the baby had not been crying previously, it would not be appropriate to say that it had stopped crying, (6-14a); if the speaker had not given the donation, it would be inappropriate to say that they regretted doing so, (6-15a); and if he had not been tricked, he could not realize this (6-16a). Thus in each case the b. sentence is presumed true in order for the a. sentence to be sensibly uttered.

A good test for presuppositions is that they remain constant under negation: each of the b. sentences above remain true if the a. sentence is negated:

(6-13) c. *The bus driver didn't manage to stop in time.*

(6-14) c. *The baby hasn't stopped crying.*

(6-15) c. *I didn't regret giving them the donation.*

(6-16) c. *He didn't realize that he had been tricked.*

Words like *another*, *again*, *more* and the like also invoke presuppositions. The humour of the following passage from *Alice's adventures in Wonderland* is based on the Hatter's claim that *more* does not presuppose some previous quantity.

(6-17) *'Take some more tea,'* the March Hare said to Alice, very earnestly.
'I've had nothing yet,' Alice replied in an offended tone: *'so I can't take more.'*
'You mean you can't take less,' said the Hatter: *'it's very easy to take more than nothing.'*
(Carroll 1927/1866: 101–102)

The negative test reveals that Alice is right: *Take some more tea* presupposes that the addressee has already had some – it remains true for *Don't take any more tea*.

In a sense presuppositions allow us to produce efficient discourse, as can be seen from (6-17), where use of presupposition invoking *more* reduces considerably what needs to be said. In a similar way, (6-18) presupposes that France has a king, otherwise it seems a strange thing to say (and some philosophers have argued that without this presumption the sentence can't be said to be either true or false).

(6-18)   *The present king of France is bald*

The examples we have just discussed would seem to suggest that presuppositions concern semantics rather than pragmatics, and there is disagreement among scholars as to which domain they belong to. I have discussed it under pragmatics because presuppositions can be cancelled under certain conditions. For instance, the presupposition (6-13b) does not always hold for (6-13c) – as shown by (6-13d) – and nor does the corresponding presupposition hold for (6-19). (6-20) shows that the same cancellation is possible for *more*.

(6-13)   d. *The bus driver didn't manage to stop in time, in fact he didn't even try to.*

(6-19)   *How can five students have managed to fail such an easy test?*

(6-20)   *Alice didn't have more tea, if indeed she had any.*

Summing up

Meaning is that which is expressed by linguistic units and conveyed by the use of linguistic units in speech, writing and signing. It is a multifaceted phenomenon, embracing two domains, semantics and pragmatics. **Semantics** is concerned with the meanings expressed or encoded by linguistic forms, that is, with the meaning aspect of the linguistic sign. **Pragmatics** is concerned with meanings that are not encoded, but are inferred. Semantics is thus concerned with **sentence meaning**, pragmatics with **utterance meaning**. Sentence meaning is largely **compositional**, whereas utterance meaning is not.

The major concern of semantics is with **sense**, which involves **value** and **intension**. A linguistic item can be used either **literally** or **figuratively**; metaphor, metonymy and synecdoche are examples of figurative meanings.

We dealt with three issues in semantics. First was the relations between the senses of a lexical item: **polysemy**, **vagueness** and **homophony**. Second was the identification of the range of semantic relations among lexical items: **synonymy**, **antonymy**, **hyponymy** and **meronymy**. Third was how to specify the semantics of a linguistic unit; we outlined one approach, **componential analysis**, which factors the semantic meanings of lexical items into atomic components or features.

We also dealt with four issues in pragmatics: speech acts, reference, the cooperative principle and presuppositions. **Speech acts** are what speakers do when they utter a sentence; speech acts have an **illocutionary force**. Some speech acts overtly specify their illocutionary force; these are **performatives**. When the illocutionary force is directly indicated by linguistic form we speak of **direct speech acts**; otherwise it is an **indirect speech act**. Direct and indirect speech acts differ in terms of politeness. **Reference** is concerned with the link between utterances and people, things, places and times that are being referred to. **Deictic elements** play an important role in establishing reference. The **cooperative principle** is a principle of interpretation and inferencing shared by speakers and hearers, permitting the utterance meaning intended by a speaker to be reliably inferred by the hearer. It is constituted by four **maxims**: **Quantity**, **Quality**, **Relevance** and **Manner**. **Presuppositions** are implicit assumptions invoked by certain sentences as required truths in order for utterance of the sentence to be appropriate or reasonable.

Guide to further reading

A good basic textbook on semantics is Hurford and Heasley (1983). Saeed (1997) and Löbner (2002) provide more detailed treatments of the subject; aside from lexical semantics (the focus of this chapter), they deal with sentence semantics and discuss a number of modern theories. (An important difference between the approach to sentence semantics in these books and the approach taken in this book is that they treat roles such as Actor and Undergoer as purely semantic, rather than both grammatical and semantic.) Goddard (1998) is the only theoretically coherent introduction I know of; unlike most other semantics textbooks, it contains numerous illustrations drawn from languages other than English. Lyons (1977) remains the most comprehensive treatment of the subject; however, it is a highly technical work and demands careful reading.

Ruhl (1989) shows in a number of case studies how many (Ruhl would doubtless say 'all') apparent polysemies of lexical items can be accounted for as different contextualizations of a single abstract sense.

Despite its now derogatory title, Malinowski (1923/1936) is well worth reading as a serious attempt by a brilliant anthropologist to understand the meanings of utterances in an 'exotic' language. Malinowski adopts a 'meaning is use' semantics, effectively rejecting the division between semantics and pragmatics. For more recent arguments against the division see Matthews (1995).

Kempson (2001) is a good place to begin reading on pragmatics. Good introductory textbooks are Levinson (1983/1992); Blakemore (1992); Thomas (1995); Mey (1993) and Yule (1996).

The cooperative principle and conversational maxims are dealt with in detail in Grice (1975, 1989). Stephen Levinson has developed Grice's ideas in important ways; the most accessible outline of his proposals is Levinson (1995); Levinson (1999) applies the framework to positional verbs ('stand', 'sit', 'hang') in the Papuan language Yélî Dnye.

Issues for further thought and exercises

1. What semantic relations are involved in the following pairs of lexemes?

   a. *maximum*   *minimum*   h. *single*   *married*
   b. *left*   *right*   i. *open*   *shut*
   c. *east*   *west*   j. *converse*   *chat*
   d. *mad*   *crazy*   k. *learned*   *erudite*
   e. *borrow*   *loan*   l. *appear*   *disappear*
   f. *brotherly*   *fraternal*   m. *mobile*   *cell phone*
   g. *parent*   *child*   n. *sane*   *insane*

2. Find synonyms (try and find at least two for each) for the following English words: *faithful*, *believe*, *stretch*, *break*, *ground*, *before*, *injustice* and *habit*. Are your synonyms exact or approximate? In the case of approximate synonyms, explain the meaning differences, and comment on any differences in their syntactic behaviour.

3. English has a number of verbs relating to cooking, among them the following morphologically simple ones: *cook*, *fry*, *boil*, *steam*, *bake*, *sear*, *grill*, *barbeque* and *toast*. Suggest a set of semantic features that distinguish these verbs from one another, and provide a full feature description of each verb.

4. Suggest semantic features that will distinguish the following verbs of motion: *walk*, *fly*, *go*, *jump*, *swim*, *hop*, *run*, *crawl*, *drive*, *roll* and *move*. Give a full feature description for each verb.

5. List as many hyponyms as you can of *furniture*. Draw a hierarchical diagram showing the hyponymic relations among these words.

6. Make up a list of meronyms of *car*, and show the meronymic relationships among them on a hierarchical diagram. Are there any instances of transitivity in these terms? (As a test for meronymic relations, check whether the two terms X and Y can occur in the frames *X has Y* and *the Y of X*. If so, then Y is a meronym of X. Thus *seat* is a meronym of *car* because we can say *a car has a seat*, and *the seat of the car*.)

7. How would you explain the meaning of *mouse*? Make an attempt at writing an explicit definition. Now do the following:

   a. Think of actual uses of the word in sentences – or check in a corpus if you have one readily available. What other senses do you need to identify to account for your examples; attempt to give sharp definitions of each of the senses you find.

   b. Which senses would you identify to be polysemies of a single lexical item, and which would you suggest belong to another lexeme. Do you think any of your polysemies might be better treated as instances of vagueness? Why or why not? Compare your treatment of *mouse* with the treatment in your dictionary.

8. Look up some word (for example, *try*, *finish*, *game* etc.) in your dictionary. Find the lexical items in the definition (focus on the first sense if more than one is given) that are most closely related semantically to the word, and look up their definitions in the dictionary. Continue this process, and see how long it takes you to get back to your original word. Draw a diagram to show how the headwords are linked – for example, if *try* has *attempt* in its definition, draw a line connecting them.

9. Think of contexts in which the following sentences can be used with the illocutionary force indicated:

   a. *It's cold in here*   command/request for action
   b. *Do you know the way?*   rejection of advice
   c. *The refrigerator is full*   refusal of offer
   d. *The cat hasn't been fed*   denial of permission
   e. *Do you know what time it is?*   complaint
   f. *Can you pass the salt?*   yes/no question

10. A good way of testing for a performative is to see whether *hereby* can be inserted and the resulting sentence makes sense. *I resign* is a performative by this criterion, since *I hereby resign* makes perfect sense. But *I understand* is not, since you would not say *I hereby understand*. Using this test, decide which of the following are performatives.

    a. *I swear that I have never been out with her.*
    b. *You are requested not to feed the animals.*
    c. *I swore that I had never been out with her.*
    d. *I welcome you all tonight.*
    e. *You are nominated as head of the commission.*
    f. *I promise to work harder in future.*
    g. *We nominated him as head of the commission.*
    h. *I dismiss the story as malicious gossip.*
    i. *You know that I have never been out with her.*

11. Using the Gricean maxims, explain the following: (a) how *the tree* in Figure 6.1 can have the utterance meaning indicated; and (b) why I said *for animals and people* on p. 144, when I might more economically have said *for animals* (and thus satisfying the Maxim of Quantity).

12. Consider the following conversational fragment:

    > Carol: *Did you see the new Spielberg movie on TV last night?*
    > Barry: *I've got an important exam today*

    What is the pragmatic meaning of Barry's reply? Can you explain this meaning by inference governed by the Gricean maxims? Think of other utterances Barry could use to mean either 'yes' or 'no', and explain how that meaning can be inferred.

13. Identify at least two presuppositions of each of the following sentences:

    a. *Harry was surprised that the postman arrived so early.*
    b. *Harry's younger brother wanted more ice-cream.*
    c. *When Harry arrived he began to argue with his brother.*
    d. *Those dogs are barking again.*
    e. *When will Harry ever grow up?*
    f. *The postman doesn't like dogs either.*
    g. *What's happened to my glasses?*
    h. *I hope we have another warm day before September.*
    i. *Only Harry knows the combination to the safe.*
    j. *He still regrets being married.*
    k. *Harry has gone back to Stockholm, because I was speaking to him on the phone yesterday.*

Part II
Language: A Human Phenomenon

Sociolinguistics: Language in Its Social Context

7

Our orientation up to now has been to language as a structured system of signs. In this and the following three chapters we aim to place language firmly its human environment, and attend to it as a human phenomenon. We begin in this chapter by considering language from the perspective of the uses speakers put it to in their social lives. We will be concerned, that is, with the social aspects of the meaning-making potential of the language system in its context of use. This area of investigation is called sociolinguistics.

Chapter contents

Goals

The goals of the chapter are to:

- describe how languages vary systematically according to social factors, and identify the main types of variation;
- show how speakers vary their ways of speaking – including the language they choose to speak – to construct personal identities and social roles for themselves in speech interactions;
- identify some of the factors relevant to language choice in bilingual communities;
- discuss how and why habits of language use can change over time, and possible consequences of these changes to the vitality of a language; and
- overview the increase in rate of language endangerment and extinction in recent centuries, and concerns of speakers and linguists to arrest the processes.

Key terms

accents	gender variation	language maintenance/revival	secret varieties
accommodation	identity		social varieties
bilingualism	isogloss	language shift	speech community
code-switching	language choice	register	standard dialect
dialects	language endangerment/ obsolescence/death	registerial variation	style
dialectal variation		respect varieties	

7.1 Language as a social phenomenon

Social domains of language use

All speech occurs in an interactive context in which interactants – speakers and hearers – make choices from the linguistic system. These include lexical and grammatical choices that express appropriate experiential meaning, that is, meaning concerned with the construal of the world of experience (see §5.4). This is only part of the story. As discussed in §4.5, words are not always neutral signs, but often express attitudinal values, as for instance when one says *pass away* instead of *die*. This is not the only way that words can be charged with non-experiential meaning. Words can also convey social information about the speaker. For instance, if an Australian is thanked for doing someone a favour, they would be likely to respond with *No worries*, while an American is likely to say *You're welcome*. On one level these expressions mean the same thing, but choice of one rather than another is consistent with the norms – the typical speech patterns – of Australian English versus American English.

A person's membership in a social groups – for example, the British community, a rural farming community, or an immigrant community in an urban area – will correlate with the use of certain linguistic forms and patterns of behaviour in preference to others. Some linguistic forms and behaviours interactants use represent part of the relatively stable aspect of a person's social identity; these forms indicate who the speakers are. Here variation in language is according to the speaker.

But not all choices are like this. A speaker of Australian English might say *Please take a seat* or *Grab a chair* when offering the addressee a place to sit. These forms do not mark the speaker as being an Australian so much as correlate with the particular aspects of the immediate context of speech, and the temporary roles they adopt. Imagine a university lecturer and student in a formal interview concerning the student's failure in a test. After a greeting, the lecturer might invite the student to sit down with *Please take a seat* – which could well sound ominous to the student, and hint that something unpleasant was to follow. Later, the two may happen to meet in a bar; the lecturer might invite the student to join her with *Grab a chair*. Here the choice of different expressions has to do with the speech context, and the respective roles the interactants take on; it does not concern the speaker's social identity in the sense of their group membership. This is variation according to use.

These two social features and their linguistic correlates are summarized in the first two columns of Table 7.1. In the third column are indicated the most general social functions or macro-functions associated with the linguistic devices within their domains of use. The languages and social varieties one controls, as well as the varieties associated with uses, go together to construct a participant's identity as a person: they concern who the person is, the dimension of 'being'. This contrasts with the 'doing' dimension where the concern is with how the language system is used to accomplish things in speech. In this chapter we focus on the former dimension, 'being things with words', ignoring the latter, 'doing things with words', which is dealt with in part under pragmatics (§6.3) and in part in the chapter on discourse on the accompanying website.

These rather terse observations will be elaborated more fully in the remainder of this chapter, beginning with the 'being; construction of personal identity' macro-function. To be sure, Table 7.1 gives an oversimplified picture: the distinction between social varieties and

Table 7.1 A model of the major phenomena relevant to the sociolinguistics of language use

Social phenomenon	Linguistic manifestation	Social macro-function
Community	Languages and social varieties	Being; construction of personal identity
Interactive context	Varieties according to use	Being; construction of social role

varieties according to use is not as clear cut as a simple contrast between temporary social role and permanent personal identity. Nevertheless, it provides a useful initial perspective on the complex phenomena of language variation and use. Before embarking on this enterprise, however, it is important to say a few words about the notion of speech community, since it plays a crucial role in the story.

The speech community

A **speech community** is a coherent group of people who share the same language or languages and more or less the same norms of language use. The members of a speech community form a network of interacting individuals who communicate linguistically with one another frequently, and more intensively than they engage with outsiders.

The term 'speech community' is somewhat elastic, and may be used of groups of radically different sizes depending on one's focus. From the broadest perspective, the speakers of English form a single speech community, with overall more frequent in-group interactions than out-group interactions; they also share what is in some sense the same language, and use it in at least some common ways, even if there are some differences in how they use it in specific circumstances. So also might the speakers of British English or Cockney be regarded as forming speech communities. What is required for a group of speakers to represent a speech community is a degree of unity and cohesiveness both on the level of the language system(s) and on the level of interpersonal interactions. A random selection of a million speakers of English drawn from the UK, the USA, New Zealand and India would fail to meet this condition, and does not form a speech community. Nor do the speakers of English and Cantonese together form a speech community.

7.2 Social varieties and variation

Regional variation

No language with a reasonable number of speakers spread over a relatively wide territory will have a completely homogenous the grammar and lexicon, and differences in pronunciation, words or grammar are likely to be associated with different regions. Such variation is called **dialectal variation**; varieties of a language with their own peculiarities of grammar, phonology, phonetics or lexicon and associated with particular geographical regions are **dialects**. The term **accent** is used in reference to varieties that differ only phonetically or phonologically; the term 'dialect' is used more generally when there are differences in lexicon and grammar, and possibly also phonetics as well.

The Austronesian language Taba, spoken by some 30,000–40,000 people living mainly on Makian Island, near the island of Halmahera in Indonesia, shows minor dialectal differences in each village. These include a small number of lexical differences; a phonological difference (in the speech of some villages an /o/ is found where others have /a/), and a grammatical difference (in some dialects the singular/plural contrast is made only on human nouns, while in others it is made for all animate nouns).

The differences between neighbouring dialects of a language are insufficient to make speech in one dialect unintelligible to speakers of another; dialects are variant forms of a single language, not distinct languages (see also §13.1). However, if a language is spread over a very large region, speakers from opposite extremes of the region may not be able to understand one another, or may experience difficulties in understanding one another, and misunderstandings may be frequent. Nevertheless, neighbouring varieties will be mutually intelligible, and the language can be seen as a chain of mutually intelligible dialects. Such situations are called dialect continuums. An example is the so-called Western Desert language (Pama-Nyungan) spoken over the vast desert region of Australia shown in Map 7.1. The named varieties in this map differ from one another mainly in lexicon, and slightly in grammar. Geographically close varieties are similar enough to be mutually intelligible; distant ones such as Yulbarija in the far north-west and Kukata in the extreme south-east are more divergent, and not everything said in one would be immediately understood by a speaker of the other.

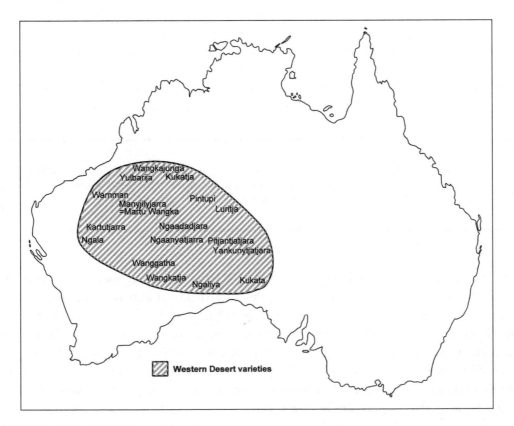

Map 7.1 Varieties of the Western Desert language.

> Mutually unintelligible forms of speech like Mandarin Chinese and Cantonese are thus separate languages; they are not dialects in the linguistic sense, contrary to popular usage, and terminology in common use in Chinese linguistics in China.

Standard dialects

Sometimes one dialect of a language will be recognized as the most important or **standard dialect** of the language. This is usually the most prestigious dialect, and regarded as the most 'correct' form of speech. For languages with longish traditions of writing such as English and French, the standard is the variety promoted in schools, and children are usually taught to write in; it is also the variety most likely to be heard on national broadcasting networks. The standard is usually the variety that is codified in grammars, dictionaries and style guides. In the case of English, somewhat different standards have emerged in different countries, so we have Standard American English, Standard Australian English, Standard British English, Standard New Zealand English and so on. If a general Standard English can be identified, it would be something of an abstraction, characterized by features common to the national standards.

Not all languages have standard dialects. The traditional languages of Australia did not have standard varieties; it is only in post-contact times that some traditional languages have acquired standard varieties. These are often the varieties that have, by a quirk of history, been the ones that missionaries have worked on, and perhaps produced bible translations in, or that educators have happened to choose as the standard for literacy materials.

> Notice that linguistic usage of the term *dialect* differs from popular usage, where a dialect is understood to be a non-standard or substandard variety of a language and the standard variety is not regarded as a dialect. In linguistics, both standard and non-standard varieties are dialects.

Isoglosses

In dialectology, the study of dialects, it is standard practice to use **isoglosses**, lines drawn on a map to mark the boundaries of regions in which a particular feature is found, whether it is a particular lexical item, a characteristic feature of pronunciation, grammatical feature or whatever. These are a bit like isobars on a weather map, which bound regions of the same barometric pressure. Map 7.2 shows the isogloss for the Danish stød,[1] which runs in an east–west direction. It also shows isoglosses for genders,[2] which run in a north–south direction. As this indicates, isoglosses do not always coincide. Generally, however, boundaries of major dialects are marked by bunching of isoglosses.

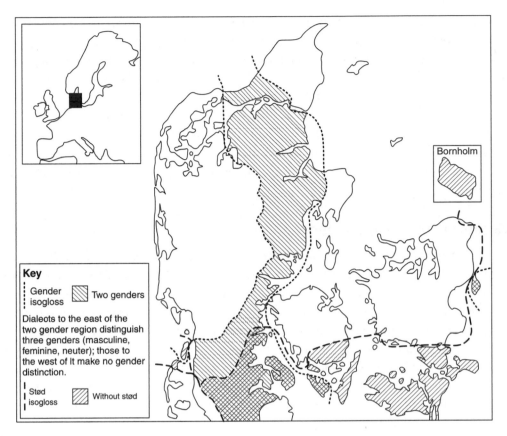

Key

Gender isogloss — ▨ Two genders

Dialects to the east of the two gender region distinguish three genders (masculine, feminine, neuter); those to the west of It make no gender distinction.

Stød isogloss — ▨ Without stød

Bornholm

Map 7.2 Two isoglosses in Danish.

Variation according to social group

Many societies in today's world are stratified according to socio-economic status. In industrialized Western societies stratification depends on income, education, occupation and so on. Sociolinguists commonly identify two classes according to these variables: working class (generally with lower levels of education and in manual or semi-skilled employment) and middle class (generally with higher levels of education, and working in non-manual professional jobs). Both of these can be further divided into upper, middle and lower. Sometimes lower and upper classes are also distinguished. These classes (in Western societies) form a scale of variation rather than a set of rigidly distinct and precisely delimited classes.

One investigation, undertaken by William Labov in the late 1960s, studied social stratification in the speech of New York City residents according to a number of linguistic variables (Labov 1972). One was the phonetic realization of /θ/, which in New York City has three variants, [θ], [t̄θ], and [t̠]. Across various styles of speech, Labov found a consistent correlation between social class and the phonetic variable. For a given level of formality, the higher the speaker's socio-economic status the greater was the tendency to use the fricative allophone [θ], and the lower the speaker's status, the more affricate and stop allophones they used. Moreover, there was a fairly large gap between lower- and working-class speakers on the one hand, and middle-class speakers on the other.

Use of these linguistic variables is a matter of frequency; it is not an all or nothing affair. No social class in New York City is totally consistent use of any of the allophones. Furthermore, for each class, use of the prestigious variant [θ] increases with the degree of formality of speech. The variation thus concerns the notion of style (see the box on p. 165).

Variation according to gender

Men and women probably speak differently in all human societies. Some differences have a biological foundation: across populations males tend to have larger vocal folds than females, and thus the fundamental frequency tends to be lower in the speech of males than females. However, biology does not fix even this, and the differences can be exaggerated, as is the case in Japanese where the pitch differences between the genders are more marked than in English, due to female Japanese speakers tending to use higher pitches than English-speaking females. This has been confirmed experimentally by Y. Ohara, reported in Coulmas (2005: 37). Ohara recorded conversations and sentences read in Japanese and English by the same speakers, and found that the women used higher pitch when speaking Japanese than English, while men used the same pitch in both languages.

Differences in speech between the genders are often a matter of degree rather than kind, although in some languages there are features that are unique to either males or females.

In English the situation is of the former kind, that is, a matter of degree rather than kind. A number of linguistic features tend to pattern differently for men and women. It is documented, for instance, that women tend to have, and habitually use, larger vocabularies of colour terms than men, including terms such as *mauve, lavender, crimson, violet, beige* and so on. Differences also exist in usage of non-standard grammatical forms such as double negatives (as in *I never did nothing*), use of the /ɪn/ allomorph of the -*ing* verb suffix (as in *eating*), and non-standard past tense forms such as *seen* instead of *saw* (as in *I seen it the other day*). Numerous studies have shown these non-standard features to be more common in the speech of males than females.

In some languages categorical differences are found in the speech of males and females, certain forms being peculiar to one gender. In Gros Ventre (Algonquian, USA) alveolar and palatal affricates in men's speech correspond with velar stops in women's speech. Sidamo (Afroasiatic, Ethiopia) has lexical items peculiar to men's and women's speech. For example, the word for 'four' is *rore* in women's speech, and *foole* in men's speech.

In Japanese there are differences in grammatical morphemes. For example, the first and second person pronoun forms are *atashi* 'I' and *anata* 'you' in women's speech, but *boku* 'I' and

Table 7.2 Bound pronouns in women's and men's varieties of Yanyuwa

	Women		Men
	Male	**Masculine**	**Male-Masculine**
Nominative	*ilu-*	*inju-*	*ilu-*
Accusative	*anya-*	*i-*	*ø-*

kimi 'you' in men's speech. There are also a number of lexical differences: *kite* 'come' of female speech corresponds to *koi* in the speech of males. Japanese also has a number of sentence-final particles used for expressing politeness. Some of these are unique to the speech of males, others to the speech of females. In addition, a range of particles are used by both male and female speakers, but in different frequencies: some are used predominantly by males, some predominantly by females and a few with about the same frequency by both.

In the Australian language Yanyuwa (Pama-Nyungan) there is an even more fundamental grammatical difference between male and female speech. In the variety spoken by females seven noun classes (see note 2) are distinguished, while in the variety of male speakers just six are distinguished. The contrast between male and masculine classes made by women is lost in men's speech. (The nature of the difference between the male class and the masculine class in the variety spoken by women need not concern us.) This difference shows up in a number of places in the grammar of the two varieties, including in the bound pronouns (see Table 7.2). It also shows up in the gender prefixes to nouns and their modifiers: where the prefix *ki-* is found in the speech of males, either *nya-* (male class) or *ji-* (masculine class) is found in females' speech

Other dimensions of variation

Other social dimensions of social variation include age, ethnicity and religion. Let us look briefly at each of these.

Different generations of speakers often show differences in speech, for instance in use of slang terms (see Question 8, Chapter 4) such as *buck* 'dollar', *wicked* 'good', *cool* 'good, up to date'. Some slang terms (e.g. *buck*) have long lives, and may end up as standard lexemes; *dwindle* is an example: it was a slang term in Shakespeare's time. Many do not survive long, and their use can be characteristic of a particular generation group, the youth of a certain time. This is the case for terms such as *cool* vs. *wicked*, or *sick* for 'good'.

Different ethnic groups in countries such as the USA, Britain and Australia, often speak slightly different varieties of English, showing divergences in phonetics/phonology, lexical items and/or grammar. Perhaps the best-studied ethnic variety is the English of African Americans, sometimes called African American Vernacular English (AAVE). This variety shows characteristics distinguishing it from Standard American English. (a) The auxiliary *be* is usually absent where standard English has an unstressed *be*, as for instance in *He fast in everything he do*. (b) The verb *be* is used to indicate habitual activity, as in *He be late*, which means 'he is always late'; *He late* by contrast refers to a single instance. (c) Word-final consonant clusters of Standard English are often absent in AAVE, the cluster being typically replaced by its initial consonant, as in *foun* (*found*) and *lef* (*left*). Although this happens in casual speech in other varieties of English, it is more general in AAVE.

Sometimes religious differences are associated with differences in language varieties. Hindi (spoken in India) and Urdu (spoken in Pakistan) are mutually intelligible varieties of a single language, often referred to as Hindi/Urdu. They differ somewhat in lexicon, and employ different writing systems. But the contrast is based ultimately on religion: Hindi is associated with the Hindu religion, Urdu with Islam.

Accommodation

Speakers often change the way they speak according to the person they are speaking with, adopting features of one another's speech – or what they believe to be characteristics of one another's speech. Thus they adjust the variety they use so as to be more like the variety of their addressee. This is called **speech accommodation**, and is a way of reducing the social distance between the interlocutors. Speakers of any dialect of English who reside for long periods of time in a region where a different dialect is spoken normally accommodate to the dialect of their region of residence; on return to their home region, they reaccommodate to their native dialect. Their speech tends to converge to the dialect spoken around them. I notice this in my own speech when returning to Australia every second year, and then on my subsequent returns to Denmark. When the sociolinguist Peter Trudgill examined his own speech in interviews with Norwich informants, he found that his use of some accent features closely resembled those of the accent of his informants (Trudgill 1986).

Speakers can also choose to emphasize their social distance from an interlocutor by refusing to accommodate, by diverging from the patterns of the other's variety. A person who speaks both a standard and a non-standard dialect of English might shift from speaking the standard to speaking the non-standard in order to signal social distance from their interlocutor, for instance, to underline a refusal to comply with a request.

7.3 Varieties and variation according to use

Where variation in language depends on the more immediate context of the utterance rather than characteristics of the speaker, we speak of different **registers** or **registerial variation**. Registers thus do not construct the speaker's personal identity, but rather their and their addressee's role in that speech interaction. They are linguistic varieties according to use.

According to Michael Halliday (e.g. 1978), three factors are relevant to the specification of registers:

- **Field**, the subject matter of the discourse. For instance, the field of this book is linguistics.
- **Tenor**, the relations among the interactants in the discourse. This includes for example the degree of distance or formality they adopt.
- **Mode**, the medium or channel employed. This can include the choice between speech and writing; it can also include the manner of speaking, for instance, speaking over the telephone rather than in person, and the role of other systems such as gesture.

Different values for these factors (according to Halliday) give rise to different registers or registerial variants.

Examples of different registers in English include legal, bureaucratic, scientific, religious and medical 'Englishes', which are characterized by lexical peculiarities. Differences in the frequencies of use grammatical constructions or categories may also exist: scientific English shows heavy use of nominal modes of expression and nominalizations (nominal stems derived from roots of other parts-of-speech, for example, *variation* from *vary*). The other two factors are also relevant: there will be differences according to the relation between the interactants and whether speech or writing is used. For instance, the register of this book, a written piece, differs from the register I use in lecturing.

Other registers found in some languages include secret varieties, respect varieties, baby-talk and animal talk (speech directed to animals). In what follows we discuss the first two of these.

> The notion of **style** overlaps with the notion of register. A style is a variety associated with a particular social context of use, and differs from other styles in degree of formality. Thus styles in a language can be ranged from the most informal and colloquial to the most formal.

Secret varieties

Professional and occupational registers like those mentioned in the previous section serve gate-keeping functions: non-members of the group are excluded from full understanding of the message due to the technical terminology and possibly arcane modes of expression. In some cases this function comes to the fore, and a register's motivation is principally to exclude outsiders and render the meaning obscure. Registers of this type are called 'secret languages' or 'anti-languages'.

An example is the secret register called *kpéléméíyé* used by young Kisi men in Liberia. Based on Kisi (Niger-Congo, Sierra Leone), only males of a certain age use it, and no female speakers or non-Kisi speakers understand it. The words of this secret register are formed from ordinary Kisi words by a variety of somewhat obscure processes of modification, the most obvious of which is reversal of syllables. Examples illustrating the latter process include the secret variety lexeme *ndòtún* 'dog' deriving from the ordinary term *tùŋndó*, and *yòɲáá* 'cat' coming from *ɲààyó*. There are also semantic and grammatical differences, including replacement of some items by their opposites, and reordering of words in clauses.

Other examples of secret registers include Pig Latins, sometimes used by school children in Western societies; secret initiands' and ritual varieties of some Australian Aboriginal groups; and secret varieties used by criminals, for example, in West Bengal. A common characteristic of these registers is the replacement of a lexeme by a lexeme opposite or nearly opposite in meaning; this is also quite commonly employed in slangs, as in the use of *wicked* and *sick* for 'good'. Also common is the reversal of the order of syllables.

Respect varieties

Many, perhaps all, languages have means of showing respect, deference, distance and politeness by lexical or grammatical choices. For instance, it is common in the languages of Europe (and elsewhere) for a speaker to address a single hearer with the second person plural pronoun form to indicate respect; in French, for instance, the plural *vous* is used in addressing a single person to show respect, distance or politeness. Japanese and Korean (isolate, Korea) have systems of honorifics, lexical and grammatical choices that mark respect. For instance, in Korean the ordinary word for 'meal' is *pap*; the corresponding honorific is *cinci*. Ordinary verbs in Korean can be made honorific by adding the infix *-si-*, as in *o-si-ta* 'to come', corresponding to ordinary *o-ta* 'to come'.

Traditional Australian Aboriginal societies were egalitarian, and respect was shown not to an individual because of their higher social rank, but rather to particular relatives. In most cases this applies to individuals related as mother-in-law to son-in-law (sometimes brothers-in-law) who should not engage in familiar or intimate interactions with one another, and should be circumspect in their interactions with one another. In many cases special speech varieties are used among interlocutors so related, sometimes also when speaking about the in-law. These varieties were used as a sign of social distance and respect, and are here called **respect varieties** (they are also called avoidance styles and mother-in-law languages).

Respect varieties generally have the phonology and grammar of the everyday language – though there can be divergences – and differ mainly in lexicon. Often the vocabulary of the respect variety is quite small, sometimes covering only a limited range of meanings; the lexemes are typically vague in meaning compared with everyday words. For example, Bunuba and Gooniyandi respect varieties have just over a hundred words. Some respect words have a more general sense than their everyday counterparts, so that one avoidance term corresponds to a few different everyday terms. In the Bunuba variety *jayirriminyi* covers the meanings of the ordinary words *thangani* 'mouth, language, speech, story' and *yingi* 'name', while *jalimanggurru* covers three distinct boomerang types, referred to in ordinary speech as *baljarrangi* 'returning boomerang type', *gali* 'returning boomerang type', and *mandi* 'non-returning boomerang type used for hunting'. However, only a fraction of the everyday lexicon has corresponding respect terms: absent are terms for genitals and sexual activity, topics inconsistent with respect and distance!

Generally, an utterance in the respect variety consists of just a single respect lexeme, as illustrated by Gooniyandi example (7-1), which shows the respect verb *malab-* 'make' instead of the ordinary verb *wirrij-* 'dig'.

(7-1) *malab-mi*   *goorrgoo*   Gooniyandi respect variety
       make-he:effected:it   hole
       'He dug a hole.'

Some respect varieties apparently have somewhat larger lexicons than the Bunuba and Gooniyandi ones, some fewer. At one extreme is the Dyirbal (Pama-Nyungan) respect variety, which apparently had lexemes covering the entire range of semantic domains, though less precisely than the everyday lexemes. At the other extreme are respect varieties with just a single characteristic lexeme, as in the case of Jaru, where it is *luwarn-*, identical with the ordinary verb meaning 'shoot'. This verb replaces every verb of everyday speech, and is completely general in meaning. Respectful utterances are formed in Jaru by replacing the verb by *luwarn-*, as illustrated by (7-2), which may be compared with the near minimal pair in everyday Jaru, (7-3).

(7-2) *maliyi*   *nga-lu*   *luwarnan*   *murla-ngka*   Jaru respect variety
       mother:in:law   they:are   be:doing   here-at
       'Mother-in-law is sitting here.'

(7-3) *ngawiyi*   *nga*   *nyinan*   *murla-ngka*   Everyday Jaru
       father   he:is   be:sitting   here-at
       'Father is sitting here.'

Respect varieties often show differences in manner of delivery, being spoken more slowly or softly than normal, and without eye-contact. Use of pronouns is often different: the 'you-plural' form is normally used for a singular addressee, the 'they' form in reference to a single avoidance relative. Furthermore, respect speech is typically vaguer than ordinary speech; it is rare for speakers to elaborate on vague avoidance utterances to make the meaning more precise.

7.4 Language use in bilingual communities

A speech community is not always made up of speakers of just a single language. Many speech communities around the world are constituted of individuals who speak two or more shared languages. I use the term **bilingualism** to refer to such situations, allowing that more than two languages may be involved; sometimes the term *multilingualism* is used instead as the cover term. Most Aboriginal language speech communities in Australia were traditionally, and still are, bilingual. Almost everyone in the Gooniyandi speech community traditionally spoke, in addition to Gooniyandi, at least one of the following: Bunuba, Kija (Jarrakan), Nyikina (Nyulnyulan, Australia) and Walmajarri; some gifted individuals spoke other languages as well. In more recent times, Kriol (a creole – see §13.4) has been added to the typical inventory. The Danish speech community is also a bilingual one, with English and German among the languages shared by many Danes.

Speakers in bilingual speech communities need to choose between two or more languages on any occasion of speaking. The choice of language is perhaps never entirely random, and like lexical and grammatical choices, usually conveys meaning. We deal first with the most general level of language choice, the level of the speech interaction. Then we look at choices made at the level of utterances, and the ways in which, and reasons why, speakers adopt now one language, now another at different points in the speech interaction. The fundamental idea underlying the discussion is that languages express aspects of speaker's social identity (the 'being' macro-function).

In some cases a speech community uses two distinct forms of one language, one form learnt via education, the other acquired as the first language. The variety learnt at school, the 'high' (H) variety, is usually used in more formal contexts such as in church, on the radio, in serious literature and so on. The other variety, the 'low' (L) variety, is associated with less formal contexts, such as family conversations. This is known as **diglossia**. The German-speaking community in Switzerland is a diglossic speech community. Standard German is the H variety, learnt at school; Swiss German is the L variety, learnt in the home. Comparable situations in which different languages are involved, as in the case of Spanish (H) and Guaraní (L) in Paraguay are also referred to as diglossic.

Language choice

In bilingual communities, speakers tend to speak each language in particular interactive contexts, depending on who they are talking to, the topic of conversation and so on. The clusters of contextual factors that influence the habitual choice of language are called **domains**. Examples of domains could include the domestic domain, the educational domain, the administrative domain and so on.

The association between a language and a domain, it should be stressed, is a tendency not a rule: the claim is only that certain choices of language correlate statistically with certain domains. Bilingual speakers can and often do vary their language within a single discourse, or across discourses of the same type (see next section).

It has been proposed that broad patterns of language choice in many African countries correlate with social domains (Myers-Scotton 1993). In urban regions in Kenya many people are trilingual in their own mother tongue, Swahili and English. Mostly they use their mother tongue in the home, and with members of their own ethnic group. At work again, speakers may use their mother tongue with others in their own ethnic group, and otherwise Swahili or English (especially in white-collar occupations). Outside of the workplace, English and Swahili are also used with people from other ethnic groups, with English associated with more formal and public interactions.

Another trilingual speech community is Sauris, a small community in the Carnian Alps in north-eastern Italy. Here a dialect of German is used in the home; Italian is the language of education and organized religion; and Friulian (a Rhaetian Romance language) is used by men in the local bars.

Code-switching

Code-switching is the phenomenon, common in bilingual speech communities, in which speakers switch from one language to another within the same conversation. Indeed, code-switching often occurs even within the same utterance, as in (7-4) – quite unremarkable in casual conversation – from a bilingual speaker of Malay (Austronesian, Malaysian peninsular and many nearby islands) and English. (Malay words are bolded.)

> (7-4) *This morning I **hantar** my baby tu **dekat** babysitter tu **lah***
> 'This morning I took my baby to the babysitter.'

In many bilingual situations the languages in the speaker's repertoires include one or more local or minority languages associated with local ethnic groups, and a majority language that has no such local associations, such as a national language or international language like Swahili and English in Kenya. Broadly speaking, choice of the local language underlines solidarity between the conversational partners, while choice of the national language serves a distancing function, emphasizing the social distance.

By making choices among the available languages within the progress of a conversation, speakers strategically manipulate solidarity and distance to more effectively serve their goals at that point in the interaction. Susan Gal found that bilingual speakers of Hungarian and German in the Austrian village of Oberwart might switch to German in an argument conducted largely in Hungarian to add extra force to a particular point (Gal 1979). It is not that German is always chosen to help win an argument; rather, at certain points in an interaction it can be used in a bid to achieve this communicative purpose; at other points it might be used to achieve different ends.

Code-switching is common in Australian Aboriginal communities today, though only a few careful investigations have been undertaken. One notable example is Patrick McConvell's (1985) close study of code-switching in an interactive event in which a small group of men from Daguragu, a small community in the Northern Territory, are butchering a bullock. The men spoke 'standard' Gurindji (Pama-Nyungan), as well as a local regional variety such as Wanyjirra (Pama-Nyungan) and Kriol (see p. 325).

Within this interaction the men constantly switch between using the local variety, standard Gurindji and Kriol. They do not do this at random, however. McConvell shows that the choice depends to a large extent on which social group(s) the speaker wishes to stress membership of at different points in the interaction. Choice of the local variety Wanyjirra highlights the interlocutors' membership of a small local group: using this variety a speaker can declare their social proximity to the addressees, that they are co-members of a small speech community. This might pave the way for a request. By contrast, choice of Kriol would serve to downplay the alliances among the interactants, indicating no more than that they are all members of the large Kriol speech community. Choice of Kriol could reinforce denial of a favour, or stress wider community needs over the needs of an individual. The speaker as it were smooths the way for such problematic speech acts as denials by distancing themselves from the addressee.

This is illustrated by (7-5), a short excerpt of three speech turns of two of the butchers. (Here the vertical line | indicates switch of language; capitals indicate Kriol words; bolding indicates words specific to Standard Eastern Gurindji; small capitals mark specifically Wanyjirra forms; and plain italics indicates forms common to Gurindji and Wanyjirra.)

(7-5) G: *MINE* | PAMPIRLA | *THERE AGAIN, OLD MAN* | KUMA-WU
                        shoulder   shoulder

           WAKU NYARRA? | *kankurla-pala-nginyi*   *ngu-yi-n* | KUMA-WU
           which   way   above-across-from   will-me-you   cut-will

       J: | **laja** | -ma   ngartji   ma-ni   W-rlu
               shoulder   -topic   choose   get-did   W-by

       G: | NGANINGA | -ma
               my   -topic

       G: 'MINE | THE SHOULDER | THERE AGAIN, OLD MAN | THE SHOULDER, OR WHAT? | *From across the top you have to for me* | TO CUT IT.'

       J: | '**the shoulder** | *W- picked it out.*'

       G: | 'MINE | (*it is*).'

McConvell comments on the code-switching in this interaction as follows:

> G begins in Kriol, but switches to Wanyjirra to emphasise the close local bond between himself and J, in relation to J's giving him the shoulder, and the cutting action which will provide G with the shoulder. J however responds by shifting back to the wider community arena by using SEG [Standard Eastern Gurindji], and emphasising the rights of a non-Wanyjirra community member. G reasserts his claim within the narrower arena by using the W [Wanyjirra] term for 'mine'.
>
> (McConvell 1985: 111)

7.5 Language shift and endangerment

Languages do not remain constant for long: indeed they change rapidly. In later chapters we deal with changes that happen over time to the lexicons and grammars of languages. Sociolinguistic patterns are not immune to change either, as societies change and languages are put to new uses. New styles of speech or writing emerge for use in new social interactions and purposes. The wide availability of email, instant messaging, SMS and the World Wide Web has resulted in new patterns of use of many languages.

Nor are things static in the domain of linguistic varieties and their social-identity values. New dialects emerge as populations move into new regions and countries, as happened to English in America, Australia and New Zealand; in some circumstances new languages eventually emerge (see §13.4). Moreover, over time people change their habits of choosing between the languages and varieties at their disposal in the speech community, and thus the social values associated with these varieties change.

When changes in habits of language use become particularly pronounced, and one language or language variety comes to be used in a significantly smaller or wider range of circumstances in a speech community we speak of **language shift**. In extreme cases, what was once the major language of a community – the language used as the primary vehicle of communication and the mother tongue of most community members – may be replaced by another language. When this process affects the entire speech community of a language, we speak of language **endangerment** or **obsolescence**; when it reaches the point where no speakers remain, we refer to language **death**.

Rate of language shift, endangerment and death

The rate at which language shift or death progresses varies considerably from case to case. In some cases of **gradual shift** the domains in which one language is used contract gradually, and it may take many generations before it is replaced by another language (if it ever is). The replacement of Scots Gaelic or Gàidhlig (Indo-European, Scotland) by English has been ongoing for hundreds of years, and remains incomplete.

At the opposite extreme, a language can completely disappear within a generation or less. Such cases of **sudden death** are rare, and are often associated with the death of all speakers within a short period of time. In 1226 the Xixia or Tangut population of Western China, speakers of a Tibeto-Burman language, were annihilated by the Mongolian emperor Genghis Khan. But perhaps the clearest example of sudden death is that of Tambora, spoken on the Indonesian island of Sumbawa. All speakers of this language were wiped out in a volcanic eruption in 1815.

Sometimes political circumstances can give rise to sudden death of a language without the death of the entire speech community. Following a massacre of thousands of Indians in El Salvador in 1932, the survivors abandoned their traditional languages so as not to be identified as Indians.

Causes of language shift

Language shift and death can happen for many reasons. Usually it is not possible to isolate a single cause for an instance of language shift; rather, a number of factors typically conspire. The wider social circumstances are also relevant, as none of the factors separately or together guarantees that language shift will occur. Nevertheless, across diverse cases certain factors tend to recur.

Disruption of the speech community – physical or social separation of speakers so that there are fewer opportunities for interaction among them – is a factor in language shift. This can come about in many different ways: decimation of the speech community; enforced resettlement together with others who do not share the language; widespread dispersal of the community for employment and other reasons; influx of significant numbers of immigrants; and separation of children from the adults (e.g. by segregation in dormitories). The Nyulnyul speech community was affected in almost all of these ways during the first 60 or 70 years of contact with Europeans. First, it was significantly reduced in the late nineteenth and early twentieth centuries through killings by unscrupulous Europeans and diseases they brought with them. With the establishment of the Beagle Bay Mission in Nyulnyul territory in 1890 began influxes of Aborigines from outside, few of who spoke the language. When dormitories were established on the mission in the early twentieth century, Nyulnyul children were separated from their parents who they saw only on weekends; use of Nyulnyul in the dormitories was forbidden. From the first decades of the twentieth century, many mission educated Aborigines of Nyulnyul descent were sent to employment outside of the mission.

Economic considerations underlie many of the above considerations. Also relevant are numbers of speakers and their patterns of marriage. The larger the speech community of a language, the better chance it will have of survival, other things being equal. But other things are not always equal, and some languages have survived for a long time without large speech communities, while others appear vulnerable even with many thousands of speakers. If marriages tend to be outside of a smallish community of speakers, fragmentation of the community may well result. This consideration was also relevant in the case of Nyulnyul: in the early decades of the twentieth century missionaries strongly encouraged marriage between local Nyulnyul men and women from outside, the majority of who had been forcibly taken to the mission as young children.

Attitudes to the languages can also be decisive. Speakers might shift their speech habits in favour of a language enjoying higher status, especially if it is politically advantageous to do so. Attitudes can be relevant in other ways as well. In some Australian Aboriginal communities the traditional languages have come to be regarded by speakers as too difficult for children, and suitable only for adults. And in some cases last speakers have withheld their language from younger generations because they fear it will not be adequately valued.

The symbolic value of a language can also have a bearing. In some instances the language of the colonizers is associated with the modern world and desirable commodities, while the traditional language might be associated with old ways of life no longer practised. An association with traditional culture can, on the other hand, sometimes be an advantage, giving the language at least one domain in which its survival is enhanced. The Nyulnyul situation is interesting in this regard: as a result of missionary translations of religious materials, it seems that the association between Nyulnyul and traditional cultural practices was weakened, so that no longer was the language identified with traditional practices. As a result, Nyulnyul was left with no positive symbolic value.

Structural changes accompanying language shift and endangerment

In language endangerment situations, especially when shift is gradual, simplifications of grammar and lexicon often occur. For instance, the Gurindji of 5–8-year-old children in the Daguragu and Kalkaringi communities in the Northern Territory shows evidence of simplification in various grammatical features, and loss of infrequent words.[3] Bound pronouns have been lost entirely, and the allomorphy of some case suffixes has been reduced, as can be seen from the two case inflections presented in Table 7.3. (For explanation of the term ergative see §11.3.)

As mentioned in §3.3, Nyulnyul has a set of some fifty bound nouns indicating parts of the body that require a prefix indicating the owner of the part. By the last decades of the twentieth century, only one speaker used this system. The others (most of who did not speak the language fluently) used the third person singular form of the noun as the root form; the system of prefixes had been lost entirely, and possession was indicated by a possessive pronoun. Thus whereas in traditional Nyulnyul one would say *nga-marl* 'my hand', in modern speech 'my hand' is expressed as *jan nimarl*, literally 'my his-hand'.

Table 7.3 Some allomorphs of two case suffixes in Gurindji (after Dalton et al. 1995)

Cases	Children's Gurindji	Traditional Gurindji
ergative	-*ngku* after a vowel	-*ngku* after a vowel in words of two syllables
		-*lu* after a vowel in words of more than two syllables
	-*tu* after a consonant	-*tu* after an alveolar consonant
		-*ju* after a palatal consonant
		and others
locative	-*ngka* after a vowel	-*ngka* after a vowel in words of two syllables
		-*la* after a vowel in words of more than two syllables
	-*ta* after a consonant	-*ta* after an alveolar consonant
		-*ja* after a palatal consonant
		and others

Intriguingly, this system of pronoun prefixes to nouns was not entirely absent from late-twentieth-century Nyulnyul. Some speakers retained it on the one or two exceptional prefixing nouns that do not denote body parts. Thus it was retained in the speech of some on -*mungk* 'belief, knowledge', as in *nyi-mungk* 'your belief/knowledge' and *nga-mungk* 'my belief/knowledge'. One guesses that preservation of the feature for this lexical item may have been supported by the fact that -*mungk* expresses a meaning closer to that of a verb rather than a noun; note, however, it was not actually reanalysed as a verb, and given verbal inflections.

With decreasing use of a language in specialized social domains and disappearance of social domains such as ritual, registers can be lost, and along with them lexical items peculiar to them. For instance, in the late twentieth century speakers of Nyulnyul appear to have known few terms for secret-sacred law and ritual objects. These words almost certainly disappeared with the generation who were adolescents in the 1890s: this was the last generation to undergo initiation, a prerequisite to acquisition of sacred religious knowledge.

Language maintenance and revival

Language endangerment and death have always occurred; however, the rate at which languages are becoming endangered and dying has been steadily accelerating over the past few centuries. Many languages of Australia and the Americas have become seriously endangered in post-colonial times. In Australia, for example, no more than 20 traditional languages are presently being learnt as a mother tongue of children, or have a thousand or more speakers. This represents less than a tenth of the number of languages that were spoken by viable populations of speakers on the continent at first colonization in 1788, although many even then perhaps had fewer than 1,000 speakers.

Some linguists have predicted that if present trends continue unabated as many as 90 per cent of the presently spoken languages will either become extinct, or at least endangered, within the next century. Opinions differ, however, and it is a fact that linguists' prognoses have often been wide off the mark (Vakhtin 2002).

Many speakers of endangered languages and many linguists are concerned about this situation, and efforts have been proposed or adopted to arrest the processes of shift in communities around the globe. These efforts are referred to by a range of terms, including language **maintenance** and **revival** (other terms are also used; sometimes the terms are used to refer to different things, sometimes as synonyms). For instance, in Australia a number of Aboriginal-controlled language centres have emerged since the mid-1980s, that are concerned with determining community attitudes to the traditional languages, and how best to serve them. In a number of cases communities have expressed determination that their traditional languages survive, or that a previously spoken traditional language be reintroduced. Slightly earlier, in New Zealand, 'language nests' or *kohunga reo*, were established by the Maori community in an attempt to promote the acquisition of Maori by children. In these language nests older Maori-speaking adults, typically from the generation grandparental to the children, worked as voluntary caretakers speaking Maori to the children. (This strategy has subsequently been tried elsewhere.)

Unfortunately, it is difficult to determine which strategies are likely to succeed either in general or in particular cases, and few attempts have enjoyed much success. Widely regarded as the most successful is the revival of Hebrew – which had not been used as a medium of everyday communication for over a thousand years – in the late nineteenth and early twentieth centuries. (See, however, Zuckermann (2006) for a different view.)

Summing up

Any language with a viable **speech community** is heterogeneous, showing varieties and variation in phonetics, phonology, lexicon and/or grammar associated with differences among speakers along social dimensions.

Languages are often divided into different **dialects** and **accents** according to region. They also show **dialectal variation** across regions, which sometimes cuts across dialects. Dialectal variation is represented by **isoglosses** on a map. Other social dimensions that language variation and varieties may be associated with include social class, age, gender, ethnicity and religion. The linguistic variant spoken by a speaker serves as a badge of group membership. Speakers tend to **accommodate** to the variety of their interlocutor, reinforcing social ties with them.

Languages also vary according to the use speakers put them, different forms of speech being associated with different functions of language in interaction. This gives us **registers** and **registerial variation**, which include legalese, secret languages, respect varieties and the like. **Styles** are similar to registers, but the term is usually used for varieties differing in terms of formality.

Many speech communities are **bilingual**. In such communities the choice of language can express a speaker's social identity. In many bilingual communities language choice is at least partly motivated by **domain**; but domains do not usually determine the language spoken. In most bilingual communities **code-switching** occurs, often to strategically manipulate feelings of solidarity and distance.

Speech communities change over time, sometimes radically: their language repertoire may change with the introduction of a new language, as may the habits of using them. **Language shift** happens when a language comes to be spoken in fewer domains, in a more restricted range of social circumstances. In extreme cases, a language can become **endangered** or **obsolescent**; ultimately we may have language **death** or **extinction**. These processes happen at vastly different rates. Language endangerment is often (though not always) accompanied by changes, usually simplifications, in the grammar and lexicon of the language.

There is currently considerable concern amongst linguists and others, including speakers of endangered languages, about the loss of the world's linguistic diversity; this has led to the development of **language maintenance** efforts in various countries.

Guide to further reading

Two of the best textbooks on sociolinguistics are Mesthrie et al. (2000) and Coulmas (2005). Also worth reading are Holmes (1992) and Coulmas (2001); for a rather different approach, see Halliday (1978). One type of sociolinguistic investigation we did not mention, the ethnography of communication, is concerned with how language is used in different cultures; Saville-Troike (1989) provides an excellent textbook introduction.

On use of corpus studies to identify registers according to statistical patterns in distributions of lexical items see Biber (1995) and Biber et al. (1998). Chapter 5 of Mithun (1999) deals with various speech registers in North American languages (though not under the term register); for fuller treatment, Silver and Miller (1997) is recommended.

There is a large literature on gender differences in language and language use in English and other languages; see Holmes and Meyerhoff (2003) for an excellent collection of articles. Finlayson (1995) discusses 'women's language of respect' in Xhosa (Niger-Congo, South Africa); Bradley (1988) deals with grammatical and lexical differences between men's and women's varieties in Yanyuwa.

Books dealing with social aspects of bilingualism and multilingualism include Myers-Scotton (1993) and Romaine (1995); see also Romaine (2001).

A short overview of language shift and endangerment can be found in Chapter 8 of Mesthrie et al. (2000). For fuller treatments see Grenoble and Whaley (1998) and Tsunoda (2005); Grenoble and Whaley (2006) deals with language maintenance and revitalization. McGregor (2003) provides fuller details on the language situation of Nyulnyul. Abley (2003) presents a non-technical and very readable travelogue of his journeys searching for endangered languages. However, be warned that Abley adopts an extreme Whorfian stance (see §8.1), and shows considerable linguistic naivety.

Issues for further thought and exercises

1. Below are some words characteristic of different major dialects of English, including British, American, Australian and New Zealand. Identify which dialect(s) each belongs to. (Columns do not show dialects.)

   a. *faucet*   *tap*
   b. *dyke*   *toilet*   *bathroom*
   c. *truck*   *lorry*
   d. *g'day*   *hi*   *hello*
   e. *gas*   *petrol*
   f. *drugstore*   *chemist*
   g. *diaper*   *nappy*

2. Which dialects do you think the following pronunciations represent?
   a. [fɪʃ]   'fish'
   b. [mɔɪnɪŋ]   'morning'
   c. [səi]   'see'

    d. [tʃips]   'chips'
    e. [næɒ]   'now'

3. List as many gender differences as you can in English or another language you speak. Classify the differences according to whether they are phonetic, phonological, intonational, lexical, grammatical, pragmatic or interactive (i.e. differences in the organization of speech interaction).

4. In one of his investigations Labov was interested in post-vocalic *r* as a sociolinguistic variable: in New York English it is a prestige feature. He visited three department stores in New York and asked the attendant a question that would elicit the answer *fourth floor*; for example, he might have asked *Excuse me, where are women's shoes?* Both words *fourth* and *floor* could of course be pronounced with or without the rhotic following the vowel. The three department stores varied from lower to higher prices, which he expected would correlate with the socio-economic status of the clientele. Labov pretended he did not hear the answer, and asked for a repetition. He found that there were more instances of post-vocalic *r* in *floor* than *fourth*. Why would this be? He also found more instances of post-vocalic *r* in the speech of attendants in the more expensive stores, and a higher frequency of this variable on the repetition. Labov interprets this as indicative of differences in the frequency of post-vocalic *r* across the social varieties of New York speech. Given that the attendants in all of the stores would presumably be working class, how would you account his conclusions?

5. Compile a list of lexical items characteristic of some professional register (such as education, law, music, medicine). Give an explanation of each term in informal style. Do you think that use of informal style rather than the professional register would be helpful in making professional writing in these domains more accessible to the layman? Do you think that the professional register could be entirely replaced by an informal style: or to put things another way, is the only function of professional registers to exclude non-members of the profession? Explain your reasons.

6. What linguistic features (such as modes of delivery (i.e. in terms of the phonetic properties of delivery of the message), lexicon and grammar) do you think would characterize the difference between the registers of spoken science and sports commentating? Listen to an example of each on television, and test your expectations. Be alert also for other differences than those you expected.

7. Below are examples of words in a Pig Latin variety of French called Verlan. Explain the way Verlan words are formed from the corresponding French words.

	French	**Verlan**	**English**
a.	*blouson* /bluzõ/	*zomblou*	'jacket'
b.	*bloquer* /blɔke/	*québlo*	'to block'
c.	*père* /pɛːʀ/	*reupé*	'father'
d.	*zonard* /zonaːʀ/	*narzo*	'person who lives in a suburb of Paris'
e.	*jeter* /ʒ(ə)te/	*téjé*	'to throw'
f.	*cresson* /kʀɛsõ/	*soncré*	'watercress'
g.	*démon* /dɛmõ/	*mondé*	'demon'

8. Discuss the different opinions on language death embodied in the following two quotes:

    a. The last fluent speaker of Damin [a secret language spoken by initiated men among the Lardil of Mornington Island, North Queensland] passed away several years ago. The destruction of this intellectual treasure was carried out, for the most part, by people who were not aware of its existence, coming as they did from a culture in which wealth is physical and visible. Damin was not visible for them, and as far as they were concerned, the Lardil people had no wealth, apart from land. (Hale et al. 1992: 40)

(Continued)

Issues for further thought and exercises—Cont'd

b. As a linguist I am of course saddened by the vast amount of linguistic and cultural knowledge that is disappearing, and I am delighted that the National Science Foundation has sponsored our UCLA research, in which we try to record for posterity the phonetic structures of some of the languages that will not be around for much longer. But it is not for me to assess the virtues of programmes for language preservation versus those of competitive programmes for tuberculosis eradication, which may also need government funds . . .

Last summer I was working on Dahalo, a rapidly dying Cushitic language, spoken by a few hundred people in a rural district of Kenya. I asked one of our consultants whether his teenaged sons spoke Dahalo. 'No', he said. 'They can still hear it, but cannot speak it. They speak only Swahili.' he was smiling when he said it, and did not seem to regret it. He was proud that his sons had been to school and knew things that he did not. Who am I to say that he was wrong? (Ladefoged 1992: 810–811)

Notes

1. The stød, or creaky voice, is an effect produced by slow and irregular vibrations of just one end of the vocal cords; it sounds a bit like the noise of a door swinging on unoiled hinges. The Danish stød is a prosodic feature associated with certain syllables.

2. Genders or noun classes are systems in which the nouns of a language are divided into different groups according to the forms taken by syntactically related items such as demonstratives and adjectives in the NP. For example, standard Danish distinguishes two genders (sometimes called common and neuter) that are indicated by the form of articles, determiners and adjectives. Thus the article *en* 'a' goes with nouns such as *mand* 'man', *kvinde* 'woman', *øl* 'beer', indicating that these nouns are of the common gender; by contrast the article *et* 'a' goes with nouns like *land* 'country', *hæfte* 'notebook' and *tog* 'train'.

3. More recently, it has been argued that the variety now spoken by children at Daguragu and Kalkaringi is a new language variety, a mixed language (see §13.4) involving components of Gurindji and Kriol, rather than a simplified form of Gurindji (Meakins and O'Shannessy 2004).

Psycholinguistics: Language, the Mind and the Brain 8

In this chapter we develop our second take on language as a human phenomenon, considering it from the perspective of the individuals who use it. Our focus is on human beings as speakers and hearers, and the biological and psychological attributes that on the one hand are requirements for our possession of language, and on the other hand permit us to engage effortlessly and rapidly in the production and comprehension of speech. Another important set of concerns are the relations between language and other cognitive phenomena, the question of where language fits within our mental system.

Chapter contents

Goals

The goals of the chapter are to:
- explore the relation between language and thought, and discuss the Sapir-Whorf hypothesis, that the structure of the language we speak influences how we think about the world;
- mention some modern revisions to the Sapir-Whorf hypothesis;
- present some fundamental facts about speech production and perception, and comment on what they indicate about the mental organization of language;
- introduce some important experimental methods used in studying speech processing;
- overview the basic physiology of the brain;
- introduce the main questions in the study of neurolinguistics; and
- outline the main methods of investigating neurolinguistics.

Key terms

anomic aphasia

arculate fasciculus

Broca's area

Broca's aphasia

categorical perception

cerebral cortex

conduction aphasia

contralateral control

dichotic listening test

electroencephalo-
grams (EEGs)

exchange errors

functional magnetic
resonance imaging
(fMRI)

garden path
sentences

global aphasia

lateralization

lexical lookup

localization

magnetoencephalo-
grams (MEGs)

neurolinguistics

neuron

positron emission
tomography (PET)

psycholinguistics

Sapir-Whorf
hypothesis

slips of the tongue

split-brain patients

spoonerisms

Wada test

Wernicke's area

Wernicke's aphasia

8.1 Language and cognition

We begin with the relation between language and other forms of cognition. On this hotly debated issue there is as yet no consensus amongst linguists or psycholinguists. At one extreme is the notion that language forms a distinct module separate from other cognitive processes; this view tends to be associated with linguists and psychologists working within formal theories of language, for example, Noam Chomsky, Jerry Fodor and Stephen Pinker. At the other extreme is the idea that there is no distinction between the cognitive processes employed in language and those employed in other domains of thought; this view is associated with investigators working within functionally oriented paradigms, including Ronald Langacker, George Lakoff and Talmy Givón. We will not enter this debate, but merely comment that the balance of evidence seems to favour an intermediate position: a degree of separateness, along with commonalities with other cognitive phenomena.

Language and thought: the Sapir-Whorf hypothesis

We discuss instead a related question: is there a relationship between the language one speaks and the way one thinks about and conceptualizes the world? One highly influential idea holds that the answer is in the affirmative: the structure of the language we speak does correlate with the way we think. This idea goes back a long way, at least to Wilhelm von Humboldt (1767–1835), and more recently to Franz Boas (1858–1942), Edward Sapir (1884–1939) and Benjamin Lee Whorf (1897–1941). It is now referred to as the **Sapir-Whorf hypothesis**, often just the **Whorfian hypothesis**.

The Sapir-Whorf hypothesis can be separated into two components. The first is the principle of **linguistic relativity**, according to which lexical and grammatical differences between languages correlate with non-linguistic cognitive differences. For instance, the existence of a number of terms for similar objects in a language – say 'mound', 'ridge', 'hill', 'mesa', 'plateau', 'cape' and 'mountain' – will correlate (according to this principle) with different ways of habitually thinking about geographical projections, while if a single term is used it is likely that the range of objects will be regarded as the same. The principle of relativity holds that language and habitual modes of thought are correlated; it does not presume a causal relation between them.

The second aspect of the Sapir-Whorf hypothesis is the stronger principle of **linguistic determinism**, the notion that differences in cognitive styles between cultures, differences in their habitual ways of thinking, are due to differences in the grammatical and semantic systems of the languages. Thus thinking about the geographical features 'mound', 'ridge', 'hill', 'mesa', 'plateau', 'cape' and 'mountain' as either different or the same would be a consequence of the language system, in this case the lexicon.

Whorf is usually understood to have advocated linguistic determinism, though his stance was often equivocal. His thinking was more sophisticated than simple examples like the above might suggest. He considered that it was not only lexical features that are relevant, but, more importantly, grammatical structures. Thus he contrasted the linear notion of time shared by speakers of English, in which time progresses ever onwards into the future, with a cyclic view of time he attributed to speakers of Hopi (Uto-Aztecan, USA). An aspect of this difference, Whorf suggested, was related to the presence of tenses in English, which is consistent with a time line extending indefinitely into the future, and their absence in Hopi. (His analysis of Hopi as a tenseless language has been criticized by some later investigators, notably Malotki 1983.)

This single difference between Hopi and English is not telling: absence of tenses does not logically imply a cyclical view of time. Whorf sought not just single isolated lexical or grammatical features, but sets of linguistic phenomena that interlock in a system. In the case of the Hopi notion of time, he linked the absence of tenses with other facts about the language, including expressions used for quantifying time. Rather than measuring by numbers of units such as days, they used expressions like 'the fourth day'. This, Whorf averred, was consistent with the notion of cyclical time, repetition of events of the same type in cycles of days.

Revisions to the Sapir-Whorf hypothesis

The Sapir-Whorf hypothesis was subjected to intensive empirical testing by linguists, anthropologists and psychologists in 1950s and 1960s. One semantic domain that was tested early on was colour terms, since languages were known to differ in the range of distinctions they make. A classic study by Eleanor Heider investigated colour perception among the speakers of Dani (Papuan, Papua), which distinguishes just two colour terms (Heider 1972). The investigation revealed that Dani speakers could distinguish colours not distinguished lexically, and recognized focal colours (the shades considered to be the most typical of the colour in a language that has a lexical item for it) better than non-focal colours.[1]

This argues against an extreme determinism, that the structure of one's language determines perception. It does not, however, refute a weaker version that language may affect the ease of distinguishing and remembering colours. And indeed, the weaker version has been supported by some empirical findings. One experimental study (Kay and Kempson 1984) involved speakers of English and Tarahumara (Uto-Aztecan, Mexico), a language that does not have separate terms for 'blue' and 'green'. Three colour chips were presented to each participant on each trial, from which the participant was to pick the odd one out. In some trials two chips were quite close in actual physical colour (i.e. wavelength of reflected light), but would be classified as *blue* and *green* by speakers of English; a third chip was a focal green, but more distant in physical colour from the other green than the green was from the blue. Whereas the Tarahumara speakers chose the chips that were closest in physical colour, speakers of English selected the two chips that would be labelled *green*.

Following something of a lull from the early 1970s, the Sapir-Whorf hypothesis has recently made a comeback, and reappeared in new guises, stimulating some intriguing new research. One revision that has yielded interesting results is encapsulated in Dan Slobin's aphorism **thinking for speaking**: the nature of the language we speak influences the way we think for speaking (Slobin 1996a). The focus is on the dynamic processes of thinking rather than on 'thought' as an abstract phenomenon.

Slobin examined stories told by children about a wordless picture book, and showed that speakers of different languages attend to different aspects of the depicted situations in constructing stories. They are forced to do so by grammatical features of their language. Thus, speakers of English attend to whether an event is in progress, and pay a good deal of attention to paths of motion; speakers of Spanish, by contrast pay attention to whether an event is completed or not. This is a consequence of differences between English and Spanish in the semantic structure of motion verbs, and the grammatical categories distinguished in verbs.

If the thinking for speaking version of the Sapir-Whorf hypothesis can be sustained, one could then look beyond, and examine whether there are extensions beyond, to other cognitive domains. Recent work by Stephen Levinson and John Haviland has advanced this style of argument for spatial terms in some languages: that the spatial distinctions and categories speakers need to attend to for speaking are carried over to other aspects of cognition.

Many Australian languages resemble the Pama-Nyungan language Guugu Yimithirr in using the cardinal direction terms 'north', 'south', 'east' and 'west' to specify relative locations of objects and directions of travel rather than body-centred terms 'left' and 'right'. The system of cardinals is used even for identifying parts of the body: if I was facing north, I would refer to an itch in my west ear rather than my left ear. To speak Guugu Yimithirr properly requires that you pay attention to the cardinal directions. Levinson argues that this extends beyond thinking for speaking, and that Guugu Yimithirr people carry this type of thinking over to spatial behaviour generally (Levinson 1997). For example, suppose you are facing a table on which three objects have been laid out, as shown in Figure 8.1. You are asked to turn around 180° to face the other table, and place the three objects in the same arrangement on this table. How do you place them?

Most speakers of English and Dutch orient the objects on the second table according to a body-centred system, so that the donut goes in the centre, with the star to the right, and the pencil to the left of it. But speakers of Guugu Yimithirr tend to place the objects so they maintain their absolute cardinal orientations. So if you were facing west to begin with,

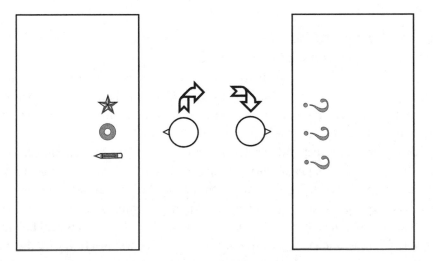

Figure 8.1 A version of Levinson's spatial arrangement experiment.

the star will be placed to the north on the second table, the doughnut in the middle, and the pencil to the south. Speakers of Guugu Yimithirr and English (or Dutch) tend to place the star on opposite sides of the doughnut. It seems that the cognitive system employed for speaking about space also influences thinking about space for other types of behaviour.

8.2 Language processing

Imagine a communication system in which there is a fixed set of symbols and a fixed set of meanings that they can convey, such as a system of semaphore flags signalling messages about a limited range of movements of a vehicle. Production and understanding of signs within such a system by a human operator might be a simple process of linking existing meanings with pre-determined flags or flag positions. Such a psychological process could not work for speech production or comprehension, where the range of possible meanings is not laid out in advance: speakers make new meanings that have never been made before, occasionally using new forms not previously used or not yet conventionalized. Speakers must have mental models that permit them to construct and interpret novel forms, as well as to assign appropriate meanings to them. For language processing therefore, human beings must have not just an internalized lexicon, but also grammar of their language, that they access in production and comprehension.

A major concern of psycholinguistics is to develop models of these mental grammars and lexicons, and the psychological processes by which they can be accessed in speech production and comprehension. In this section we outline some of the basic features of speech processing that must be accounted for in any model.

Comprehension

Perception of speech sounds
Four difficulties in perception of speech sounds
A crucial component of the comprehension of speech is processing the sounds that reach the hearer's ears. This is no trivial task. Recall from §2.1 and Figure 2.1 that speech sounds form a continuous stream, rather than a sequence of discrete sounds; the boundaries between the sounds are indistinct, as are the boundaries between words.

True, there are sometimes indications of boundaries in the speech signal. Words are occasionally separated from neighbouring words by pauses. And an allophone of a phoneme can indicate the position of the phoneme within a word. For example, *great ape* and *grey tape* could be distinguished by an aspirated [tʰ] in *grey tape*, that would not normally occur in *great ape*. On the other hand, realization of the /t/ as [d] or [ɾ] would be most likely in *great ape*. (This is not to say that these minimal pairs would always be distinguished in pronunciation.) By the same token, allophony also contributes to processing difficulties since it means that quite different stretches of sound – for example, [nɒtʔætʔɔːɫ], [nɒtætɔːɫ] and [nɒdədɔːɫ] – must be recognized as representing the same sequence of words, *not at all*. The third form, moreover, admits another interpretation. (What is it?)

Another source of difficulty in processing comes from the extreme variations within the sound wave between speakers. The sound waves of *The farmer kills the duckling* spoken by a child, a woman, a speaker of British English and a speaker of New Zealand English, would be quite different to the sound wave for my production. The hearer has to factor out the differences in the acoustic signal that reaches their ears, and recognize that the distinct sound waves represent the same sentence – while at the same time recognizing that other equally minor differences in the sound wave indicate different sentences.

The fact that speech often occurs in a noisy environment gives rise to a further difficulty in processing. We must ignore large components of the sound that reaches our ears (the TV blaring, children screaming, traffic on a nearby highway, etc.) in processing speech, while at the same time not necessarily ignoring them entirely.

> An interesting variant on the observation that speakers ignore components of the sounds that reach their ears as irrelevant to language is that if you listen to speech in a click language such as Zulu (Niger-Congo, South Africa), the clicks will probably sound like non-linguistic noises going on at the same time as the spoken word. Speakers of non-click languages have strategies for separating speech sounds from non-speech sounds that do not always give the correct results when applied to a click language.

Categorical nature of speech perception

An important feature of the perception of speech sounds is that it is **categorical**. When you hear a stretch of speech you categorize the phones as phonemes, ignoring the physical differences between them. You do not perceive a bilabial stop as now having a long VOT (see §2.3), now an average length VOT, now an very short VOT: a speaker of English perceives it as either a /b/ or a /p/; a speaker of Warrwa would, by contrast, categorize it as the single phoneme /b/, regardless of the length of VOT.

Experiments have been done in which aspects of the sound signal of speech (or artificial machine-generated speech) are modified by small degrees, and presented to experimental subjects. For instance, the VOT of the initial stop of [ba] might be varied in increments of 10 ms from −10 to +80 ms. When you listen to the sequence of syllables, you do not hear a gradual increase in VOT; rather, at a certain point you hear a definite switch from [ba] to [pa]. By contrast, if you listen to a musical tone that varies from 200 Hertz (cycles per second) to 1000 Hertz, you don't hear it as suddenly jumping at some point from low to high pitch.

Role of vision

In a face-to-face conversation you not only hear your interlocutor, you also see them. Indeed, conversational partners typically spend a good deal of time looking at their interlocutors' faces while speaking to them. The visual channel provides additional information to the hearer that can assist in the perception of the spoken word, especially in a noisy environment. Try turning your television sound down to a point where you can only just hear what is being said by a newsreader, and then turn away. What do you notice? A particularly good illustration of the relevance of visual cues comes from the so-called McGurk effect, named after Harry McGurk, the psychologist who first observed it.

Identification and recognition of words

Recognition of words involves more than just **bottom-up processing**, processing of the incoming sound waves on a phoneme-by-phoneme basis. Hearers also use clues from the wider context, including the sentential environment, to help identification of words. Processing involves **top-down** aspects as well. Experimental subjects make fewer errors in identifying words in sentences than when the same words are presented in isolation. Further evidence is provided by experiments in which segments of speech are removed without affect on comprehension. In one study the [s] representing the plural morpheme -*s* in sentences such as *Cats like fish* was replaced by a cough. Hearers reported hearing the fricative even though it was not present in the actual sound wave; in fact, when told that a sound was missing, they could not accurately identify which one it was.

Other factors are known to affect the identification of words. Frequency is one: high-frequency words are processed more quickly and easily than low-frequency words, and are more readily identified in noisy conditions. Also relevant is the existence of phonologically similar words, which have the effect of slowing down identification through interference. In one experiment it was shown that if word frequency is held constant, words with many phonologically similar neighbours – that is, words differing from the target word by a single phoneme – are identified more slowly than words with few neighbours.

Recall from §6.2 that words often have a number of different senses, and may be homophonous with other words. Experimental evidence suggests that even when they appear in a sentence, words immediately invoke a range of polysemous senses, as well as homophonous words; the appropriate sense or lexical item is selected only after a slight delay. The experiments use lexical decision tasks, in which sentences with a polysemous word like *bug* are presented to subjects through headphones; shortly after the word *bug* is heard, a target form is presented on a screen, to which the subjects should respond by indicating (usually by pressing a button) as quickly as possible whether or not it is a word. The word *bug* in a sentence such as *For several weeks after the exterminator's visit they did not find a single bug in the apartment* immediately facilitates the recognition of both *insect* and *spy*, decreasing the time taken to recognize them as words. However, after a few hundred milliseconds only *insect* is facilitated, suggesting that within this very brief space of time the other interpretations have been discarded as irrelevant.

Comprehension of sentences

Comprehension of sentences involves not just **lexical lookup**, the identification of the component words (as discussed in the previous subsection), but also **parsing**, the assignment of a grammatical structure to the sentence.

Parsing begins immediately from the very beginning of an utterance: hearers do not wait until the entire utterance has been produced before they begin processing it, as any self-respecting grammarian would. Evidence from conversational interaction indicates that interactants continually monitor what is being said, projecting what is to follow; they switch speaker and hearer roles so rapidly that there is often no gap in speech. This would be impossible if processing was delayed until the end of utterances.

There is a downside to beginning parsing so soon. In sentences like *The horse raced past the barn fell* – called **garden path sentences** – beginning parsing from the start of the sentence results in *raced* being interpreted as the main verb in the intransitive clause *the horse raced past the barn*. But then the next word is inconsistent with this analysis; the only possibility is that *raced past the barn* is part of an NP with *the horse* (i.e. *the horse that was raced past the barn*).

Intonation and prosody sometimes provide cues to parsing sentences, including garden path sentences.

Production

Production of sentences does not proceed on a one-phone-at-a-time or a one-word-at-a-time basis, with each phone or word being processed sequentially, in their order in the utterance. Rather, entire sentences are planned ahead of time, before the any part is produced. That this is so finds support in speech errors or **slips of the tongue**. As it turns out, these are not random. Many errors involve exchanges with later elements, indicating that larger units must have already been conceptualized.

Exchange errors occur at all levels. At the phonological level are **spoonerisms**, named in honour of the Oxford don Reverend A. Spooner (1844–1930), who was renowned for this type of error. Among the famous spoonerisms attributed to him are *Let us drink a toast to our very queer dean*; and *You've hissed all my mystery lectures and tasted the whole worm*. The transpositions of these two examples are typical, and involve switching of phonemes from identical positions in syllables in nearby lexical words, indicating the significance of the syllable as a processing unit. One does not find errors like *to our very near queed*, where the transposed phonemes are from different syllabic positions. Moreover, it is typically consonants in syllable-initial position that are transposed.[2]

At the morphological level are errors in which lexical morphemes are transposed; the bound morphological markers normally remain in place, as in *slicely thinned* for *thinly sliced*, where each lexeme gets the morphological marking appropriate to its position and role in the phrase.

At the syntactic level are transposition of lexemes within syntactic constructions, as in *He is writing a mother to his letter*. Such errors are like spoonerisms in that transposed words normally come from the same phrasal position.

These errors reveal another important characteristic of speech errors: choice of phonologically conditioned allomorph (see §3.4) is in accordance with the replacing item, not the replaced item. Thus the allomorph of *-ed* in *thinned* is /d/, the allomorph appropriate to *thin*, not to *slice* (which takes voiceless /t/); and if instead of *mother* in the example of the previous paragraph we had *aunt*, *an* would have been chosen as the allomorph of the indefinite article, not *a* – *He is writing an aunt to his letter*, not *He is writing a aunt to his letter*.

Exchange errors are not the only types of error that occur in speech. Another type is anticipatory errors, where a later form is anticipated, as in *kindler and gentler*. There are also wrong word choices, where a phonologically or semantically similar word occurs instead of the intended word, for example, *sexton* instead of *sextant*. Errors can also be mixed, involving both phonological and semantic components, as in *The competition is a little strougher* where *strougher* is a blend of *stronger* and *tougher*.

Based on speech errors, it has been suggested that syntactic constructions are planned about two clauses in advance, whereas phonological structures are constructed about one clause ahead (Garrett 1988). Of course, the content of the message to be communicated must also be planned ahead, a task which is typically more attention-demanding than the relatively automatic and unconscious processes involved in linguistic planning. But the two must be carefully coordinated so that the right information is processed and expressed in language at the right time. The language production system and more general processes of cognition must work together in concert, and cannot be entirely separate.

Relations between production and comprehension

Speech comprehension and production are both complex processes that are only partly understood. They are not mirror-images – comprehension is not production put into reverse; the available evidence suggests that at least some of the psychological mechanisms involved are different. For one thing, as we have seen, in production entire utterances are planned ahead of time; in comprehension, by contrast, parsing appears to be at least to some extent incremental, beginning with the first word. If it were the precise reverse of production, it would operate on complete utterances.

On the other hand, comprehension and production cannot be entirely separate processes. Speakers monitor their own speech production and correct errors – recall the feedback loop in the speech chain model (see §2.1). This suggests that the comprehension system is involved at least to some extent in speech production. Conversely, according to one theory of speech perception, the motor theory, processing does not just involve processing of acoustic signals reaching the brain from the ear. It also involves matching these signals against mentally reconstructed sub-vocalized sequences of articulations; thus the acoustic signal would be analysed at least in part via reconstruction of its production.

8.3 Language and the brain

Basic structure of the human brain

The human brain, which is roughly spherical in shape, is divided into two hemispheres, the left hemisphere and the right hemisphere; these are connected by a bundle of nerves called the corpus callosum. Bodily experiences and control are largely **contra-lateral**; that is, each hemisphere manages the opposite side of the body.

The outer layer of the brain, the **cerebral cortex**, is a layer about 2–4 millimetres in thickness, made up of the cell bodies of several billion brain cells or **neurons**. Many cognitive functions are located in the cortex. The cerebral cortex is deeply folded and fissured, and is divided into four main lobes (in each hemisphere), the frontal lobe, the parietal lobe, the occipital lobe and the temporal lobe. These are shown in Figure 8.2.

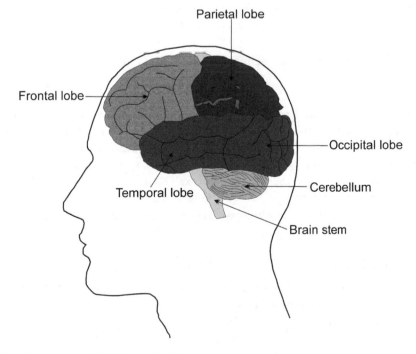

Figure 8.2 Major structures of the human brain.

Also shown in Figure 8.2 are the brain stem, which controls the automatic functions necessary to keep the body alive (e.g. the beating of the heart), and the cerebellum, which helps control movement and cognitive processes requiring precise timing.

The branch of psycholinguistics concerned with the brain is called **neurolinguistics**.

Localization and lateralization

In 1848 in Vermont in the USA, Phineas Gage, a railway foreman, was tamping gunpowder into a blasting hole in a rock, when it exploded. The three-and-a-half-foot (a bit over a metre) long tamping rod was projected through Phineas' left cheek and out through the top of his forehead, falling some fifty metres distant. Remarkably, Phineas never lost consciousness, was fully aware of what had happened, and survived for many years after the injury. His language abilities were unaffected; however, within a few months of the accident his personality had changed dramatically.

This story is consistent with **localization** of certain cognitive functions in particular regions of the brain. In particular, it suggests that the extreme front part of the brain is the site for emotions; language ability must be localized elsewhere, as must vision and motor control of the limbs.

Although there are disagreements concerning the precise details and extent, it seems certain that language is localized to some degree. Thus, in most individuals the left hemisphere is more dominant in language processing than the right. Most right-handers show left hemisphere domination, as do most left-handers (thought the proportion is slightly lower). This is **lateralization**.

Two areas in the dominant hemisphere are particularly important in language processing:

- **Broca's area**, named after Paul Broca, a nineteenth-century French physician and anthropologist, is a small patch in the anterior (front) part of the temporal lobe of the language-dominant hemisphere about two centimetres across. If you put your finger to your head just above the left temple, that's about where it is. Broca's area is believed to be associated with speech production.
- **Wernicke's area**, named after the German physician Carl Wernicke, is a slightly larger area than Broca's, and located further towards the posterior (back) of the brain. Put your finger just above and slightly behind the left ear. Wernicke's area is believed to be associated with speech comprehension.

Figure 8.3 shows the approximate locations of Broca's and Wernicke's areas, as well as some other major brain areas of the left hemisphere. Broca's and Wernicke's areas are connected by a bundle of nerve fibres called the **arculate fasciculus** (not shown).

As mentioned already, investigators are not in universal agreement as to the extent to which language is localized in the brain. There is evidence of a fair degree of plasticity in the human brain, whereby one region can take over the functions of another region that has been damaged. There is also evidence of considerable variation among individuals.

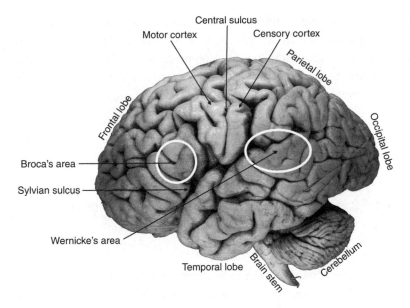

Figure 8.3 (a) and (b). Some of the major areas of the left hemisphere of the brain. (Source http://brainmuseum. org/, supported by the National Science Foundation.)

Evidence for localization

Much evidence has been adduced in favour of some degree of localization of language functions in the brain. Below we discuss five different types of evidence. This evidence is mostly indirect, coming from circumstances in which things fail to function properly.

Aphasia

Aphasia is an impairment of language function (as distinct from muscular paralysis of the speech organs) due to brain damage, often as a result of a stroke, a tumour, or head injury. The original evidence for Broca's and Wernicke's as language centres came from post-mortem studies of aphasic patients. Broca and Wernicke both found associations between certain types of aphasia and damage to the regions of the brains of their patients named after them.

Broca's aphasia

In 1861 Paul Broca described the results of an autopsy he performed on a patient by the name of Leborgne, who had suffered severe aphasia for more than two decades. Leborgne was able to utter no more than a few swear words and the syllable Tan, after which he is often named. By use of gestures, however, he was able to answer some questions, and he understood much of what was said to him. The autopsy revealed extensive damage in the area now known as Broca's area.

Broca subsequently found similar damage to the brains of almost a score of other aphasic patients displaying similar impairments in speech production. In this type of aphasia – called

Broca's aphasia or **agrammatic aphasia** – the person experiences difficulties in the production of fluent speech and the almost exclusive use of lexical words at the expense of grammatical morphemes, which are rarely used. Comprehension of speech by Broca's aphasics is typically much better than production. These features are illustrated in the following utterance by a patient who was asked why he had returned to hospital:

(8-1) *Ah . . . Monday . . . ah Dad and Paul . . . and Dad . . . hospital. Two . . . ah . . . doctors . . . and ah . . . thirty minutes . . . and yes . . . ah . . . hospital. And er Wednesday . . . nine o'clock. And er Thursday, ten o'clock . . . doctors. Two doctors . . . and ah . . . teeth*

Deaf patients with damage to Broca's area show similar deficits in sign language, namely, dysfluency and agrammaticism, but relatively intact comprehension. This suggests that Broca's area is specialized for language, rather than speech as such.

Wernicke's aphasia

Not long after Broca's studies, Carl Wernicke investigated a number of aphasic patients, and found extensive damage in what is now called Wernicke's area. This type of aphasia, called **Wernicke's aphasia** or **fluent aphasia**, is characterized by severe difficulties in comprehension, but quite fluent speech, which is often incomprehensible and may include nonsense words. The following example is an attempt to refer to a kite. Notice that the speaker is clearly trying hard to convey meaning, and that their difficulty lies primarily in finding appropriate words.

(8-2) *It's blowing, on the right, and er there's four letters in it, and I think it begins with a C – goes – when you start it then goes right up in the air – I would I would have to keep racking my brain how I would spell that word – that flies, that that doesn't fly, you pull it round, it goes up in the air.*

Other types of aphasia

Wernicke also described a third type of aphasia, now called **conduction aphasia**, in which the arculate fasciculus (connecting Broca's and Wernicke's areas) suffers damage. Comprehension and fluency of the speech of conduction aphasics is usually little affected. However, sufferers experience difficulties in repeating words spoken by another person, and in monitoring their own speech, thus leading to frequent hesitations and pauses.

Anomic aphasia is the inability to name things seen. Strangely, this does not necessarily extend to things perceived by other means, for example, by touch or smell. This type of aphasia manifests itself in a variety of different forms: some people lose words for only vegetables, or just words for inanimates. One case reported is of two women who had no trouble with nouns, but severe difficulty with verbs. For words with dual membership, such as *milk*, they experienced no difficulty with the word used as a noun, but couldn't cope with it as a verb. There is no evidence of any specific site for brain damage giving rise to anomic aphasia. In the following example, notice that the patient cannot find the noun *comb*, although she uses the verb *comb*.

(8-3) Doctor: *Can you tell me what this is?* [Showing, a pen]

Patient: *Geez, you know . . . isn't that funny, oh I know, it's one of those things, . . . it's. . . . it's funny, you know . . . I know that it is . . . you know . . . it's hummmm . . . it's one of those things.*

Doctor: *How about this?* [Produces a comb]

Patient: *Ooohhh. . . . isn't that funny . . . I'm getting old . . . it's so terrible, ohhh . . . you know . . . I just . . . it's that funny, oh geez . . . you know . . . I know, it's that thing you use to comb your hair with.*

Mark Ashcraft, a cognitive psychologist, describes an episode in which he suffered from a temporary restriction of blood flow to part of his brain while working late in the office one evening. He suddenly found himself unable to understand familiar labels on the computer printouts, and could not remember any of the terms of his profession. He describes the episode as follows:

> The most powerful realization I had during the episode, and the most intriguing aspect to me since then, was the dissociation between a thought and the word or phrase that expresses the thought. The subjective experience consisted of knowing with complete certainty the idea or concept I was trying to express and being completely unable to find and utter the word that expresses the idea or concept. (Ashcraft 1993: 49)

Global aphasia, as the label suggests, involves disturbance to all language functions, to all processing components. Global aphasia typically involves damage to large portion of frontal and temporal lobes.

Summary of aphasia types

Table 8.1 summarizes the main features of the five types of aphasia, according to the standard or classical model.

Table 8.1 The five classical types of aphasia

Syndrome	Symptoms	Location of brain lesion
Broca's aphasia	Utterances typically short, with grammatical morphemes usually omitted; speech effortful and non-fluent. Comprehension much better.	Broca's area; front part of the temporal lobe and back part of the frontal lobe
Wernicke's aphasia	Poor comprehension, but fluent production that is often incomprehensible. Use of nonsense words common.	Wernicke's area; back part of temporal lobe
Conduction aphasia	Problems with repetition of speech, though comprehension is usually good. Sound and meaning appear disconnected. Reasonably fluent, though rhythm of speech may be disrupted by pauses and hesitations.	Arculate fasciculus; bundle of connect-ing Broca's and Wernicke's areas
Anomic aphasia	Inability to name things or events. Use of circumlocutions.	No specific location
Global aphasia	Disturbance to all language functions.	Large part of frontal and temporal lobes

Problems of interpretation

The account of aphasia presented in the previous subsections that links the type of aphasia with language centres in the brain can be criticized on more than one count. As Sigmund Freud pointed out, we can't conclude that a function is localized in a certain area of the brain because damage to that area results in aphasia. It could be that the area is involved in a crucial way in the task that is widely distributed across areas of the cortex; for instance, it could be where several lines of connection cross.

Henry Head, who studied language disturbances resulting from gunshot wounds to the head in the 1920s, found a wide range of aphasic symptoms among individuals with similar injuries. He concluded that the classification into Broca's, Wernicke's and conduction aphasias was not clear cut.

One can also question the extent to which it is valid to draw conclusions about localization of brain function from autopsies. It could be that many changes to brain functions, as well as to the damage itself, took place between the onset of aphasia and the death of the patient. Indeed, aphasics often develop ways of compensating for their injuries, revealing a remarkable degree of plasticity in brain function.

Split-brains

Studies of patients who have had one of their hemispheres removed provide some evidence of lateralization of language processes. Removal of the right hemisphere, an operation sometimes performed in cases of malignant brain tumours, usually does not result in the loss of language, though other cognitive processes may be affected.

Another clinical procedure that used sometimes to be used on patients suffering from epilepsy was to surgically cut the corpus callosum connecting the two hemispheres of the brain, in the hope that this would prevent the spread of the seizure from one hemisphere to another. It also prevents the sharing of information between the two parts of the brain. With the corpus callosum severed, the two hemispheres are effectively separate mental entities; this condition is called **split-brain**. Certain information will reach only the right hemisphere, and other information only the left hemisphere.

If the image of an object is presented to the right visual field of a split-brain patient, this will be processed by the left hemisphere, and the object can be named. If it is presented to the left visual field, it will be processed by the right hemisphere, and cannot be named. In one experimental study, a word was presented to the left visual field of a split-brain patient, who was to select by feel the correct object from a group of objects behind a screen. This could be done, though when asked what the object was, the person would reply 'I don't know.' This was their left hemisphere doing the talking, unaware of what the right hemisphere knew. This experiment reveals that the right hemisphere is capable of at least some linguistic processing, such as identifying an object by name. Some studies have shown that the right hemisphere is capable of processing concrete lexemes, but poor at more abstract items, though this finding is controversial.

Dichotic listening

The **dichotic listening test** is an experimental technique for determining which hemisphere is dominant in language processing in an individual. It relies on the contralateral processing of sensory input by the brain. The subject wears a set of headphones through which two different signals – which might be syllables, numbers or words – are input simultaneously.

Most people show a right-ear advantage: that is, it is the signal played into the right ear that most people tend to correctly identify. If *boy* is played in the left ear, and *girl* in the right, it is most likely that the subject will report hearing *girl*, the word played in their right ear. This is consistent with left-hemisphere dominance for language processing for most people. This is because the signal received through the left ear will be sent first to the right hemisphere, and only then via the corpus callosum to the left hemisphere for processing. The signal coming from the right ear will be processed earlier, since it goes directly to the left hemisphere.

By contrast, when the sounds played in the headphones are not speech sounds, for example, music, coughs, traffic noise and so on, a left-ear advantage tends to be shown. So, if the sound of laughing is played in the left ear, and coughing in the right ear, subjects are more likely to perceive the laughing input.

The specializations of the two ears may have more to do with the nature of the processing than the physical type of sound that is input. Thus speakers of Thai, a tone language (recall §2.5), reveal a left-hemisphere advantage when distinguishing CV syllables contrasting in tone, whereas English subjects show a right-hemisphere advantage. It has been suggested that the real distinction is between the analytical processing performed in the left brain (which includes many aspects of the processing of the linguistic signal) and the holistic processing of the right brain of most people.

Wada test

The Japanese neurosurgeon Juhn Wada devised a test to determine which hemisphere is dominant in language processing by injecting sodium amytal into the carotid arteries of neck. The result is deactivation of the ipsilateral (same side) hemisphere of the brain, and immediate contralateral paralysis of the body. The patient is asked to count backwards, beginning as the injection is given. Counting is always interrupted when the sodium amytal takes affect, momentarily if it affects the non-dominant hemisphere, for a longer period of one to three minutes if it affects the dominant hemisphere.

Studies such as Rasmussen and Milner (1977) reveal evidence of correlations between handedness and language lateralization. One study conducted by Loring and others in 1990 using tasks such as counting, comprehension, naming and repetition showed that of 103 patients, 79 had exclusive left hemisphere language representation, 2 had exclusively right hemisphere dominance and 22 had bilateral language representation (Loring et al. 1990). Bilateral representation was much higher in left-handers than right-handers.

Brain scanning

Recent advances in technology permit us to study the human brain in operation in relatively normal circumstances. Four technologies are described below that have been used fairly extensively in investigations of brain activity in performing linguistic tasks.

Electroencephalograms

Electroencephalograms or **EEGs** measure electrical activity in the brain resulting from the firing of neurons through electrodes placed on the scalp. In experimental studies involving this technology, the subject is presented with a language task, and the brain activity recorded over a number of trials to determine whether there are consistent changes in activity associated with performing the task.

In one experimental procedure subjects are presented with sentences that end in either expected or unexpected ways – for example, *the pizza was too hot to eat*, or *the pizza was too hot to drink*. A large change in electrical activity is observed some 400 milliseconds following the presentation of an anomalous word, that does not occur following an expected word. This change, known as the N400 component (the N stands for negative), is a reliable indication of an incongruent or unexpected stimulus.

A variant of EEG technology is magnetoencephalography. Magnetoencephalograms (MEGs) measure magnetic fields rather than electrical fields. EEGs and MEGs give very precise indications of timing of brain activity. EEGs give quite imprecise indications of the location of the activity in the brain; MEGs provide more accurate indication of location. The other two technologies, to be described next, give quite precise information about the location of brain activation, but a less precise indication of its timing.

Positron Emission Tomography

Positron emission tomography scanning or **PET scanning** involves injection of a harmless radioactive isotope (often oxygen-15) into the blood stream. Since neurons in the more active areas of the brain require more oxygen, blood flow to that region increases. The PET scanner detects the locations of the radioactive isotope; greater concentrations will be recorded in regions where blood flow is higher. Thus the regions of the brain that are most active in the performance of a task can be mapped in three dimensions.

One PET investigation studied processing of single words under different conditions (Petersen et al. 1989; see also Petersen and Fiez 1993). In the first condition the subject fixated visually on a small point on a monitor while brain activity was measured. In the second stage the subjects fixated on the same point, while words were either presented on the monitor just below the point, or aurally through headphones. In each case, the words were presented at the rate of 40 per minute. Next, subjects were required to say the words they read or heard. And in the final stage, the subjects were requested to give a verb describing an appropriate action for each displayed noun. For example, they might say *eat* in response to the word *cake*. The brain activity associated with the various component tasks can be determined by subtraction. Thus, taking away the level of brain activity associated with the perception of the fixation point from the level of activity associated with the visual or aural perception words can be expected to give an indication of the activity associated with the comprehension of the spoken or written words. Taking the level of activity involved in perception from the level involved in speech production will indicate the activity involved in production of the words, and so on. With this sort of experimental design it is possible to determine the regions of the brain that are most active in specific language-related tasks.

Unsurprisingly, the visual and auditory regions were active in the viewing and hearing conditions; Wernicke's area and large parts of the sensory cortex were also involved in the hearing condition. Broca's area was active in the task of generating verbs, as was an area in the temporal lobe. The speaking words condition was associated with activation in a region between Broca's and Wernicke's areas, and involving parts of the motor and sensory cortexes.

PET scanning suffers from certain disadvantages, most of which are too technical to discuss here. One that we can mention is that since it involves the injection of a radioactive isotope, ethical considerations limit the number and duration of tests an experimental subject can be exposed to.

Functional Magnetic Resonance Imaging

Unlike PET scanning, **functional magnetic resonance imaging** or **fMRI** is a non-invasive technique: that is, it does not require the injection of anything foreign into the blood stream. In fMRI, brain activity is measured indirectly through changes in oxygen levels in the blood stream, measured via different magnetic properties of oxygenated and deoxygenated blood. fMRI has certain advantages over PET: it is faster, gives better spatial resolution, and does not suffer from such severe restrictions on the amount of time, or number of times, a patient can be in the scanner. It is also cheaper.

fMRI is a more recent technology than PET, and a number of investigations carried out with PET have been repeated with fMRI, using the same experimental designs and methods, including cross-task subtraction. The results of the two imaging techniques appear to be in general agreement.

Among the exciting recent developments is the combination of fMRI with EEG or MEG in an attempt to match the high spatial resolution of the former with the excellent temporal resolution of the latter.

Like all technologies fMRI is imperfect, and suffers from disadvantages and limitations as far as neurolinguistic research is concerned. The machinery is noisy, thus decreasing its usefulness in speech perception. Worse, the subject must remain virtually immobile: even tiny movements of the head resulting from jaw movements in speech can affect determination of the location of activity.

Concluding comments

Modern technology permits of observation of the normal human brain in action in conditions increasingly approaching those of natural speech production. Findings from neuroimaging techniques such as PET and fMRI are in overall agreement with findings from earlier post-mortem dissection studies of aphasic patients, and show that Broca's and Wernicke's areas are active in language production and comprehension tasks. This does not argue, as mentioned above, that these areas are **the** language areas. The evidence suggests that language processing and other cognitive tasks are intertwined in the brain, and that strict localization is likely only for elementary cognitive processes, not complex processes such as language. There is growing evidence that language processing is not completely restricted to the dominant hemisphere; the non-dominant hemisphere plays important roles as well, for instance in interpreting metaphoric and figurative language, and humour. One fMRI study revealed a more prominent degree of lateralization in males than females in a rhyme-judgement task.

The role of other brain structures than the cortex is increasingly recognized. Subcortical structures are also important. Damage to some of these areas can lead to certain types of aphasias; moreover, aphasia resulting from damage to Broca's area seems not to be long-lasting if it is restricted to the cortex. There is also evidence that the cerebellum plays a role in language processing beyond mere motor control and coordination.

The human brain shows a degree of plasticity in relation to language and other cognitive functions. It is capable of recovery at least to some extent from damage through deployment of other areas (the neurons themselves are not normally replaced). Studies of individuals who had one hemisphere removed in early childhood have revealed that the other is capable of taking over most language functions.

Summing up

Psycholinguistics enquires into such issues as the relation between language and other mental phenomena, and the processes by which we comprehend and produce speech. It is characterized by major differences of opinion and approach. According to some, language is represented by a distinct **mental module**, largely separate from other modules. Others hold that there is nothing unique about language. Many hold views in between these two extremes.

Another hotly debated issue concerns the relation between language and thought. According to the **Sapir-Whorf hypothesis** the structure of the language one speaks influences one's conceptualization of the world; it comes in stronger and weaker versions: **linguistic determinism** and **linguistic relativity**. A recent reinterpretation is Slobin's **thinking for speaking**.

Speech **comprehension** involves recognition, integration and identification of units and information at all levels. Experimental findings support the idea that comprehension involves both **top-down** and **bottom-up** processing. Evidence from **garden path sentences** indicates that parsing begins immediately, at the first word of an utterance. Sentence **production** is more difficult to study than comprehension, and much of the evidence comes from **slips of the tongue**, which reveal that utterances are planned ahead.

The study of language in the brain and the brain functions involved in speech processing is **neurolinguistics**. Two areas of the left (or language-dominant) **hemisphere** are especially important in language processing: **Broca's** and **Wernicke's areas**. Evidence for this **localization** comes from studies of **aphasia** and **brain scanning**.

Different types of aphasia – including **Broca's**, **Wernicke's**, **conduction**, **anomic** and **global** – are identifiable according to impairments to different aspects of language; these tend to be associated with damage to different brain regions.

Brain scanning technologies permit language processes to be studied online, though all have limitations. **Electroencephalography** (EEG) and **magnetoencephalography** (MEG) provide excellent information about timing, but poor locational information; **positron emission tomography** (PET) scanning and **functional magnetic resonance imaging** (fMRI) provide accurate information about the location of brain activity, but are imprecise on timing events. Findings from experiments with PET and fMRI agree quite well with results of post-mortem studies of aphasics.

Guide to further reading

Probably the best place to begin reading about the Sapir-Whorf hypothesis is with Whorf (1956). This hypothesis has engendered an enormous literature, both pro and con. Lee (1996) attempts to come to grips with what Whorf was really saying. Gumperz and Levinson (1996) and Gentner and Goldin-Meadow (2003) contain many articles exploring and extending Whorf's ideas.

Good introductory textbooks on psycholinguistics are Aitchison (1989, 1997); Gleason and Ratner (1998); and Whitney (1998). Aitchison (2003) is a useful glossary that explains psycholinguistic terminology clearly. Garrod and Pickering (1999) contains articles on various aspects of speech perception and comprehension. Traxler and Gernsbacher (2006) provides comprehensive coverage of the field, though at an advanced level; it is not recommended for beginners.

On slips of the tongue, see Fromkin (1973a, 1973b, 1988) and Cutler (1982). See also Fromkin (1980) for a range of error types, and Bond (1999) on slips of the ear.

The story of Phineas Gage is told engagingly in Fleischman (2002), though the details are not always entirely accurate. Calvin and Ojemann (1994) tells a fascinating story of conversations with an epileptic patient before, during and after neurosurgery. Donald (1991: 82–86) provides a detailed account of a man (pseudonym Brother John) who experienced temporary aphasic seizures in which he would go through stages resembling different types of aphasia. During these seizures other cognitive processes were unaffected; he was fully aware of what was going on around him and could later remember and describe what had happened.

Good popular introductions to the brain are Carter (1998/2000) and Greenfield (2000), which is based on a six-part BBC2 television series. For a more detailed and technical treatment, see Kolb and Whishaw (1980/2003).

For an overview of neurolinguistics see Caplan (2001); Obler and Gjerlow (1999) and Ingram (2007) are good textbook treatments of the subject.

Issues for further thought and exercises

1. Some languages have grammatical systems of gender for nouns, which are generally indicated by agreement of verbs, determiners and/or adjectives. For example, French nouns are either masculine or feminine; Danish and Swedish nouns are either common (*en*) or neuter (*et*); and Bantu languages are known for large gender systems. One interpretation would be that in thinking for speaking, speakers of such languages would employ an isomorphic system of classifying things. To what extent do you think this is likely to be so? Assuming that such a system is used in thinking for speaking, how could you test whether it extends to other aspects of thought, to thinking in other cognitive domains?

2. What is the Stroop effect? (You can find information about it on the web, and in many books on psycholinguistics.) Write a paragraph description of the effect, explaining what it shows. Try it out on yourself and your friends.

3. An important experimental technique used in psycholinguistics is known as **priming**. Find out what it is, and write a paragraph description of the technique (in your own words); explain the nature of the technique, a simple experiment using it, and why it is believed to show what it does.

4. Record examples of speech errors over the next few weeks. (Carry a notebook around with you and note the errors down as soon as you can to avoid forgetting or mis-remembering them.) How would you classify the types of error you have found?

5. We've spoken of slips of the tongue, but slips of the ear also occur, speech errors of perception and comprehension. These are more difficult to identify in actual speech, but there are certain conditions under which it is possible to notice or infer them. Think of some such conditions, and then over the next few weeks attempt to observe examples. What types of error are represented, and how do they compare with the types of speech errors mentioned in the text?

6. One example of a common phonological error is the pronunciation of *ku klux klan* as *klu klux klan*. What sort of error is this? Can you think of any other examples of similar phonological errors? Steve Mirsky's column 'Antigravity' in *Scientific American* February 2004 reports the following humorous exchange from a radio conversation:

   'The Klu Klux Klan.'
   'It's not Klu. It's *Ku*. Its not Klu Klux Klan, it's Ku Klux Klan.'
   'I didn't say Klu Klux Klan,' I said '*Klu* Klux Klan.'
   'You said it again, you said Klu.'
   'I did not say Klu Klux Klan,' I said '*Klu* Klux Klan.'
   'You said it again, you said Klu.'

   What does this dialogue suggest about language processing?

7. I recall as a child hearing one child say to another *Heads I win, tails you lose*. He threw a coin, and of course won. The other child looked puzzled. The same thing continued over a number of throws, with the second child getting increasingly confused as he lost every time. What type of error is this? Can you think of (or have you observed) similar errors? What (if anything) does it reveal about language comprehension?

8. Below are some examples of speech by aphasics. Which type of aphasia do they appear to represent? Give your reasons.

   a. *Well this is . . . mother is away here working her work out o'here to get her better, but when she's looking, the two boys looking in other part. One their small tile into her time here. She's working another time because she's getting, too.*

   b. *Lower Falls – Maine – Paper. Four hundred tons a day! And ah – sulphur machines, and ah wood – Two weeks and eight hours. Eight hours – no! Twelve hours, fifteen hours – working working – working! Yes, and ah – sulphur. Sulphur and – ah wood. Ah . . . handling! And ah sick, four years ago.*

c. *I felt worse because I can no longer keep in mind from the mind of the minds to keep from mind and up to the ear which can be to find among ourselves.* [Uttered by a patient in response to a question about his health.]

d. Examiner: *What kind of work have you done?*

   Patient: *We, the kids, all of us, and I, we were working for a long time in the . . . You know . . . it's the kind of space, I mean place rear to the spedawn . . .*

   Examiner. *Excuse me, but I wanted to know what kind of work you have been doing.*

   Patient: *If you had said that, we had said that, poomer, near the fortunate, porpunate, tamppoo, all around the fourth of martz. Oh, I get all confused.*

9. Some aphasics substitute words for written words when asked to read them. Compare the following list of written word and read words (from two different occasions of reading), and state what the words have in common and how they differ. What does this suggest about the way words are stored in the brain?

Written word	First read response	Second read response
act	play	play
applaud	laugh	cheers
example	answer	sum
heal	pain	medicine
south	west	east

10. Supposing you were to give a Broca's aphasic the following list of homophonous words to read, what differences would you expect in the reading of the words from the two columns?

ewe	you
bee	be
eye	I
hymn	him
four	for

11. Find out about one or more of the following disorders: jargon aphasia, dyslexia, acquired dyslexia, Specific Language Impairment (SLI) and autism. Write a brief description of the disorder, mentioning its physiological manifestations and causes, and typical effects on language.

Notes

1. Heider's interpretation of her data has been challenged by Roberson et al. (2005).

2. Transposition of the endings ('rhymes') of syllables (e.g. V, VC) does sometimes occur. Thus Jacques Hadamard mentions writing *will she* instead of *we shall*, which mistake he puts down, probably correctly, to an error in phonological processing that was subsequently written down (Hadamard 1996/1945: 79). (Note that there is a further change in the vowel quality of the first item. Can you suggest an explanation?)

9 Language Acquisition

This chapter is concerned with the processes by which human beings acquire a language, how they attain the ability to comprehend and produce utterances in it. We begin with first-language acquisition, the processes by which children learn to speak the language of the community they are born into. While there is considerable individual variation in the acquisition process, this variation falls within limits and acquisition follows regular patterns. We discuss four general learning strategies that have been suggested to be relevant to the acquisition of language by children. Finally, we deal with the acquisition of language by adults, enquiring into the extent to which this process resembles first-language acquisition, and the extent to which adults can acquire native-like command of a language.

Chapter contents

Goals

The goals of the chapter are to:
- describe the milestones of language acquisition by the child;
- describe common patterns in the child's acquisition of phonetics, phonology, lexicon, morphology, syntax and semantics;

- discuss learning strategies that have been proposed for the child's acquisition of language;
- identify developmental patterns in acquisition of a second language by adults;
- discuss the effects of age on adult acquisition of a language, and raise the question of whether an adult can acquire native-speaker competence in a language; and
- mention some ways in which second-language learning processes vary among individuals

Key terms

babbling	critical period	object scope	syntactic
basic mastery	hypothesis	one-word	bootstrapping
caretaker speech	hypothesis testing	holophrastic stage	telegraphic speech
conditioned-response	imitation	overextension of	transfer/interference
learning	innateness	meaning	two-word stage
continued acquisition	L1	overgeneralization	underextension of
cooing	L2	second-language	meaning
	mismatch in meaning	learning	

9.1 Major features of child language acquisition

General characteristics of language acquisition

Preliminary remarks

Normal children in all societies acquire, within the space of a few years, fluent control of a language, sometimes two or more. By the time they are five years old they know several thousand words, have acquired the major phonological and grammatical systems of their language(s), as well as the fundamentals of the semantic and pragmatic systems, and how the language is used in its social context. Exceptions are few: children with severe physical handicaps such as extreme mental retardation, or Down's syndrome, may not acquire a language fully; very rarely a child is not exposed to sufficient speech.

The language(s) a child acquires depends on the languages habitually spoken around them, by their parents and other community members, including other children they interact with. Children have no genetic predisposition to speak a particular language: if removed from their biological parents at an early age, and brought up by foster parents who do not speak the language of the natural parents, the child will learn the foster parents' language like any native-born child. Although a good deal is known about the processes of acquisition of language by children, about what and when (in what sequence) the child learns, many questions relating to how and why remain unanswered. There are major disagreements on the issues of whether or not we are genetically programmed to speak, and the learning processes by which language is acquired.

In no society are children explicitly taught to speak their first language(s). They acquire spoken language spontaneously, in everyday interactive situations; explicit instruction is unnecessary, and, if given, usually has little effect. Deaf children, of course, are unable to perceive the acoustic input of languages spoken around them. But, if exposed to a sign language, they also acquire it spontaneously. This spontaneous acquisition of speech and signing contrasts with writing, which is usually learnt through explicit instruction; most children learn to write in school, or are taught by parents or siblings.

Acquisition of all languages is believed to proceed through similar developmental stages. However, it must be cautioned that intensive investigations of acquisition have been carried out in a vanishingly small fraction of the world's approximately 7,000 languages. Most studies have focussed on major languages of Europe (especially English) and Asia (particularly Mandarin Chinese and Japanese). Comparatively few studies have been undertaken of acquisition of indigenous languages of Australia, Papua New Guinea, the Pacific islands or North and South America. This represents a serious limitation in our knowledge.

Basic schedule of acquisition

The child's acquisition of language is a staged process. The stages, which are similar across the range of languages in which acquisition has been investigated, are as follows:

- pre-language stages of cooing, beginning at about two or three months; and babbling beginning at around six months;
- one-word stage, beginning at about a year or so;
- two-word stage, beginning at 18 to 20 months;
- telegraphic speech, beginning at two to three years of age;
- basic mastery, at around four or five years;
- elaboration and expansion especially of lexicon – also to some extent grammar – continuing throughout life.

Children vary considerably as regards the times they reach the various stages, some entering the stages very early, some very late – for example, Albert Einstein is said not to have begun talking until five years of age. Regardless of whether the child is fast or slow in the acquisition of language, in the long run it seems not to matter: late talkers end up with full control of the language. Moreover, it should not be presumed that the stages are rigidly distinct; they merge into one another. Below we discuss these six stages in order.

Pre-language stages

The earliest stages of child language acquisition are the pre-language stages, which last from about two months to a year of age. At around two months the child typically begins to produce vocalizations called **cooing**. These vocalizations consist of syllables, often repeated, made up of a velar consonant plus a back vowel, like [kuː], [gaga] and [guː].

By about six months the child is generally sitting up, and producing a wider range of sounds, including stops, nasals and fricatives. In this stage, **babbling**, the child produces word-like utterances, typically CV syllables, though they are not recognizable as words of the language. The phones are not necessarily restricted to those of the surrounding language; for example, children in an English-speaking environment sometimes produce retroflex stops and bilabial fricatives. But as time goes on the phones in babbling tend increasingly towards the phones heard in the language environment. In the later stages, towards the end of the child's first year, babbling becomes more controlled, and different intonation patterns may be used.

Deaf children also babble vocally, though they usually cease to do so by about nine months of age, due to lack of auditory feedback. Deaf children exposed from birth to a sign language babble manually from about ten to fourteen months. They produce a range of hand gestures that are not necessarily found in the sign language to which they are exposed. According to some investigators, hearing children also produce manual babbles, rhythmic motor actions produced as part of the process of gaining control of bodily movements. These are different to the babbling of deaf children exposed to a sign language.

One-word stage

At around 12 to 18 months children produce their first recognizable words. These words occur alone, in single-unit utterances, and thus the term **one-word stage** or **holophrastic** stage. A one-word utterance can be given different intonation contours to express different speech acts, for example, falling intonation for a statement, rising for a question or request.

The first words tend to be similar both phonetically and semantically, regardless of the language. They tend to consist of CV syllables, and rarely contain consonant clusters. The first words are lexical rather than grammatical, and generally label concrete objects or individuals that the child interacts with, like *mummy*, *daddy* and *kitty*. Also common in this stage are words for negation (used in refusal, *no*), non-existence (remarking on disappearance or absence of something, for example, *allgone*), recurrence (used in requesting more, *more*), and attention (drawing attention to something or someone, for example, *hi*).

In the one-word stage, language tends to be closely tied to the interactive context, and shows little displacement (see §1.3). Utterances tend to be interpersonally oriented, engaging the child interactively with the parent (or caregiver).

The two-word stage

By 18 to 20 months or so the child typically has an active vocabulary of some 50 words; this increases dramatically over the next few months, so that by two years of age the child's vocabulary will normally increase to around two to three hundred. When a child has a vocabulary of around 50 words, they begin to put the words together in two-word utterances. Before this, children often string together sequences of separate utterances, with pauses in between them.

The first two word utterances tend to express the same kinds of meanings as in the one-word stage, but do so more explicitly: negation or refusal, for example, *no bed*; recurrence, as in *more milk*; non-existence, as in *allgone doggie*; and attention, for example, *hi daddy*.

New kinds of meaning begin to appear later in this stage, including: actor-action, as in *mummy eat* or *eat mummy*; quality-thing, as in *bad kitty*; possession, as in *baby chair*; thing-location, for example *doggy table*; action-location, for example, *go park*; action-undergoer, as in *eat brekky*, and actor-undergoer, as in *mummy dinner*. At this stage in the speech of many children, words specifying things occur in second (i.e. final) position.

Telegraphic speech

Multiple word utterances usually make their first appearance sometime during the third year of life. Multiple word utterances begin, at least in English, as strings of lexical words, without grammatical words or morphemes. This is called **telegraphic speech**, after the style of expression that used to be used in telegrams.[1]

In this stage, function words and morphemes, such as prepositions (in languages like English) and inflectional morphemes, begin to appear. The acquisition of inflected forms of words differs depending on the morphological complexity of the language: in a morphologically simple language like English it lags behind that of more morphologically complex languages, where the morphology is more salient.

Basic mastery

By four or five years of age most children have acquired a basic mastery of their language. Their vocabulary will stand at well over 1,000 items, and the basic systems of phonology, morphology and syntax will be in place.

Continued acquisition

Language acquisition continues throughout life. This is especially true of lexical items, which continue to be acquired in adulthood, although at a much slower rate than for the two-year-old child. Certain registers, such as scientific and legal registers in Western cultures, may not be acquired until late adolescence or even adulthood.

Some aspects of grammar take a longer time than others for children to acquire. For example, the numeral classifiers of many South-East Asian languages – words that specify the semantic type of an object and have to occur in NPs with numerals (e.g. for two pencils one might say 'two long-objects pencils', for two coins, 'two round-objects coins') – are often not fully acquired until the child is ten or more years of age. One study of ten-year-old Thai speakers revealed only about 90 per cent of correct usage of numeral classifiers, according to adult norms. My own adventitious observations suggest that tag questions in English (see §5.3) may not be fully acquired until adolescence. Thus children of ten or twelve may use negative tags to negative clauses (as in *He didn't go yesterday, didn't he?*) in circumstances where adults would use positive tags (as in the unmarked *He didn't go yesterday, did he?*).

Caretaker speech

As mentioned in §7.2, many languages have special speech registers for talking to young children; adults do not speak to infants, or interact with them, in the same ways as with other adults. These registers, variously called **baby-talk**, **motherese**, **child-directed speech** and **caretaker speech** – we will use the last term – have characteristics that assist (or are believed to assist) the child's acquisition of language.

Caretaker speech in Western cultures tends to be characterized by a slow rate of delivery, exaggerated intonation, high pitch, palatalization of consonants, repetition, high frequency of diminutive forms (like the English *-ie* ~ *-y* ending in *doggie*, *kitty*), simple syntax, short utterances (one study found that the average length of sentences addressed by mothers to two-year-olds was less than four words), and simple and concrete lexical items. Sometimes unusual or complex phonemes are replaced by more common or simpler ones, and sometimes special lexical items peculiar to caretaker speech are used, often involving simpler syllabic structures (e.g. *tummy* instead of *stomach*), and repeated syllables (e.g. *wee-wee*, *poo-poo*, *choo-choo*).

These characteristics tend to be broadly associated with caretaker speech in many cultures. Some studies suggest that the intonation patterns used by mothers (or other caretakers) when talking with young infants carries information about approval and disapproval, and that similar patterns are used in different societies to encourage or discourage the child to do something (Fernald 1985). But prosodic features are not universal. High pitch is not always a feature of caretaker speech: in Quiche Mayan (Mesoamerica) caretaker speech is characteristically low pitched, high pitch being used in speech to socially dominant individuals.

Who primarily uses caretaker speech to the child differs from culture to culture. In Western cultures it tends to be parents, especially mothers, and close relatives of the infant (such as grandparents and siblings). In Western Samoa it tends to be siblings, adult neighbours and adult relatives other than parents.

The role of caretaker speech in language acquisition – to what extent it really does facilitate acquisition, or is tailored to the needs of the child – is an issue on which there is considerable difference of opinion. Experimental evidence suggests that infants tend to prefer caretaker speech to ordinary adult-to-adult speech. Unfortunately, caretaker speech has not been studied across a representative sample of languages.

Acquisition of phonetics and phonology

Before the end of their first year children recognize a number of words, involving a range of different consonants and vowels, although they are unable to produce more than a few of them themselves. The perception of speech sounds begins very early, some phonetic differences being perceived from a very young age. Even one-month-old babies are able to perceive the difference between [pa] and [ba], regardless of their language environment. Very young babies show preferences for the voice of their mother over the voices of other women; they also prefer the language the mother speaks: a baby of a French-speaking mother prefers to hear French over other languages. Before the child can produce any words, he or she has acquired some of the basic intonation patterns and auditory characteristics of the language. By a year of age, the child's ability to hear sound contrasts that are phonemic in the language being acquired is enhanced, while the ability to hear sound differences that are not contrastive begins to deteriorate.

Nasals and stops are generally among the earliest consonants acquired (as in *mama* and *papa*), [ɑ] and [i] the earliest vowels, with [u] appearing slightly later. Labial consonants tend to be mastered earlier than consonants at other places of articulation. By the age of four, children learning English are generally able to produce all the contrasting vowels and diphthongs, though a few consonants still cause difficulty. These include the fricatives [θ] and [ð], which are unusual across the world's languages and are the last consonants to be fully acquired, as well as affricates ([tʃ] and [dʒ]) and some fricatives (the alveo-palatals [ʃ] and [ʒ], and the voiced [v] and [z]). In some phonetic environments, [l] and [ɹ] remain problematic.

The position of a consonant in a word is relevant to its acquisition. Consonants are more likely to be correctly produced at the beginning of words than elsewhere. Final consonants generally emerge latest in production.

A characteristic of language acquisition is that perception precedes production: children are often able to perceive contrasts that they are unable to produce. This is nicely revealed in the following quote:

> One of us, for instance, spoke to a child who called his inflated plastic fish a *fis*. In imitation of the child's pronunciation, the observer said: 'This is your *fis*?' 'No,' said the child, 'my *fis*.' He continued to reject the adult's imitation until he was told, 'That is your fish.' 'Yes,' he said, 'my *fis*.' (Brown and Berko 1960: 531)

Trends are also discernible in the ways in which children change the sound-shape of words they produce, replacing certain phones by non-adult ones. Among the trends are the following:

- Velars are often replaced by alveolars; for instance, *gone* might appear as [dɒn].
- Fricatives tend to be replaced by stops; thus *see* might be pronounced [tiː].
- Word final consonants tend to be omitted; for instance, *kick* might be pronounced as [ti] (with replacement of the velar stop by an alveolar stop).
- Unstressed syllables are often omitted, as in [naːna] for *banana*.
- Consonant clusters tend to be avoided; thus *sky* might be produced as [kaɪ].
- There is a tendency for phones to harmonize within words. Thus *dog* might appear as [gɔg], where the first consonant has fully harmonized with the second; *thumb* could appear as [nəm], showing partial harmonizing of the initial consonant with the following nasal.
- Laterals and rhotics tend to be replaced by glides: [l] might be replaced by [j], as in [jɛg] for *leg*.

Acquisition of lexicon

We mentioned above that the child acquires their first words at around a year of age. Between 18 and 36 months, the child's vocabulary increases rapidly, doubling every 6 months; it doubles again over the next year. By four years of age, a typical child is estimated to have a vocabulary of around 1,600 words.

The early lexicon of children acquiring English tends to be made up of a high proportion of nouns. This has been thought to reflect the inherent conceptual simplicity of nouns over verbs; it could also reflect a greater salience of nouns in caretaker speech in English. The early lexicons of children acquiring languages in which verbs occur more frequently than in English, and in languages in which they tend to occur finally in the clause, sometimes show a higher proportion of verbs (Snow 1995), though other studies have detected no such difference.

As in the acquisition of phonetics and phonology, perception precedes production. By about 18 months of age, when a child has an active vocabulary of around 50 words, some studies have revealed that they can understand up to five times as many words. This difference remains throughout life: adult speakers recognize and understand many more words than they actively use.

Acquisition of semantics

Acquisition of a lexical item is more than learning a phonetic or phonological form. The child also has to acquire the meaning associated with the form. This is not a straightforward process; the meaning of a word is not directly perceptible. Children do not however use lexemes meaninglessly; they assign some content to the lexemes they acquire, and there is a surprisingly good correlation between the meaning assigned by children and the meaning in the adult language. Errors in meaning assignment are of three main types.

Overextension refers to the child's generalization of the meaning of the word beyond the sense in the adult language. The word might be extended to all things sharing a general feature of colour, shape, size or whatever. For example, the word *daddy* might be used to refer to any man, *doggy* to all four-legged hairy animals, or *moon* to all round things. Overextension need not necessarily apply equally to the production and comprehension of a word. For example, one child used the word *apple* to refer to other similar round objects like balls and tomatoes, but was able to correctly pick out the apple from a collection of such items when asked to identify *the apple*.

Less common is **underextension**, where the child assigns a narrower meaning to the word than in the adult language, using it to designate a more restricted range of objects or events. For example, the word *doggy* might be reserved for just the pet dog, or *duck* to just a toy duck.

Rarely, children assign a completely mistaken meaning to a word; this is referred to as **mismatch**. Mismatches are often syntagmatically motivated: they involve assignment of some meaning present in the context in which the word was heard to the wrong item. Thus one child who saw his first bicycle at a party for a child named Mikey for some time afterwards called all bicycles and tricycles *mikeys*.

The meanings of some words are more difficult for children to acquire than others, both in comprehension and production. Concrete vocabulary is easier to acquire than abstract vocabulary, and lexemes expressing relative meanings. Children tend to assign absolute meanings to adjectives such as *big* in their first few years. Kinship terms tend to be first given ego-centred meanings: *mother* and *father* being reserved for just the child's parents; the relational nature of kinship terms may not be fully understood until the age of seven or more. English-speaking children often do not acquire the relative use of *left* and *right* (as in *the dog is to the left of the tree*) until 11 or 12. Children under about eight years of age generally do not appreciate that many words are ambiguous, and thus may not be able to understand puns and jokes that rely on lexical ambiguity.

Acquisition of morphology

Cross-language differences are prominent in the acquisition of morphology. In English it begins rather late; in languages with richer morphologies, such as Hungarian, Spanish and Turkish, acquisition of morphology begins earlier. In English words often appear in their root or stem form, which is the most salient form. But in more morphologically complex languages the bare root or stem form may not be free; the lexical item might be encountered only in different inflected forms. This is the case for Spanish verbs, which are encountered in forms such as *como* 'I eat', *comes* 'you eat', *comía* 'I ate', *comías* 'you ate', but never in the uninflected root form *com*, which is not a free morpheme. The child acquiring Spanish acquires verbal suffixes earlier than does the child acquiring English because they are more pervasive in Spanish, and one is always present on a verb. In general, the more pervasive a morphological category is in a language the more rapidly it tends to be acquired.

Children tend to acquire the grammatical morphemes of their language in relatively consistent orders. Table 9.1 shows the acquisition sequence of the ten first-learned grammatical

Table 9.1 Typical order of acquisition of first ten grammatical morphemes in English (based on data presented in Brown 1973: 271)

Position in acquisition	Morpheme	Frequency position in adult speech	Approximate age of acquisition in months	Examples
1	Verb suffix -*ing*	2	24	*walking, playing*
2	Prepositions *in, on*	4	24	*in box, on bed*
3	Noun plural suffix -*s* ~ -*z*	3	24	*trucks, dogs*
4	Irregular past tense of frequent verbs		30	*went, saw*
5	Noun possessive clitic '*s*	5	30	*kitty's, daddy's*
6	Verb *be* in questions		30	*Is Kitty here? Was it?*
7	Definite and indefinite articles, *the* and *a* ~ *an*	1	36	*a dog, the dog*
8	Regular past tense suffix -*ed* ~-*d* ~ -*t*	6	42	*walked, played*
9	Regular third person singular present tense suffix -*s* ~-*z*	7	42	*walks, plays*
10	Irregular present tense of frequent verbs		42	*has, does*

morphemes in English based on an investigation of three children by Roger Brown (1973: 271). Similar patterns have been observed in acquiring English morphemes in a number of children from different family environments, although there is some individual variation in the order and especially the age of acquisition.

It will be noticed that the order of acquisition does not perfectly reflect frequency in adult speech. Thus, the most frequent word in adult English, *the*, does not appear until the child is three years of age, in the seventh position.

The regular nominal plural morpheme *-s ~ -z ~ -əz* is one of the earliest acquired morphemes in English. However, the morphology of number marking in English shows irregularities, and the acquisition of plural marking of nouns is a staged process. The typical stages are as follows (based on Moskowitz 1978):

a. First no nouns distinguish number: a single form is used regardless of how many things are referred to.
b. Next, the child has a single noun that distinguishes number, usually the irregular *foot ~ feet*; other nouns do not distinguish number. The singular and plural forms of this word are both highly frequent, and are saliently different phonetically.
c. Third another high-frequency irregular plural form is acquired alongside its singular form, typically *man ~ men*.
d. Following this, the regular allomorph *-s* appears on nouns ending in voiceless consonants, and *-z* on nouns ending in voiced segments; the third allomorph *-əz* is not yet in use, and nouns like *house* that end in a sibilant appear in just one form. The two regular allomorphs are overgeneralized, and appear also on the irregular plural forms – so the plural of *man* becomes /mænz/. For *foot*, many children have two plural forms, /fʊts/ and /fiːts/.
e. In the fifth stage the allomorph /əz/ appears on words ending in sibilants, such as *house*. However, it is overgeneralized to all nouns, so that the child is producing plural forms like /kætsəz/ or /kætəz/ instead of /kæts/.
f. Sixth, most overgeneralized plural forms, with the exception of /mænz/, are corrected.
g. Finally, all overgeneralizations are corrected.

Notable in this sequence is the fact that adult irregular plural forms of high frequency words are acquired early (though not necessarily with the plural meaning); subsequently non-adult forms involving the regular allomorphs appear. These regular forms coexist for some time with the irregular forms, before being completely replaced. Observe also that when they appear, the regular plural allomorphs are overgeneralized. Acquisition of the past tense of English verbs follows a similar sequence of stages.

Acquisition of syntax

We have already noted some of the major features of the earliest stages of acquisition of syntax, beginning at around 18 months of age, when the child starts to combine words into longer utterances. The earliest stages, as we saw, are characterized by a lack of grammatical morphemes; these do not begin appearing until the child's third year. In the following subsections we outline the acquisition of three syntactic constructions in English.

Negative constructions

Three main stages have been identified in the acquisition of negative constructions in English. These stages overlap, and the child shows steady progress towards the adult norm.

In the first stage, at around 18–26 months, negative markers *no* and *not* are put at the beginning or end of the utterance, as in *No drink, No I can go* and *Gone no*. In the second stage, which begins during the child's third year, the negative word starts to be used between the subject and verb, as in *You no do that*, and *I no eat it*; in verbless clauses it occurs between the two noun phrases, as in *That not mine*. At about the same time, negative forms such as *don't* and *can't* appear as unanalysed elements, also within utterances, as in *I can't see*, and *I don't want it*. The third stage sees the appearance of other auxiliary forms with attached negative markers (*isn't, won't*), and their morphological analyses. Some examples are *She won't let go, She isn't going* and *You've not got one*.

Some of the more advanced negative constructions are not acquired until the early school years. For example, the correct use of *some* and *any* in *I've got some* and *I haven't got any*, and of *hardly* and *scarcely*.

Interrogatives

A well-studied aspect of the acquisition of English syntax is how children learn interrogatives (see §6.3). Three main stages, again not discrete, have been identified. The first stage employs just intonation: high rising tone on an utterance signifies that it is a question. For example, *Daddy there* or *I can go* with high rising tone is used in requests of information. The second stage occurs during the child's second year, when he or she begins to use interrogative words, first *what* and *where*, and later *who, why, when* and *how*. These words are put at the beginning of the clause, which is uttered on a rising intonation contour, as in *Where horse go* and *What you doing there*. In the third stage children acquire the auxiliary verbs *be, have* and *do*, and interrogative structures involving auxiliary verb followed by subject. This is learned first for yes-no interrogatives (as in *can I go* and *did he go*), and somewhat later for information interrogatives (as in *When can I go* and *Where are you going*).

Complex sentence constructions

At about the age of three, sentences begin to appear that consist of more than one clause. To begin with, most of these are coordinate constructions using the conjunction *and*. Subordinate constructions (e.g. *when* and *if* clauses, and relative clauses) are increasingly used from this age, though they remain rarer than coordination constructions. Words like *so, if, after, what, because* and *when* are used in these constructions, though not necessarily in the adult way. An **order of mention strategy** is employed whereby the event of the first clause is presumed to occur before the event of the second, as in *I fell down because I hurt my knee*. The same strategy is used in the child's comprehension of complex sentences.

Children under six years of age experience difficulties in correctly interpreting complex sentence constructions, especially subordinate constructions. And more sophisticated conjunctive items, such as *really*, *anyway*, *though*, *actually* and *of course*, do not emerge until even later, perhaps not until the child is seven years old.

9.2 Strategies for child language learning

In this section we discuss some learning strategies that have been suggested to explain how children acquire their mother tongue. We begin with four major proposals, briefly mentioning evidence for and against. Following this, we discuss some specific mechanisms that have been proposed for the acquisition of the meaning of lexical items.

Broad strategies for language leaning

Conditioned-response learning

Conditioned-response learning is a theory of learning associated with the psychological theory of behaviourism, which was applied to language acquisition by B. F. Skinner (1957). According to behaviourism, language develops from adult reinforcement and shaping of the babbling of the infant, and subsequently like other learned behaviour. Two types of conditioned-response learning are involved: classical conditioning and operant conditioning.

In **classical conditioning** a stimulus (e.g. presentation of meat to a dog) that invokes a natural response (salivation) is consistently accompanied by another stimulus (e.g. ringing a bell). Eventually, the accompanying stimulus (the bell ringing) invokes the response (salivation), even in the absence of the former stimulus (presentation of meat). Learning the meaning of a word was believed by Skinner to follow this process: if an object is presented to the infant accompanied by the word for it, the child begins to associate the word with the object, ultimately responding to the word in the same way as to the object. When this happens, the child has learnt the word.

Operant conditioning involves rewarding certain behaviour, which is thereby strengthened; unrewarded behaviour eventually disappears. The individual behaves in such a way as to obtain rewards. According to Skinner, children are reinforced by adults who reward their early attempts to speak with smiles, attention and the like. As time goes on, adults become more demanding, and reward only the best approximations to adult speech. This selective reinforcement, it is suggested, gradually shapes the child's behaviour in the direction of the adult norm.

Although conditioning might account for some aspects of language acquisition, there is much it cannot account for, and it has been severely criticized by linguists (beginning with Chomsky's excoriating review (1959) of Skinner's *Verbal behavior*). One criticism is that children acquire the grammar of their language despite the fact that they are rarely if ever reinforced for producing grammatical utterances, or receive negative reinforcement (punishment) for ungrammatical utterances. By contrast, children are not infrequently reinforced for telling the truth and punished for lying; yet they often end up as inveterate liars as adults! Another criticism is that conditioning cannot account for comprehension, which, as we have seen, precedes production throughout language acquisition – how could it be conditioned? A third criticism is that it cannot account for the facts of acquisition of irregular morphology (see p. 211). Finally, conditioned-response learning cannot account for the child's production of word forms and sentences they've never heard before.

Imitation

Another strategy for language acquisition is **imitation**. Human beings are excellent imitators, surpassing other primates. Imitation is a common means by which children (and adults) learn many things, including aspects of language. Children actively imitate the speech of those in their social environments, sometimes at inappropriate times, to the embarrassment of their parents. Caretakers often encourage their charges to imitate what they say, providing especially clear models of what should be said in the form of caretaker speech (see p. 207).

Children frequently imitate new lexical items. Imitation may also be relevant to the acquisition of grammar. Children often imitate sentence patterns they are unable to produce spontaneously, and later stop imitating them when they are able to produce them. Imitation may thus serve to link comprehension with spontaneous production.

But although some aspects of language acquisition can be accounted for by imitation, not all can be. Four pieces of evidence are often cited against imitation. The first is the overgeneralization that occurs at one stage in the acquisition of morphology, where former correct irregular forms are replaced or augmented by incorrect regular forms. The latter forms, such as *wented*, are said to be unlikely to have been imitated from adult speech. Second, children are sometimes unable to imitate adult utterances exactly, even when encouraged to do so. A good illustration of this is the following dialogue, reported by McNeill, in which the child is unable to imitate a pattern, despite numerous repetitions by the adult:

(9-1)	CHILD:	*Nobody don't like me.*
	MOTHER:	*No, say 'Nobody likes me.'*
	CHILD:	*Nobody don't like me.*
		(Eight repetitions of this dialogue.)
	MOTHER:	*No, now listen carefully: say 'Nobody likes me.'*
	CHILD:	*Oh! Nobody don't likes me.* (McNeill 1966: 69)

It seems that children ignore aspects of the utterance that lie beyond their competence. Third, if children learn largely by imitation, why don't they learn grammatical morphemes such as *the* and *a ~ an*, which are among the most frequent morphemes in English, much earlier than they do? Fourth, imitation does not explain why comprehension precedes production in acquisition, and why children can perceive phonetic differences they are unable to produce.

None of these objections is entirely telling. Studies of what is actually said to children are few and limited, making it difficult to evaluate the claim that they are not exposed to overgeneralized forms like *wented*. Furthermore, imitation can never be precise repetition in all details, and it could be rejoined that a child acquiring a language is still learning what is a significant feature vs. what is not. Put in another way, comprehension may be a critical component of 'accurate' repetition.

Elicited imitation is a technique sometimes used to determine a child's competence in a particular domain of grammar. Here the experimenter reads out a sentence to be repeated. If the child changes anything in their repetition, or fails to correct an error in the model sentence, this is presumed to indicate that it is an aspect of the grammar that has not yet been acquired.

Hypothesis testing

In adopting the strategy of **hypothesis testing** the child is presumed to be behaving like a scientist, making guesses about how the language works, and testing these guesses against the evidence from speech, and the reactions of interlocutors. According to this theory, the child acquires a language through their attempts at analysing it grammatically.

One piece of evidence for hypothesis testing comes from overgeneralized forms such as *wented* and *feeded* that are believed to be inventions of the child, formed according to regular morphological processes. The child has apparently figured out the general rule, and applied it in a novel case: the child hypothesizes that past tense is formed by adding *-ed*, and tests it on the verbs *go* and *feed*.

But it seems implausible to attribute to babies and young children the abstract styles of thinking and experimentation employed by scientists, and honed over many years of training. It is not clear that children actively seek empirical confirmation or disconfirmation of their hypotheses – that they really do test their hypotheses against actual empirical data.

Another criticism concerns where their hypotheses come from: on what basis are infants capable of making their guesses, given their lack of experience, and that they are rarely given explicit training and when they are, are often unable to make effective use of it?

The hypothesis testing approach to language acquisition also ignores the fact that language is a skill, that acquisition of a language is not just acquisition of knowledge about the grammar and lexicon of a language, but the ability to use the language to produce utterances meaningful in the context.

Innateness

A fourth proposal, developed in the 1960s by linguists working within generative grammar (see p. 19), is **innateness,** the notion that children are born with an innate capacity to acquire language, and that much of our knowledge about language is genetically encoded. The child has little to learn since much of the knowledge about language is hardwired in the brain. When children are exposed to a language, general principles of discovering the structure of the language are automatically put into operation; these principles constitute the **language acquisition device** (LAD) of the child.

The LAD is deployed to make hypotheses about the grammar of language being acquired, thus answering one of the difficulties raised for the hypothesis testing account: the guesses of the child are based on innate knowledge. Given that the grammatical structure of languages varies considerably from language to language, what is innate must of course be very abstract.

One frequently cited argument for innateness is the speed and accuracy at which language is acquired by the child, despite serious inadequacies in the language sample the child is exposed to. This notion is referred to as the **poverty of the stimulus**. It is further argued that there are certain errors that children never make, that could not be inferred from the evidence available to children from utterances they hear. The problem with these claims is that they are not backed up by empirical evidence. Increasingly investigators are finding evidence that the data available to the child is not as fragmentary and unruly as suggested. Moreover, it turns out that children do make some of the errors that they have been claimed never to make.

The exact nature and properties of the LAD are highly controversial and are in constant flux due to theoretical changes in generative grammar. While the innateness theory has dominated in language acquisition studies over the past 40 or so years, there are signs of dissatisfaction with it. Increasingly investigators are exploring alternatives in which language is not seen as unique among human cognitive phenomena, and requiring a dedicated acquisition device.

Strategies for learning meaning of words

It is no trivial matter for the child to determine what lexical items mean, how they should be used and what part-of-speech they belong to. The following six principles have been proposed as strategies for determining the meaning of words (Golinkoff et al. 1994):

- **Reference**: assume that words refer to things, events and qualities.
- **Extendibility**: assume that words apply to more than just the specific thing, event or quality referred to in the first-observed instance – assume they label types, not tokens.
- **Object scope**: assume that words denoting objects denote whole objects, not portions of objects.
- **Categorical scope:** assume that words can be extended to objects in the same basic-level category as the thing referred to in the originally observed usage.[2]
- **Novel name-new category**: assume that novel word-forms apply to things, events or qualities that you do not yet have a name for. This principle is based on a dispreference of synonymy: a new label will more likely denote something new than be an alternative term for something already known.
- **Conventionality**: assume that speakers prefer specific over general lexemes.

These strategies can be thought of as heuristic principles for children to operate with so as to quickly and effectively learn the meanings of new words. They resemble the Gricean maxims (see §6.3) more than grammatical rules, in that they are effective (but not infallible) operating principles.

Another strategy is to infer word meanings from grammatical properties of the utterance. This strategy, called **syntactic bootstrapping**, was tested in an experiment in which preschool children were shown a depiction of an unfamiliar action, such as a person doing something to a pile of materials with an unfamiliar tool (Brown 1957). One group of children were told *In this picture you can see nissing*; a second group were told that they could *see some niss*; and a third group, that the picture showed *a niss*. Children from each group were then asked to select another picture showing *nissing*, *niss* and *a niss*. The result was that the children selected a picture depicting the same action, the same material and the same tool, respectively.

> Researchers disagree as to whether inferring word meaning is assisted by the syntax (syntactic bootstrapping) or the meaning of words provides children with cues to the grammatical analysis of sentences (semantic bootstrapping). Most likely the two processes interdigitate.

9.3 Second-language learning

In many parts of the world children grow up speaking more than one language, having acquired them during childhood by processes described in §9.2. Sometimes a person acquires, or attempts to acquire, another language as an adult. We will refer to such a language as a **second language** (L2), regardless of whether it is the person's second, third or later language. We will refer to the process of its acquisition as **second-language learning** (or L2 learning); it is also called adult language learning.

Developmental stages in second-language learning

Like L1 acquisition, L2 learning is a staged process; the stages are not, however, exactly the same. In this section we outline some aspects of L2 learning of English, a major focus of research on L2 learning.

Phonetics and phonology

The phonological system of the learner's L1 may be reflected in errors in pronunciation of L2, particularly in the early stages of acquisition. For example, the lack of voicing contrast in word-final stops in Dutch, Danish and German may be carried over to L2 English, and final voiced stops replaced by the corresponding voiceless stops. The absence of a velar nasal phoneme in Hungarian – [ŋ] occurs only preceding a velar consonant – can be reflected in the pronunciation of words such as *singer* as [sɪŋgə]. One investigation of the acquisition of stress in English by Polish and Hungarian L2 learners revealed that 95 per cent of the errors in stress assignment were the result of influence from L1. (Stress placement in both languages is predictable.)

This phenomenon, referred to as **interference** or **negative transfer**, is not restricted to phonology, but is also found in the L2 acquisition of morphology and syntax. For instance, Spanish speakers learning English as a second language often transfer their possessive construction involving *de* 'of' as in *el libro del profesor* 'the teacher's book', using the corresponding construction *the book of the teacher* instead of the possessive with *-s*. Negative transfers are more easily corrected in morphology and syntax than in phonology.

L2 acquisition of morphology

One investigation of adult L2 learners, including speakers of 16 different L1s, revealed that they acquired 11 English grammatical morphemes in roughly the same order: (1) progressive *-ing*; (2) singular copula *is ~ 's* (as in *Bush is the president*); (3) plural *-s ~ -z ~ -əz*; (4) articles *the* and *a*; (5) singular auxiliary *is ~ 's* (as in *the dog's barking now*); (6) irregular pasts of some frequent verbs (e.g. *went*); (7) third person singular present verb suffix *-s*; and (8) the possessive enclitic *-s ~ -z ~-əz*. This sequence is remarkably similar to the sequence of L1 acquisition of English morphology (see Table 9.1).

Acquisition of syntax

L2 acquisition of English negative and interrogative constructions is similar to their acquisition in L1. Regardless of the learner's L1, L2 learners typically begin by putting the negative particle *not* or *no* in clause-initial position, then before the main verb, and finally, in the correct position, with the correct choice of auxiliary verb, although tense marking may be imperfect, as in *he didn't felt it*. Similarly, L2 acquisition of interrogative constructions progresses from rising intonation on an ordinary declarative structure, through use of initial WH words, to use of auxiliary verbs, and ultimately the correct ordering of subject and auxiliary. Interference from the speaker's L1 can affect the order of the stages, and the length of time the learner remains at the stage; it can also result in additional stages, such as *Saw you that?* by German L1 speakers, following the pattern of interrogative constructions in German.

Effects of age on L2 acquisition

Everyone learns their first language with apparent equal facility and ease; differences among adult L2 learners are more apparent: some L2 learners acquire a high level of command of the second language, while others do not. The Polish-born author Joseph Conrad (1857–1924), who wrote a dozen or more novels in English including *Lord Jim*, is frequently cited as someone who acquired a high level of command of English as an L2 learner – although Bertrand Russell said that he spoke it with a very Polish accent. Age is generally considered to be the most important factor affecting L2 acquisition. It is widely accepted that adults acquire an L2 more rapidly in the short term, while children start off more slowly, but overtake adults within about a year or so. This claim has, however, been criticized, among other things on the grounds of the limited range of L2 learning environments in which it has been tested.

That adult L2 learners cannot acquire a native-like accent has also been challenged. Some investigations reveal that a small proportion of adult learners can acquire native-like accents, and fall within the range of native speakers; moreover, they cannot be reliably distinguished as second-language speakers by native speakers of the language. Likewise, a small proportion of adult L2 learners can apparently acquire native speaker-like competence. These observations contradict the frequently heard claim that it is impossible for an adult learner to gain full control of a second language. But they do not contradict the generalization that the older one is when exposed to the L2, the more difficult it is to acquire the language, and the less successful the learner is likely to be.

A widely held view is that there is an optimal age for acquisition of language, which ends around puberty. According to the **critical period hypothesis**, there is a biologically determined window for the full acquisition of language, that extends from about 2 months of age to about 13 years (Lenneberg 1967). After this age, the neurophysiological ability for language learning is lost or significantly impaired. The biological evidence for this hypothesis is weak. And age could be relevant for other reasons. For instance, adults are unlikely to acquire an L2 in environments remotely like the environments in which a child is reared and acquires their L1; they are also superior in abstract thought, and already have knowledge of another language.

Transfer

Aside from influences of the grammatical systems of L1 on L2, pragmatic functions such as manners and strategies of asking for information, requesting action, refusing offers, and the like, can also be transferred from L1 to L2.

More interestingly, the L2 system may have an inverse influence on the L1 system. For example, VOT (see §2.3) for stops in English is longer than the VOT of corresponding French stops. The VOTs of stops in the speech of French speakers who learnt English as an L2 tends to be longer than the VOTs for monolingual speakers of French. They have a VOT in between the VOTs of the two languages, regardless of the language they are speaking at the time, though the actual values of the VOT may depend on the language spoken. Evidence suggests that such bilinguals have two phonological systems, though both systems differ from the systems of monolinguals. By contrast, for bilinguals who learnt both languages in childhood the respective systems are apparently indistinguishable from the systems of monolingual speakers.

The meanings of words in L1 can also be affected by an L2. Monolingual speakers of Korean use the term *paran skej* 'blue' for colours that are greener than colours covered by the same term when used by speakers who learnt English as an L2 in adulthood. Whether these L2 bilingual speakers have a single lexical system for both languages, or two separate systems – one for each language, and each possibly different from the respective mono-linguals' systems in the languages – is a moot point. Evidence is conflicting: some investigators argue for two possibly overlapping systems, others that the L1 system is still operating while the bilingual individual is speaking the L2.

Factors relevant to L2 acquisition

Many factors are relevant to the success of L2 acquisition, including personality factors. One is **motivation**, the need or desire to learn the L2, which can be a desire for proficiency for the purpose of participating in the life of the community, or for more practical purposes such as getting a job or promotion. A second factor is **aptitude**: adult L2 learners differ in their talent for acquiring a second language. A third consideration is the learner's **attitude** to the second language. Negative attitudes are likely to lead to decreased motivation, and to failure to attain proficiency in the L2, while positive attitudes are likely to be associated with increased motivation and greater likelihood of success. A fourth factor is **empathy**, the ability to take another person's perspective. It has been suggested that empathetic persons are more likely to succeed in language learning in natural communicative situations. Being less inhibited than others, they may be less embarrassed by making mistakes.

Also relevant are the circumstances and manner in which the L2 is learnt. Sometimes a distinction is drawn between foreign-language learning (in which the L2 is learnt outside of the community of speakers, for instance, Hungarian and Finnish (Uralic, Finland) in Denmark) and second-language learning (where the language is learnt in its speech community). It seems reasonable to believe that the latter situation is more conducive to L2 acquisition than the former. But things are not always as simple as this. In the Netherlands and Scandinavian countries adult monolingual speakers of English can experience difficulties in entering into speech interactions in the language of the country because speakers immediately switch to English when a foreigner is present.

Summing up

Human beings are predisposed to acquire a language, and it is evident that something is genetically coded. There is considerable disagreement amongst investigators as to what it is that is genetically determined. According to some, specific knowledge about the grammar underlying all human languages – universal grammar – is a part of our biological heritage. Others argue that nothing specific to language is genetically coded, that we have merely a language-ready brain (and body).

Language acquisition proceeds by a consistent sequence of **stages**, though children differ according to when they reach the stages. They are: **cooing** and **babbling**; the **one-word holophrastic** stage; the **two-word** stage, and **basic mastery**. Some aspects of grammar are not acquired until adolescence, and **continued elaboration** occurs throughout an individual's life.

Regularities exist in the acquisition of all aspects of language. In all domains **perception precedes production**. The child's acquisition of lexical semantics is surprisingly accurate, though errors of **overextension** and **underextension** occur. To explain the accuracy of acquisition of semantics, a set of strategies have been proposed: **reference**, **extendibility**, **object scope**, **categorical scope**, **novel name-new category** and **syntactic bootstrapping**.

More general mechanisms for the child's acquisition of language are **conditioned-response learning**, **imitation** and **hypothesis testing**. None of these explain all aspects of language acquisition. According to a widely held view, language is too complex to be learnt by the child from the imperfect model it is exposed to. This notion, the **poverty of the stimulus**, has it that there is an innate **language acquisition device** guiding the child in its construction of the grammar of the language it is exposed to.

Second-language learning is also a **staged** process. **Age** is perhaps the important factor in success of L2 acquisition. The **critical period hypothesis** has it that there is a biologically determined window for acquisition of native speaker competence. Also important to the success of second-language learning are **personality factors** including **motivation**, **aptitude**, **attitude** and **empathy**.

A recurrent feature of L2 acquisition is **transfer** or **interference** from the L1 system. Transfer can also proceed from the L2 to the L1.

Guide to further reading

Good article-length accounts of first-language acquisition are chapter 8 of Gleason and Ratner (1998), MacWhinney (2001), and chapter 10 of O'Grady et al. (1989). Surveys of topics in acquisition can be found in Fletcher and MacWhinney (1996). Three good anthologies are Bloom (1996), Bowerman and Levinson (2001) and Lust and Foley (2004).

Ochs (1988) describes first-language acquisition in a non-Western culture, and Dan Slobin's multi-volume collection (1985a, 1985b, 1992, 1997a, 1997b) deals with first language acquisition in many languages. Chapter 5 of Emmorey (2002) deals with first-language acquisition of deaf sign languages, primarily American Sign Language.

Michael Halliday (1975/1977) and Michael Tomasello (2003a) set out very different socialization theories of acquisition. Elman et al. (1997), Gopnik et al. (2001) and Sampson (1997, 2005) take non-innatist perspectives on acquisition; Crain and Lillo-Martin (1998) and Pinker (1994) represent the innatist side.

The Child Language Data Exchange System (CHILDES), at http://childes.psy.cmu.edu/, contains acquisition data – including audio and video recordings and transcriptions – from children in various languages.

Cook (2001) provides an excellent account of current issues in second-language acquisition. Also worth reading are chapter 11 of O'Grady et al. (1989) and chapter 10 of Gleason and Ratner (1998). Recent textbooks on L2 acquisition include Bialystok and Hakuta (1994) and Gass and Selinker (1994). Evidence for the critical period hypothesis is discussed in Strozer (1994); Birdsong (1999) is a collection of articles presenting both sides of the argument. An alternative proposal, the perceptual magnet effect, is elaborated in Kuhl and Iverson (1995); see also Gopnik et al. (2001).

Issues for further thought and exercises

1. Two experimental methods that have been used to study speech perception in pre-speaking infants are the high amplitude sucking paradigm and the conditioned head-turn procedure. Find out about these two methods, and write a paragraph description of each, explaining their motivations (why do they work?).
2. How would you explain the use of the word-form *Mikey* as a term for bicycles and tricycles by the child referred to in §9.1 by the strategies for determining the meaning of words given in §9.2?

(Continued)

Issues for further thought and exercises—Cont'd

3. Below are some utterances produced by three children at different stages of development. What is the most likely order of the stages of development of the children based on these examples? Justify your ordering.

   a. *You want eat?*
      I can't see my book
      Why you waking me up?

   b. *Where those dogs goed?*
      You didn't eat supper
      Does lions walk?

   c. *No picture in there*
      Where momma boot?
      Have some?

4. What is the *wug*-test? Describe the test (the original is described in Berko 1958, available online at http://childes.psy.cmu.edu/topics/wugs/wugs.pdf) and its motivations (i.e. what was the reason for developing it). Design a *wug* test to explore the acquisition of other grammatical categories such as: agentive derivations (-*er* as in *farmer*); the progressive aspect (the -*ing* form of verbs); and nominative and accusative cases (for a language with nominal cases as an inflectional category).

5. We mentioned that deaf children babble vocally, and later with their hands. See what you can find out about the acquisition of sign language by deaf children. What stages does it follow, and are the stages comparable to the stages of acquisition of spoken languages? (Some references are Meier and Newport (1990) and Newport and Meier (1985); a very basic outline can be found at http://www.cms-kids.com/SHINE/documents/ASL_Stages_Development_I.pdf.)

6. What is the *gavagai* problem? Give a brief description and comment on how serious a problem you think it might be to first- and/or second-language learners. Could the strategies mentioned in §9.2 assist in its resolution? What other factors might be brought into account?

7. The following is a small selection of two-word utterances of a child of two years and nine months age (cited in Blake 2008: 237). Describe the morpho-syntax of this child's speech as revealed by these examples.

a. *Bubble coming*	'a bubble is coming'
b. *Bubble come*	'a bubble is coming'
c. *Smack daddy*	'I'm going to smack daddy'
d. *Naughty me*	'I am naughty' [Reply to 'Why did you hit Lawrence?']
e. *Gone pencil*	'my pencil has gone'
f. *Smack Laurie*	'smack Lawrence!'
g. *Sockie here*	'your socks are here'
h. *Study bed*	'he is studying in his bedroom'
i. *Finish tea*	'have you finished tea [evening meal]?'
j. *Near daddy*	'I'll put this chair near daddy'
k. *Out bed*	'I want to get out of bed'
l. *Clothes wet*	'her clothes are wet'

8. What is foreigner talk? Compare it with caretaker speech, identifying similarities and differences. Do you think that foreigner talk is useful to the acquisition of an L2? Explain your reasons.

9. Find out about the immersion approach to second-language learning. Describe the method briefly (in a few paragraphs) and comment on its usefulness; do you perceive any inadequacies?

10. George Birdsong's introductory chapter to his *Second Language Acquisition and the Critical Period Hypothesis* (1999:1–22) outlines evidence for and against the critical period. Summarise the evidence he presents, and comment on its relevance to the critical period. How might proponents of the hypothesis deal with the counterevidence? What do you conclude from Birdsong's discussion?

11. The following is a transcription of a description of a classroom scene by an L2 speaker of English whose native language is Spanish. What 'errors' are represented? Which do you guess result from interference from Spanish, and which would you attribute to overgeneralization or other processes? Check a grammar of Spanish to see whether your guessed interference error is reasonable.

In a room there are three womens . . . one is blond . . . blond hair . . . there are three womens . . . one woman is the teacher . . . and the other two womans are seat in the chair . . . one of them are . . . are blond hair . . . and the other woman . . . is black hair . . . the teacher is made an explanation about shapes . . . triangle circle

Notes

1. Telegrams were costed by the number of words, and so function words were kept to a minimum. Thus *We arrived safely and are having a good time* in telegram form would be *Arrived safely having good time*. Who would want to pay for *we*, *and*, *are* and *a*?

2. Basic-level categories are neutral levels in taxonomies, the levels that are most cognitively prominent. Examples are the categories of dogs, cats, horses – in most everyday circumstances one refers to members of these species with the terms *dog*, *cat* and *horse* rather than the more generic *animal* or more specific terms like *poodle* or *labrador*.

10 Language in Its Biological Context

We have now explored language in its social context, in the context of individual speakers, and in the context of learners. To complete our project of situating language in human life, we adopt the widest perspective and consider it in its biological context. The main issue concerns the status of language in relation to communicative systems employed in the non-human animal world: is language unique to human beings? If so, is it a system without precedents in the biological world – possibly the result of a fortuitous genetic mutation – or was language an evolutionary development from some simpler system of communication?

Chapter contents

Goals

The goals of the chapter are to:
- describe some systems of communication used in the animal world;
- evaluate the extent to which natural animal communication systems satisfy the design features of human language;
- discuss the ability of members of other species to learn human language; and
- introduce some theories of the origins of human language.

Key terms

alarm calls	bonobos	gestural origins of language	language evolution
ape gestures	chimpanzees		language origins
ape vocalizations	feral children	gorillas	primates
bee dances	FOXP2 gene	grooming and gossip hypothesis	signing
bird calls	genetic encoding of language		Specific Language Impairment (SLI)
bird songs		indexical signs	
bodily signs		joint attention	vervet monkeys

10.1 Natural communication systems of other animals

We explore the question of the uniqueness of human language from two different angles. First, in this section, we examine human language in relation to the natural communication systems of other animals:[1] what properties do they share, and to what extent are they different? Second, in §10.2, we discuss the ability of animals to learn and use human language: to what extent are they capable of acquiring human languages?

These two questions are of interest in relation to the origins of human language, which we deal with in §10.3. If we can show that non-human animal communication systems exist that share features of human languages, and that our closest biological relatives have systems that most resemble human language, this would count as evidence in favour of the evolution of language from animal communication systems, and that language differs in degree rather than kind from these other systems. Even if we could find evidence that other species can learn human language to a significant degree, this might count in favour of the evolutionary development of human language from systems of animal communication. Not finding such evidence does not, however, argue against an evolutionary story: it may be that there are no living species sufficiently close to us biologically to reveal the continuity. Our lineage diverged from our closest biological relatives the chimpanzees some five to six million years ago; the only remains of the intermediate species that emerged and lived during these millions of years are fossils; the species themselves are extinct.

Our two questions are of interest for other reasons as well. If animals have the capacity to acquire human languages this would count as evidence that language is not a peculiarity of human beings, or a genetic endowment of our species. It would argue in favour of the idea that language is not encoded in a module in the brain entirely separate from general intelligence. Again, if it is found that animals do not have this capability, it does not follow that language is encoded in our genes, or that it is stored and processed separately in the brain.

It could only be concluded that animals lack the necessary genetic or neurological requirements.

Many stories have appeared over recent decades, and continue to appear, in the popular media about apes and other animals with amazing talents for human language. Popular magazines, papers, and television series talk of animals with large vocabularies, with grammar, with the ability to create novel utterances that they have not previously heard, with the ability to communicate their thoughts and feelings to their human trainers and so on. Such claims are often highly exaggerated and emotional; critical scientific evaluation is required before they can be accepted.

Commonalities of signs in communication systems of humans and animals

Certain bodily signs indicating emotions are shared among humans and animals. For example, Charles Darwin describes in his *The Expression of the Emotions in Man and Animals* the involuntary erection of feathers in birds and hair in mammals when angry or fearful (1898: 94-101). These involuntary behavioural events can be interpreted (not necessarily consciously) by other animals, and not only members of the same species, as indicators of the animal's emotional state; the other animal might as a consequence adopt an appropriate mode of behaviour – for instance, flight from a gorilla displaying such signals.

> Involuntary signs like the erection of hair or feathers are **indexical signs** or **indexes**, according to the classificatory scheme developed by the American philosopher Charles S. Pierce (1955). Indexical signs are characterized by association between form and meaning that arises through habitual co-presence; the form as it were points to the meaning. Other examples are smoke, which is an index of fire, and the first person pronoun *I*, which is an index pointing to the speaker.

Many animals signify submission by lowering their bodily position below that of a dominant animal, for example by cowering or curling up. Conversely, a dominant animal may raise its position – or the position of its head – above that of a subordinate. Similar bodily signs are employed by human beings. Thus, a person might bow their head as is sign of submission, or stand erect over another in an attempt to intimidate them.

Lower-pitched vocalizations are universally associated with aggression and dominance. This is based on an association between lower pitch and a larger vocal tract and bigger vocal folds, which in turn correlate with larger body size. A number of animal species – including red and fallow deer, koalas, lions and tigers – have a descended larynx, or at least a larynx that can be lowered by the animal during vocalization. This results in lowering of the resonances of the sound, thus exaggerating the perceived size of the vocalising animal, intimidating rivals and perhaps attracting females.[2]

Bodily signs carry important messages, often unconsciously and involuntarily; this is perhaps part of their usefulness, since they preclude deliberate deception. On the other hand, they can form the basis for deliberate signs expressing similar meanings, as for instance when an animal threatens or warns another with bared teeth, or higher bodily position, while not necessarily experiencing the naturally associated emotion. The conscious use of these systems is well developed among human beings, who can smile deceptively, or deliberately modify their height with items of clothing (shoes, or hats) to communicate dominance. Bodily positions and characteristics are also characteristics that, as in the case of lowering of the larynx, are amenable to evolutionary development.

Natural communication systems of some animal species

Aside from the systems of bodily signs that indicate the internal state of the individual, many animal species have communication systems that are used to convey information about the external world. In the following subsections we describe four such systems.

Bees

Some bee species have a system of communication that is used by foraging bees on their return to the hive to convey information about the location of nectar sources. The system of European honeybees, discovered by Karl von Frisch (for which he was awarded a Nobel Prize), involves two different types of dances. If the nectar source is close to the hive, a round dance is performed; other bees perceive the scent of the nectar on the dancing bee, and set off in all directions looking for it. If it is at some distance from the hive (over about 50 metres or so) the bee performs a tail-wagging dance that follows a figure 8 shape. The angle of the diagonal of this shape indicates direction of the nectar source. Usually it is performed in relation to the vertical; the angle of the diagonal of the figure to the vertical indicates the direction of the nectar source in relation to the sun. Thus if the diagonal is at 40° to the left of the vertical, as shown in Figure 10.1, the feeding place will be in a direction at an angle of 40° to the left of the current direction of the sun.

The speed of the tail-wagging dance indicates the distance of the nectar source from the hive: the more distant the source, the slower the rhythm of the dance. The bee also brings along attached to its body minute particles of the pollen from the flower; only those bees that gather from that type of flower will take any notice of the dance. Similar dances are performed by scouting bees to indicate a new site for the hive.

The bee's dance shows displacement (see §1.3), since the source of nectar may be some distance removed in space and time. However, displacement is limited in the sense that only an immediately relevant source is indicated, not a source that the bee visited on a previous foraging trip. There is also a minor degree of productivity in the system, in that the bee is not restricted to conveying information about known sources, and can modify the dance parameters so as to convey fairly precise information about a new source. But the message remains constrained to indicating horizontal direction, distance and type of nectar; the system does

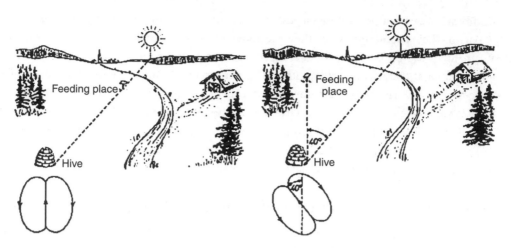

Figure 10.1 Indication of direction of nectar source by honey bee's tail wagging dance (from von Frisch's Nobel lecture, 1973 (Frisch 1992/1973), © The Nobel Foundation 1973)

not permit indication of vertical direction. Thus when von Frisch showed some honeybees a supply of sugary water at the top of a radio beacon, they duly performed the round dance in the hive at its foot. Other bees searched around for honey in the vicinity of the hive, looking everywhere except upwards. Eventually they gave up the search.

Bees improve their interpretation of the signs with increased age, perhaps suggesting some degree of cultural transmission. However, transmission is primarily genetic. Thus cross-breed offspring of different varieties of bees tend to know the dance of just one variety. And bees raised in isolation can interpret and perform the dance correctly when introduced to the hive.

Birds

Most birds have systems of communication employing vocalizations; many birds also communicate by non-vocalized sounds such as beak clapping, and by visual displays of objects (e.g. bower-birds), or dances (e.g. brolgas). Vocalizations fall into two types.

First, there are **calls**, brief bursts of sound such as whistles, screeches and chirps. These are generally of just a few syllables duration, and include alarm calls, food calls (indicating the location of food), signals between parents and offspring, and flocking calls.

A second type of vocalization are **songs**, which are more complex sequences of sounds that together form units that are typically separated from other songs by a relatively long pause. Experimental and observational evidence shows that bird-songs are used mainly by males, and often for one of two purposes: to attract a mate, or to mark out territory. Songs may be produced either individually, or by groups of two or more birds, as in the case of kookaburras. Some species have large inventories of songs, perhaps in the order of 200 for nightingales.

The songs of some song-bird species appear to be innate. In other species there is evidence of learning, although a genetic template for the song may also be present. In such species young birds learn by copying adult birds; if prevented from hearing the songs of adult birds, they still sing, but their songs are slower, simpler and more variable than the normal songs of their species. This suggests some measure of cultural transmission, which is supported by two further types of evidence. First, there is a critical period for acquisition of song in male zebra finches and various other species, a developmental period during which a bird must be exposed to adult songs in order for it to master the song. Second, some species, including the white-crowned sparrow, show dialect variation in their songs.

Dialect variation permits birds to recognize members of different groups. This identifying function is also one of the motivations for bird-song. Cues to sex and age can also be provided by voice-quality, which can also permit recognition of individual birds. For example, a sea-bird returning to a large colony may be recognizable to its family members by its distinctive voice quality.

In some species productivity is also apparent: birds may improvise on heard songs, perhaps to attract a mate. Female birds of various species (e.g. red-headed parrot finches and zebra finches) show definite preferences for males with elaborate courtship songs.

Vervet monkeys

Many species of monkeys use vocalizations as well as facial expressions and posture to communicate with one another. Vervet monkeys, which live in a variety of habitats in southern, eastern and western Africa, use bodily signs including head-bobbing (in threat displays), rapid glancing towards and away from another individual (communicating subordination), penile displays (demarcating territory) and tail-signals (indicating the degree of assuredness by degree of erection).

Vervet monkeys also have a system of vocalizations including at least 20 different sounds. Among these are alarm calls warning of the presence of predators. A high-pitched chutter warns of the presence of a snake; a chirp (short but loud barking call) gives warning of leopards and lions; a *rraup* or short cough-like call warns of an eagle; an *uh* warns of a minor predator such as a hyena; and a *nyow* indicates the sudden appearance of a minor predator. These warning signs elicit immediate defensive action: on hearing the 'eagle' warning call, vervets look skywards, and run for cover; on hearing the 'snake' call, they raise themselves on their hind-legs, and search the ground for a snake. In one experiment alarm calls were played through a concealed loudspeaker, resulting in the appropriate evasive action.

Vervet monkeys also have vocalizations that inform about the monkey's emotional state. A low-pitched chutter expresses an aggressive threat, or solicits support from other group members; a *woof-whoof* by subordinate males indicates submission; a series of nasal grunts are emitted by group members when the group starts to move.

The vocalizations of vervet monkeys appear to be arbitrary. They are also to some extent culturally transmitted: the vocalizations of young vervets increase in accuracy with age, and infants check adult responses before responding themselves. Adult vervets also react differently to alarm calls of adult and young individuals: on hearing an alarm signal by a young monkey they first check for themselves whether a predator is present before initiating evasive action. Comprehension also precedes production.

Alarm calls are given only when danger is present. The system shows no displacement, for example, use of the calls in reference to predators present on other occasions. However, signs are occasionally used deceptively: one monkey might give a sign of submission, then bite a rival. Vervets are not creative in combining signs to form new and more complex signs, or inventing new signs to make new meanings. Also unlike human language is the fact that all vocal signs are concerned with regulating the behaviour of other vervets; no vocalizations are used purely for the conveyance of information about the state of the world. Thus there are no vocalizations for informing of the presence of harmless species that pose no threat.

Apes

Apes also have systems of communication that include vocalized and non-vocalized signs, including bodily gestures.

Chimpanzees have at least a score of vocalized calls that have been described by Jane Goodall (1986). These constitute indivisible whole utterances, and cannot be combined into sequences or decomposed; they show no duality of patterning (§1.3). Moreover, chimpanzee vocalizations, like the vocalizations of other apes, appear to be largely involuntary, and beyond conscious control. Goodall describes an instance in which a chimpanzee found a cache of bananas. He wished to keep it to himself, but was unable to suppress the pant-hoot vocalization; nevertheless he deliberately muffled it by placing a hand over his mouth. Conversely, 'production of sound in the *absence* of the appropriate emotional state seems to be an almost impossible task for a chimpanzee' (Goodall 1986: 125). This is presumably an adaptive advantage: since most ape vocalizations are warning signals, or signals relating to territory and mating, being involuntary makes them difficult to fake.

Gestural communication is better developed and more flexible in apes than vocalizations. Some gestures are involuntary bodily displays expressing emotional states (see p. 226). But there are others. Studies of gorillas and chimpanzees in relatively free-ranging naturalistic zoos have revealed the use of systems of gestural communication containing over 30 signs. In contrast with vocalizations, manual gestures are voluntary, and can be controlled. Moreover, unlike vocalizations, they are intentionally directed to specific recipients, and are generally produced when the intended recipient is watching.

According to Michael Tomasello, chimpanzees employ two main types of intentional gesture in natural communication with other chimpanzees. One type is an attention attractor, a gesture aimed at getting another to look at the gesturer. The second type is a stylized gesture signifying an incipient or desired action. For example, many young chimpanzees use a stylized gesture to their mother, such as a brief touch on the top of the rear end, to request her to lower her back so they can climb on. These gestures are idiosyncratic, and used exclusively with the individual's mother; many attention attractor gestures are also idiosyncratic rather than conventionalized at the social group level.

Chimpanzees employ gestures for social-regulative purposes, attracting attention to the self or to request action, but not purely for purposes of informing about the world. They do not use gestures to direct attention to something for the purpose of sharing interest in it; thus they do not draw other chimpanzees' attention to an object by pointing at it.

10.2 Teaching human language to animals

The animal communication systems discussed in §10.1 all fail to satisfy one or more of Hockett's design features of human language (see §1.3). In all of the cases we discussed, displacement was either absent, or minimal – if the animal could communicate about something that was not physically present, it had to be something of current relevance. Moreover, animal communication systems seem to be used to convey a rather limited range of meanings, from a predetermined set.

Perhaps it is a mere accident that animals did not develop communicative systems as elaborate as human language; maybe some animals actually do have the capability of acquiring human language. Numerous instances have been reported over the past century of animals acquiring human language, as well as of performing a range of other complex mental operations, such as arithmetic, that one thinks of as uniquely human. In this section we focus on attempts to teach a human language – or a simplified version of a human language – to apes. But before we embark on this, we look briefly at the linguistic ability of one non-primate species, one with a long history of domestication.

Dogs' understanding of human language

Dog owners often speak to their pets, which they believe are capable of understanding much (if not everything) that is said to them. For example, an owner says *heel*, and the dog returns to its owner; or *fetch* and it fetches a thrown ball.

An investigation by Juliane Kaminski and associates examined a border collie, Rico, reported by its owners to know words for over 200 different items, which it would fetch when instructed (Kaminski et al. 2004). The dog had been trained from ten months of age to fetch items placed in different locations around the owners' flat, and had been rewarded for fetching the correct object.

In order to circumvent the 'Clever Hans' effect,[3] the experimenters had the owner request Rico to fetch two items randomly selected from the 200 that the dog was allegedly familiar with from an adjacent room. The owner and experimenter were both out of sight of the dog when it selected the items. Rico performed well on the task, and the experimenters conclude that he did know the labels for the items.

More strikingly, the dog could rapidly learn names for unfamiliar toys. The owner would first ask Rico to bring a familiar object. Then Rico was asked to bring an unfamiliar item with a name that he had not previously heard. He was able to fetch the novel object from a group of eight items consisting of seven familiar objects, performing this accurately in seven out of ten attempts. It appears that Rico was operating on the principle that a new word would belong to an unfamiliar and hitherto unnamed object (see 'Novel name–new category' principle in §9.2). Furthermore, after a period of a month during which he had no access to the new object, he was able to remember many of the new labels, fetching the correct thing from a group of novel and known objects on half of the occasions.

Does this study show that 'dogs understand language', as a CNN headline on Thursday 10 June 2004 put it? Certainly not, if by language is meant human language. Two hundred words for material objects is a far cry from the rich lexicons of human languages, which consist of many thousands of words, including words for events as well as things. Rico's understanding of words for objects is based on fetching. One wonders whether he could perform an instruction to do something other than fetch the object, not to fetch something, or learn a word for something not fetchable, such as a sofa. Could he, for instance, understand and perform *Bite the cushion and lie on the sofa*?

Apes

Not surprisingly, the most serious attempts to teach a human language to animals have been made with our closest relatives, the apes. The earliest attempts were made in the first half of the twentieth century, and were resounding failures. In the 1920s, Robert Yerkes attempted unsuccessfully to teach chimps to speak, and proposed that sign language be taught instead. In the 1930s Winthrop and Luella Kellogg acquired a seven-month old chimpanzee Gua, which they brought up like a human child, alongside their own son. Although Gua was able to understand over 70 words, she never spoke. In the late 1940s Keith and Cathy Hayes acquired Viki, who they attempted to teach English. Despite intensive coaching over a period of three years, she learnt to say just four words – *mama*, *papa*, *cup*, and *up* – though she was able to recognize around 100 words.

These attempts failed partly for physiological reasons. The human vocal tract is adapted for speech, with its short jaw, rounded tongue and lowered larynx with the right angled bend between the pharynx and oral cavity; chimpanzees lack these physiological adaptations (compare Figure 10.2 with Figure 2.2), and are incapable of articulating the range of sounds of human languages. In particular, the high front and back vowels, [i] and [u], are outside of their range. Moreover, as has already been mentioned, vocalizations in apes are largely involuntary. For all these reasons, recent experiments have attempted to teach apes signs of ASL (American Sign Language) or invented systems employing plastic tokens or keys on a computer keyboard.

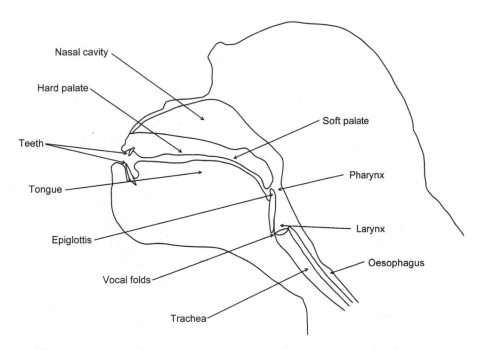

Figure 10.2 Vocal tract of the chimpanzee.

Teaching ASL to chimpanzees

The first attempt to teach ASL signs to a chimpanzee was made in the mid-1960s by Beatrix and Allen Gardner. They and their research assistants raised a female chimpanzee named Washoe, acquired in 1966 at about a year in age, in a domestic environment. Washoe was not subjected to rigorous training schedules, but left to acquire ASL in a relatively 'natural' way. The humans around her communicated with one another and with Washoe in ASL. By 1975 Washoe had learned to use around 150 signs. Washoe was also able to combine signs to express more complex meanings. She made a number of two and three sign sequences of her own invention, such as *listen eat* for 'listen to the dinner gong', *open food drink* for 'open the refrigerator', and *gimme tickle* for 'tickle me'. She is also said to have made novel words, such as combining the sign for 'water' with the sign for 'bird' on seeing a swan. Similar abilities were reported a short time later for a gorilla called Koko.

Another famous attempt to teach a chimpanzee ASL was made by Herbert S. Terrace and colleagues. Beginning in 1973, Nim Chimpsky was taught ASL under controlled conditions from the age of four months; detailed records were kept of his progress, including video recordings. Like other chimpanzees, Nim acquired an active vocabulary of around 125 signs, and comprehension of some 200. He put the signs together into sequences, as shown in Figure 10.3, which illustrates a three-sign sequence. These sequences showed some

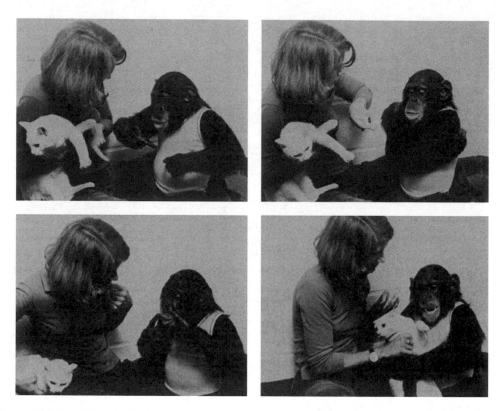

Figure 10.3 Nim Chimpsky signing *me hug cat* to trainer. (Terrace, et al. 1979: 892; reprinted with permission from AAAS, Herbert S. Terrace and coauthors.)

regularities of ordering. For example, in two-sign sequences *more* occurred in initial position about 80 per cent of the time, and the verb preceded the object with about the same frequency. Closer examination revealed that Nim's signing showed preferences for ordering particular words – for example *more* was preferred at the beginning of a sequence, *Nim* at the end. Many other words showed random distribution. In Nim's two-sign sequences involving *eat*, the order *eat Nim* occurred 302 times as against 209 instances of *Nim eat* and 237 of *me eat*; in all instances Nim was the eater. It cannot be concluded from Nim's utterances that he was using a consistent ordering of signs to distinguish who is acting on who.

Nim's average utterance length remained at about 1.5 signs. Furthermore, his multi-sign utterances were characterized by a high degree of repetition. About 20 per cent of his three-sign utterances involve repetition of a sign; another 28 per cent involve both the sign for *Nim* and the sign for *me*. Nim's longest utterance, consisting of 16 signs, *give orange me give eat orange me eat orange give me eat orange give me you* is highly repetitive, and contains just five different sign types.

Terrace also found that a high proportion of Nim's utterances were full or partial imitations of signs recently given by his trainers. Nim rarely initiated a conversational exchange.

Almost 90 per cent of his utterances were given in response to his teachers. Re-examining films of Washoe's and other apes' use of signs, Terrace concluded that the same held true of them: all were producing a high proportion of prompted repetitions of the signs made by their trainers. It seemed that the chimpanzees were producing signs in order to receive rewards.

Teaching chimpanzees to use tokens or keys

Other investigators have employed, instead of ASL, systems of arbitrary signs made up of plastic tokens or keys on keyboards labelled with symbols. In 1966 David and Ann Premack began to train their chimp Sarah to manipulate plastic tokens as signs. Many of these tokens were quite arbitrary: for instance, the sign for 'banana' was in a square shape, for 'chocolate', an X shape with a vertical line through the middle. Sarah understood over 100 signs, and is reported to have understood conditional sentences such as *if apple, then chocolate* – given the choice between taking an apple and a banana she would choose an apple in order to get the (greatly desired) chocolate reward.

More recently plastic tokens have been replaced by light-up keys on keyboards connected to computers. Sue Savage-Rumbaugh and colleagues trained bonobos (pygmy chimpanzees) to use such symbols on a portable keypad. Their most notable success was with Kanzi, who acquired proficiency in the system not through direct training, but by observing his mother's less than successful training. He eventually acquired a vocabulary of some 250 signs, and is said to use key order to express meaning – *Kanzi tickle Sue* to mean that he would do the tickling, vs. *Sue tickle Kanzi* to mean that he wanted Sue to tickle him.

Another bonobo in Savage-Rumbaugh's training program, Panbanisha, is reported to have been strolling along with a group of scientists when she suddenly pulled one of them aside and repeatedly pressed the keys *fight*, *mad* and *Austin* in various combinations on her keyboard. It was understood that she meant by this that there had been a fight in Austin's building (Austin was another chimp). On investigation this proved to have been the case. According to Savage-Rumbaugh, Panbanisha had never before put these three symbols together; moreover, the message was manifestly not motivated by a desire for a food reward, and was initiated by the chimpanzee. Notice, however, that Panbanisha was employing the same strategy as Nim Chimpsky in her longer utterances: repetition of a few signs, with no attempt to elaborate or reformulate the message.

Evaluation of apes' language abilities

Investigators disagree on whether use of signs by apes is comparable with human language. Nevertheless, differences are manifest, and it cannot reasonably be claimed that the systems that apes have learnt show all of the features of human languages. No ape has been demonstrated to actively use anything like the many thousands of signs that the average speaker of any human language controls; and the utterances produced by apes, as we have seen, tend to be short and, beyond a few symbols, highly repetitious. Whether the combinations of symbols follow a grammatical system is uncertain.

The communication systems taught to apes fail to satisfy two of Hockett's six design features discussed in §1.3. No study has demonstrated that the signs show either duality of patterning or reflexivity. However, the other four properties are satisfied to some degree at least: the signs are arbitrary; at least some degree of displacement is evident (e.g. in the case of Panbanisha's communication about Austin); the systems are culturally transmitted and learned; and there is indication (not uncontested) of some degree of productivity.

It also seems that chimpanzees are more prone to interrupt utterances by their teachers than usually occurs in human conversational exchanges. They rarely initiate communicative acts, though they are not incapable of doing so. In an experiment described in Menzel (1999), a female chimpanzee called Panzee observed an experimenter hide an object (e.g. food) in the trees outside her enclosure over a number of trials. After delays of up to 16 hours she could interact with a human who did not know about the hidden object. From the beginning of the experiment Panzee did whatever was necessary to gain the person's attention, used her keyboards to indicate the type of object hidden, and manual pointing to indicate the location of the object.

It cannot be concluded from either studies of animal communication systems or attempts to teach apes and other animals to use human language that the evidence favours the evolution of human language from animal communication systems. Nor does it favour the evolution of our language production and comprehension abilities from the general cognitive abilities of our ancestors. Nevertheless, as observed at the beginning of §10.1, this lack of evidence does not argue for a non-evolutionary scenario, or for a separate language module in the mind. Indeed, overall it seems that the language abilities of human beings differs from the abilities of animals in degree rather than kind. The evidence suggests that some of the cognitive mechanisms involved in speech comprehension and production may have been in place prior to the emergence of human language. Perhaps the apparent qualitative differences between human language and animal communication systems are the result of the piling-up of quantitative differences. This brings us naturally to our next topic, the origin and development of human language.

10.3 Origins and evolution of human language

Divine origins and the 'original' human tongue

Our unique ability to speak has inspired wonder and attempted explanations from time immemorial. Many, if not all, religions have myths accounting for language origins and/or diversification. Often a divine source is proposed. According to the Judea-Christian tradition, God gave Adam the power to name things; the Tower of Babel story accounts for the subsequent diversity of languages. Babylonians attributed language to the god Nabu, Egyptians to the god Thoth and Hindus to Sarasvati, wife of Brahma. According to some Australian Aboriginal societies, languages were implanted in particular tracts of country by Dreamtime beings during the Dreamtime, a formative stage in which the world came to be as it is.

Operating within the parameters of such divine notions of language origins, various experiments have been carried out to determine what the original language was. According to the Greek historian Herodotus, around 600 BC the Egyptian pharaoh Psammetichus segregated two newborn infants in an isolated mountain hut with a shepherd who was instructed to allow no one to speak in their presence. The pharaoh's idea was that in isolation from linguistic input they would speak the original human language. The first word they produced was reported to have been *bekos*. This was discovered to be the word for 'bread' in Phrygian, a now extinct Indo-European language spoken in the north-west of modern Turkey. Around 2,000 years later King James IV of Scotland did a similar experiment in which children were isolated. They, however, allegedly started speaking Hebrew; this was taken as evidence that Hebrew was the language spoken by Adam. A variety of other languages have been proposed for one reason or another as the original tongue of humans (including German, Aramaic and Chinese).

Experiments like those performed by Psammetichus and James IV are not, of course, repeated by linguists in this day and age. Occasionally, however, children grow up in virtual social isolation, in circumstances in which they have been exposed to little or no language. Some of these 'feral' children were apparently reared by animals, as in the case of two children found in India in 1920, said to have been brought up by wolves. A recent case is Genie, discovered in 1970 at the age of 14. Genie had been confined to a small room and had experienced only minimal human contact from the age of 18 months. None of these children spoke a language when they were discovered, nor did they subsequently learn one fully. Genie did, however, learn a relatively large vocabulary, though her syntax remained quite simple. She apparently went through many of the same early stages of acquisition that children normally go through (see §9.1).

Nineteenth-century theories of language origins

The nineteenth-century linguist Max Müller suggested a famous classification of theories of language origins, distinguishing the 'la-la', the 'bow-wow', the 'ding-dong', the 'pooh-pooh' and the 'yo-heave-ho' theories.

The 'la-la' (or 'sing-song') theory sees the origins of human language in a communication system resembling bird-song (see §10.1). The Danish linguist Otto Jespersen favoured this theory, presenting an idyllic Rousseauan view of human-kind's origins:

> The genesis of language is not to be sought in the prosaic, but in the poetic side of life; the source of speech is not gloomy seriousness, but merry play and youthful hilarity . . . In primitive speech I hear the laughing cries of exultation when lads and lassies vied with one another to attract the attention of the other sex, when everybody sang his merriest and danced his bravest to lure a pair of eyes to throw admiring glances in his direction. Language was born in the courting days of mankind. (Jespersen 1922: 433–434)

The 'bow-wow' theory proposes that human language began with mimicry of natural sounds of the environment. A bird's or animal's call might be imitated, and this imitation used to refer to the creature; or a noise might be imitated and used as a verb to denote an event associated with the noise – for example, *splash*, *bang* and *crash*. According to this view, language origins lie in iconic rather than arbitrary signs.

The 'ding-dong' theory also suggests that language originated in natural connections between meanings and sounds. These could be iconic connections, as in the imitation of physical sounds. Alternatively they might be indexical connections, as in the case of *mama* for 'mother', supposedly deriving from the sound made by a baby as its lips approach its mother's breast.

According to the 'pooh-pooh' theory language originated in natural cries of emotion such as anger or pain, as when someone utters *yow* or *ouch* in pain, or *yuck* as an expression of distaste. Darwin championed this theory.

The 'yo-heave-ho' theory proposes that the sounds uttered by persons when engaged in strenuous physical exertion provide the source of earliest language. The grunts and groans that are naturally emitted in circumstances of exertion might then have taken on other meanings or senses in social contexts, perhaps being interpreted by hearers as requests for assistance.

While the 'bow-wow', 'ding-dong', 'pooh-pooh' and 'yo-heave-ho' theories may account for some words in human languages, it is difficult to see how they can explain much more. It is not clear why morphology should have arisen at all. As for the 'sing-song' theory, why would we have anything but unanalysable songs (holophrases) used in a delimited range circumstances? Why didn't these songs remain the domain of one of the sexes, as in the case of birds? What drove the emergence of utterances analysable into components?

More recent theories of language origins

In 1866 the Linguistic Society of Paris imposed a ban on papers on the origins of human language, a restriction it reaffirmed in 1911. Linguists have by and large supported the sentiments of the ban ever since on the grounds that investigations of origins can only be speculative and, in the absence of technology for time-travel, unverifiable.

Anthropologists, archaeologists, geneticists, psychologists, neurobiologists and others have been more daring, and have not shied from speculation informed by findings in their disciplines. It is only recently that linguists themselves have turned attention again to the question of origins. While it is true that one can only speculate, speculation does play a role in science. And serious speculations will perforce be constrained and informed by the fields within which the investigator works. If there is convergence in the findings across different fields one may feel more confident in a speculation. The area provides a good domain for interdisciplinary research, provided one enters it with an open mind, and does not adopt the rhetorical stance of some linguists that only linguists have the warrant to make statements about language – for surely this is an area where we cannot rely on a single discipline.

In the following subsections I outline with a very broad brush a few of what seem to me to be the more interesting recent proposals about language origins. No attempt is made to be comprehensive: there are far too many theories to mention in an introductory survey; some are too complex to summarize in a few paragraphs, and have been left out for that reason. Nor do I attempt to be critical – all the proposals are based on circumstantial evidence, and can be fairly easily critiqued on the grounds that they leave unexplained a rack of known facts about the structure and/or functions of human language. In other words, at best they might account for the emergence of a communicative system of complexity less than that of human language; all take recourse to much hand-waving.

Gestural origins

One popular notion, with a long history, is that human language originated in bodily gestures that were later transferred to the vocal medium. Our ancestors such as the australopithecines may have communicated with bodily signs before their vocal tracts were capable of speech. One attraction of this idea is that apes have intentional control of manual gestures but not of vocalizations (see §10.2), and the same was presumably true of our common ancestor, and likely also of some of the descendant hominid species. Following Max Müller's lead, we will refer to this theory as 'noddy'.

The main problem with 'noddy' is how to account for the switch from manual gestures to vocal gestures. Perhaps over a long period of time manual gestures became increasingly accompanied by vocalizations, that may have begun with grunts; this process may have continued until the point was reached where the balance shifted from primacy of the visual to primacy of the vocal. This shift could have been sustained and enhanced by practical advantages such as the possibility of using vocalizations in the dark, and the freeing up of the hands for other tasks, thus allowing one to carry out manual activities at the same time as speaking. But it would have necessitated biological changes to both the vocal organs and brain. The advent of bipedalism some five or six million years ago was, according to some (e.g. Corballis 2003; Lieberman 2003), a crucial first step in these biological changes. Alternatively, a genetic mutation that occurred some time in the last 100,000 years may have been responsible (Corballis 2003).

Michael Arbib (2003) has suggested that biological evolution led to a language-ready brain, a key development being the evolution of the system of mirror neurons that link production and perception of motor acts of grasping (see §8.2). Intriguingly, these are found in a region of the cortex of a monkey's brain that is considered to be the analogue of Broca's area. As Arbib observes, it is not that a switch occurred in the development of human language from the manual to the vocal medium; rather, the relative load of the latter increased. Facial and manual gestures arguably form with speech a single multi-modal communication system, as also argued by gesture specialists such as David McNeill.

The grooming hypothesis

Robin Dunbar (1996) proposes the grooming hypothesis – the 'yackety-yack' theory – which assigns primacy to the interpersonal and social dimensions in the emergence of language. He observes that grooming is the favoured bonding mechanism amongst primates.

However, human groups tend to be too large – the order of 150 members – for grooming to be viable. Individuals would need to spend about 40 per cent of their waking day grooming; given that this is time during which they could do little else, it is far too much to be practical. (The highest proportion of time observed among any primate is half of this, among Gelada baboons.) Speech provides a means of grooming at a distance; it can also be done while engaged in other activities, and is not restricted to pairs – multiple partners can be groomed simultaneously. As Dunbar observes, much of our everyday use of language is in gossip, which can be seen as an investment in the verbal servicing of social relationships.

Language as a genetic predisposition

Everyone agrees that we are genetically adapted for speech: although both the baby and the rattle are exposed to the same linguistic input, only the baby acquires language. The human brain and/or mind cannot be a *tabula rasa*. What investigators disagree on is the extent of our genetic endowment, whether the minimal view that our genes give us a language-ready brain or the maximal view that we have a genetic blueprint for language.

Two divergent opinions are held by those who maintain the maximal position, which we'll call the 'just genes' theory. On the one hand there are those who, like Chomsky, suggest that language arose in one unique and isolated biological event, as the result of a single genetic mutation and not by the normal evolutionary process of natural selection (Chomsky 1986) – the 'Oops!' theory. On the other hand there are investigators like Stephen Pinker who argue that language is a biological adaptation that evolved in the human species via the normal evolutionary process of natural selection. Language is, according to Pinker's story – the 'chatting-up' theory[4] – an innate specialization that evolved for the encoding of propositional information in a form that permits it to be conveyed from one individual to another.

If the 'Oops!' theory is correct, a single gene ought to be responsible for language. A possible candidate for this is the FOXP2 gene, the first gene to be shown to be relevant to language. A mutation in this gene was shown by geneticists in 2001 to be associated with a type of language disorder – called Specific Language Impairment (SLI) – characterized by articulation difficulties and grammatical impairments. However, it seems increasingly likely that it cannot be a single gene that is responsible for language,[5] which counts against the single mutation scenario, and in favour of the natural selection scenario. Thus, language is not completely wiped out in those individuals showing the mutation in FOXP2, and other genes have been shown to be associated with SLI. Furthermore, an investigation by a team of geneticists into the distributions of the FOXP2 gene across a range of animal and human populations revealed that the most likely scenario is that the gene has been the target of selection during recent human evolution (Enard et al. 2002).

Language and social cognition

Many investigators now consider that the last and perhaps most significant steps in the evolution of language – in particular the development of complex syntax – were cultural rather than biological, and focus on the social and cultural environment in which language arose.

According to this view, there was no specific biological adaptation for human language in the shape we find it today; rather, we reached a stage of having a brain that was ready for language, before we had language. Language evolved in a cultural, not biological, setting.

Michael Tomasello has proposed (1999, 2003b) that a crucial aspect of this was the emergence of a type of social cognition that enabled the development of human culture, and human symbolic communication within it. Crucial in this was the evolution of the ability to recognize other individuals as intentional agents who one can share attention with. According to this 'looky-look' theory, the capacity for joint attention is crucial to the development of sharing of experience – and thus information – as well as collaborative action. Fully modern human languages developed, according to 'looky-look', via processes of grammaticalization (roughly, the emergence of grammatical elements from lexical elements – see §12.5) operating over periods of millennia on the grammatically less complex communicative systems that arose in the biological evolution of our species.

Concluding remarks on language evolution

It is fair to say that the majority viewpoint is tending towards the notion that our genetic make-up permits us to acquire language, rather than that language is genetically encoded. To use a computer analogy, our genes gave us the necessary biological hardware, but not the software, which emerged more recently, after the biological machinery was in place, in the human cultural context. Many investigators now situate the final steps in the evolution of language in human culture, in the interpersonal context. It is also widely accepted that unanalysable and independent symbols emerged first; syntax came much later.

Although investigations of the communicative systems and abilities of animals does not unassailably support the gradual evolution of language from other communication systems, it cannot be doubted that the majority of fundamental biological components and processes involved in vocal production and perception are shared with animals. They are modifications of existing features, rather than entirely novel. Given this, it is difficult to disagree with those who hold that comparative investigation of non-human communicative systems is a fruitful perspective for the exploration of the evolution of human language.

Another point of widespread (though not universal) consensus is that investigation of the evolution of language is not the prerogative of linguistics, but is best approached from many different disciplinary perspectives. We have mentioned anthropology, archaeology, psychology, genetics and neurobiology. Computer and mathematical modelling have recently come to prominence as means of testing theories, especially where multiple factors are involved.

Summing up

Many animals species have **natural systems of communication** employing bodily gestures and vocalizations to express emotional states, to warn conspecifics of dangers, to demarcate territorial boundaries, and for mating. These systems do not satisfy all of the design features of human languages. This does not mean that other animals are incapable of producing or comprehending human language, and many attempts have been made to teach human language to other species. The most successful have focused on apes. The systems apes have learnt show some of the design features of human languages, though duality of patterning and reflexivity are conspicuously absent.

Studies of natural communication systems of animals and attempts to teach animals human language do not argue strongly either for or against the evolution of language from animal communication systems. However, some cognitive mechanisms of language appear to have been in place prior to the evolution the modern humans.

Speculations on the **origins** of human language go back into prehistory. The nineteenth century saw the emergence of many theories, including 'bow-wow', 'ding-dong', 'pooh-pooh', 'yo-heave-ho' and 'la-la'. Recent years have seen the emergence of more sophisticated theories. According to 'noddy', language has its origins in **gestures**; 'yackety-yack' suggests that language emerged to facilitate **gossip** and as a replacement for manual **grooming**.

'Just genes' proposes that language is **genetically encoded**. According to one variant, 'chatting-up', language evolved by the normal evolutionary processes of natural selection; an alternative variant, 'oops', maintains that language emerged as an accidental genetic mutation. **Specific Language Impairment** (SLI) is associated with a mutation of the **FOXP2 gene**, which was for a time heralded as the 'language gene'. However, recent evidence indicates that FOXP2 gene is not specific to language.

A clutch of recent theories consider the final steps in the emergence of human language to have been **cultural**: biological evolution gave us a **language-ready brain**, but language arose in a socio-cultural setting. One such theory is 'looky-look', which argues that **joint attention** was the critical development.

Guide to further reading

Animal communication systems are surveyed in Bright (1984), and Morton and Page (1992). The communicative dances of honeybees are nicely described in Karl von Frisch's 1973 Nobel lecture (Frisch 1992/1973, available online at http://nobelprize.org/nobel_prizes/medicine/laureates/1973/frisch-lecture.pdf). Vocal communication of birds is described in Kroodsma et al. (1982). Cheney and Seyfarth (1990) deals with communication systems of monkeys, while Goodall (1986) treats chimpanzee communication.

Attempts to teach language to chimpanzees are described in Hayes (1951); Gardner and Gardner (1971); Premack and Premack (1993); Savage-Rumbaugh and Lewin (1994); and Terrace (1979). For a critical overview see Seboek and Umiker-Seboek (1980). On the Clever-Hans effect, see Seboek and Rosenthal (1980).

Genie's acquisition of language is described in Curtiss (1977), and Curtiss et al. (1974) (reprinted in Lust and Foley 2004); see also Rymer (1994).

For a brief survey of some of the main approaches to the evolution of human language see Carstairs-McCarthy (2001). Slightly older but still good overviews of the field from the perspective of linguistics are Aitchison (1996), and chapter 2 of Foley (1997). The classic work dealing with biological aspects of language evolution is Lenneberg (1967); this book is now dated, and many of the ideas it presents have been challenged. Fitch (2000) is a more recent overview; also interesting is Lieberman (2000). Christiansen and Kirby (2003), is a collection of articles covering a variety of different perspectives on language evolution; I recommend it as a starting point for anyone who seriously wants to find out more about current ideas on language evolution. Other recent edited collections are Hurford et al. (1998), Knight et al. (2000), Givón and Malle (2002) and Wray (2002). Johansson (2005) identifies a number of facts that must be taken into account in any viable theory of the evolution of language.

Issues for further thought and exercises

1. It is sometimes suggested that linguists' attempts to show that other animals' communication systems are not human languages reflect neurotic desires to prove that human beings are superior to other animals. Do you think this is a valid criticism? Why or why not? (Why don't linguists concern themselves with the proposition that barking is restricted to dogs, or meowing to cats, for instance?)
2. The involuntary erection of hair and feathers was classified as an indexical sign in §10.1. Can you explain why in more detail? It is also possible to regard it as an iconic sign. Explain how. Use your explanation to suggest an evolutionary account of the development of this involuntary action.
3. To what extent do the systems of bodily signs discussed in the section 'Commonalities of signs in communication systems of humans and animals' in §10.1 satisfy the properties of human language? Evaluate them in relation to Hockett's design features.
4. To what extent are the signs of the bee's dance arbitrary or otherwise? What aspects are arbitrary, iconic and indexical?
5. Evaluate the animal communication systems described in the section 'Natural communication systems of some animal species' in §10.1, in terms of the full set of Hockett's design features. Tabulate your findings and discuss whether the differences from human language are a matter of degree or kind.
6. Review the notion of duality of patterning, and explain in a few sentences what it means. Do you think that duality of patterning is a useful design feature for all communicative systems? If not, when – under what conditions – do you think that this becomes a relevant consideration? Explain your reasons.
7. The table below shows a number of Nim Chimpsky's most frequent three- and four-sign combinations (from Terrace et al. 1979: 894, reprinted with permission from AAAS, Herbert S. Terrace and coauthors). What is the frequency of repetition in these combinations? Calculate the frequency both in terms of the combination types and their tokens, and in relation to the length of the combination. Is repetition more frequent in four-sign combinations than in three-sign combinations? What other generalizations can you make about the utterances listed? What other information would you like to know about these combinations if you were going to write a description of the grammar of Nim's utterances?

Three-sign combinations	Frequency	Four-sign combinations	Frequency
play me Nim	81	*eat drink eat drink*	15
eat me Nim	48	*eat Nim eat Nim*	7
eat Nim eat	46	*banana Nim banana Nim*	5
tickle me Nim	44	*drink Nim drink Nim*	5
grape eat Nim	37	*banana eat me Nim*	4
banana Nim eat	33	*banana eat me banana*	4
Nim me eat	27	*banana me Nim me*	4
banana eat Nim	26	*grape eat Nim eat*	4
eat me eat	22	*Nim eat Nim eat*	4
me Nim eat	21	*play me Nim play*	4

(Continued)

Issues for further thought and exercises—Cont'd

Three-sign combinations	Frequency	Four-sign combinations	Frequency
hug me Nim	20	drink eat drink eat	3
yoghurt Nim eat	20	drink eat me Nim	3
me more eat	19	eat grape eat Nim	3
more eat Nim	19	eat me Nim drink	3
finish hug Nim	18	grape eat me Nim	3
banana me eat	17	me eat drink more	3
Nim eat Nim	17	me eat me eat	3
tickle me tickle	17	me gum me gum	3
apple me eat	15	me Nim eat me	3
eat Nim me	15	Nim me Nim me	3
give me eat	15	tickle me Nim play	3
nut Nim nut	15		

8. Find out about attempts to teach a system signs to dolphins. (Some references are Evans and Bastian 1969; Herman 1980:178–180; Herman, et al. 1984; and Richards et al. 1984.) Write a brief description of one attempt, and discuss the extent to which the animal appears to have acquired a system comparable to human language. Compare the dolphin's ability to use the signs system with that of chimpanzees.

9. What are some possible motivations for replacing signs of American Sign Language by signs made up of plastic tokens and computer keyboards? Can you think of any disadvantages in the latter systems? Discuss the extent to which they resemble human languages, whether sign languages, speech, or writing. Do the differences render comparisons with human language spurious or difficult to interpret? (For instance, does the fact that the entire system of symbols is visible facilitate production, making the animal's ability appear better than it otherwise would?)

10. Which notion do you favour, the idea that language is genetically encoded, or that our genetic make-up permits language, but does not determine it? Identify and discuss evidence for and against your preference.

11. We mentioned in various places in the text bonobos (sometimes called pygmy chimpanzees). What are they? Why do many researchers use bonobos in preference to chimpanzees?

Notes

1. For simplicity we will henceforth drop the qualifier *other* and, following everyday parlance, use the term *animal* in the sense 'non-human animal'.

2. The same thing happens in human beings: at puberty the larynx of males increases in size and lowers. This sexual difference has no analogue in our primate relatives, which have by contrast a larger difference in overall body size between the sexes.

3. This effect is named after the German horse Clever Hans that lived around the turn of the twentieth century. Clever Hans appeared to be capable of reading, spelling and performing arithmetical sums shown on a blackboard by his trainer. He tapped out the answer with a hoof. It was eventually demonstrated that he was responding to subtle visual cues provided unintentionally by his trainer: on calculations that were concealed from the trainer, Hans' performance was no better than chance.

4. This name is suggested by a standard evolution-by-natural-selection story whereby language would be selected for as a way of attracting a mate, and is reminiscent of the old 'sing-song' theory favoured by Jespersen. According to this theory, language is to human beings as long-elaborate-tail is to peacocks. It functions to attract a mate – the better you are at talking, the better your chances at finding a mate.

5. On the other hand, given the relatively small number of genes making up the human genome, it is unlikely that a single gene could be dedicated to language. In addition, people with the FOXP2 mutation show other types of impairment.

Part III
Language: Uniformity and Diversity

Unity and Diversity in Language Structure **11**

The main theme running through the remainder of the book is variation. In this chapter we deal with the range of variation in the grammatical structures of the world's languages. We explore the extent to which languages are similar phonologically, morphologically, syntactically and semantically; we also investigate the parameters of variation, limitations on variation and correlations between variable characteristics. A few comments are also made on possible explanations of the similarities and differences.

Chapter contents

Goals

The goals of the chapter are to:
- introduce the notions of linguistic universals and typology;
- discuss empirical requirements for investigations of universals and typology;
- distinguish and exemplify four main types of linguistic universal;

(Continued)

Goals—Cont'd

- describe two widely used typologies of human languages;
- discuss some important typologies of the phonology, morphology, syntax and lexicon of the world's languages;
- introduce the notion of markedness and illustrate its relevance to linguistic typology; and
- discuss reasons for the similarities and differences among human languages.

Key terms

absolute universals

absolutive case

accusative case

agglutinating languages

alienable possession

animacy hierarchy

argument structure

case systems

ditransitive

ergative case

fixed word order languages

free word order languages

fusional languages

implicational universals

inalienable possession

intransitive

isolating languages

markedness

motion verbs

neutralization

nominative case

non-absolute universals

non-implicational universals

number

polysynthetic languages

prefixing languages

suffixing languages

tone systems

transitive

typology

universals

11.1 Preliminaries to the study of the unity and diversity of languages

Two complementary perspectives on variation in language

It is difficult not to be impressed by the extraordinary diversity within the world's languages. Some languages distinguish just three vowels, while others distinguish a score or more. There are languages with no more than ten phonemes, and languages with over ten times as many. English and French use only the pulmonic airstream mechanism in 'ordinary' words, while Goemai uses the glottalic airstream as well. In Mandarin Chinese words are morphologically simple, while Yup'ik words show great complexity, and a single word may express what requires a multi-word sentence in Mandarin Chinese.

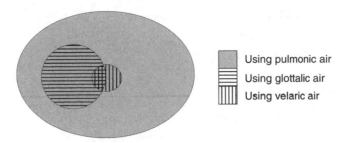

Using pulmonic air
Using glottalic air
Using velaric air

Figure 11.1 Language types according to airstream mechanisms used contrastively.

Yet the variation is not unlimited. There are certain properties that most or all languages share; these are known as **language universals**. To give a simple example, all languages use egressive pulmonic air; no language uses only ingressive pulmonic air, only velaric or only glottalic air. No language contrasts sounds produced with any of these airstreams and sounds made with esophageal air (air from the stomach). These are universal properties of the sound systems of human languages. Discovering language universals is an important task of modern linguistics; so also is explaining them.

Another slant on the airstream mechanism data is that some languages use velaric and/or glottalic airstreams to make phonemic contrasts, while others do not. Figure 11.1 depicts the situation graphically, and shows that we can group languages into types according to whether all phonemes contrast on the pulmonic airstream, or they contrast glottalic and/or velaric airstreams as well.

Language typology deals with grouping together or classifying languages in ways like this. Some linguists classify languages into click languages (in which sounds produced on velaric air contrast with sounds produced on pulmonic air) and non-click languages. Thus Zulu and Xhosa would be click languages, English, Saliba and Warlpiri (Pama-Nyungan, Australia) non-click languages. You might reasonably question whether presence vs. absence of contrasting airstream mechanisms in a language really is a useful way of grouping languages. Perhaps it is like classifying animals according to whether they have fur, hair or bristles – possible, but of no great interest because few other characteristics cluster with them.

Typologists also investigate the classification of component systems of languages. For instance, one could classify vowel systems into nasal (having a phonemic contrast between vowels with nasalization and vowels without) and oral (without such a contrast). This approach is sometimes referred to as **linguistic typology**, to maintain a terminological distinction from the classification of entire languages (language typology). Typologists today mostly do linguistic typology.

Typology and universals are really just different perspectives on the same thing: how to get a handle on the limitations on variation among languages. Typology views it from the perspective of variation within commonality; universals, from the perspective of unity within variation. For convenience, I will use the term *typology* as a cover term for both perspectives; it is usually be clear which sense is relevant.

Requirements

Claims about cross-linguistic variation and similarity must be based on and evaluated in reference to not just one single language, but many languages. Ideally you might say they should be based on **all** languages of the world. Otherwise, perhaps the one language you omitted is the exception. But given that the world's languages number almost 7,000 and many of them have not been described at all, the ideal is beyond our present reach.

Granted that we must be selective, how do we choose the languages? To begin with, it will depend on the sort of question one is asking: there is no single all-purpose procedure that works for all types of question. For instance, we can ask questions about languages of the world generally, the languages of a particular region, the languages of a family (see §13.2), or languages that have a particular property (e.g. have clicks, or nominal cases). Your sampling procedure will be different for each of these questions: if you are enquiring into the languages of a region it would make no sense to include many languages outside of it.

Let us suppose we are interested in questions about the world's languages generally. Two considerations are pertinent:

(a) A selection of languages can't be judged as good or bad merely on how many languages are included. A selection of 50 very different languages is more representative than a selection of 100 quite similar ones. We can make a selection that maximizes diversity by choosing languages that are widely distributed geographically and belong to different families (see §13.2).

(b) Considerations of diversity alone are insufficient. You obviously need to select languages for which you have access to good data, which generally means a language for which a comprehensive grammar is available. What is comprehensive will depend partly on what you are investigating. For some studies (e.g. possession of nasal vowels) even the briefest sketch grammar might be adequate. On the other hand, if you are investigating noun cases or parts-of-speech systems you will need more comprehensive grammars.

Even if you are able to find languages with excellent grammars, your investigation can be hampered by terminological and theoretical differences. For instance, descriptive linguists use the term *subject* in a range of ways, and to disregard this would be fatal to your study.

11.2 Universals of language

A distinction can be drawn between characteristics that are shared by all languages (so far as we know) and characteristics that are exhibited by many though not all languages. Thus we can talk – with some poetic licence – of **absolute** and **non-absolute** universals. The shared characteristics can be either specific linguistic features such as vowels, or logical relationships

Table 11.1 Four types of language universal.

	Absolute universals	Non-absolute universals
Non-implicational universals	A characteristic shared by each and every language without exception. *All languages have X*	A characteristic shared by many (or most) languages, a tendency *Languages tend to have X*
Implicational universals	A logical relation of implication between two characteristics that is found in every language *In all languages if X then Y*	A logical connection between two characteristics that is found in most/many languages *If a language has X it tends to have Y*

between features such as 'if a language uses the velaric airstream, it also uses the pulmonic airstream'. (Note that the inverse implication does not hold: if a language uses the pulmonic airstream it need not use the velaric airstream.) Correspondingly we can distinguish **non-implicational** from **implicational** universals.

Table 11.1 shows the four types of universals these distinctions give rise to, and summarizes their distinguishing attributes. In the following subsections examples will be given of each of the four types.

Absolute non-implicational universals

Some examples of absolute non-implicational universals are:[1]

- All languages have syllables, consonants and vowels.
- All languages have at least one stop phone.
- All languages have lexical words and distributional words (minimal free forms).
- All languages distinguish between grammatical units of at least three sizes, word, phrase and clause.

These probably seem quite unexciting. Nevertheless, they are not logical necessities, and systems can easily be imagined that do not display the properties. They may therefore be more significant than first appears.

Non-absolute non-implicational universals

Non-absolute universals are robust tendencies, that admit some exceptions. Here are a few:

- Most languages have CV syllables.
- Most languages have nasal phones.
- Most languages have an alveolar stop, and most have the high front vowel.
- In most languages a part-of-speech distinction can be drawn between nouns and verbs.

These generalizations hold for a high proportion of the world's documented languages. A few exceptional languages have no CV syllables: Breen and Penselfini (1999) argue that in Arrernte (Pama-Nyungan, Central Australia) all consonants occur in final position. Some Lakes Plain languages (Papuan, Papua) lack nasal phones entirely, while in some Asmat languages (also Papuan, Papua) nasals and corresponding stops are in allophonic variation. Hawaiian (Austronesian, Hawai'i) lacks alveolar stop phones. Some languages lacking the noun-verb distinction were mentioned in §4.1.

Absolute implicational universals

Absolute implicational universals are not easy to find, but here are three:

- If a language has phonemic mid-vowels it has phonemic high vowels.
- If a language has voiceless nasals it also has voiced nasals.
- If a language distinguishes dual number (a grammatical category indicating 'two') in pronouns it also distinguishes plural number.

> There are two things to be wary of when formulating implicational universals. First, if the 'if' clause expresses an absolute universal, then the consequence will also be an absolute universal. It is preferable to simply state the latter as an absolute universal. Thus rather than 'if a language has vowels, it has consonants' it would be preferable to state the absolute non-implicational universal 'all languages have consonants', since even though the implicational universal is valid, the non-implicational universal makes a stronger claim. Second, if the consequence is an absolute universal, then it makes little sense to formulate an implicational universal. Occasionally, one sees an implicational universal like 'if a language has voiceless vowels, it also has voiced vowels', or 'if a language uses the velaric airstream, it also uses the pulmonic airstream' (p. 251). Since we have already seen that all languages have vowels and use pulmonic air, it is preferable to state the stronger absolute universal that all languages have voiced vowels and use the pulmonic airstream. Logically, (almost) anything could serve as the condition for an absolute truth: 'if a language has duals, it has voiced vowels'! (Even 'if pigs could fly, a language has voiced vowels'!) Note that our second absolute implicational universal above almost runs foul of this: it is saved by the fact that there are a small number of languages without nasals.

Non-absolute implicational universals

Non-absolute implicational universals are abundant. Here is a sample:

- If a language has front rounded vowel phones, it will usually have front spread and back rounded vowels.
- If a language has phonemic affricates, it usually has phonemic fricatives as well.
- If one of two number categories is marked by an affix to a noun, it tends to be the plural.
- If a language has bound morphemes marking number and case in nouns and either both follow or both precede the noun, the marker of number almost always comes between the noun and the case morpheme. In other words, if they are adjacent the number-marker is always closer to the noun.

There are exceptions to each of these implications, though they are few. In such circumstances it pays to look carefully at the exceptions to see whether they really are exceptions, or to try to specify the condition in another way. Some grammars fail to make the distinction between affixes and clitics, and this could be the source of exceptions. Alternatively, it might be that the markers in question are not genuine number or case makers – that is, they might mark similar though not identical categories.

11.3 Typology

The bulk of this section deals with morphological typology, one of the most fully studied areas of typology. We begin in the first subsection with two morphologically based classifications of languages. Following this we explore (in the second subsection) the typology of three morphological categories, number, possession and case. Syntactic typology has also attracted a considerable amount of attention. However, our treatment (in the third subsection) is brief, partly because a greater knowledge of syntax is required than presented in Chapter 5, and partly due to analytical and theoretical problems that render the empirical basis somewhat shaky. Actually, the division between morphological and syntactic typology is made here for expository purposes, and many phenomena can be equally treated either way: what is represented morphologically in one language may be expressed syntactically in another.

Rather less attention has been devoted by typologists to phonetic/phonological typology and lexical/semantic typology, and I restrict myself to a few brief remarks on these underdeveloped but fascinating domains.

Two morphological typologies of languages

Morpheme integrity

A widely used typology of the world's languages, with roots in the nineteenth century, distinguishes four morphological types:

- **Isolating** languages have no (or few) bound morphemes. Every word is monomorphemic. Haitian Creole (a French-based Creole spoken on the island of Haiti) is an isolating language, as the following example illustrates:

(11-1)	*m*	*pa*	*konprann*	*sa*	*l(i)*	*ap*	*di*	*m*	*lan*	Haitian Creole
	1sg	not	understand	what	3SG	PROG	say	1sg	DET	
	'I don't understand what he/she is telling me.'									

- **Agglutinating** languages allow morphologically complex words, which are easy to segment into morphemes. The boundaries between morphemes are clear cut: it is obvious where one morpheme ends and the next begins. Hungarian, Finnish and Turkish are agglutinating languages; so also is Guaraní (Tupi, Bolivia and Paraguay):

(11-2) *pe-mitā-kuña*   *o-u-va*   *hína*   *che-nupā*   Guaraní
        that-child-woman   3SG:ACT-come-REL   PROG   1sgINACT-hit-VOL
        kuri
        RPST
        'That young woman who is coming wanted to hit me.'

- **Fusional** or **inflectional** languages have morphologically complex words in which it can be difficult to separate morphemes from one another: the boundaries between them are blurry. In contrast with agglutinating languages words are not easily analysed into morphemes that follow one another like beads on a string. The extinct Indo-Aryan language Pali (India) was a fusional language. Consider the following case forms of the noun *kaññā* 'girl':

(11-3)

	Singular	**Plural**	Pali
Nominative	*kaññā*	*kaññā, kaññāyo*	
Accusative	*kaññaṃ*	*kaññā, kaññāyo*	
Instrumental	*kaññāya*	*kaññāhi*	
Genitive	*kaññāya*	*kaññānaṃ*	
Dative	*kaññāya*	*kaññānaṃ*	
Ablative	*kaññāya*	*kaññāhi*	
Locative	*kaññāya, kaññāyaṃ*	*kaññāsu*	
Vocative	*kaññe*	*kaññā, kaññāyo*	

Although it is easy to distinguish a root *kaññā* 'girl' that remains largely invariant, the affixes are not easily segmented into separate morphemes marking number and case.

- **Polysynthetic** languages are morphologically rich languages with long and complex word forms that often convey information requiring a multi-word clause in other languages. Yup'ik is a polysynthetic language; so also are many other languages of North America, including Koyukon (Athabaskan, Alaska):

(11-4) *to-ts'eeyh-ghee-ø-tonh*   Koyukon
        water-boat-PRF-CL-put:long:object
        'He launched a boat.'

The above examples illustrate some reasonably clear-cut instances of languages of the four morphological types. However, the reality is messier, as can be seen from the data and discussion in Box 11.1, which gives translations of 'I'll bring back the honey' – in some cases slightly modified because of absence of a word for 'honey' – in 21 languages. It is better to see the four types as ideal points along a continuum between the extremes of isolating and polysynthetic languages. Based on our sample clause, the languages in Box 11.1 can be placed roughly as shown in Figure 11.2. Of course, one would want to take more than a single sentence into account in locating languages in this morphological 'space'. With more data, Mandarin Chinese would doubtless end up closer to the isolating end of the scale than English.

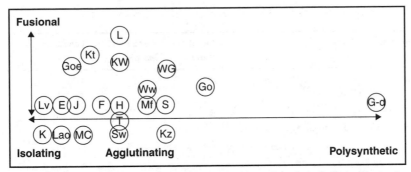

Key: E–English; F – Finnish; G–d – Gun-djeihmi; Go – Gooniyandi; Goe – Goemai; H – Hungarian; J – Japanese; K – Kisi; KW – Ku Waru; Kt – Kuot; Kz – Kwaza; L – Latin; Lao – Lao; Lv – Laven; MC – Mandarin Chinese; Mf – Michif; S – Sabaot; Sw – Swahili; T – Taba; WG – West Greenlandic; Ww – Warrwa.

Figure 11.2 Location of the 21 sample languages on two dimensions of morpheme integrity.

Box 11.1 *'I'll bring back the honey' in a small selection of languages*

'I'll bring back the honey'			Morphs: Words	Fused morphs: Morphs	Language
nga-yiuk-yi-rrurnde-ng 1SG-honey-APP-return-NPST			5/1 = 5	0	Gun-djeihmi (Gunwiny-guan, Australia)
ngalinya honey	*barn-ja-wi-l-arri* return-SUB-FUT-1SG>3SG/CL		6/2 = 3	1/6 = 0.17	Gooniyandi
nü'ty honey	*waje-'nǎ-da-ki* bring/get.back-FUT-1SG-DEC		5/2 = 2.5	0	Kwaza (isolate, Southwestern Amazon)
mǎ-ǎ-ket-u FUT-1sg-bring-hither		*beenyto* meat	5/2 = 2.5	0	Sabaot (Nilo-Saharan, Africa)
neqi meat	*oqquti-ssa-ara* bring:home-FUT-1SG>3SG/IND		4/2 = 2	1/4 = 0.25	West Greenlandic (Eskimo-Aleut, Greenland)
warna honey	*nguy* return	*ka-na-ngka-ya-ngany* 1SG/FUT-CL-FUT-say-APP	7/3 = 2.3	1/7 = 0.14	Warrwa
li the	*myel* honey	*ni-wii-ashee-peet-aw* 1SG-FUT-back-bring-3SG	7/3 = 2.3	0	Michif (Mixed language, Canada)
re-fer-ebo back-carry-1SG/FUT		*mel* honey/ACC/NEUT	4/2 = 2	2/4 = 0.5	Latin
po-yl sugarcane-DEF *ya-d* here-DAT	*lyi-p* get-NF/1 *o-bu* come-FUT/1SG	*me-b* carry-NF/1	10/5 = 2	3/10 = 0.3	Ku Waru (Papuan, New Guinea)

(Continued)

Box 11.1—Cont'd

'I'll bring back the honey'						Morphs: Words	Fused morphs: Morphs	Language
k-mul-ak		madu				4/2 = 2	0	Taba
1SG-return-APP		honey						
vissza-hoz-om		a	méz-et			6/3 = 2	0	Hungarian
back-return-1SG		DEF	honey-ACC					
ni-ta-let-a		asali	hapa/huko			6/3 = 2	0	Swahili
1SG-FUT-bring-IND		honey	here					
tuo-n	hunanja-n	takaisin				5/3 = 1.7	0	Finnish
bring-1SG	honey-ACC	back						
eba	inə	t-ana-ŋ				6/4 = 1.5	2/6 = 0.3	Kuot
FUT	again	1SG/FUT-bring:back-3SG/FUT						
ilumə								
honey								
wǒ	yào	ba	mìfēng	ná-húi-lái			0	Mandarin Chinese
1SG	FUT	CON	honey	take-back-moving		7/5 = 1.4		
watashi	ga	hachimitsu	o	tot-te		9/7 = 1.3	0	Japanese
1SG	NOM	honey	ACC	get-GER				
ku-ru	yo							
come-NPST	PART							
I'll	bring	back	the	honey		6/5 = 1.2	0	English
1SG-FUT	bring	back	the	honey				
hen	t'ong	mang	nshi	wa		7/6 = 1.17	2/7 = 0.29	Goemai
1SG	IRR	take/sg	honey	return:home/SG				
n-ni								
comitative-3SG								
kuu³	si⁰	qaw³	nam⁰-pheng⁵	khn²		7/6 = 1.17	0	Lao (Tai-Kadai, Laos)
1SG	IRR	take	liquid-bee	return				
maa²								
come								
ì	có	lìáŋ	cùùwó	nánùn		5/5 = 1	0	Kisi
1SG	FUT	honey	bring	here				
ʔaj	ma	cɔk	tbɨh	daak	sut	6/6 = 1	0	Laven (Austro-Asiatic,
1SG	FUT	take	bring	water	bee			Laos)

Qualifications

i. A single example is given for each language; there will always be other ways of expressing the same meaning, for example, in Gun-djeihmi the word 'honey' could appear outside of the verb; the free pronoun 'I' could also occur. The clauses given are minimal expressions of the meaning in the language, in the absence of context.

ii. Zero morphemes (see §3.6) have been excluded.

iii. Some word boundaries are uncertain: the nominative and accusative postpositions in Japanese, for instance, are sometimes treated as bound morphemes.

Discussion

The fuzziness of the boundaries between the four morphological types is apparent. For example, English and Mandarin Chinese both have a single complex word made up of easily separated pieces. Thus they are not strictly isolating, but have some agglutinative tendencies. And while most of Gooni-yandi's morphology is agglutinative, there is a fusional tendency: the form *-l-* in the verb means 'I (acted on) it', 1sgNOM/3sgACC; it cannot be divided into two separate morphemes.

Each clause has between one and seven words, with the two extremes instanced just once. It seems reasonable to use the ratio of morphs per word to give a rough idea of the degree to which a language is isolating or polysynthetic. These are shown in the second column; the figures suggest that this ratio varies continuously rather than takes discrete values; with a larger set of languages we would expect to find many more intermediate values. The languages are listed in the table in order of decreasing value for this ratio.

In the third column are figures suggesting how fusional the language is. This figure is the proportion of morphs that are fused: that is, the ratio of the complex or fused morphs to the total number of morphs. However, since 1sg is fused in every language – often also with NOM – 1sg and 1sgNOM were treated as single morphs; to do otherwise would result in losing the distinction between the language that combine just these categories, and those that combine one or more others with them. By this index, Latin emerges as a good example of a fusional language, both grammatical morphs expressing complex components of meaning.

Affixing typology

The examples in Box 11.1 reveal an unexpected pattern. Within a word, grammatical morphemes are much more likely to follow a lexical root than to precede it. Using terminology loosely, suffixes outnumber prefixes by a considerable margin: there are some 29 readily segmentable suffixes, but only 12 prefixes, less than half the number. This pattern is not an accident of the small and unrepresentative selection of languages in our sample. Bybee et al. (1990) found suffixes outnumbered prefixes by almost three to one in a larger and more representative corpus of languages.

The difference between prefixes and suffixes is so striking that some linguists have proposed it as a typological parameter, though of course it is limited to languages that are not strictly isolating. The exact manner of defining the two categories varies, but what seems to work best (and was first formulated by Capell 1938) is: suffixing languages have suffixes only; prefixing languages have prefixes and/or suffixes. A range of other characteristics tend to correlate with this distinction.

The other types of affix – infixes, circumfixes and suprafixes (i.e. prosodic 'affixes') – are far less frequent than prefixes or suffixes.

Morphological typology

Grammatical number

We mentioned in §11.2 an absolute implicational universal that if a separate dual number is distinguished in the pronoun system of a language there will also be a plural category.

No pronominal systems distinguishes dual against an undifferentiated non-dual (i.e. everything else, singular and plural). Duals only emerge if there is already a category contrast between singular and non-singular pronouns.

We can extend this generalization with the observation that if a language has a trial category (specifying 'three') or a paucal category (specifying 'a few') in its pronouns then it will also have the dual category. A useful way of summarizing these linked generalizations is in terms of a **hierarchy**, as shown in (11-5).

$$(11\text{-}5) \quad \text{singular/non-singular} < \text{dual} < \begin{Bmatrix} \text{trial} \\ \text{paucal} \end{Bmatrix}$$

The hierarchy shown in (11-5) is interpreted as follows: if a pronoun system distinguishes a certain number category, it will also make all number distinctions to the left of it. The categories trial and paucal are unordered (the curly brackets indicate 'or') with respect to one another: a language can have trials without paucals, paucals without trials. Notice also that at the leftmost end of the hierarchy is shown not a single category, but two in contrast. This is because 'singular' and 'non-singular' only make sense in contrast to one another.

This hierarchy also captures generalizations about number inflection in nouns. But there is an important feature of number marking that it does not capture. Recall that in §11.2 it was observed that if a number category is marked by an affix, it will usually be the plural: few languages express singular by an affix, while the plural has none.

This brings us to the important notion of **markedness**, the idea that grammatical categories are not equal, that some are more 'natural' than others. The notion of markedness is a complex one, that brings together a number of considerations that we cannot delve into here. Instead we outline properties that tend to distinguish unmarked categories from marked categories, using the category of grammatical number for exemplification.

In the case of number inflection of nouns, the plural category is **marked**, while the singular is **unmarked**:

- the unmarked category tends to be realized by shorter or simpler forms than marked categories (singular forms are usually the shorter; in the typical case, they have no formal representation);
- the unmarked category tends to be used most often within a language (singulars are more frequent than plurals in English discourse);
- the unmarked category tends to admit the most distinctions on cross-cutting dimensions (e.g. more case distinctions are usually made in the singular than in the plural; gender distinctions are often restricted to the singular);
- the unmarked category is the one that tends to occur in contexts where the contrast does not apply, or is **neutralized** (in English there are a few nouns where the number contrast is not manifested in ordinary count expressions (e.g. *sheep* and *fish*); such words are typically singular in form).[2]

These characteristics do not always go together, they just tend to. In Welsh, there is a smallish set of nouns whose singular is marked by an overt morpheme, but whose plural is not. And in English there are nouns like *trousers* and *oats* which occur only in plural form.

Returning to (11-5), the categories to the right of the hierarchy are more marked than those to the left, and the singular/non-singular contrast is unmarked. Two other features are notable:

- the unmarked category/contrast tends to be found most frequently across languages (more languages distinguish singular from non-singular than make the other distinctions);
- the unmarked member tends to appear in the most contexts in a language, and has fewest restrictions on environments of use (the dual category is more likely to be restricted than the singular/non-singular opposition, for example, to humans or animates).

Hierarchies and the notion of markedness have proved to be very useful in typology, and we will see them again as the story unfolds.

Nominal possession

Many languages use different constructions for expressing two different types of possession, alienable and inalienable. **Inalienable** possession refers to things that are inherently possessed, like one's eyes and one's mother: eyes and mothers are in normal circumstances eyes and mothers of some person. **Alienable** possessions by contrast are things that are not inherently possessed, like tools, one's books, and so on. Such objects do necessarily have to be owned, or be in anyone's possession.

If a language makes the distinction between these two types of possession, inalienable possession will be expressed by a more closely integrated construction, a construction in which the form for the possessor and the possessed are close together. Alienable possession will be expressed by a construction in which the forms indicating the possessor and possessed are more separated. This is illustrated by the following Paamese examples. In the inalienable construction, (11-6), the morphemes for possessor and possessed are tightly fused together, the former being a suffix to the latter. But in alienable possession, (11-7), they fall into two distinct words, the suffix for the possessor being attached to a form (glossed POSS) that indicates alienable possession (different POSSs distinguish different types of alienable possession).

(11-6)	*aha-n*	*viṽi-n*		Paamese
	brain-3SG	cheek-3SG		
	'his/her brain	'his/her cheek'		

(11-7)	*vakili*	*ona-k*	*ani*	*emo-n*	Paamese
	canoe	POSS-1SG	coconut	POSS-3SG	
	'my canoe'		'my coconut'		

Notice that in these examples the inalienable construction has fewer morphemes. This is a universal tendency, further illustrated by the following examples:

(11-8)	*cing*	*lyec*	*yewi*	*laco*	Acholi (Nilo-Saharan, Sudan)
	hand	elephant	hair	man	
	'elephant's trunk'		'man's hair'		

(11-9)								
dyang	*pa*	*rwot*		*jami*	*tuku*	*pa*	*latin*	Acholi
cow	POSS	chief		things	play	POSS	child	
'chief's cow'				'child's play things'				

Conceptually, an inalienable possession is more intimately connected with its possessor than is an alienable possession. This correlates iconically with closer connection in linguistic form in inalienable possession constructions.

Languages differ as to what are treated as inalienable possessions, although body parts and kin are usually included. Also likely to be treated as inalienable possessions are parts of inanimates (e.g. plants), and culturally significant items such as one's land, cattle, or one's most personal and intimate belongings (e.g. clothing, personal tools). However, these items can't be put on a universal hierarchy of likeliness to be treated as inalienable. Some languages, for instance, treat both body parts and kin as inalienable possessions, while others treat body parts as inalienable and kin as alienable, and still others treat only kin as inalienable. In some languages a body part term can be treated as either alienable or inalienable according to cir-cumstances. A body part of an animal being eaten, or a disembodied hand found on the ground, might be treated as an alienable possession of the finder or eater, whereas on a living being it would be treated as inalienable.

Case systems

When nominals or pronominals are given different morphological markings according to their grammatical role we speak of case marking. Many languages employ a nominative-accusative system of case marking, a system in which, as in Latin (§3.3), the subject of a clause occurs in nominative case, the object in accusative case.

Typically the nominative case is the unmarked case: formally, it often has no overt marker, in contrast with the accusative, which is usually marked by a morpheme with phonological form. In Hungarian, for example, the nominative form of a noun is its citation form (the form used when you mention the word), whereas the accusative is marked by the suffix *-(V)t* – thus *vonat* 'train' is the nominative and citation form, the accusative form being *vonat-at*. (The formal unmarkedness of the nominative aligns with other characteristics typical of unmarked categories – see pp. 260–261.)

An alternative system of case marking, found in fewer languages, uses the same morpho-logical marking for the subject of an intransitive clause and the object of a transitive clause, and different marking for the subject of a transitive clause (the terms 'subject' and 'object' are used loosely here and are not meant to imply that these are genuine grammatical relations). The case of the transitive subject is called **ergative**, and of the intransitive subject and transi-tive object, **absolutive**. Such a case system is found in Chukchee (Chukotko-Kamchatkan, northeastern Siberia): in (11-10) the intransitive subject is marked by zero, as is the transitive object in (11-11), but the subject of the transitive clause is marked by *-nan*. This is typical of an ergative-absolutive system: it is generally the absolutive that is unmarked.

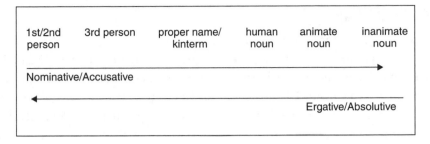

Figure 11.3 The animacy hierarchy.

(11-10) *ŋinqeq-ø*   *gətg-etə*   *qət-gʔi*   Chukchee
         boy-ABS/SG   lake-DAT   went-3SG
         'The boy went to the lake.'

(11-11) *gəm-nan*   *walə-ø*   *tə-mne-gʔen*   Chukchee
         I-ERG   knife-ABS/SG   1SG-sharpen-3SG
         'I sharpened the knife.'

Languages are not always consistent in their case-marking systems, and it is not uncommon to find a nominative-accusative system in one part of the grammar, and an ergative-absolutive one elsewhere, or even complete absence of case marking on some subjects and objects. Thus, Latin's daughter languages French, Spanish and Italian have nominative-accusative case marking for pronouns, but not nouns. In Anguthimri (Pama-Nyungan, Australia) nouns inflect on an ergative-absolutive basis, while pronouns inflect according to a nominative-accusative system.

The distribution of the two case-marking systems is not random. In cases like those just mentioned, the **animacy hierarchy** of Figure 11.3 accounts for the case-marking system used on a nominal or pronominal. The way this is to be read is that if a nominative-accusative case system is used at some point, it will be used everywhere to the left of that point, and correspondingly if an ergative-absolutive system is used at some point, it will be used everywhere to the right. This is in agreement with the Anguthimri facts mentioned above, and with Malayalam (Dravidian, India), where nominative-accusative marking covers the whole range of animate nouns, but not inanimate nouns.

This hierarchy has proved useful beyond case-marking. It is also relevant to the grammatical category of number. If a number contrast is obligatory at some point, it will be maintained everywhere to the left of that point. Some languages – for example, Kharia (Munda, India) – distinguish number for animates, but not inanimates, or for pronouns, but not nouns.

Syntactic typology

Universality of grammatical relations

Whether or not grammatical relations are universal is highly contentious. Many linguists would agree that having grammatical relations is a universal property of human languages, that no language lacks them. Disagreements centre on the identity and definitions of the relations, and no set is unanimously agreed to. This is partly because of theoretical differences: recall that some linguists regard grammatical relations as purely formal and meaningless categories, whereas others regard them as meaningful. Adopting such fundamentally different perspectives, two linguists describing the same language would come up with quite different descriptions, and identify different grammatical relations. Even if our two linguists shared the same theoretical perspective, they might well come up with different defining criteria.

Whatever criteria we adopt, it is unlikely that any two languages will share precisely the same grammatical relations. The best we can hope for is sufficient similarity to allow certain relations in different language to be equated. The universality of grammatical relations is thus a claim about things that are sufficiently alike to be regarded as instances of the same category.

Many linguists consider Subject and Object to be universal grammatical categories in this sense. In any language we can find grammatical relations with enough in common with subject and object in, say, English, to allow us to regard them as instances of the same categories. Other linguists – myself included – consider the roles Actor and Undergoer to be better candidates for universality.

We will not pursue the issue of the universality of grammatical relations further, but turn instead to word order, and outline a word order typology that enjoys a perhaps too prominent place in linguistic typology.

Word order typology

Argument structure

A clause consists of obligatory or essential elements that must be there in the structure, along with optional elements that may or may not be present. In *They followed his dripping blood until nightfall* three elements are structurally essential, the NP *they*, the VP *followed* and the NP *his dripping blood*; the final PP *until nightfall* is not essential. (See §5.3 on phrase types.)

It is important to note that we are not claiming that essential elements cannot be omitted: for example, there is nothing wrong with *They saddled the horses and followed his dripping blood until nightfall*. But in such instances, *they* is presumed, and filled in, so to say, by the hearer (see §5.4). The NP *his dripping blood* can also be left out, as in *They followed until nightfall*; but if it is, we have a different type of clause, referring to an event we might gloss 'come after', where it is not implied that they were directing their motion towards anyone else as a goal. The NP is essential in a transitive construction. The situation for *until nightfall* is clearly different.

The obligatory elements form the **core** of a clause. The core of the majority of clauses in most languages is made up of a VP plus one or two, sometimes three, NPs, as in the following examples:

(11-12)   *omushaija*   *a-naaba*   Nkore-Kiga (Niger-Congo, Uganda)
   man   he-wash
   NP   VP
   'The man washes.'

(11-13)   *enjangu*   *y-aa-rya*   *eshonzi*   Nkore-Kiga
   cat   it-PST-eat   fish
   NP   VP   NP
   'The cat has eaten the fish.'

(11-14)   *mugimba*   *a-ka-ha*   *ishe*   *ekitabo*   Nkore-Kiga
   Mugimba   he-PST-give   father   book
   NP   VP   NP   NP
   'Mugimba gave his father a book.'

These three types of clause are called **intransitive, transitive** and **ditransitive** respectively, according to the number of obligatory NPs. Let us group together the first obligatory NP in each clause – denoting the most active entity in the event – and call it S (short for notional subject). We also group the last NP in (11-13) and (11-14) as O (notional object) – it is the thing that is the least active in the event. The second NP in (11-14), the IO (notional indirect object), will be henceforth left out of account to simplify the story.

This operation we could perform in any language, basing the grouping primarily on meaning. The word order typology we discuss in the next subsection is concerned with the order of these notional elements – S, O, and IO are not grammatical relations, but labels for convenience groupings of obligatory elements – and the lexical verb (V).

Order of essential elements

Some languages, like English, Irish Gaelic (Indo-European, Ireland), Ewe and Mandarin Chinese, have a **basic word order**: an ordering of the elements S, V and O that is strongly preferred in ordinary neutral declarative clauses (see §6.3). In English this word order is of course SVO; exceptions do occur (e.g. *That I do not like* and *Believe you me*), but are relatively rare, and are pragmatically marked.

But not all languages show this degree of rigidity the order of words. Some are quite flexible or free, showing few grammatical restrictions, and no overwhelming preference for any particular order. Languages like this can be called **free word order** languages, in contrast with **fixed word order** languages, that have a basic word order. These labels are not to be understood literally: word order in free word order language is never totally chaotic; and in fixed word order languages some variability is always possible (e.g. thematization may be relevant – see §5.4).

Table 11.2 Frequencies of word order types (data from Tomlin 1986: 22 and Haspelmath et al. 2005)

Word order	% of languages	Examples
SOV	40.5%	Amharic, Japanese, Hindi, Kurmanjî Kurdish (Indo-European, Turkey), Malayalam, Mende (Niger-Congo, Liberia), Mongolian (Altaic, Mongolia), Nama (Khoisan, South Africa), Georgian (South Caucasian, Georgia), Cherokee (Iroquoian, USA), Hittite (Indo-European, Anatolia), Korean
SVO	35.4%	English, Danish, Spanish, Ewe, Kinyarwanda (Niger-Congo, Rwanda), Hungarian, Mandarin Chinese, Hausa, Finnish, Lingala (Niger-Congo, Democratic Republic of Congo), French, German
VSO	6.9%	Biblical Hebrew (Afro-Asiatic, Israel), Irish Gaelic, Ge'ez (Afro-Asiatic, Ethiopia), Tamazight (Afro-Asiatic, Algeria), Welsh, Tagalog
VOS	2.1%	Malagasy, Tzotzil (Mayan, Mexico)
OVS	0.7%	Hixkaryana (Carib, Brazil), Panare (Carib, Venezuela)
OSV	0.3%	Urubú (Tupi, Brazil), Nadëb (Maku, Brazil)
Free	14%	Acehnese, Pipil (Uto-Aztecan, El Salvador), Kisi, most Australian languages

The majority of Australian languages are free word order languages in this sense. Indeed, many allow not just any order of S, O and V, but also permit the actual words to occur in any order. Thus, words belonging to the S NP need not necessarily appear next to one another, as in the following Jiwarli (Pama-Nyungan, Australia) example, where the words of the bolded NP are separated by the verb:

(11-15) ***kutharra-rru***   ***ngunha***   *ngurnta-inha*   ***jiluru***   Jiwarli
         two.NOM-now   that.NOM   lie-PRS   egg.NOM
         'Now those two eggs are lying (there).'

Not all of the six possible orders of S, O and V are equally preferred in fixed word order languages. Table 11.2 the word order types together with an indication of their approximate frequency, and some languages with the orders. Notice that S precedes O in about 96 per cent of fixed word order languages.

What makes the word order typology interesting is that there are correlations with other grammatical features. For example, among languages with adpositions (prepositions and postpositions), those with VO order tend to have prepositions, while those with OV order tend to have postpositions. English and Japanese illustrate this correlation, respectively. Another correlation is that VO languages tend to position the negative before the V, while OV languages tend to place the negative after the V.

Phonological typology: tone systems

One characteristic frequently employed in typologizing languages and phonological systems is phonemic tone. Tone systems themselves are not unitary phenomena, and two types are often recognized, following Pike (1948): **contour tone** systems, and **register tone** systems.

In contour tone systems direction of tone movement is relevant, not just its relative level. Thai, Lao, Mandarin Chinese, Hakka (Tibeto-Burman, China), Cantonese and many other languages of South East Asia are contour tone languages. Mandarin Chinese for example distinguishes four contour tones: high level, high rising, low falling rising and high falling. Cantonese distinguishes nine contour tones.

In register tone systems it is the relative height of the tone on a syllable that is crucial, not the direction of movement. Many African languages have register tone systems, including Yoruba (Niger-Congo, Benin), Twi (Niger-Congo, Ghana), Bemba, Sango (a Creole, Central African Republic), among others. Bemba, for example, has two phonemic tones, high and low, illustrated by the minimal pair *ímbá* 'sing' and *imbá* 'dig'.

Another type of tone system, **pitch accent**, uses pitch differences to mark accented vs. unaccented syllables. Languages with pitch accent systems include Ancient Greek, Japanese, Una (Papuan, Papua) and many other languages of the island of New Guinea.

In contour tone systems and register tone systems, usually each syllable of a word has a tone value (in some cases, none), whereas in pitch accent systems usually just one syllable of a word has a distinctive tonic value.

Lexical-semantic typology: verbs of motion

A motion event is made up of four main components: (a) the Motion component itself, the change in location from one position to another; (b) the Figure that moves; (c) the Path over which it moves; and (d) the Manner in which it moves. All languages allow expression of these four components in a sentence referring to a motion event, with component (a), the Motion pure and simple, being represented in the verb. Leonard Talmy has suggested (e.g. 2007) that a lexical-semantic typology of languages is possible based on which of the three other components typically and colloquially conflate with (a) Motion in the verb.[3] The three types are: Motion+Figure, Motion+Path, and Motion+Manner.

English and other Germanic languages (including, for example, German, Dutch, Frisian, Danish, Norwegian and Swedish) typically make the Motion+Manner conflation. In English, aside from basic motion verbs like *walk*, *swim*, *fly* and *crawl*, many other verbs allow the combination of these components: *float*, *roll*, *limp*, *stumble*, *slide* and so on.

This conflation of Motion and Manner is not a preferred pattern in Japanese, Korean, Turkish, Tamil or Romance languages. In Spanish, there is no verbal expression conveying the combination 'move+float', as in *the bottle floated into the cave*. Instead, the notion of floating is expressed by a separate word:

(11-16)	*La*	*botella*	*entró*	*a*	*la*	*cuerva*	*flotando*	Spanish
	the	bottle	entered	to	the	cave	floating	
	'The bottle floated into the cave.'							

In Spanish, in contrast to English, the typical conflation is of Motion with Path: *salir* 'move out', *subir* 'move up', *bajar* 'move down', *cruzar* 'move across', *volver* 'move back' and others.

Although English has a number of such verbs, including *return*, *pass*, *ascend*, *descend*, these are not the most frequent or colloquial expressions in the language, and indeed these have been borrowed from Romance languages.

The third pattern, the Motion+Figure conflation, is represented in just a few English verbs, like *ooze* and *flow*, that specify liquid Figures. Languages like Navajo (Athapaskan, USA) and Atsugewi (Hokan, USA) typically manifest this conflation. According to Talmy, Atsugewi has a series of verbs referring to different types of moving Figure: *lup* 'a small, shiny, spherical object such as an eyeball, or hailstone to move', *qput* 'dirt to move', *swal* 'a linear flexible object suspended at one end (e.g. a sock on a clothes line, a flaccid penis) to move', *caq* 'a slimy lump-ish object (e.g. a toad, a cow turd) to move', etc.

> Interesting as this typology is, one can raise questions as to its viability. For one thing, it can be questioned whether it is sensible to construe it as a typology of entire languages: this might get around the rather unsatisfactory dismissal of English Motion+Path verbs as 'less colloquial' modes of expression. One can also question whether the Motion component really is located in the verb in clauses like *the bottle floated into the cave*. Perhaps it is the expression of direction (e.g. *into the cave*, *away* etc.) that engenders the Motion sense, which might rather be located at the level of the construction itself. That is to say, the typology might be better regarded as a typology of constructions than a lexical-semantic one.

11.4 Explaining unity and diversity of language structure

Suggesting explanations of the observed range of variation across languages is an important part of the work of a typologist. Knowing 'what' is essential to any scientific investigation, but we also want to know 'why': how can we account for the observed restrictions on structural variation? Three main types of explanation are commonly invoked: (a) common origins; (b) the shared biological structure of human beings; and (c) the shared uses of language. We discuss these in the following subsections.

Common origins

One possible explanation of the unity of human languages is that they all come from a single language spoken in the long-distant past. Retained structural characteristics of that language might account for the universal features. Since we do not know whether or not all languages have a common ancestor, this is a highly speculative explanation. It is also difficult to see how the various correlations between features that we observed above can be explained. Thus, an explanation by common origins does not shed any light on why, across languages, the distribution of nominative-accusative and ergative-absolutive case marking of nouns and pronouns follows the animacy hierarchy. For these reasons, explanations by common origins are usually given little credence.

Human biology

Human physiology imposes constraints on what is possible in language. Given the structure of our speech organs, apico-pharyngeal consonants and glottal nasals are impossible. Likewise the difficulty of making certain tongue gestures could either rule out certain phones (e.g. apico-velars), or render them less likely than phones produced with simpler gestures (e.g. co-articulated stops involve more complex gestures than stops produced at one place of articulation, and are less common cross-linguistically). The universality of pulmonic phones can probably be explained physiologically: the lungs provide the largest and most convenient source of air. The universality of consonants and vowels and the near universality of CV syllables might also have physiological explanations.

But biological explanations are not limited to phonetic and phonological universals. Some lexical, morphological and syntactic universals also have biological explanations, though these are rooted in the structure of the human brain and psychology rather than the vocal tract.

A psychological explanation for the predominance of suffixing over prefixing has been proposed by Cutler et al. (1985). It goes like this. The brain begins processing the acoustic information it receives immediately, rather than waiting for an entire utterance to be received (which is why we can be garden-pathed – see §8.2). Thus the brain begins to attempt to guess a word (indeed more) before it has been heard in its entirety. This strategy is most efficient when the most significant information occurs early. Experimental evidence indicates that information in the root is more critical to comprehension than information in affixes (Cutler et al. 1985; Hawkins and Cutler 1988), making processing most efficient when affixes follow the root.

The fact that sentences are not mere ordered strings of morphemes, but are hierarchically structured into word, phrase and clause units also has its basis in human cognition. A general property of human cognition is that processing of sequences is facilitated by the imposition of structure. Once a sequence has more than a handful of items, it must be structured for us to work efficiently with it. (Think for example of how you express telephone numbers by dividing them into groups, rather than treating them as undifferentiated lists.) An unstructured sequence of morphemes of the length of a typical sentence would be an unprocessable jumble of signs.

Functional unity of language

All languages serve similar functions in human life, including conveying information, and expressing social relations; they also have similar communicative demands put on them, for example, the necessity of keeping track of who is doing what to who. It seems plausible to expect some universals of language to be explicable in terms of such considerations. Here are two universals that could be explained functionally.

All languages recognize a category of negative clause that contrasts grammatically with a positive or affirmative category. This can be plausibly attributed to the fact that language is used to communicate information about what did not happen, to enquire about what did not happen, to issue commands not to do things, to express surprise that something did not happen and so on. Moreover, it is presumably essential to also make it perfectly plain that it did not happen and so on. Thus, it would not do to have a vague category that covered both negative and positive, and distinguish between them pragmatically.

In all languages there are ways of grammatically signalling that what is said is someone else's utterance, for example by using clauses of speech (as in *He said 'the farmer killed the duckling'*), and/or by quotative morphemes (generally particles or enclitics that go inside a clause and mean something like 'it is said' or 'allegedly' as in *the farmer allegedly killed the duckling*). There are functional reasons for such constructions and morphemes: speakers need to be able to signal, and not just allow the interpretation, that an utterance is not their own. Here again, a single vague category would not suffice communicatively.

Summing up

Linguistic **universals** and **typology** provide two complementary perspectives on variation in language structure. Both must necessarily be based on empirical evidence from the world's languages. Which languages one includes depends on the question being asked. If one is making universal or typological generalizations about the world's languages, this should be based on a **representative sample** of languages.

Universals are categorized into four types, according to two independent contrasts: **absolute** and **non-absolute**, and **implicational** and **non-implicational** universals.

A widely used (though imperfect) **language typology** is morphological, distinguishing four types of language according to **morpheme integrity**: **isolating**, **agglutinating**, **fusional** and **polysynthetic**. Another morphological typology distinguishes languages according to the type of affix they prefer, giving a contrast between **prefixing** and **suffixing** languages.

Linguistic typology is concerned with classifying linguistic phenomena such as constructions, rather than languages. Such typologies can be concerned with any linguistic level. Three morphological typologies were discussed, **number**, **possession** and **case**. Our syntactic typology distinguished **free word order** languages from **fixed word order** languages, and within the latter, six types according to the possible orders of subject, object and verb. This typology is interesting because there are correlations with other aspects of grammar. We briefly discussed a phonological typology of **tone systems**, which distinguishes **contour tone** systems, **register tone** systems and **pitch accent** systems. We also discussed a lexical-semantic typology of **motion verbs**, according to whether the verb conflates **manner**, **path** or **figure** with the motion component.

One way of representing cross-linguistic correlations between linguistic categories is by a **feature hierarchy**. These show the relative **markedness** of the features, from most **marked** to **unmarked**. Markedness is a complex notion, that takes into account a range of considerations including formal size and complexity, frequency of use in a language, frequency of occurrence across languages and number of cross-cutting dimensions distinguished.

Linguistic typology and universals demand explanation; three main considerations are: common origins, human biology and psychology, and functional unity.

Guide to further reading

Of the textbooks on language typology and universals, Whaley (1997) is the most accessible; Croft (2001) gives a good if somewhat dense overview of the subject. Fuller treatments can be found in Comrie (1981); Croft (1990); Shopen (2007a, 2007b, 2007c); and Song (2001). The classic work, which still repays study, is the four-volume *Universals of Human Language* (Greenberg et al. 1978). *The World Atlas of Language Structures* (Haspelmath et al. 2005) is an important reference-work; a web version is freely available at http://wals.info/.

The morphological typology of languages is widely used, and mentioned in most introductory textbooks; Sapir (1921); Whaley (1997: 128–136) and others have remarked on the need to separate the two dimensions shown in Figure 11.2, fusion and synthesis. On the typology of affixing, see Bybee et al. (1990). Word order typology is treated extensively in Tomlin (1986). Dryer (1997) is a staunch rejection of the universality of grammatical relations. The typology of possession is treated in a wide variety of works, among them Seiler (1983); Chappell and McGregor (1995); Heine (1997); Payne and Barshi (1999); and Baron and Herslund (2001). Comrie (2003) gives a clear overview of explanations of language universals.

On the typology and universals of phoneme systems see Crothers (1978); on phonetic universals and typology see Ladefoged and Maddieson (1996) and Maddieson (1997/1999). Universals and typology of tone systems are dealt with in Maddieson (1978), and Donohue (1997).

For more on Leonard Talmy's typology of motion verbs see Talmy (2003, 2007); and Slobin (1996b). Particularly well developed in semantic typology and universals is the domain of colour terms, where the classic work is Berlin and Kay (1969); see also Heider (1972); Davidoff (1991); and Roberson et al. (2005).

Useful websites for language typology and universals include: http://ling.uni-konstanz.de/pages/proj/sprachbau.htm, http://noam.philologie.fu-berlin.de/~gast/tdir/, and http://linguistics.buffalo.edu/people/faculty/dryer/dryer/.

Issues for further thought and exercises

1. It was mentioned in this chapter that almost all languages have an alveolar stop (where this is to be interpreted to include a range of places from dental to alveolar); furthermore, if a language has nasals, it probably has /n/. This suggests that alveolars may be unmarked with respect to consonants at other points of articulation. Test this in English by examining the other features of unmarked categories. For the purpose of frequency in English, take a sample 200–300 word paragraph from a newspaper, and examine the distribution of alveolars relative to other points of articulation. (Beware of the mismatch between English orthography and phonology.)
2. Do frequency by word type (i.e. as listed in the dictionary) and by word token (as in use) always correlate? Test this by comparing the frequency of /ð/ in the 100 most basic English words (see the Swadesh list included on the website for this book), and its frequency in the paragraph you used in Question 1.

(Continued)

Issues for further thought and exercises—Cont'd

3. How representative is the sample of languages given in Box 11.1? Did I need a representative sample of languages to make my point about the morphological typology? One language that is badly placed in Figure 11.2 because of the way we measured the degree of agglutination and fusion is West Greenlandic. What morphological type is this language usually assigned to, and why? Why do you think our measurement was so poor in this case – after all, it seems to give reasonable results for most other languages (e.g. Latin, Lao and Mandarin Chinese). Can you suggest some better way of determining the placement of the languages on the scales?

4. Below is data on four grammatical features in a dozen languages of the far north-west of Western Australia. The choice of languages was principled: one language was chosen from each group of each family (see §13.2), and where possible no languages were geographically contiguous.

	Genders	Case-affixes	Case enclitics	Number of short vowels
Ngarinyin	Yes	No	No	5
Gooniyandi	No	No	Yes	3
Kukatja (Pama-Nyungan)	No	Yes	No	3
Walmajarri	No	Yes	No	3
Miriwoong (Jarrakan)	Yes	No	No	4
Bardi	No	No	Yes	4
Yawuru	No	No	Yes	3
Kija	Yes	No	No	4
Bunuba	No	No	Yes	3
Nyangumarta (Pama-Nyungan)	No	Yes	No	3
Wunambal (Worrorran)	Yes	No	No	6
Yawijibaya (Worrorran)	Yes	No	No	5

Suggest universal generalizations on the basis of this data, giving at least one of each of the four types we distinguished in §11.2. Say which type each of your generalizations is. (For the purposes of this question, universals are understood as generalizations that hold for all languages in the sample; ignore all other languages of the world!)

Which correlations appear motivated, and which do you think are accidental? That is, if you were going to extend the investigation to a more representative set of the world's languages, which would you think most likely candidates for universals.

5. According to a universal tendency known as Behagel's third law, elements belonging to the same linguistic unit tend to be adjacent – that is, discontinuity of grammatical units is disfavoured. How would you explain this generalization?

6. An explanation was suggested in §11.4 for the widespread preference for suffixing over prefixing. That explanation would seem to suggest that infixes might be preferred over prefixes, yet we know that this is not so. Why not? Can you suggest an explanation that also accounts for the dispreference for circumfixes?

7. Which of the following categories or units do you think are more marked of the pair in English? Explain your reasons.

    a. affirmative   negative
    b. masculine   feminine
    c. present tense   past tense
    d. stops   nasals
    e. definite (e.g. 'the') indefinite (e.g. 'a')

f. /i/   /a/
g. /i/   /ɛ/
h. apico-alveolar stop   retroflex stop
i. possessive pronouns   reflexive pronouns
j. *old*   *young*
k. *full*   *empty*

8. Below is a table showing the consonant phonemes of Gooniyandi. Discuss the system in relation to universals of phoneme systems and markedness. Identify the segments you expect to be most and least marked.

	Labial	Lamino-dental	Apico-alveolar	Apico-postalveolar	Lamino-palatal	Velar
Stop	b	d̪	d	ḍ	ɟ	g
Nasal	m	n̪	n	ṇ	ɲ	ŋ
Lateral			l	ḷ	ʎ	
Rhotic			r	ɻ		
Glide	w				j	

9. Does case-marking in English satisfy the animacy hierarchy of Figure 11.3? Does the data raise any problems for the hierarchy? (In answering this question you should identify the range of words in English that show nominative-accusative case-marking, and place them on the hierarchy.)

10. Some languages show optional case marking, whereby the case marker may be present or absent on certain NPs, or in certain environments, without affecting grammaticality or interpretation. Granted that optional case marking tends to follow the animacy hierarchy (Figure 11.3) how would you expect it to be distributed? For instance, given that a language shows optional accusative case marking at a certain point on the hierarchy, what conclusions would you expect to be able to draw?

11. Here are some further activities to attempt in relation to the languages listed in Box 11.1:

    a. Which languages are prefixing and which are suffixing, according to Capell's definition? What is the relative proportion of each type?
    b. Assuming that they are all fixed word order languages (not all are, as a matter of fact), determine the relative frequency of OV and VO. (S has been left out because many of the examples do not have an S NP – why do you think this would be?)
    c. What percentage of the languages mark accusatives on 'honey' overtly?
    d. What percentage of languages use verb agreement with the S and/or O?
    e. A few languages have a morpheme labelled APP for applicative. Check a dictionary of linguistics to find out what this category is. What do you conclude about the semantic features of the verb in these example sentences?
    f. Examine the lexical expressions used in the languages, and make a list of the range of lexical means you find of expressing the notion 'bring back'. Can you suggest any way of categorizing these modes of expression?

Notes

1. For simplicity, here and throughout the rest of the chapter we restrict attention to spoken languages, excluding sign languages.

2. We know that they are singular in form not because they do not end in /s/ or /z/, but because there are regular plural forms that can be used in referring to multiple types – *there are many sheeps in New Zealand* means 'many sheep varieties'.

3. By the expression 'colloquially conflate' what is meant is that the conflation is not necessarily found in all lexical items and expressions, but rather is found in the most common, informal and conversational means of expressing the meaning.

Language Change

12

Just as languages vary from region to region, they change over time. In this chapter we outline some of the major ways in which change over time happens. We discuss changes in phonetics and phonology, morphology, syntax and semantics. We also discuss some reasons why language change occurs. Chapter 13 examines some of the consequences of change in language systems over time.

Chapter contents

Goals

The goals of the chapter are to:
- explain how and why languages change over time;
- introduce some of the main types of change in phonology, morphology, syntax and semantics;
- introduce the notion of regularity of sound change;
- give examples of some important changes in the historical development of English and other Indo-European languages; and
- identify some of the ways by which languages acquire and renew their grammatical resources.

Key terms

amelioration	cognates	insertion	sound change
analogical change	deletion	metathesis	structural pressure
assimilation	dissimilation	morphological change	syntactic change
bifurcation	extension	pejoration	taboo
bleaching	grammaticalization	reanalysis	understatement
borrowing	Grimm's law	regularization	
chain shifts	hyperbole	regularity	

12.1 Major characteristics of language change

Language change is ubiquitous; with the exception of extinct languages; no language remains static over a long period of time. You are probably aware of changes that have occurred in your own language within your lifetime: new words that have come into use, and others that have gone out of use, or at least out of fashion. You are probably also aware of differences between the speech of your generation and that of your parents' and grandparents' generations.

Modern human beings have changed relatively little biologically since they first appeared in Africa 150,000–200,000 years ago. Languages change much more quickly, so that they are usually recognizably different within a few centuries, and certainly over a period of a millennium. Compare the following three versions of the Lord's Prayer from different periods in English: **Old English** (from around 450 to about 1100), **Middle English** (about 1100–1500) and **Modern English** (around 1500 to present). (Note that þ and ð represent the voiceless and voiced dental fricatives (IPA θ and ð), y represents the high front rounded vowel in the Old English version, and c usually indicates the voiceless velar stop (IPA k).)

(12-1)   *Fæder ure þu þe eart on heofonum; Si þin nama gehalgod to becume þin rice gewurþe ðin*
         willa on eorðan swa swa on heofonum. urne gedæghwamlican hlaf syle us todæg and for-
         gyf us ure gyltas swa swa we forgyfað urum gyltendum and ne gelæd þu us on costnunge
         ac alys us of yfele soþlice.

Old English, 11th Century

(12-2)   *Oure fadir þat art in heuenes halwid be þi name; þi reume or kyngdom come to be. Be þi*
         wille don in herþe as it is doun in heuene. yeue to us today oure eche dayes bred. And fory-
         eue to us oure dettis þat is oure synnys as we foryeuen to oure dettouris þat is to men þat
         han synned in us. And lede us not into temptacion but delyuere us from euyl.

Middle English, Wycliffe, dated 1384

(12-3)   *Our Father which art in heaven, hallowed be thy name. Thy kingdom come. Thy will be*
         done in earth as it is in heaven. Give us this day our daily bread. And forgive us our tres-
         passes, as we forgive them that trespass against us. And lead us not into temptation. But
         deliver us from evil. Amen.

Early Modern English, from *Book of Common Prayer* 1559

You probably experienced little trouble understanding the third version, even though there are a few words that are no longer in common usage (*art*, *thy*, *trespasses*), and some of the grammar is a little unusual. Knowing the meaning of the passage, you will probably not experience enormous difficulties in reading the Middle English version, though it is clearly more divergent from Modern English. But the Old English version is likely to remain largely uninterpretable – 1,000 years have seen sufficient changes to result in effectively a new language: to speak Old English a speaker of Modern English would need to learn it just as they would Spanish or Finnish.

How fast do languages change? This is a bit like asking how fast do cars go. It is impossible to give a figure: the rate of change varies considerably; languages sometimes change rapidly, sometimes slowly. Thus, the changes in the 500 years from Early Modern English as represented in (12-3) seem less striking than the changes in the 400 years separating (12-2) from (12-1). It also depends on what aspect of the language you are considering. Some parts of languages tend to be more resistant to change than others: for example, some lexical items are more susceptible to change than others (see p. 307); pronouns tend to change rather slowly compared with the average lexical item; and bound morphemes tend to change more slowly than free morphemes.

The speed of change can also depend on other factors. Nick Reid has documented a case of particularly rapid change that occurred in the Australian language Ngan'gityimerri (non-Pama-Nyungan) verbal construction in the 50 years from 1930 to 1980 (Reid 2003). He suggests that one reason why the change could happen so rapidly is because of the small size of the speech community: a drastic change such as occurred might be expected to take considerably longer to travel through a larger speech community, say the community of Mandarin Chinese speakers.

Any aspect of a language can change over time: phonetics, phonology, morphology, syntax, semantics, pragmatics and lexicon. We have already encountered in Chapter 4 processes of extending the lexicon of a language, including acronyming, compounding, reduplication, borrowing and invention. These processes represent – along with the loss of words – the major means by which lexical changes occur.

12.2 Sound change

In the seventeenth century, speakers of Parisian French began to pronounce their rhotic as the uvular trill [ʀ], instead of the apico-alveolar trill [r]. This phonetic change subsequently spread by **diffusion** to other languages in Western Europe, hopping from urban area to urban area, and gradually spreading from the urban areas to adjacent rural areas. Today a uvular or pharyngeal rhotic has replaced, or partly replaced, the former apical rhotic in many dialects of French, German, Danish, Dutch, Swedish and Norwegian.

Speakers were probably aware of this phonetic change as it was in progress. Not all phonetic changes are like this. Many are slow and imperceptible at first, and become apparent only with the passage of time.

Grimm's law

Grimm's law[1] – named after Jacob Grimm (1785–1863) who formulated it in 1822, based on work by others, including Rasmus Rask (1787–1832) – describes some important sound changes that happened to stops in proto-Indo-European, the language from which most European languages ultimately derive (see §13.3), in the development of the Germanic languages. Three interrelated sets of changes occurred.

- Voiceless stops became voiceless fricatives: *p, t, k* became *f, θ, h.*
- Voiced stops became voiceless stops: *b, d, g* became *p, t, k.*
- Voiced aspirated stops became plain voiced stops: *bh, dh, gh* became *b, d, g.*

These changes did not occur in the developmental history of other Indo-European languages, for instance, Romance languages. Thus if we examine words in say English and French that derive from the same word in proto-Indo-European – such words are called **cognates** – we should find voiceless fricatives in English where there are voiceless stops in French, voiceless stops in English where there are voiced stops in French and voiced stops in English where there are voiced aspirated stops in French. In fact, however, the Romance languages also underwent their own sets of sound changes, complicating the picture. In Table 12.1 we give one cognate in English and French illustrating the first two sets of changes, omitting *b* which was rare in proto-Indo-European. In this table we follow the standard convention of prefixing a star to forms in the proto-language.

Table 12.1 Some cognates in English and French illustrating Grimm's law

Grimm's law sound change	English	French cognate
*p > f	foot	pied
	fish	poisson
*t > θ	three	trois
	thou	tu
*k > h	heart	cœur
	hound	chien (initial /ʃ/ from /k/)
*d > t	two	deux
	tooth	dent
*g > k	knee (/ni/ from /kni/)	genou (initial /ʒ/ from /g/)
	corn	grain

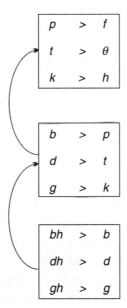

Figure 12.1 Grimm's law chain shift.

The three sets of sound changes in Grimm's law are interrelated. If the voiced aspirated stops first changed to plain voiced stops, and then later these changed to voiceless stops, then these to fricatives, all Proto-Indo-European stops would show up as fricatives in Germanic languages. Since this did not happen, the changes must have been linked together in a **chain shift**, as depicted in Figure 12.1. We can imagine either the top change dragging the other changes along after it, as it were, filling the spaces left over as a result of the changes; or alternatively the bottom change could be imagined as pushing the other changes ahead of it, preventing massive collapse of phonemic contrasts.

Some common types of sound changes

This section mentions and exemplifies five common types of sound change.

Loss or deletion

Loss or **deletion** of segments is a not uncommon type of sound change. English examples include loss of voiced stops following nasals at the end of a word: the final /b/ of *thumb* has been lost (although it remains in *thimble*, where it is not word-final) as has been the final /g/ of *strong* (cf. *stronger*). Loss of word-final segments is called **apocope**. Loss of a segment from the beginning of a word is **aphaeresis**; word initial /k/ preceding an /n/ in English has been lost, as in *knife* and *knee*, the spellings of which reflect previous pronunciations. Segments can also be lost within a word – this is called **syncope** – as happened to the middle consonant of many three-member consonant clusters in Scandinavian languages. For example, the Swedish place name *Väsby* derives from *väst* 'west' and *by* 'town'.

Insertion

Insertion or **epenthesis** involves the addition of phonological segments into a word. The stops in *thunder* and *number* are epenthetic; speakers of English often add an epenthetic schwa between the two final consonants of *film*. Latin words beginning with an *s* followed by a stop began in the second century AD to add an initial short *i* vowel: *scola* became *iskola* (cf. French *école* 'school'), and *stabula* 'stable' became *istabula*.

Assimilation

Assimilation is the process whereby a segment changes to become more like a nearby segment, usually adjacent to it. This is a very common type of sound change. Latin *octo* 'eight' became *otto* in Italian, *noctem* 'night' became *notte*, and *factum* 'done' became *fatto*. (The letter *c* in Latin represents /k/.) The first stop in the consonant cluster in these words has changed to become more like – indeed, identical with – the following stop by adopting its place of articulation. This is called **regressive assimilation** because it is as though a property – place of articulation – of the second stop moves backwards (regresses) to the preceding stop in the cluster.

An example of **progressive assimilation**, where the phonetic characteristic shifts forward, is the change in the history of Icelandic from **findan* 'find' to *finna*, and **munθ* 'mouth' to *munn*. Here the nasal component of articulation has shifted forward from the nasal to the following stop or fricative, resulting in a double nasal consonant.

The above examples illustrate total assimilation – one segment becomes identical with another. Partial assimilation is when one segment becomes more like, but not identical with, another. Regressive partial assimilation is illustrated in the change from the velar stop /k/ to the alveo-palatal affricate /tʃ/ before front vowels in the history of English. For instance, **kinn* changed to *chin*, and **kɛːsi* to *cheese*.

Do you understand why the change from /k/ to /ʧ/ is assimilation? Recall that front vowels have the high point of the tongue forward in the mouth, whereas velar stops have the back of the tongue relatively high in the mouth, making contact with the velum. The articulation of the stop changed so as to closer approximate the following vowel by anticipating its tongue position. (Remember that when velars precede front vowels they tend to shift their point of articulation forward to the pre-velar region, as in words like *key*. Alveo-palatal articulation is a more extreme form of assimilation.)

Dissimilation

Dissimilation is the reverse of assimilation: neighbouring segments become less alike. Dissimilation is most frequent with laterals and rhotics. Notice how the second rhotic in the Latin words *arbor* 'tree' and *rôbur* 'strength' changed to a lateral in Spanish *arbol* and *roble*.

Metathesis

Metathesis is the inversion of the order of adjacent or nearby phones. English examples include *ask* from Old English *acsian* (in fact, *aks* was regular until the seventeenth century, and is still found in some dialects), *bird* from Old English *brid*, and *horse* from Old English *hros* (other sound changes have affected the last two words in many dialects).

Metathesis is not common. But occasionally it is systematic. In Ilocano (Austronesian, Philippines) word initial /t/ and word-final /s/ have been fairly consistently switched. Corresponding to Tagalog *taŋis* 'cry' and *tigis* 'decant', which preserve the original sequence of these two phonemes, are Ilocano *sa:ŋit* and *si:git*.

Generality of sound changes

Sound changes can be limited to particular phonological environments, though they are sometimes unconditional, and apply everywhere. For instance, at some point in time the palatal lateral /ʎ/ in Hungarian changed unconditionally to /j/.

Sound changes are generally regular. If /k/ changes to /ʧ/ before front vowels, this usually happens to every /k/ in this environment, and not just to a scattering of them. Metathesis and dissimilation are the most frequent exceptions to the regularity of sound change.

If sound changes are so regular, why do we have exceptions to Grimm's Law such as *genuflect* and *pedicure*, which are obviously related to the French words *genou* 'knee' and *pied* 'foot' cited in Table 12.1? Shouldn't these words show up with initial *k* and *f* respectively? (See end of chapter for answer.)

12.3 Morphological change

Acquisition and loss of bound morphemes

One way of acquiring new bound morphemes is through borrowing of words, and later factoring out of common components. Following the Norman invasion of England in 1066 English acquired a large number of lexical items from French, many of which had derivational affixes attached to them. As the borrowings became increasingly numerous and integrated into the language, these affixes were identified, and came to be attached to native English words as well. Derivational morphemes such as -*able*, -*ment*, *dis*- and *re*- entered the English language in this way.

This is not the only way new bound morphemes can appear. Sometimes bound morphemes are borrowed as such, and not as parts of lexical items. Jeffrey Heath's seminal study (1978) identifies a number of bound morphemes borrowed between languages of Arnhem Land. Among his examples is the verbal derivational morpheme -*thi* 'become', borrowed into Ngandi (non-Pama-Nyungan) from its unrelated neighbour Ritharrngu (Pama-Nyungan). And in the Kimberley region, the bound comitative postposition -*ngarri* 'with' has been borrowed as an independent item across languages belonging to at least three different families.

Another important process of morpheme acquisition is grammaticalization, discussed in §12.5.

Morphemes can also be lost over time, going slowly out of use until they completely disappear, or only relics remain. Old English verbs took a third person plural agreement marker -*n* as in *stodon* 'they stood', which was lost over time as a result of a regular sound change.

Analogical change

Languages often regularize their morphology, replacing irregular forms by regular forms, thus making the regular morphological rules more productive. For instance, *shoe* once had plural *shoen*, which is now completely replaced by *shoes*; and in Middle English the plural of *cow* was *kine*, which has completely gone in most dialects, being replaced by the regular *cows*.

What is going on here resembles the process of solving a simple mathematical equation involving proportions: *shoe* is to x as *loo* is to *loos*. Clearly x must be *shoes*:

$$\frac{shoe}{x} = \frac{loo}{loos} \quad \text{therefore} \quad x = shoe \times \frac{loos}{loo} = shoe \times s = shoes$$

The new form is constructed on analogy with another morphological opposition; this is called **analogical change**.

The term **analogical levelling** is used for regularizations in which an irregular morphological opposition is replaced by another opposition modelled after a more regular pattern. Another type of analogical change is **analogical extension**, whereby a minor morphological pattern is used as the basis for analogical remodelling. Otto Jespersen once cited a now famous example of a Danish child 'who was corrected for saying *nak* instead of *nikkede* ["nodded"], [and] immediately retorted "sticker ["prick"], stak ["pricked"], nikker, nak," thus showing on what analogy he had formed the new preterit'. In some dialects of American English the past tense of *dive* is *dove* rather than the regular *dived*. This form is formed by analogy with a minor pattern, as in *drive* ~ *drove*.

> The word *mouse* has recently been extended to an item of computer equipment. The usual plural of this *mouse* is the regular *mouses*, not *mice*. But *mice* remains as the standard plural of *mouse* in its ordinary sense. This is an illustration of the process of **bifurcation**. Both regular and irregular plurals remain, but they have acquired different meanings.

Reanalysis

Reanalysis refers to the process by which a word with a certain morphological structure comes to be analysed differently over time (see also §4.3). *Quince* was originally the plural of *quin*, but the plural suffix was reanalysed as a part of the stem; the plural is now *quinces* – which historically has two instances of the plural suffix! Likewise for the Dutch word *schoenen* 'shoes', the earlier plural form of which was *shoen*. The auxiliary verb *have*, pronounced as /əv/ in many environments, appears to be in the process of being reanalysed in some varieties of English as *of* following a modal auxiliary (e.g. *may*, *could* etc.). Thus it appears as /əv/ when stressed in expressions like *would have gone*, pronounced (and sometimes written) as though *would of gone*. The verbal suffix -*ing* is in some environments reanalysed as the participial -*en*.

In some Austronesian (see §13.3) languages of the Pacific, ordinary nouns are preceded by a free morpheme *a* that indicates the following word is a noun. It seems that the proto-language also had a similar morpheme **a*. But in Paamese it has been reanalysed as part of the root form of some nouns, as in *atas* 'sea' from **tansik*, and *ani* 'coconut' from **niu*.

12.4 Syntactic change

Changes in word order

Latin had relatively free word order. The three words of our earlier Latin example (3-2) (repeated as (12-4) below) can occur in any order, and the result is an acceptable sentence with the same meaning:

(12-4)	*serv-ī*	*consul-em*	*audi-unt*	SOV
	slave-PL:SUB	consul-SG:OBJ	hear-they:PRS	
	'The slaves hear the consul.'			

(12-5) *serv-ī*   *audi-unt*   *consul-em*   SVO
        slave-PL:SUB   hear-they:PRS   consul-SG:OBJ
        'The slaves hear the consul.'

(12-6) *consul-em*   *serv-ī*   *audi-unt*   OSV
        consul-SG:OBJ   slave-PL:SUB   hear-they:PRS
        'The slaves hear the consul.'

(12-7) *consul-em*   *audi-unt*   *serv-ī*   OVS
        consul-SG:OBJ   hear-they:PRS   slave-PL:SUB
        'The slaves hear the consul.'

(12-8) *audi-unt*   *serv-ī*   *consul-em*   VSO
        hear-they:PRS   slave-PL:SUB   consul-SG:OBJ
        'The slaves hear the consul.'

(12-9) *audi-unt*   *consul-em*   *serv-ī*   VOS
        hear-they:PRS   consul-SG:OBJ   slave-PL:SUB
        'The slaves hear the consul.'

In the modern daughter languages, the Romance languages, however, word order is fixed SVO, as in:

(12-10) *les*   *esclaves*   *entendent*   *le*   *consul*   French
         the:PL   slave:PL   they:hear   the   consul
         'The slaves hear the consul.'

This rigidification of word order doubtless results from loss of noun cases in modern Romance languages. With the loss of cases, word order was apparently pressed into service for distinguishing between subjects and objects. A similar thing happened in the history of English.

> Saying that languages like Latin and Old English had 'free word order' should not be interpreted literally. First, in these languages it was phrase order rather than word order as such that was 'free': words belonging to the same phrase usually remained together. Second, different word orders conveyed different pragmatic nuances. Third, it is usually the case that not all word orders in a language are equally common: often one is preferred in use, even if all are grammatically acceptable.

Word order can also be borrowed. In parts of Papua New Guinea, some Papuan languages have apparently borrowed SVO word from neighbouring Austronesian languages, while some Austronesian languages have borrowed SOV word order from their Papuan neighbours. Thus it is believed that word order in the Austronesian languages of the Central and

Milne Bay Provinces was originally SVO, but this changed to SOV under the influence of nearby Papuan languages.

Changes in grammatical constructions

Grammatical constructions can, like morphology, change as a result of borrowing, reanalysis and extension.

Borrowing of grammatical constructions

Pipil, has borrowed the Spanish comparative construction, including the morphemes *más* 'more' and *que* (/ke/) 'than' (Campbell 1998: 230–231). Thus compare (12-11) with the Spanish counterpart (12-12). Prior to contact with Spanish, Pipil had different ways of expressing comparatives, all of which have been replaced by the Spanish-style construction.

(12-11) *ne*   *siwa:t*   *mas*   *galá:na* *ke*   *taha*   Pipil
       the   woman   more   pretty   than   you

       'That woman is prettier than you.'

(12-12) *esa*   *mujer*   *es*   *más*   *linda*   *que*   *tú*   Spanish
       the   woman   is   more   pretty   than   you

       'That woman is prettier than you.'

Reanalysis of grammatical constructions

Mandarin Chinese has a special grammatical construction called the *bǎ*-construction, a type of passive in which the word order is SOV instead of the normal SVO, and the object is marked by the preposition *bǎ*, as in:

(12-13) *wǒ*   *bǎ*   *zhāng-sān* *dǎ*   *le*   Mandarin Chinese
       I   OBJ   Zhang-san   hit   PFV

       'I hit Zhang-san.'

Written records show that *bǎ* was a verb meaning 'take' in Archaic Chinese. Gradually it developed into a preposition, while retaining its use as a verb until the Tang dynasty (618–907 AD). The modern construction comes from a sentence involving two verbs forming a so-called serial verb construction – in the case of (12-13), this would have had a meaning like 'I took Zhang-san and hit him'. This also accounts for the unusual word order of the construction: the object is in the expected place for the erstwhile verb *bǎ*.

Extension of grammatical constructions

A frequent type of extension is for a reflexive construction to extend to cover passive senses. Old Spanish had a reflexive construction involving the reflexive morpheme *se*, as in (12-14).

(12-14) *Juanito*   *se*   *vistió*   Old Spanish
       Johnny   reflexive   dresssed

       'Johnny dressed himself.'

Over time this construction came to be used in contexts where a passive interpretation was also possible, and ultimately in contexts where only the passive interpretation is possible, as in (12-15) – which does not mean that the 2,000 people captured themselves!

(12-15)	*cautiváron-se*	*quasi*	*dos*	*mil*	*personas*	Spanish
	they:captured-reflexive	almost	two	thousand	persons	

'Almost two thousand persons were captured.'

12.5 Grammaticalization

The English adverbial derivational suffix *-ly* derives from Middle English *lic* 'like', and ultimately from Old English *gelic*. This is an example of **grammaticalization**, a process by which a lexical word becomes a grammatical item.

One of the Danish passive constructions involves a suffix *-s* to the verb, as in (12-16). This suffix derives from an earlier free reflexive form *sig* 'self', which later cliticized and extended to reciprocals ('do to one another') and middles (so called because they are intermediate between actives and passives). The clitic ultimately reduced to the verbal inflectional suffix *-s*, and extended to cover passive senses.

(12-16)	*dørene*	*låse-s*	*klokken*	*seks*	Danish
	the:doors	lock-passive	o'clock	six	

'The doors will be locked at six o'clock.'

Grammaticalization generally involves **phonological reduction** and **semantic bleaching**, reduction in the meaning of the item, whereby the meaning becomes less concrete. Both are illustrated in the grammaticalization of English derivational *-ly* and the Danish passive suffix *-s*.

Some examples of common types of grammaticalizations are:

- Verbal derivational morphemes sometimes come from lexical verbs. For example, most varieties of the Western Desert dialect continuum (see p. 159) have a verbal derivational morpheme *-rri* 'become', which comes from a verb meaning 'to fall', which previously occurred in compounds.
- Complementizers (elements used as connectives in certain types of complex sentence, like *that* in *I regret that he is sick*) often come from the verb 'say', as in Ewe *bé* 'that', 'say'.
- Copulas (words like *to be* that connect subject and predicate in clauses like *John is sick*) often derive from verbs of position or stance, like 'stand', 'sit', 'lie': Quechua *tiya-* 'to be' comes from **tiya* 'to sit'.
- Copulas often come from demonstratives or pronouns: the copula *shì* of Mandarin Chinese derives from *shì* 'that, the afore-mentioned'.
- Auxiliary verbs often derive from main verbs, as in the case of English auxiliary verbs *have* and *will* which were once used exclusively as main verbs meaning 'to possess' and 'to desire'.
- Definite markers often come from demonstratives: the Danish definite markers *-en* (as in *mand-en* 'the man') and *-et* (as in *bord-et* 'the table') derive from postposed demonstratives.

- Indefinite articles often grammaticalize from 'one', as in the case of English indefinite *a ~ an*.
- Relative pronouns (as in *the child **who** was hit*) often come from *wh*-question words, as in the case of English *who*, *where* and *when*.
- Future tense markers often have a source in verbs like 'want', 'go' and 'have': for example, French and Spanish inflectional futures derive from the Latin verb *habere* 'to have'.

Processes of grammaticalization are generally **unidirectional**: they proceed in one direction only. For example, verbs like 'want' and 'go' often become future tense markers, but the reverse does not occur. Free lexical words become bound affixes, and show reduction in semantic content. The reverse process is rare, though not impossible: the English derivational suffix *-ism* has recently become an independent word meaning 'doctrine, belief system'; and the possessive enclitic *-s ~ -z ~ -əz* probably derives from an inflectional genitive case marker. Such processes are the exception not the rule.

12.6 Semantic change

It is not just the forms (signifiers) of linguistic signs that change over time, but also the meanings (signifieds); indeed, these can change drastically. As a result, cognates can be obscured, and appear unlikely. For instance, English *silly* is cognate with Danish *salig* and German *selig* both of which mean 'blessed, blissful'. In fact, *silly* comes from Old English *sælig* 'happy, blessed, blissful', which took on the sense 'humble, simple' in Middle English, then 'feeble, week', and then 'weak minded, stupid' in Early Modern English.

Semantic changes are not random, although they are not as regular as sound change, and are frequently restricted to individual lexemes. Like other changes, semantic changes can be classified into a number of recurrent types. We have encountered some of these already: extension (§4.3); narrowing (§4.3); bifurcation (§12.3); and bleaching (§12.5). Four other types of change are common.

Pejoration

Pejoration is the process by which a word acquires negative connotations. Speakers come to evaluate the word less positively, ultimately giving it a more negative meaning. The changes in meaning of *silly* illustrate this. Pejoration is also involved in the development of the modern words *moron*, *negro* and *midgit*. A considerable number of terms for women in English (and other languages) began as relatively neutral terms, and acquired increasingly negative connotations over time. *Hussy* was originally a shortened form of *housewife*; *slut* previously denoted a woman of untidy habits; *mistress*, a borrowing from Old French *maistresse* 'woman in control', at one time denoted a 'woman who employed others in her service'; and *madam* began as a polite term of address to women. For the first two terms the pejorative senses triumphed; for the second two, both neutral and pejorative senses are still available.

Amelioration

The reverse process, in which a word comes to acquire (more) positive connotations, is **amelioration**. *Fond* comes from the past participle of *fonnen* 'to be silly, foolish' in Middle English. *Knight* comes from Old English *cniht* 'boy', which shifted to 'servant', then 'military servant', and thence to its modern meaning 'member of lower nobility'. Parallel developments are found in other European languages. Spanish *caballero* 'knight, nobleman' began as a term for 'horse-rider'; *caballo* 'horse' in turn comes from Latin *caballus* 'workhorse, nag'.

Hyperbole

In **hyperbole** a word loses a strong aspect of meaning through frequent exaggerated use. Intensifying adverbs like *terribly*, *awfully* and *horribly* have, through overuse, lost the senses of the words from which they are derived, *terrible*, *awe* and *horrible*, and are now general intensifiers meaning little more than 'very'. *Starve* comes from Old English *steorfan* 'to die', and *quell* from *cwellan* 'to kill, to slay, to put to death'.

Understatement

Understatement is another type of exaggeration that can lead to semantic change through overuse. Verbs of killing sometimes derive from weaker verbs of violence that do not necessarily imply death, via understatement: *kill* derives from a verb meaning 'to hit, strike, knock'; French *meurtre* 'murder' from a verb meaning 'to bruise'. Another example is *bereaved*, from Old English *be-rēafan* 'to rob, plunder'.

Direction of semantic change

What typically happens in semantic change is that an additional meaning is acquired in a certain restricted context of use; this new meaning tends to increase in frequency of occurrence, until it takes over and the original sense goes out of use. English *write* can be traced back to a proto-Germanic lexeme meaning 'to cut, scratch'. The meaning was extended to include also 'to write', the context being through runic writing, which were scratched on stone and wood. This is reflected in Old English *wrîtan* 'to cut' and 'to write', and Old Norse (Indo-European, Europe) *ríta* 'to score' and 'to write'. In Modern English the original sense 'to scratch' has been lost, and only the extended sense 'to write' remains. As this illustrates, to establish an extended meaning and context for a lexeme often requires understanding of technology and cultural practices.

We conclude this all too brief discussion of semantic change by mentioning a few instances of not-infrequent changes that tend to go in a single direction, typically from more concrete to less tangible, and more abstract.

- Body-part terms often develop into spatial terms (e.g. *at the foot of*).
- Spatial terms frequently acquire temporal senses (e.g. *after* and *before*).

- Perception verbs often develop into verbs of comprehension (e.g. from *see* or *hear* to 'understand').
- Terms for handedness and/or sides of the body often develop into terms of moral evaluation or qualities; typically the left side develops in the negative direction to badness and evil (for instance, *sinister* derives from a Latin word meaning 'left'), the right to goodness and virtue (think of *right*).
- Terms for obligation, ability and permission often develop into terms expressing degrees of probability (e.g. *must*, which originally indicated obligation, has developed a sense 'necessarily true').

12.7 Causes of language change

Why do languages change? Numerous reasons have been put forward over the centuries, some plausible, others quite fanciful. Among the latter are anatomical, ethnic, racial and geographical factors. To give one example, it has been suggested that consonants in languages spoken in mountainous regions change more rapidly than they do in languages spoken in coastal regions because of the greater breathing effort required. Yet Danish has undergone extensive consonantal changes, although its primary speech community resides on a very flat coastal terrain. Perhaps, as Otto Jespersen suggested (1922: 257), it is due to the number of Danes holidaying in Switzerland and Norway (these days on Crete)!

In the following sections we outline some of the more plausible reasons why languages change. In most cases, a change is likely to be motivated by a combination of factors, rather than just a single factor. Before we begin discussing the causes, it may be well to remark that changes over time are generally considered to emerge from variation that existed in earlier varieties of the language, prior to the change. This synchronic variation serves as it were as fuel for diachronic change, which did not happen instantaneously.

Physiological tendencies

Simplification or ease of articulation has often been suggested as a reason for sound changes. Loss of segments results in shorter words, and less effort in production; assimilation reduces the difference between segments in sequence, and so also the effort in production. It is not far from this view to the idea that laziness, sloppiness and indolence are the major causes of sound change. Speakers of English will be familiar with these as everyday explanations of the contemporary changes in the language, habitually remarked on by media watchdogs of 'correct' English.

But there are problems with simplification and ease of articulation as explanations of sound change. To begin with, what is simple or easy? Crowley (1992: 201–202) observes that the two segments in the sequence /gl/ in Kuman (Papuan, New Guinea) were fused together to form the velar lateral /ʟ/. This 'simplification' results in a segment that is relatively unusual in the world's languages, and which is far from easy for non-native speakers to articulate. A similar 'simplification', this time at the allophonic level, is found in some dialects of Australian English where the lateral /l/ of *milk* is realized as the velar allophone [ʟ]. (In some dialects /l/ has become even more like the high back vowel in some positions, and lost its consonantal features.)

As in these examples, simplification in one place often leads to complexity elsewhere. Loss of final vowels or initial consonants in a language will result in shorter words, and less production effort. But it can lead to complexity in syllable shapes – for instance, the emergence of V and CVC syllables, where previously all syllables were CV.

It is not that the simplification explanation is totally misguided. Rather, it needs reformulation in more explicit and physiologically appropriate terms. We can think of speech production as involving muscular gestures or movements that are coordinated in a complex way, rather like the instruments in a symphony. A variety of physiologically and psychologically natural processes affect the gestures when they are put together; these concern the nature of the gestures, their presence and their timing. We can see these in the emergence of the Kuman velar lateral: the velar gesture and the lateral gesture (i.e. lower the sides of the tongue) have been retimed from sequential to simultaneous, and along with this the stop gesture and the apical gesture have disappeared. Nasalized vowels arose in French in a similar fashion. Between the ninth and fourteenth centuries final /n/ began to be lost in words like *bien* 'well' and *fin* 'end'. The lowering of the velum was retimed to occur during the vowel; the final gesture, the blockage of air through the oral cavity, eventually disappeared.

A similar explanation accounts for the insertion of segments in some circumstances. It is difficult to coordinate the articulatory gestures in sequences such as [ml] and [mt] so that the velum is raised at precisely the same time that the bilabial contact is released and the apical contact initiated. Closure of the nasal cavity prior to the opening of the lips in the production of the [m] will result in insertion of a [b]. The English word *bramble* acquired its second bilabial stop in this way.

This type of explanation is based on physiological processes for which no further explanations are proposed – we have not attempted to explain why some gestures were lost, some gained and others became simultaneous: they just happened. The actual changes are not predictable like the motion of the planets; at best they are more or less explicable in hindsight. In most circumstances different outcomes could have eventuated, some more likely, others less likely. It is not suggested that all sound changes can be explained in this way.

Functional considerations

Languages change to meet new needs and purposes. We have already seen illustration of one such process in the acquisition of new items of vocabulary for new and novel things and meanings. In a similar way lexemes can be lost – or undergo meaning change – as the objects they denote become outmoded. Thus a *lure* was originally a special pipe used to call back hawks in the medieval sport of falconry; now it refers to anything used as an enticement.

Morphological and syntactic change can also be motivated at least in part by functional considerations. The shift from free word order in Old English to fixed word order in Modern English (see §12.4) has a functional motivation: the need to keep the subject and object distinct, in the face of loss of case-marking on nouns.

With endless repetitions of lexical items, they tend to lose whatever expressive value they may once have had. Some instances of morpho-syntactic change are motivated by considerations of expressiveness, which can be considered as a type of functional motivation for change. Many Australian languages have compound verb constructions involving compounding of a morphologically almost invariant preverb and an inflection-taking verb, as in Miriwoong *dilyb ge-ma-n-tha* (break he-it-get-past) 'he broke it off'. There is no reason to suppose that these compound expressions were introduced into the languages because of lexical gaps in ancestor languages. Rather, it seems that they began life as constructions involving an ideophone – a sound-symbolic word like *bang!* – paired with a verb. Over time this mode of expression came to dominate and eventually won out over plain verbs, which had become lifeless old ways of talking about events.

Identity

An important motivation for language change is to establish and maintain group identity and cohesiveness on the one hand, and on the other hand, to signal its distinctiveness from other groups. Youth and occupational groups often employ some lexical items peculiar to themselves, or give existing lexemes new senses. Youth 'slangs' or jargons distinguish members from older people because they change so rapidly. But it is more than mere fashion that motivates such lexical changes: the fashion serves to distinguish group members from outsiders.

Phonetic change can also be motivated by identity considerations. In a pioneering study of the centralization of the beginning of the diphthongs /aɪ/ and /aʊ/ in Martha's Vineyard, a small island off the coast of Massachusetts, USA, William Labov showed that the extent to which the change is employed is correlated with social attitude. The change has taken greatest hold on speakers who identify themselves as islanders, and have the most negative attitudes to mainlanders. It has been adapted to a lesser degree by speakers with more neutral attitudes, or more positive attitudes to mainlanders.

The idea here is that a minor variation in speech can be adopted by speakers as a marker of their identity as a group; the variation can then spread through the language variety of the speech community. The variant itself is effectively arbitrary; it is the expansion of the variation leading ultimately to change in the variety that is explained, not the particular variant that emerged.

Foreign influence

Extensive contact between speakers of different languages can result in language change. This is especially the case when speakers of one language are politically dominant, and there is widespread bilingualism or multilingualism in the speech community. The widespread changes that happened to English in the aftermath of the Norman invasion of

England in 1066 resulted from the political dominance of French, and its high status in the public domain. In this case, English was the **substratum** language, the language of the politically subordinate group. In colonial times, English was usually the **superstratum** language. The new Englishes that arose in colonial contexts show features of the substratum languages. This is the case for Indian English, which shows phonetic characteristics of the substrate Indo-European and Dravidian languages. Some features of the English of African Americans that are not shared with standard American English have been put down to influences from the languages spoken by the slaves transported to America centuries ago, such as Ewe and Mandinka (Niger-Congo, Senegal).

In situations of extensive community-level bilingualism it often happens that lexemes, morphemes, grammatical constructions and even phonemes are borrowed. Such borrowing has happened on a large scale in Aboriginal Australia, where multilingualism was the norm in traditional times. In such environments, even bound morphemes are not infrequently borrowed between unrelated (or very distantly related) languages. In the small village of Kupwar in southern India three languages have been in close contact for some six centuries, Kannada (Dravidian), Urdu (Indo-European) and Marathi (Indo-European). Many villagers are bi- or tri-lingual. While the lexical items of the three languages have tended to remain separate, and few lexical borrowing have occurred, their syntax has converged; the local varieties of the languages are rather different grammatically from the standard varieties, and more similar to one another.

Taboo

Lexical replacement is sometimes motivated by phonological similarity to a taboo word. The word *coney* was the word for 'rabbit' in Middle English. It came to be used as a term first of endearment then of abuse of women; ultimately it was used for the female genitals. Because of this association, it was dropped as a term for 'rabbit', and now remains only in the last sense. A similar thing has happened to *cock* 'rooster' in many dialects of English, with its extension to 'penis'; perhaps *pussy* will also follow a similar trajectory.

Another example is provided by Proto-Uralic *kuńcɛ ~ *kuće 'star' and *kuńće ~ *kuće 'urine', which merged together in Old Hungarian, becoming homophones *húgy* 'star' and *húgy* 'urine'. The former lexeme became obsolete, and was replaced by *csillag*; the latter remained. These examples illustrate a general tendency, namely that the term denoting the taboo or 'touchy' body part or product is retained at the expense of the other term, which is replaced by a new term.

We mentioned in §4.5 tabooing of names of recently deceased persons and similar sounding words in Australian languages. While the tabooed word usually comes back into use within a few years, it is likely that in some cases the replacement term sticks, and the original tabooed term is dropped for good.

Social upheaval

It is sometimes suggested that major linguistic changes correlate with periods of social upheaval. With rapid breakdown of the existing social system, and the communication networks constituting it, the language system might also show disruption and rapid change. There is doubtless some truth to this suggestion. The Norman invasion of England was such an event, and it did give rise to a number of quite substantial changes in English. The decimation of many indigenous groups in Australia and the Americas led to the obsolescence and ultimately death of many languages; in some cases the languages were only partially learnt by children, and survived as varieties with simplified grammar and reduced lexicons.

However, it is unlikely that all cases of rapid language change (the rate languages change is variable, as mentioned at the beginning of the chapter) can be put down to social upheaval, or that social upheaval inevitably leads to rapid language change, except perhaps in the lexicon. The so-called information revolution of recent years has given rise to numerous new lexical items, even new ways of using language. But it does not seem that the phonological and grammatical systems of English have simultaneously undergone substantial changes.

Regularization

Languages often change so as to regularize their grammar, reducing the number of irregularities and partially regular patterns in the morpho-syntax. The processes of neatening and extending the patterns characteristically occur at certain points in first language acquisition (see §9.1). Speech 'errors' of adult speakers sometimes result from over-regularization, for instance when an adult says *strived* instead of *strove* or *striven*. Such 'errors', especially when they occur in infrequent words, may become the accepted forms, ousting the existing irregular form, and giving rise to analogical levelling (§12.3). The result is greater transparency in the system.

Structural pressure

There is some tendency for paradigmatic systems within a language to be regular or symmetrical. That is, languages tend to prefer regular systems such as the Sanskrit system shown in (12-17) over irregular ones such as the hypothetical one shown in (12-18).

(12-17)	p	t	ṭ	c	k	Sanskrit
	p^h	t^h	$ṭ^h$	c^h	k^h	
	b	d	ḍ	ɟ	g	
	b^h	d^h	$ḍ^h$	$ɟ^h$	g^h	
(12-18)	p	t	ṭ	c	k	
	p^h		t^h			
			ḍ	ɟ		
	b^h	d^h	$ḍ^h$			

Asymmetrical systems tend to become symmetrical by filling in gaps. This is what is meant by **structural pressure** as a factor in language change. This seems to have been at least part of the motivation for the emergence of /ʒ/ in English. In the eighteenth century, English had the irregular system of fricatives as shown in (12-19).

(12-19) f θ s ʃ h
        v ð z

In the nineteenth century a partner for /ʃ/ emerged through insertion of /j/ following the original /z/ in words like *treasure* and *pleasure*; this sequence subsequently fused into the single fricative segment /ʒ/.

This leaves /h/ out on a limb. There is no evidence of any pressure in English for the emergence of its voiced counterpart /ɦ/. Instead, there is a tendency for /h/ to disappear from the phonological system of English: it has been lost completely in some varieties, and has been retained in others mainly through strong social pressures, including the influence of writing.

Presumably at least part of the reason why English has not developed /ɦ/ is because the voiced glottal fricative is unusual in the world's languages. The tendency towards regular paradigmatic systems is always balanced against such considerations. In many Australian languages we find a neat patterning of stops and nasals at each point of articulation. But laterals tend to break the pattern: velar laterals are absent, and lamino-dental laterals are rare, even in languages that distinguish this place of articulation for stops and nasals.

The best we can say is that there is some tendency for languages to fill in structural gaps. On the other hand, changes can result in gaps in what were perfectly regular systems. Proto-Indo-European *p* was lost in proto-Celtic, resulting in a less regular system in the stop consonants. The gap was filled in differently in different branches of Celtic. Motu (Austronesian, New Guinea) has recently lost its velar nasal, creating an irregularity in the otherwise regular system of nasals and stops that distinguished three points of articulation. But there is as yet no evidence of any change that might lead to removing this gap.

Summing up

No living language remains static for long, and all aspects of language are subject to change, though some features are more resistant to change than others. And, overall, language change occurs at very different rates.

Common processes of **sound change** are: **loss** or **deletion**, **insertion**, **assimilation**, **dissimilation** and **metathesis**. Sometimes a group of sounds is affected by a linked set of changes in a **chain shift**; **Grimm's Law** is an example. An important property of sound change is its **regularity**. This permits us to identify **cognates**, words in related languages that can be traced back to the same word in an ancestor language.

Morphological change can happen through **borrowing**, **analogical change** (including **levelling** and **extension**) and **reanalysis**. In some cases both the new analogized form and the original form coexist, and take on different meanings; this is called **bifurcation**. The same three types are also found in **syntactic change**. In addition, word order changes sometimes result from morphological changes such as loss of case-marking.

Semantic change tends not to be as regular as sound change. A variety of processes can result in semantic change, including: bifurcation, tabooing, euphemism, dysphemism, metaphor, metonymy and synecdoche. Types of semantic change include **extension**, **narrowing**, **bleaching**, **pejoration**, **amelioration**, **hyperbole** and **understatement**.

Grammaticalization is the process by which new grammatical words and morphemes emerge in a language, often from lexical items. Grammaticalization is normally accompanied by **semantic bleaching** and **phonological reduction**. It is normally **unidirectional**: lexical items become grammatical items, but the reverse process is rare.

Causes of language change are numerous and varied. They include **physiological** and **psychological** tendencies, **functional** and **structural** pressures, maintenance of **identity**, **foreign influences**, **social upheaval** and **taboo**.

Guide to further reading

Aitchison (1981) is an excellent and entertaining introduction to language change. The best introductory textbook is, in my opinion, Crowley (1992); Campbell (1998) is also good. More advanced textbooks include Anttila (1972) and Hock (1991). Joseph and Janda (2003) is a comprehensive collection articles, most of which are quite technical, on every aspect of language change.

See the *Guide to further reading* for Chapter 4 for works on the history of English; of these, Burridge (2004) is recommended for the variety of examples it provides of each type of semantic change, and its lively style. Etymological information on English words can be found in dictionaries of etymology, such as Ayto (1990) and Onions (1966). Simpson and Weiner (1989) also includes a good deal of etymological information, as well as extensive exemplification of word usage from written sources since the earliest times. Many useful (and not so useful) etymological resources can be found on the web, including a free online etymological dictionary of English at http://www.etymonline.com/. Also useful is Eugene Cotter's *Roots of English: An Etymological Dictionary*, Which can be downloaded from http://ablemedia.com/ctcweb/showcase/roots.html; this dictionary, however, is restricted to terms of Latin and Greek origins.

Numerous recent works deal with grammaticalization, though few are suitable for beginners. With some reservations, I suggest Hopper and Traugott (2003) and Heine and Kuteva (2002). Three articles in Joseph and Janda (2003) deal with grammaticalization: Bybee (2003); Heine (2003); and Traugott (2003).

Issues for further thought and exercises

1. In the following passage which lexical words are inherited from proto-Germanic (i.e. are 'native' English), and which have been borrowed or involve borrowed elements? What proportion of lexical items are borrowings? Identify the source language for each borrowing. Which fraction of the borrowed items has each language contributed?

(Continued)

Issues for further thought and exercises—Cont'd

The consensus among the scientific community is that the Earth is a planet orbiting a fairly typical star, one of many billions of stars in a galaxy among billions of galaxies in an expanding universe of enormous size, which originated about 14 billion years ago. The Earth itself formed as a result of a process of gravitational condensation of dust and gas, which also generated the Sun and other planets of the solar system, about 4.6 billion years ago. All present-day living organisms are the descendants of self-replicating molecules that were formed by purely chemical means, more than 3.5 billion years ago. (Charlesworth and Charlesworth 2003: 1)

Now do the same with the following passage from a novel. Comment on any differences you observe between the two excerpts.

For a full hour Bony silently watched Alice McGorr at work, effacing himself. She examined the bedclothes, the interior of the baby's cot, and the clothes in the wardrobe. She rummaged into drawers and cupboards, removed the contents of shelves and expertly looked at cooking utensils. She brought the washing in from the line. She fingered the curtains, examined the backs of the few pictures, lifted the linoleum along the edges. She glanced through the magazines and opened the covers of the few books. And when she was done, her hair was wispy with dampness and her hands were dirty. (Upfield 1953/1958: 29)

2. Sometimes *chimney* is pronounced as *chimbley* or *chimley*. What sound changes have occurred? In many dialects of English words like *due, duty, dubious, dual* and *duke* are pronounced with an initial /ʤ/; they can be traced back to forms with initial /d/. How do you think the sound change occurred, and what type of sound change is involved? (Hint: recall the emergence of /ʒ/.)

3. Spellings often provide information about earlier pronunciations of words. But this is not always so in English spelling. Find out how the bolded letters in the following words became part of the spelling: **p**sychology, **ph**otograph, enou**gh**, **ye** olde shopp**e**, dou**b**t, **gh**ost, **s**neeze, **k**nave, caug**h**t, fau**l**t, and w**h**ich.

4. Below are some words in Banoni (Austronesian, Solomon Islands) and the proto-forms they derive from. What sound changes have occurred, and what types do they represent?

Proto-form	Banoni	Gloss
*mpaɣa	bara	'fence'
*mpunso	busa	'fill'
*tipi	tsivi	'a traditional dance'
*makas	maɣasa	'dry coconut'
*pekas	beɣasa	'faeces'
*koti	kotsi	'cut'
*mata	mata	'eye'
*matua	matsua	'rise'

5. Below are some words in Portuguese (spelt phonemically) and their Latin sources. What sound changes are represented in this data?

Latin	Portuguese	Gloss
contrā	kõtra	'against'
grandis	grãdi	'big'
septem	sɛci	'seven'
tantus	tãtu	'so much'
focus ('hearth')	fɔgu	'fire'

decem	*deʒ*	'ten'
femina	*femea*	'woman'
luna	*lua*	'moon'
non	*nɔ̃*	'no'

6. Here are some cognates from two Indo-Iranian languages, Sanskrit and Pali. The forms in one language have undergone a sound change, while the forms in the other have remained unchanged. Which language do you think has changed? What type of phonological change is exemplified? Justify your answer.

Sanskrit	**Pali**	**Gloss**
bhartum	*bhattum*	'carry'
patra	*patta*	'wing, leaf'
sahasra-	*sahassa-*	'thousand'
varsati	*vassati*	'it rains'
ārya	*ayya*	'noble'

7. Find out the etymology of the following English words: *marshal, giddy, pioneer, coach, husband, wife, bowdlerize, woman, cretin, pen, avocado, assassin, phony, love* (as the zero score in tennis), *barbeque, grog* and *lord*. What sorts of sound changes and semantic changes have occurred in the documented history of these words?

8. It was mentioned at the beginning of §12.7 that changes in a language can usually be traced back to variants existing at a single point in time. Such variants can emerge for humorous purposes. For instance, from a recent letter to the Scientific American 'Freud said a few absurd things, but to ignore all his ideas would be a "phallusy"' (*Scientific American*, September 2004, p.7); I recently gave a lecture on 'phorensic phonetics'; from the Clinton-Starr affair is *fornigate*. What process is involved in these inventions? Can you think of other variants in modern English (or another language you know well) that illustrate this process?

9. What was the Great English vowel shift? Find out when it occurred, and which vowels were affected and how. What sort of change was it? (See, for example, Campbell 1998; Anttila 1972; Hock 1991; and the internet.)

10. The following sentences taken from Shakespeare's plays illustrate the way negatives were constructed in Early Modern English. Describe the negative constructions as illustrated by these examples; compare these constructions with the modern counterparts, and describe how the syntax has changed.

   a. *Be it so she will not here before your Grace Consent to marry with Demetrius* (*A Midsummer Night's Dream*, Act I, Scene 1)
   b. *I know not by what power I am made bold* (*A Midsummer Night's Dream* Act I, Scene 1)
   c. *Whether, if you yield not to your father's choice . . .* (*A Midsummer Night's Dream* Act I, Scene 1)
   d. *My soul consents not to give sovereignty.* (*A Midsummer Night's Dream* Act I, Scene 1)
   e. *Why should not I then prosecute my right?* (*A Midsummer Night's Dream* Act I, Scene 1)
   f. *Demetrius thinks not so; He will not know what all but he do know.* (*A Midsummer Night's Dream* Act I, Scene 1)
   g. *Nay, faith, let not me play a woman; I have a beard coming.* (*A Midsummer Night's Dream* Act I, Scene 2)
   h. *For, being not propp'd by ancestry, whose grace Chalks successors their way, nor call'd upon* (*King Henry the Eighth*, Act I, Scene 1)
   i. *Ladies, you are not merry.* (*King Henry the Eighth*, Act I, Scene 3)

(*Continued*)

Issues for further thought and exercises—Cont'd

j. *Was it not she and that good man of worship, Antony Woodville, her brother there, That made him send Lord Hastings to the Tower, From whence this present day he is delivered?* (*King Richard III*, Act I, Scene 1)

k. *Heard you not what an humble suppliant Lord Hastings was, for her delivery?* (*King Richard III*, Act I, Scene 1)

l. *Didst thou not kill this king?* (*King Richard III*, Act I, Scene 2)

m. *Is not the causer of the timeless deaths Of these Plantagenets, Henry and Edward, As blameful as the executioner?* (*King Richard III*, Act I, Scene 2)

n. *The saddler had it, sir; I kept it not.* (*The Comedy of Errors*, Act I, Scene 1)

o. *Dost thou not know?* (*The Comedy of Errors*, Act I, Scene 2)

p. *May he not do it by fine and recovery?* (*The Comedy of Errors*, Act I, Scene 2)

q. *Saw'st thou not, boy, how Silver made it good At the hedge corner, in the coldest fault? I would not lose the dog for twenty pound.* (*The Taming of the Shrew*, Act I, Scene 1)

r. *Would not the beggar then forget himself?* (*The Taming of the Shrew*, Act I, Scene 1)

s. *Trouble us not.* (*The Tempest*, Act I, Scene 1)

t. *He misses not much.* (*The Tempest*, Act I, Scene 2)

11. In the following semantically related pairs the words in the first column are native English stock, those in the second are borrowings from French. How would you characterize the semantic difference? Can you explain this situation?

sheep	*mutton*
calf	*veal*
pig	*pork*
cow	*beef*

Other pairs of semantically related inherited items and French borrowings include:

clothes	*attire*
gown	*negligee*
ask	*question*
climb	*mount*
arse	*derrière*

Can you modify your explanation for the first set of terms to cover these additional pairs? What other similar pairs can you find?

Answer to question on p. 281

These words were borrowed into English after Grimm's Law ceased to apply. It is the existence of words like this, that fail to observe established sound laws, that permit linguists to identify borrowings.

Notes

1. In the study of language change, the term *law* is used to describe a change that happened at some point in time to a particular language. It is not a universal generalization applying to all times and places, as in the case of the laws of physics or chemistry; nor is it a stricture that a person can decide to disobey, as in legal contexts.

13 Languages of the World

This chapter is an introduction to the diversity of the world's languages. It briefly surveys the number, distribution and viability (states of 'health') of the languages, and how they are related to one another. The notions of genetic relatedness and language family are explained, and the methods for establishing them are outlined. Some of the major families are overviewed. In the final section of the chapter we discuss some types of languages that do not fit into the family model.

Chapter contents

Goals

The goals of the chapter are to:
- overview the linguistic diversity of the world;
- show the enormous discrepancies in the numbers of speakers of the world's languages;
- discuss what it means for languages to be genetically related;

- introduce the comparative method, the principal method of establishing genetic relations among languages and two other less reliable methods;
- overview six of the world's largest (putative) families; and
- discuss three types of language that do not fit neatly into genetic groups: pidgins, creoles and mixed languages.

Key terms

Afroasiatic	families	mass comparison	Sino-Tibetan
Austronesian	family trees	mixed languages	sound
basic vocabulary	genetic relations	mutual intelligibility	correspondences
cognate sets	groups	Niger-Congo	stocks
comparative method	Indo-European	pidgins	subgroups
creoles	language isolates	proto-languages	Trans-New Guinea
expanded pidgins	lexicostatistics	reconstruction	

13.1 Number and variety of the world's languages

How many languages are spoken in the world today?

Current estimates put the number of languages somewhere around 7,000. The latest edition of *Ethnologue* (see p. 323) lists some 6,912 languages, of which just over 100 are sign languages. This is an increase of 103 languages over the previous edition; and over 700 more than the eleventh edition, dated 1988, which listed 6,170 languages. From about the same time, Ruhlen (1987: 3) speaks of around 5,000 languages. Evidence that the languages of the world are multiplying? No – in fact, quite the contrary is the case: the world's linguistic diversity is, like its bio-diversity, rapidly declining (recall §7.5).

The reason for the discrepancy in the counts is partly due to gaps in our knowledge, especially about languages spoken in inaccessible (from the Westerner's perspective) regions. Indeed, most of the world's languages lack detailed grammatical descriptions and dictionaries. But more significant is the question of what is being counted – what constitutes a single language? The word *language* is used in a variety of different senses.

In popular parlance, a political sense is usually invoked: people often speak of languages as the forms of speech that are associated with nations. Different nations, according to this view, have different languages. Italian is the language of Italy, German of Germany, French of France and so on. Different varieties of speech found within a nation would be regarded as dialects of the language. Elsewhere the relevant political unit might not be a nation, but a 'tribe', or some other unit.

Linguists usually use the term in a different way, and employ the criterion of **mutual intelligibility**. If speakers of one form of speech can understand the speakers of another without having to learn it, the varieties are said to be mutually intelligible, and they are dialects of a single language. British English and Australian English are mutually intelligible, and so are dialects of a single language, English, according to this definition.

Sometimes linguists use the term *language* to refer to forms of speech that share a certain percentage of common (or very similar) words and morphemes, and the term *dialect* for forms that share a higher percentage of common words. For example, American English, Australian English and British English share a considerable number of words, and would count as dialects according to this conception.

These three senses do not always coincide. The mutually intelligible varieties of speech spoken in Britain and Australia are associated with different nations, and would represent different languages by the political criterion – and indeed they are sometimes spoken of as different languages: e.g. 'the Australian language' as distinct from 'the British language'. Hindi and Urdu are mutually intelligible, but often regarded as distinct languages, Hindi being the language of Hindu speakers in India, Urdu the language of Muslim speakers in Pakistan.

By contrast, Mandarin Chinese and Cantonese are frequently spoken of as 'dialects' of Chinese, not only in the West, but also in China itself, even though they are not mutually intelligible. This is because of the long political unity of the speakers and their shared writing system. A similar problem arises in diglossic situations (see §7.4), where the members of a community speak mutually unintelligible varieties depending on the circumstances.

The number of languages one distinguishes in the world will depend on which sense of the term language one deploys. To make things more problematic, linguists often do not make it clear which sense they are using, and even mix senses. So someone making a list of languages cannot always be sure what sort of things the named varieties are, and be certain they are not counting chalk and cheese.

Distribution of languages

Languages are not spread evenly across the globe. As can be seen from Map 13.1, there is a high density of languages in the equatorial region, even though this spreads across continents and islands separated by expanses of sea. The density in northerly regions is significantly lower.

It is not difficult to guess that the low linguistic density in Greenland and Siberia is a result of low population densities. But population density is not the only consideration.

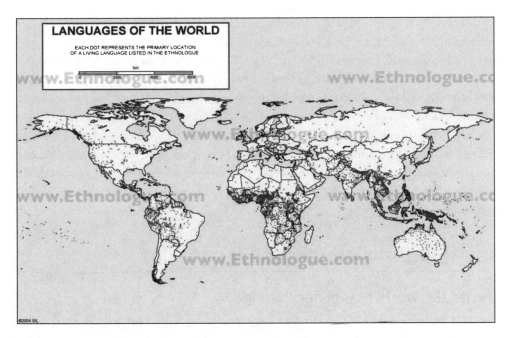

Map 13.1 Distribution of the world's languages. (*Source*: Gordon 2005; http://www.ethnologue.com/show_map. asp?name=World&seq=10)

Mainland China and Europe are much more densely populated than Australia and the island of New Guinea, but their language densities are considerably lower. In fact, over 1,000 languages are spoken in New Guinea and on nearby islands, making it the most linguistically dense region of the world.

Why so many languages?

It is believed that anatomically fully modern human beings, of the genus *homo sapiens sapiens*, emerged in east Africa some 150,000–200,000 years ago. They spread out from there to the rest of Africa, Asia, Europe, Australia (some 60,000 or so years ago), and later into America (perhaps as recently as 13,000 years ago, perhaps over 20,000 years ago). Languages change rapidly, and the physical separation of populations over time would result in the division of languages into dialects, and ultimately into mutually unintelligible languages. Even if the earliest populations in Africa spoke a single language, the social and geographical separation of human populations during the past 100 millennia or so could account for the modern diversity of languages. Perhaps we should put the question the other way around: why so few languages?

Numbers of speakers of the world's languages

It is impossible not to be struck by the enormous discrepancies among languages in terms of their numbers of speakers. A small number of languages are spoken by enormous numbers of speakers: over 40 per cent of the world's population have as their mother tongue one of the nine languages with more than 100 million speakers: Mandarin Chinese, English, Spanish, Hindi, Arabic, Bengali, Russian (Indo-European, Russia), Portuguese and Japanese.

At the other end of the spectrum, at least 3,340 languages (i.e. about half the total number of languages) have less than 10,000 speakers each – the speakers of these languages together constitute less than 0.3 per cent of the world's population. Of these languages, around 415 are nearly extinct, with just a few elderly speakers. Numerous other languages have gone out of use in recent years. In the nearly three decades during which I have been working on Kimberley languages, at least five have lost all their fluent speakers, and are effectively dead. Two or three others have reached the critical stage, and have at best a handful of speakers and part speakers.

13.2 Relations among the languages

How are the world's languages related?

Some languages belong together in the sense that they derive from a single ancestor language – called a **proto-language** – that was spoken long ago, and that subsequently split into varieties that over the passage of time became mutually unintelligible. Languages that derive from a single proto-language are said to be **genetically related**, and to belong to a single language **family**.

It is not known for sure whether or not all languages of the world ultimately come from a single ancestor language spoken in the very distant past, say at the dawn of the emergence of modern human beings. Languages change so rapidly that convincing evidence of relatedness does not remain for more than about 10,000 years – beyond that length of time, it is increasingly difficult to separate chance similarities among languages from similarities shared from a common ancestor language. The term **stock** is sometimes used for hypothetical groupings of more or less well established families into larger and more tentative sets.

We now discuss some of the methods linguists use to establish language families. It should be cautioned that genetic relatedness of languages has, in principle, nothing to do with the biological-genetic relatedness of their speakers. Speakers of genetically related languages need not be closely related biologically; a child will acquire the language spoken in its social environment, not the language spoken by its biological parents, if they are not present in the social environment. Thus, English is spoken as a mother tongue by humans of diverse biological ancestry. On the other hand, speakers of genetically unrelated languages may belong to the same genetic groups. Hungarian is not genetically related to the neighbouring languages, although the speakers of Hungarian are not distinguishable as a population in terms of biological-genetic features from speakers of nearby languages.

Nonetheless, some large-scale statistical correlations between genetic groupings of languages and biological genetic groups seem to exist: they are not totally unconnected (see Cavalli-Sforza 2001). However, the correlations are imperfect, and striking mismatches do occur.

Methods for establishing language families

Various methods have been developed and used by linguists to establish language families and thus the genetic relatedness of languages. Among them the **comparative method** is a well-honed and stringent set of techniques that provides convincing evidence for genetic relatedness. If languages can be shown to be genetically related by careful application of this method, few linguists would question their relatedness. We discuss this method in the next subsection. The following subsections then describe two more contentious and less reliable methods.

> It must be stressed that genetic relatedness is not the same thing as typological similarity. Languages sharing typological characteristics need not be genetically related; Hungarian and Walmajarri are both agglutinating languages, though there is no reason to believe they are genetically related (if they are, the connection probably goes back to proto-world, the original language of human beings!). On the other hand, languages deriving from a common ancestor language need not be typologically identical; the Indo-European languages show considerable typological diversity: for instance, while most are accusative, there are many ergative languages (see §11.3) in the Indo-Iranian branch.

Comparative method

The idea underlying the comparative method is that genetic relatedness of a group of languages can be established by **reconstructing** a proto-language that could plausibly serve as an ancestor of each of the languages, and showing in detail how the modern languages could have developed from this proto-language through a credible series of changes. Reconstruction involves hypothesising what the proto-language might have been like by attempting to undo the changes that occurred between the proto-language and its descendants.

To reconstruct a proto-language you begin by compiling sets of cognates among the languages, that is, you gather together lexical and grammatical items that are similar in form and meaning, that can be assumed to have derived from a common ancestor. From these cognate sets you identify recurrent correspondences in the forms of the cognates and propose a form in the proto-language from which the modern forms could have derived by plausible sound changes.

Consider the words cited in Table 13.1, from four languages from the far north west of Australia. (The words are spelt in the orthography for the language, which in each case is phonemic; *j* indicates a palatal stop, *y* a palatal glide, *rl* a retroflex lateral, *oo* in Bardi and Nyikina orthographies is the high back vowel (*u* in the other languages), and *rr* an apical tap; double letters (other than *oo*) indicate long vowels.)

Table 13.1 Some basic words in four languages of the north west of Australia

	Bardi	Nyulnyul	Nyikina	Warrwa
'boomerang'	jiiwa	jiib	jiba	jiiba
'camp'	booroo	bur	booroo	buru
'down'	jimbin	jimbin	jimbin	jimbin
'two'	kooyarra	kujarr	koojarra	kujarra
'be sitting'	miyala	mijal	mijala	mijala
'(his) mouth'	ni-lirr	ni-lirr	nilirr	nilirr

The forms in each row appear to be cognates; they are similar enough in phonological form and in meaning to be reasonably traced back to single words in an ancestral proto-language.

Not only are the word forms phonologically similar but also there are systematic correspondences in the phonemes that comprise them. Aside from the cases of identity of phonemes in the corresponding places in the words, we have:

- where Bardi, Nyikina and Warrwa have a final vowel, Nyulnyul has none;
- where Nyulnyul, Nyikina and Warrwa have a palatal or bilabial stop (/j/ or /b/) between vowels, Bardi has a glide (/y/ or /w/);
- where Bardi, Nyulnyul and Warrwa have the long high front vowel /ii/, Nyikina has a short high front vowel.

We can now guess what original sounds in the proto-language might have given rise to the phonemes in the modern languages, bearing in mind the principle that the sound changes that give rise to the modern forms should be credible.

First, we would guess that what remains constant across the languages – including initial /b/ and /k/ – was identical in the proto-language. No sound change is required to explain the modern forms, and there would be no reason to propose that, for instance, the recurrent initial /b/ comes from some other segment, for instance an initial prenasalized stop. (Of course, we cannot rule out the possibility that the initial /b/ did come from a prenasalized stop; but there is no evidence for this, and it is pointless to make such unwarranted and untestable speculations.)

Second, it is natural to guess that the proto-language had final vowels where Bardi, Nyikina and Warrwa have final vowels, and that these were lost in Nyulnyul. This is more likely than that the other languages gained final vowels, especially in the light of the words for 'down' and '(his) mouth' – which should have final vowels in Bardi, Nyikina and Warrwa if these languages gained their final vowels.

Third, it is reasonable to guess that the correspondence between glides in Bardi and stops in the other languages goes back to stops in the proto-language. It is more likely that stops between vowels would weaken to glides than that glides would strengthen to stops. This involves assimilation, and is attested in many other historical cases.

Fourth, the final correspondence we would naturally guess goes back to a long high vowel in the proto-language. In fact, vowel length in Nyikina is not phonemically contrastive, and it is most natural to guess that it was lost in that language rather than gained in the other languages.

With these observations in mind, we can reconstruct the words in the seven words in the proto-language as follows (recall that in historical linguistics the star before the word indicates it is a reconstructed form):

'boomerang'	*jiiba
'camp'	*buru
'down'	*jimbin
'two'	*kujarra
'be sitting'	*mijala
'mouth'	*-lirr

(The reconstruction of 'mouth' as *-lirr is based on the observation that we can also reconstruct a prefix *ni- meaning 'his, hers, its'.)

The comparative method is ultimately based on the assumption of the arbitrariness of the linguistic sign. Occasional resemblances in words are not unexpected between any pair of languages – for instance, Kaqchikel (Mayan, Guatemala) mes 'mess, disorder, garbage' and English mess. But large numbers of similarities in forms and meanings between a pair of languages is unlikely to be accidental, except in onomatopoeic words. For this reason, one initially excludes obvious onomatopoeic words from cognate sets when applying the comparative method.

A large number of lexical similarities between two languages does not necessarily mean that they are genetically related, and that the words can be traced back to a proto-language. One language might have borrowed heavily from the other. In applying the comparative method, it is important to determine whether apparent cognates are genuine, or borrowings; this can be very difficult. One additional assumption – for which there is much independent evidence – is helpful in this context. It is that basic everyday words (such as terms for the major parts of the body, everyday artefacts, low numerals, primary kinship terms, and basic observable phenomena of the world) are less likely to be borrowed than less basic words (like technical vocabulary, words for high numbers and for unusual plant and animal species). For this reason one first begins to apply the comparative method to basic vocabulary, as we did in our four-language sample.

The demand that sound correspondences be recurrent further reduces the likelihood of lexical similarities being accidental. Nevertheless, even as stringent a method as the comparative method can't be said to provide absolute proof of genetic relatedness. There remains a small chance that two languages could show numerous recurrent similarities in their basic vocabularies by accident, just as it is possible (though very unlikely) you will throw a straight sequence of a hundred, or even a thousand, heads.

Reconstructed proto-languages are idealizations; reconstructions are limited by accidents of what survives in the descendant languages, and indeed which daughter languages survive. One of the few cases where we have extensive written evidence of a 'real' ancestral language is for the Romance languages, which are known to be descendants of Latin. Proto-Romance as reconstructed from the modern languages is not the same as Latin. For instance, Latin distinguished cases for nouns, but none of the modern daughter languages do, and cases can't be reconstructed for proto-Romance.

Mass-comparison

Applying the comparative method is an exacting process, requiring a detailed knowledge of the languages being compared, not to say a considerable amount of time and effort. As a first step in determining whether a group of languages are genetically related one might relax the criteria somewhat. The method of **mass-comparison** is a way of getting an initial idea of the classification of a number of languages by comparing basic vocabulary items, excluding onomatopoeic forms. A good deal of phonetic and semantic similarity among the languages – in other words, a fair number of potential cognates – is indicative of possible genetic relatedness.

To give an illustration of the method, consider the short list of basic words in six languages of Africa presented in Table 13.2.

Table 13.2 A selection of basic words in six African languages

	Afrikaans	Bemba	Kanuri	Chichewa	Shona	Swahili
'woman'	vrou	úmwaanakashi	kámú	mkazi	mukádzí	mwanamke
'man'	man	úmwaaúmé	kwâ, kwângâ	mwamuna	murúmé	mwanamme
'sun'	son	ákasuba	kàngâl	dzuwa	zúvá	jua
'fish'	vis	ísabi	búnyì	nsomba	hóvé	samaki
'dog'	hond	ímbwa	kàri	galu	imbwá	mbwa
'bird'	voël	icúúní	ngúdò	mbalame	shiri	ndege
'three'	drie	-tatu	yàskà	-tatu	-tatú	tatu
'water'	water	ámeenshí	njî	madzi	mvúrá	maji
'big'	groot	-kulu	kúrà	-kulu	-kúrú	kubwa
'good'	goed	-suma	ngàlà	-bwino	-naka	nzuri
'tree'	boom	úmutí	kàská	mtengo	mutí	mti

Which languages would you group together as likely members of a family? Write down your suggested groupings before reading on.

Glancing through the list reveals few similarities between the Afrikaans words and any others. Nor are there many resemblances between the Kanuri words and words of any other languages, with the exception of the word for 'big'. But there are many similarities among the words in the other four languages. Particularly striking are similarities of the words for 'tree' and 'three' (identical in the four languages, except that the word is free in Swahili, but bound in the other three languages). Less obvious, but nevertheless discernible (if you make some intermediate chains of linkages), are the similarities in the forms of the words for 'sun', 'woman' and 'man'. The words for 'dog' and 'big' are each also very similar in three of the four languages. It thus seems reasonable to tentatively group these four languages together as members of a single family.

This type of evidence is less convincing than evidence of genetic relatedness obtained by application of the comparative method. Many linguists regard mass comparison as useful heuristic tool in initial hypothesis generation, but insist that it should be followed by application of the comparative method. Nevertheless, a number of language families are supported by no more than this sort of evidence – and many by even less!

A major problem with mass-comparison is that putative cognate sets obtained by eyeballing wordlists for items with similar forms and meanings will result in the inclusion of 'false friends', words that resemble one another in form and meaning, but are not genuine cognates, and exclude real cognates, the forms of which have diverged through phonological change. Thus, one would group French *feu* 'fire' and German *feuer* 'fire' together in applying mass-comparison, although the French word comes from Latin *focus* 'hearth', while the German word derives from proto-Indo-European *$p\bar{u}r$* 'fire' which became *$f\bar{u}r$-i* in proto-Germanic. These two words are not cognates: Latin *f* derives from proto-Indo-European *bh* but German *f* comes from proto-Indo-European *p* by Grimm's Law (see §12.2). (One might hope that the weight of numbers will ultimately even things out, false friends adding where distant cognates subtract. But this can only be described as wishful thinking.)

Lexicostatistics

Lexicostatistics is a statistical method for distinguishing groups and subgroups in genetically related languages. It is based on the idea that basic vocabulary is relatively resistant to change, and will be renewed rarely compared to non-basic vocabulary. If the rate of replacement of basic vocabulary is roughly constant regardless of the language, the proportion of shared basic words between a pair of related languages can give an indication of how long the languages have diverged from one another, provided borrowings are excluded.[1] From this, it is possible to determine groupings and subgroupings of the languages within the genetic set.

Application of this method depends on having first established the genetic relatedness of the languages, and that one can reliably distinguish between borrowings and shared retentions from a proto-language. This means in practice that the comparative method has already been employed to reconstruct the proto-language, its lexicon, and the historical sound changes giving rise to the modern forms.

Variants of the lexicostatistical method have been used in a number of regions in order to gain an initial picture of language relatedness, well before any application of the comparative method is feasible. One such variant was applied extensively in Australia in the 1960s, on the presumption – which still remains a hopeful guess – that the languages form a genetic unity. Pairwise counts were made of shared apparent cognates between languages, obvious borrowings being excluded. With no independent evidence of genetic relatedness, the known varieties were grouped into families, groups, subgroups, languages and dialects. Recent work by some Australianists has shown that application of this quick and dirty version of lexicostatistics sometimes gives a quite good picture of groups and subgroups, one that is in relative accord with the results obtained by the comparative method, when subsequently undertaken.

13.3 Some major families of the world's languages

The languages of the world can be divided into a number of families of related languages, possibly grouped into larger stocks, plus a residue of **isolates**, languages that appear not to be genetically related to any other known languages, languages that form one-member families of their own. The number of families, stocks and isolates is hotly disputed. The disagreements centre around differences of opinion as to what constitutes a family or stock, as well as the criteria and methods for reliably establishing them.

Linguists are sometimes divided into lumpers and splitters according to whether they lump languages together into large stocks, or divide them into numerous family groups. Merritt Ruhlen is an extreme lumper: in his classification of the world's languages (1987) he identifies just 19 language families or stocks, and five isolates. More towards the splitting end is *Ethnologue*, which identifies some 94 top-level genetic groupings, as well as 36 isolates, and 43 unclassified languages. (About two hundred other exceptional languages are identified as well, including deaf sign languages.) However, in terms of what has actually been established by application of the comparative method, the *Ethnologue* system is wildly lumping!

Some families, for instance Austronesian and Indo-European, are well established, and few serious doubts exist as to their genetic unity. Others are highly contentious. Both Ruhlen (1987) and *Ethnologue* identify an Australian family, although (as just mentioned) there is as yet no firm evidence that the languages of the continent are all genetically related. At least as contentious is Joseph Greenberg's (1987) putative Amerind stock of Native American languages.

In the following subsections, we present an overview of six major putative families: Indo-European, Austronesian, Afroasiatic, Niger-Congo, Sino-Tibetan and Trans-New Guinea. Each of these families has over 300 languages, and together they account for almost two-thirds of the world's languages, and over 80 per cent of the speakers. The website for this chapter includes a brief survey of the world's languages organized geographically.

Indo-European

The Indo-European languages have been recognized as forming a family since at least the late seventeenth century, when Andreas Jäger observed in 1686 that Persian and many of the languages of Europe are descendants of a single language. Since Jäger's time, many more languages have been shown to belong to the family. Indeed, Indo-European languages are spoken throughout most of Europe, across Iran, through Central Asia, and into India. With the colonial expansions of the fifteenth to nineteenth centuries, they spread into the Americas, Australia, New Zealand, Africa and Asia, in the process, diversifying into numerous dialects. They have become major languages in many of the former colonies, and are spoken by a staggering two and a half billion (i.e. thousand million) speakers.

The family consists of just over 400 languages (430 according to the latest edition of *Ethnologue*), which can be grouped together into a number of subfamilies or branches, as shown in the family tree representation of Figure 13.1 (p. 312). Map 13.2 shows the approximate locations of some of the main groups.

More historical-comparative work has been done on Indo-European than any other language family, and many lexemes have been reconstructed for proto-Indo-European, as well as some of its grammar. Proto-Indo-European was an inflecting language (like ancient Indo-European languages such as Latin, Hittite and Ancient Greek), with a complex verbal system with different inflections for different persons and numbers of the subject, tense, aspect, mood, as well as case-marking for nouns.

Proto-Indo-European is widely believed to have been spoken in the south-east of Europe, perhaps in the region of Turkey, some six to eight thousand years ago. Opinions differ, however, and some argue for a more northerly location in the steppes of Russia. From the homelands the language spread east and west, in the process fragmenting into numerous mutually unintelligible languages.

It is now widely believed that the early period of Indo-European expansion that took the languages as far as India in the east and Ireland in the west, was not via military style invasions like the Roman conquests of 2,000-odd years ago. One influential idea is that the expansion of the languages accompanied the spread of agriculture from a centre in the near east, beginning some six to eight thousand years ago (see Renfrew 1987, 1989). According to one version of the story, farmers gradually spread outwards, using land previously occupied by hunters and gatherers, eventually ousting them. Another version has it that agriculture and the language of the agriculturalists spread by diffusion, without major population movements. This story is not without difficulties, and it seems that there are some problems with the timing of some events. An alternative view is that Indo-European spread instead with the domestication of the horse and the invention of the wheel (e.g. Anthony 2007).

Austronesian

Austronesian is the largest universally accepted language family in the world with over 1,200 languages, spoken by some 300 million speakers from Madagascar in the west to Easter Island in the east, Taiwan in the north and New Zealand in the south, with the exception of Australia and most of the island of New Guinea. (The Niger-Congo family (see pp. 314–317) is the only larger family, but it is less well accepted.)

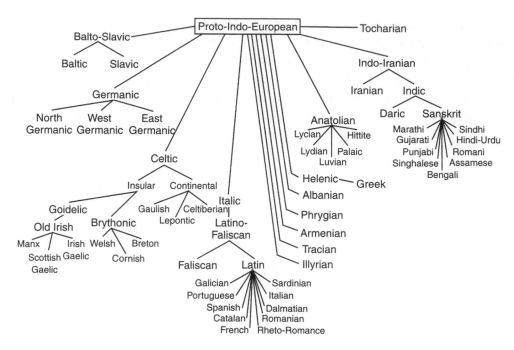

Figure 13.1 The Indo-European family tree (simplified and redrawn from Campbell 1998: 168).

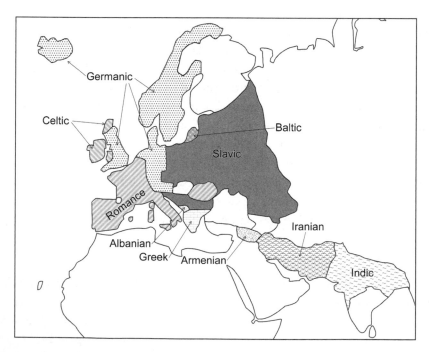

Map 13.2 Main groups of the Indo-European family.

As for Indo-European, a good deal of proto-Austronesian has been reconstructed. There are, however, differences of opinion concerning how the family is structured. One view is that it is divided into four groups, three of which – Atayalic, Tsouic and Paiwanic – are located on the island of Taiwan. Other proposals identify up to nine groups on Taiwan. Just one branch, Malayo-Polynesian, accounts for the bulk of the languages of the family, and includes all Austronesian languages outside Taiwan. Malayo-Polynesian is subdivided into four groups, Central Malayo-Polynesian, South Halmahera-West New Guinea, Oceanic (eastern group) and Western Malayo-Polynesian. Regardless of the actual structure of the family, it is clear that there is considerably greater diversity in the languages of Taiwan than in all of the rest of the languages. It is generally assumed that the region of greatest diversity is the most likely homeland, the region where the proto-language was spoken, since it is in this region that the languages have been longest that they have had the most opportunity to diversify. Taiwan is thus the most likely homeland for Austronesian.

Evidence from archaeology is largely in agreement with linguistic evidence that Taiwan was the homeland of Austronesian, and that the languages began spreading from there some 5,500 or so years ago. The languages spread via migrations of people travelling over the sea, and taking farming with them. The island of New Guinea was reached some 4,000 years ago, and New Zealand about 1000 AD. Map 13.3 gives an idea of the dispersal of Austronesian languages.

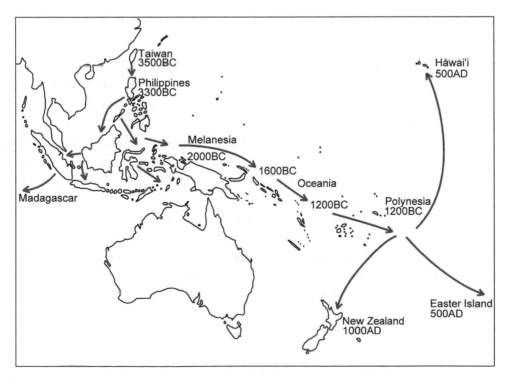

Map 13.3 Dispersal of Austronesian languages (adapted from Gray and Jordan 2000: 1053).

It has recently been proposed that the Austronesian languages are genetically related to the Sino-Tibetan languages (see pp. 317–318), forming a large Sino-Tibetan–Austronesian family. Laurent Sagart (2005) makes a plausible (though not widely accepted) case for this macro-group, identifying some 60 cognates in basic vocabulary among Austronesian and Sino-Tibetan languages, as well as recurrent sound correspondences. He avers that there is archaeological evidence in agreement with his proposals, and that the initial spread of the proto-language for this family was from mainland China to Taiwan, accompanying a migration of agriculturalists driven by population expansion. The archaeologist Peter Bellwood (2005) is in basic agreement, though he places the ultimate mainland China homeland in a different location.

Afroasiatic

Afroasiatic consists of some 353 languages (according to *Ethnologue*) spoken in northern Africa and southwest Asia by nearly 340 million people – see Map 13.4. It is regarded as the best established of the four families that African languages are now generally divided into; the other three families are Niger-Congo (on which see next subsection), and the more contentious Nilo-Saharan and Khoisan.

Afroasiatic is generally divided into six groups: Berber (consisting of 30 languages spoken in Morocco, Algeria, Tunisia, Mali, including Tamazight, Zenaga, and Kabyle); Chadic (made up of nearly 200 languages spoken in Nigeria, Chad, Cameroon, including Hausa, Miya, and Ngizim); Cushitic (with about 50 languages in Ethiopia, Eritrea, Somalia, Kenya and Tanzania, including Somali, Dahalo and Afar); Egyptian (one language, Coptic, which became extinct in the fourteenth century, though it is still used as a language of religion); Semitic (consisting of some 50 languages spoken in Ethiopia and the Middle East, including Arabic, Hebrew, Aramaic, Amharic and Tigré); and Omotic (with 20 or so languages spoken mainly in Ethopia, including Dizi, Bench and Ganza).

Semitic is the only group spoken outside of Africa. It is also the best studied group. A notable feature of Semitic languages is a root structure consisting of three consonants; grammatical information is expressed largely through intervening vowels. For instance, the root form for 'book' in Arabic is *k-t-b*; thus *kitab* 'book', and *kutub* 'books'.

It is generally believed that proto-Afroasiatic was spoken around 10,000 years ago in northeast Africa, and spread out from there, perhaps moving into southwest Asia around 8,000 years ago. Shared agricultural vocabulary is lacking across the family, suggesting that the languages dispersed before the advent of agriculture. On the other hand, cognate pottery terms are widely distributed, suggesting that pottery was known at the time of the proto-language.

Niger-Congo

Consisting of just under 1,500 languages, the Niger-Congo family is the largest language family in Africa, indeed in the world. This must be qualified by the observation that some

Map 13.4 Language families of Africa.

linguists have expressed doubt concerning its status as a genetic unit. This is because the proto-Niger-Congo has not been reconstructed, and thus the genetic unity of the language is not established fact. Nonetheless, the majority of specialists accept it as a viable genetic grouping, and regard it simply as a matter of time until this will have been convincingly demonstrated.

Niger-Congo languages are spoken over a vast area of the continent, as shown in Map 13.4, and by over 350 million speakers.

The composition of the family is not uncontroversial, and has been revised more than once. A recent classification of the family is shown in the family tree of Figure 13.2. Some nodes on this tree represent individual languages (e.g. Prɛ/Bɛrɛ), some represent small groups of languages (like Dogon), while others represent very large groups (e.g. Bantoid).

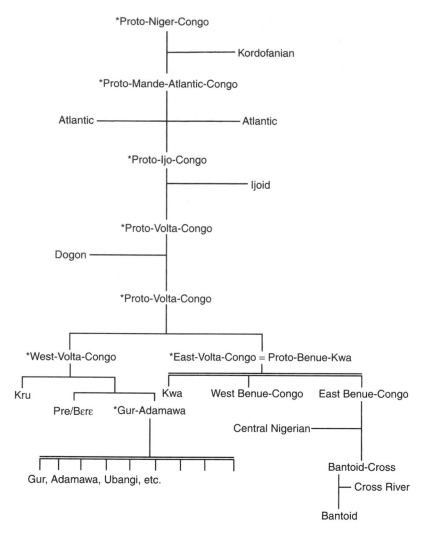

Figure 13.2 One representation of the Niger-Congo family (based on Williamson and Blench 2000: 18, redrawn and simplified).

The well known Bantu languages are a subgroup of the Bantoid group. They comprise over 400 languages (including, for example, Swahili, Fang, Tswana, Southern Sotho, Luganda and Shona), with perhaps 60 million speakers. It is believed that Bantu is a rather young group, that began diverging when speakers spread out from Cameroon perhaps only about 4,000–5,000 years ago. Bantu speaking people migrated over the next 3,000 years, taking West African yam agriculture with them. Today Bantu languages are spoken across a third of the African continent.

One characteristic of Niger-Congo languages is their possession of an elaborate system of noun classes (see note 2, Chapter 7), distinguishing humans, animals, plants, masses and liquids, abstracts and so on. The classes are marked by affixes, usually prefixes, that occur sometimes on the noun, but usually on adjectives and verbs in agreement with the noun they apply to, as shown by the following example, where *ki-* and *-ki* are the class markers:

(13-1) ***ki**-tu*   *hi-**ki***   ***ki**-kubwa*   ***ki**-lianguka*   Swahili
       ki-thing   this-ki   ki-large   ki-fell
       'This large thing fell.'

Sino-Tibetan

Made up of about 400 languages, Sino-Tibetan is the second largest language family of the world in terms of numbers of speakers, with approximately half the number of speakers of Indo-European. It includes Mandarin Chinese, the language with the largest number of native speakers.

Sino-Tibetan falls into two groups. One, Sinitic, consists of just 14 languages, including Mandarin Chinese, Cantonese (Yue), Hakka, Northern Min, Southern Min and Gan. The other group, Tibeto-Burman, has some 350 languages, mainly spoken in China, Nepal and India. Groupings within Tibeto-Burman include, according to the traditional classification: Baric (e.g. Meithei in India), Bodic (e.g. Tibetan), Burmese-Lolo (e.g. Burmese), Keren (various Keren languages spoken in Myanmar and Thailand, the most widely spoken being S'gaw Karen), Nung (e.g. Norra, Nung) and Qiang (e.g. Northern and Southern Qiang, spoken in China). Map 13.5 shows the location of the family and most of the groups.

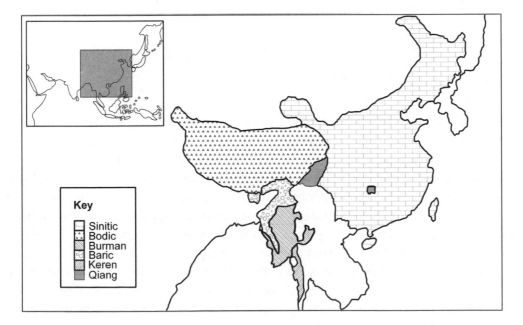

Key
Sinitic
Bodic
Burman
Baric
Keren
Qiang

Map 13.5 Location of the Sino-Tibetan family.

With the exception of Baric languages, Sino-Tibetan languages are generally tone languages. Tone cannot, however, be reconstructed for proto-Sino-Tibetan. Rather, certain syllabic endings of the proto-language gave rise to the tones of the modern languages.

Trans-New Guinea

It has already been mentioned that the region of island of New Guinea is the most linguistically diverse region in the world, populated by some 1,200 languages. These are usually divided into two groups, Austronesian and Papuan (which refers collectively to the non-Austronesian languages of the region). Papuan languages fall into 30 or more distinct genetic families and some two dozen isolates. Most of these families are quite small, with an average of 25 languages and an average of less than 3,000 speakers.

The largest Papuan family (or phylum), Trans-New Guinea, consists, according to *Ethnologue*, of some 561 languages belonging to dozen groups and spoken mainly along the mountainous cordillera of New Guinea. Proto-Trans-New Guinea has not been reconstructed; indeed, there is considerable diversity of opinion as to the structure and composition of the putative family. The *Ethnologue* grouping is a 'lumping' one basically adopting the proposal of Wurm (1975); more recently, Foley (2000) has suggested that it consists of around 300 languages, and Ross (2005) has proposed a version with 400 or so languages. Other Papuanists accept the core of the Trans-New Guinea grouping, with a good deal of uncertainty as to which languages and groups belong to it. Even in the reduced form Trans-New Guinea fits into the category of large language family, the next largest family recognized in *Ethnologue*, Australian (with 224 languages) is at least as problematic.

13.4 Problems with genetic relations and the family tree model

According to a simple model of language diversification, alluded to in §13.1, new languages emerge as the eventual result of geographical or social separation of speakers of a single language. This model underlies the notion of genetic relatedness of languages, the notion that each language has a single parent language from which it ultimately separated. The reality is more complex. Languages are not like biological species, which cannot normally interbreed; rather, languages do interact significantly with other languages spoken in their environment. We have already mentioned one way this is can happen, namely through borrowing of lexical items or grammar. Sometimes borrowing between languages is so extensive that it obscures the genetic picture. Indeed, it can render the family tree diagrams we have been using inappropriate or misleading. For some language situations linguists have proposed that, instead of the tree model, a bush model is preferable, in which there are many complex interconnections between languages.

Another thing that can happen is that new languages come into being as the result of interaction between two or more languages – or, rather, between speakers of two or more languages. The new languages thus can't be traced back to a single parent language that either split or incorporated many characteristics of a neighbouring language, and neither the tree nor the bush model is appropriate. This section focuses on cases of this type, which though in some sense exceptional are not rare – there are hundreds of them.

Pidgins

Pidgins are rudimentary or simplified forms of speech that sometimes arise in contact situations, when speakers of mutually unintelligible languages come into contact with one another in a limited range of social interactions. These interactions might be for purposes of trade or labour, including slavery, for instance, on plantations, on boats, or in mines. In keeping with their reduced range of circumstances of use, pidgins show structural reductions compared to ordinary human languages: reduced lexicons – often restricted in terms of the semantic domains they cover, though specialized in some domains – and reduced grammars, as well as diminished stylistic ranges.

Many pidgins arose in the wake of European colonialism, in the Pacific region, the Americas and Africa. The lexical items of these pidgins often derive from the language of the colonizers, but are usually pronounced according to the sound system of the languages of the colonized, who represent the majority of speakers. Pidgins often show considerable variation across speakers in vocabulary and pronunciation, depending partly on the speaker's mother tongue.

Fanagalo, a pidgin spoken in South Africa, arose in interactions between European settlers and Zulu people, and was later used in mines. Fanagalo is somewhat unusual for a pidgin in that most of its words (about 70 per cent) come from Zulu, rather than from the languages of the colonizers (24 per cent comes from English and 6 per cent from Afrikaans). Words are phonologically simplified in Fanagalo, with Zulu clicks replaced by *k*, and English interdentals replaced by either an apical stop or the labiodental fricative (e.g. *bath* appears as *baf*). The following examples are illustrative of the syntax. Note the presence of a subject pronoun between the subject and the verb (a characteristic shared with many English-based pidgins in the Pacific), the SVO word order, and the placement of the question word in initial position (as in English and Afrikaans – in Zulu it appears in the usual position for an NP in that grammatical role).

(13-2) *lo* *foloman* *yena* *funa* *lo* *nyuzipepa* *na* *lo* *ti*   Fanagalo
the foreman he want the newspaper and the tea
'The foreman wants the newspaper and tea.'

(13-3) *yinindaba* *wena* *hayikona* *shefile* *nambla*   Fanagalo
why you not shave today
'Why haven't you shaved today?'

Not all pidgins arose in contexts of European colonization. Pidgin Yimas, a pidginized form of Yimas (Papuan, New Guinea), for instance, arose in pre-contact times in the context of trade along the Arafundi River. And Hiri Motu, a pidginized variety of Motu, was once used on annual trading expeditions (called *hiri*) by Motu speakers into areas occupied by speakers of Papuan languages. The term Hiri Motu (or Police Motu) is now used for a different pidgin Motu that arose around 1900 in the predominantly Motu speaking Port Moresby area, where speakers of many different languages were brought into contact primarily in the police force.

Creoles

Sometimes pidgins become useful in a wider range of interactive contexts, and may take on the role of auxiliary languages and perhaps be given official status. Such pidgins gain extra words and grammar to cope with the additional uses they are put to; being more complex than pidgins they are called **expanded pidgins**. An example is the English based pidgin Tok Pisin, now an official language in New Guinea, and frequently used in parliament and in commerce. Tok Pisin is spoken by as many as 4,000,000 people as a second (or later) language, and is often used between speakers of mutually unintelligible Papuan languages. However, it has also become the mother tongue of a small number of people (perhaps 50,000) living mainly in urban areas of Port Moresby. When this happens – when a pidgin language acquires mother tongue speakers – it is said to have been **creolized**, and is a **creole**.

Unlike pidgins, creoles are full languages, structurally and functionally comparable with ordinary human languages. The process of creolization is associated with increases in the range and depth of vocabulary and in the structural complexity of the former pidgin (e.g. by adding subordinate clause constructions, tenses and so on), as well as expansion in stylistic range. Interestingly, creoles seem to share more with one another grammatically than they do with other natural languages, suggesting that these similarities may be attributed to general linguistic abilities shared by all people.

Also based on English is Torres Strait Creole or Broken, spoken by some 18,000 Torres Strait Islanders and Aboriginal people living on northern Cape York, Australia. Broken creolized from Pacific Pidgin English around the turn of the twentieth century. The following are a few illustrative clauses. Notice that the 'predicate marker' in (13-4) derives from English *he*, and connects the subject to the following verb, like *yena* in (13-2) above.

(13-4) *ai   luk   wan   gel   i   kam*   Broken
      I   see   a   girl   predicate:marker   come
      'I can see a girl approaching.'

(13-5) *em   pinis   skras-e   koknat   lo   madu*   Broken
      she   completive   scrape-transitive   coconut   instrumental   scraper
      'She has already scraped out the coconut with the scraper.'

(13-6)	*dem*	*piknini*	*go*	*luk*	*ama*	*blo*	*dempla*	Broken
	plural:definite	child	future	visit	mother	possessive	they	

'The children will visit their mother.'

Ethnologue lists 82 creoles, spoken by almost 30 million people in Africa, the Americas, Asia and the Pacific region. Many, like Tok Pisin, are based on European languages – that is, they derive from former pidgins that drew their lexicon mainly from a European language. A number are also based on other languages. Cutchi-Swahili and Asian Swahili are spoken in Kenya and Tanzania, and are based on Swahili (Nilo-Saharan). Tetun Dili, also called Tetum Prasa, is spoken by around 50,000 people in East Timor, and based on Tetun (Austronesian). Africa is the home of three Arabic-based creoles: Babalia, with a few thousand speakers in Chad; Sudanese Creole Arabic or Juba Arabic, with about ten times as many speakers in Sudan; and Nubi, with about 25,000 speakers in Kenya and Uganda. Six Malay based creoles are spoken in Indonesia and Malaysia.

Mixed languages

The third group of problem languages is **mixed languages**, hybrid languages components of which come from different sources. Thus some aspects (e.g. the lexicon) indicate that the language belongs to one family, while others (e.g. the grammar) suggest they belong to another.[2]

Perhaps the paradigm example of a mixed language is Michif, an endangered language spoken by a few hundred elderly people in Canada and northern USA. Michif nouns come mainly from French (about 90 per cent), and noun phrases follow the grammatical structure of French. But the verbs almost all come from Cree, an Algonquian language, and the complex verbal morphology of Cree is largely retained. Even more strikingly, two phonological systems coexist in Michif with little if any influence on one another. The Cree component retains Cree phonology, while the French component retains French phonology. Michif syntax is closer to Cree syntax than French syntax, except in the NP. The following sentence, from the beginning of a short Michif text, is illustrative. It is given in the standard orthography for each language; French morphemes are bolded.

(13-7)	**un**	**vieux**	*opahikê-t*	*ê-nôhcihcikê-t,*	*êkwa*	**un**	**matin**	Michif
	an	old	trap-he	COMP-trap-he	and	a	morning	
	ê-waniskâ-w		*ahkosi-w,*	*but*	*kêyapit*	*ana*		
	COMP-wake:up-he		be:sick-he	but	still	this:one		
	wî-nitawi-wâpaht-am	**ses**	**pièges**					
	want-go-see:it-he:it	his	traps					

'There was an old trapper who was trapping. One morning he woke up sick, but still wanted to go and look at his traps.' (Bakker 1994: 28–30)

It is not known how old Michif is, although it seems that it has been around since at least the early decades of the nineteenth century. Peter Bakker (1994: 23) observes that it could not have arisen as a contact pidgin between speakers of French and speakers of Cree. He suggests instead that the first speakers were fluent in both French, which they learnt from their fathers, and Cree, which they learnt from their mothers; he suggests further that Michif may have been invented by adolescents.

Another mixed language is Ma'a, spoken in Tanzania by Mbugu people. The Mbugu speak two languages, Ma'a and Mbugu, the latter a Bantu language. Ma'a has basically Bantu morphology and syntax, but possesses a considerable number of non-Bantu lexemes, the majority of which come from Southern Cushitic. There are also a handful of phonemic segments in Ma'a that do not occur in Mbugu. Maarten Mous regards Ma'a is a special register created by speakers of Mbugu in order to set themselves off as distinct from their Bantu neighbours (Mous 1994). Other explanations have been proposed. For instance, Thomason and Kaufman (1988) suggest it is a Cushitic language that borrowed extensively from a Bantu language.

Some varieties of Romani (Indo-European, Europe to Near East) appear to be mixed languages, including in the Near East Qirishmal (Eastern Persia) and Armenian Romani, and in Europe, Basque Romani, Norwegian Romani and now extinct Dortika in Greece. These varieties preserve Romani lexicon, but employ the grammatical structures of the surrounding languages.

Summing up

It has been estimated that some 7,000 language are spoken in the world today. This is not a precise figure, due in part to lack of accurate information especially on languages spoken in areas remote from European habitation and in part to the different criteria used in identifying languages.

The distribution of languages across the globe is not uniform, and there is a concentration of languages in the band between the two Tropics. The Pacific region is the most linguistically diverse region of the world. Languages also differ strikingly in their numbers of speakers. A few languages are spoken by large numbers of speakers, while many languages have very small numbers of speakers.

The languages of the world can be grouped into **families** of **genetically related** languages, plus **isolates**. The languages of a family can all be traced back to a single **proto-language**, which, over time and perhaps migrations of the speakers, differentiated into separate languages. Within a language family it is often possible to identify **groups** and **subgroups** of more closely related languages. The structure of a family can thus be represented by a **tree model**. Ideally the tree represents also the history of the separation of the languages. Hypothetical groups of families or **stocks** have been proposed by some linguists; these remain quite tentative.

Sometimes new languages arise through contact between two or more languages, rather than divergence of a single language over time. In such circumstances, the language cannot always be traced back to a single parent language, raising problems for the tree model. **Pidgins**, **creoles** and **mixed languages** are examples of this sort of 'hybrid' language.

The most reliable method of establishing genetic relations among a set of languages is the **comparative method**, which **reconstructs** a proto-language and shows how the modern languages could have developed from it via a series of plausible changes. Reconstruction is done by setting up sets of **cognates** in the languages on the basis of which a **proto-form** is proposed, together with regular **sound changes**. Two other methods sometimes used to establish genetic relations, **mass comparison** and **lexicostatistics**, are less reliable.

The number of language families in the world is hotly contested. Some linguists have suggested as few as 19, others around 100. Even the latter figure involves many highly dubious groupings, like Khoisan, Australian, Papuan and Amerind. Among the best supported families are Afroasiatic, Indo-European and Austronesian. In between lie a number of intermediate cases of likely families, such as Pama-Nyungan and Trans-New Guinea that remain to be validated.

Guide to further reading

Ethnologue: Languages of the World, currently in its fifteenth edition, edited by Raymond G. Gordon and published by SIL International, is intended to provide a comprehensive listing the known living languages of the world. It provides basic information on the languages, including alternative names and spellings of the names, numbers and locations of speakers, main references and family membership. This information is of varying degrees of reliability, depending on the information available on the language, and what is conveyed to the editor by experts. It appears in two versions: in print (Gordon and Grimes 2005), and on the Web (http://www.ethnologue.com).

A good overview of the linguistic diversity of the world is Comrie (2001), which provides basic information on many language families. Lyovin (1997) surveys the world's languages and gives grammatical information on a selection. Garry and Rubino (2001) contains basic information on 191 languages from all over the world, including information on the viability of the language, its use in education, genetic classification and basic grammar. Each description is by a linguist with some knowledge of the language, and it is a very useful resource. Ruhlen (1987, revised version 1991), is a highly speculative classification of the world's languages, and few of the proposed groupings are accepted by experts.

Numerous textbooks discuss the comparative method. Among them Crowley (1992) stands out for its lucid style and absence of Indo-European bias. An excellent article on the comparative method is Rankin (2003).

Numerous attempts have been made in recent years to link archaeological, biological and linguistic reconstructions of the human past, including Renfrew (1987, 1994); Cavalli-Sforza (1991, 2001); and Anthony (2007).

Good introductions to pidgins and creoles are Mühlhäusler (1986) (second edition 1997) and Arends et al. (1995). Other references include Todd (1990); and Holm (1988, 1989). Information on Fanagalo given in the text comes from Childs (2003: 207–210), which should be consulted for further details; the CD-ROM accompanying that book contains a short stretch of spoken Fanagalo.

The best sources on mixed languages are Bakker and Mous (1994), and Matras and Bakker (2003), which cover mixed languages from all over the world.

Issues for further thought and exercises

1. We have said that many of the world's languages are currently highly endangered; some hundreds are likely to go out of use in the next century. On the other hand, there are a few languages with extremely large numbers of speakers. Do you think that eventually the entire population of the world will speak a single language, perhaps Mandarin Chinese or English – if so, which do you consider more likely. Discuss your reasons.

2. Below is some additional data (slightly simplified) from the four languages we discussed on pp. 305–307. Reconstruct each word in the proto-language, and state the phonological rules required to give the forms in the modern languages. How would you account for the Warrwa words for 'sun' and 'path, road', and the Nyikina word for 'emu'?

	Bardi	Nyulnyul	Nyikina	Warrwa
'brother'	*borla*	*babarl*	*babarla*	*babarla*
'club'	*nola*	*nawul*	*nawula*	*nawula*
'man'	*amba*	*wamb*	*wamba*	*wamba*
'sun'	*alka*	*walk*	*walka*	*kidi*
'wattle type'	*irrola* ('spear')	*yirrakul*	*yirrakul*	*yirrakulu*
'path, road'	*morr*	*makirr*	*makurr*	*kaadi*
'emu'	*inini*	*winin*	*karnanganyja*	*winini* ('emu chick')

3. Below is a list of basic lexical items (written phonemically) in six different languages of the Pacific region. Apply the method of mass comparison to this lexical data, and suggest how the languages might be related to one another: how many families does it appear they form, and which languages seem to be genetically related?

	Hawaiian	Shan	Tahitian	Maori	Pangasinan	Tay-Nung	Samoan
'woman'	*wahine*	*kón jíŋ, mɛ jíŋ*	*vahine*	*wahine*	*bii*	*nhình*	*fafine*
'man'	*kaane*	*kón sáaj, phu sáaj*	*taane*	*kaane*	*toó*	*chài*	*taane*
'sun'	*laa*	*kǎaŋ wán*	*raa*	*raa*	*ágew*	*tha vàn*	*laa*
'fish'	*iʔa*	*pǎa*	*iʔa*	*ika*	*ikan*	*pja*	*iʔa*
'dog'	*ʔiilo*	*mǎ*	*ʔuri*	*kurii*	*asó*	*ma*	*maile*
'bird'	*manu*	*nôk*	*manu-rere*	*manu*	*manok*	*nộc*	*manu*
'three'	*kolu*	*sǎm*	*toru*	*toru*	*talo*	*slam*	*tolu*
'water'	*wai*	*nâm*	*vai*	*wai*	*danum*	*nậm*	*vai*
'big'	*nui*	*jáɯ, lôŋ*	*nui*	*nui*	*báleg*	*cai*	*tele*
'good'	*maikaʔi*	*lǐ*	*maitaʔi*	*pai*	*maong*	*ʔdây*	*lelei*
'tree'	*laaʔau*	*ton mâj*	*raʔau*	*raakau*	*kiew*	*may*	*laaʔau*
'long'	*loa*	*jáaw*	*roa*	*roa*	*andukey*	*rì*	*loa*
'small'	*liʔi, iki*	*ʔɔ̀n, nɔ̂j, lêk*	*riʔi, iti*	*riki, iti*	*melág*	*eng*	*liliʔi, itiiti*

4. Do a preliminary and rough lexicostatistical investigation of the same data you used in Question 3. To do this, you will need to count the number of apparent or likely cognates in each pair of languages, and fill the figures in on the table below. What do the figures suggest about the way the languages are related? In particular, are they in agreement with your proposals using mass comparison, and what (if anything) do they suggest about subgrouping in the families? (You could also do a similar investigation of the six

African languages discussed on pp. 308–309.) If you are knowledgeable in statistical methods, you could do a cluster analysis of the results to see how the languages might be grouped together hierarchically.

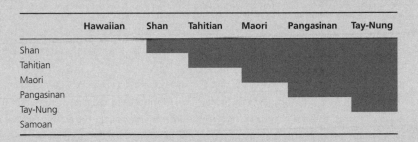

5. Find out about a language – select a language from the following list, and find out basic information on it: Acehnese, Basque, Blackfoot, Cantonese, Chamorro, Georgian, Etruscan, Ewondo, Kalkatungu, Ket, Kwaza, Lahu, Lango, Lavukaleve, Lezgian, Mundari, Navajo, Nivkh, Paamese, Slave, Squamish, Tauya, Warrwa, Yapese and Yuaalaraay. Write a short description of the language, giving information on the following: where it is spoken; approximate number of speakers and its status (healthy, endangered, dead etc.); its role in education; existence of an orthography and/or tradition of literacy; its genetic classification; basic facts about its phonology; its morphological and syntactic type. You can start by looking in *Ethnologue*, on the web, and in your linguistics library – try also to find a modern grammar of the language.

6. An alternative to the tree model for representing historical relations among languages is the wave model. Find out about this model, and write a paragraph description mentioning who first proposed it, and its main characteristics.

7. Critique the following excerpt from a speech to the Royal Society of St George by the conservative British law maker Enoch Powell, as reported in *The Independent* 23 August 1988. Identify the attitudes embodied in the quote, and discuss the notions expressed in relation to what you know about the history of English.

> Others may speak and read English – more or less – but it is our language not theirs. It was made in England by the English and it remains our distinctive property, however widely it is learnt or used.

8. Below is a short excerpt from a story in Kriol, an English-based creole spoken in northern Australia, given in the standard orthography, which is phonemic. Read it through first – without looking at the free translation into English given below – and see how much you can understand. Now read the free translation. List all of the Kriol words; using the free translation to attempt to give each Kriol word an approximate gloss. It is obvious that most of the words come from English. Which words do not come from English? Try and explain the way in which each such word is formed. Describe as much of Kriol grammar as you can based on this excerpt; you should be able to say something about word order, tense marking and complex sentence constructions.

> *Gardiya bin pikimap mipala en teik mipala langa mishin longtaim en deya wen mipala bin lil-il kid mipala yusdu tokin Walmajarri. Samtaim gardiya bin gib mipala haiding fo tokin Walmajarri. From deya mela bin lisining sampala kid bin tokin Kriol. Mela bin lisining en pikimap lilbit.*
> 'White people picked us up and took us to the mission a long time ago, and there, when we were little children we used to speak Walmajarri. Sometimes the white people would give us a hiding for speaking Walmajarri. Later, we heard some children speaking Kriol. We listened to it, and picked up a little of it.'

Notes

1. The reason why borrowings are excluded is that otherwise the proportion of shared items would be inflated between a pair of languages that both borrowed the same item, and it would not reflect a shared retention. However, it has been shown that at least in some cases it does not matter greatly to the results of lexicostatistics whether borrowings are included or excluded from the counts. (The false positives of shared borrowings might be offset by shared negatives where the languages borrow different forms.)

2. In fact, most languages can probably be described as 'mixed' to some extent, due to borrowings. Pidgins and creoles can be described as mixed; so also can English, given the number of borrowings it has admitted during its history, both into basic and non-basic lexicon, and grammatical morphemes; indeed, some phonemic distinctions could be regarded as borrowings from French (or at least the result of extensive lexical borrowings). But the technical term *mixed language* excludes cases like these. A crucial feature of a mixed language is that the contribution of each of the two major source languages is to a certain domain of the lexicon or grammar; they are not mixed in a hodge-podge. Nevertheless, doubtful cases do exist.

Glossary

ablative case The case of a noun or pronoun that indicates the source or direction from which an object or motion event begins. See also *case*.

absolute universal A generalization that holds true for all languages (although in practice usually restricted to spoken languages) without exception, for example, all (spoken) languages have vowels. See also *non-absolute universal*.

absolutive case When in a language a noun or pronoun has the same case when it is subject of an intransitive clause and object of a transitive clause but different from the case when it is subject of a transitive clause, this is called absolutive case. For example, if the word for 'window' is in the same case in 'The boy broke the window' and 'The window broke' the noun 'window' is in absolutive case. See also *case, ergative case, intransitive, transitive*.

accent A variety of speech differing phonetically or phonologically from other varieties. See also *dialect*.

accommodation Adjustments speakers make in their speech to adapt it to features of their interlocutor's speech.

accusative case The case of a noun or pronoun when it is object of a transitive clause, when this is different from its case as a (transitive or intransitive) subject. For example, in English the accusative case of the first person singular pronoun is *me*. See also *case, intransitive, nominative case, transitive*.

acoustic phonetics The study of the physical properties of speech sounds.

acronym A word formed from the initial letters of a sequence of words, for example, *Qantas* from Queensland and Northern Territory Aerial Services.

Actor The grammatical role of a noun phrase the referent of which performs the action or engages in the state designated by the clause. For example, *the farmer* in *the farmer kills the duckling*, and *the farmer is sitting in his favourite chair*. See also *Subject*.

adjectival phrase (AdjP) A grammatical or syntactic unit made up of an adjective and possibly an accompanying modifier, that occurs within a clause or noun phrase indicating a quality of some object, for example, *most difficult* in *the most difficult problem*.

adjective A part-of-speech consisting of words that typically refer to qualities or properties of things, and occur as modifiers in noun phrases, for example, *bright* in *the bright light*.

AdjP adjectival phrase

adult language learning see *second language learning*

adverb A part-of-speech consisting of words that normally qualify a verb, indicating the manner in which an action was performed, as in *she ran quickly*; the frequency of the event, as in *she runs often*; or the time or location of an event, as in *she'll come soon* and *she'll come here*.

adverbial phrase A grammatical or syntactic unit consisting of an adverb and a modifier, that specifies something about the manner, time, location, frequency of an event, as in *she ran very quickly*.

affix A bound morpheme attached to a root or stem, modifying its meaning in some way, and forming a lexical or grammatical word with it, for example, *dis-* and *-ed* in *displaced*. See also *prefix*, *suffix*, *infix*, *root* and *stem*.

affricate A sound produced by a stop followed by slow release accompanied by friction noise, for example, the first segment of *chap*, written *ch*, IPA [tʃ].

African American Vernacular English (AAVE) The variety of English spoken by African Americans.

Afroasiatic A family of languages spoken in northern Africa and the Middle East, including Semitic (e.g. Arabic, Hebrew), Chadic and Cushitic groups.

agglutinating language A language like Turkish or Hungarian in which many words are morphologically complex and consist of a root plus one or more affixes the boundaries between which are sharp.

airstream mechanisms The means of producing a stream of air for the production of speech sounds, for example, the egressive pulmonic airstream, the stream of air produced by forcing air out of the lungs.

alienable possession A grammatical category indicating a type of possession in which the possessor and possession are not linked by intrinsic ties, for example, in *my dog*, *her car*, *your bus*, *my street*. See also *inalienable possession*.

allative case The case of a noun or pronoun that indicates the intended goal or direction towards which a motion event is oriented. See also *case*.

allomorph One of the alternative phonemic forms of a morpheme, for example, the prefix *in-* in English has allomorphs /ɪn/, /ɪm/ and /ɪŋ/ depending on the first segment of the root to which it is attached, as in *inexplicable*, *implausible* and *incredible* respectively.

allophone One of the alternative phonetic realizations of a phoneme, for example, [t] and [tʰ] are allophones of /t/ in English. See also *phoneme*.

alphabet, alphabetic writing   A system of writing that uses a set of symbols each ideally representing a phonemic segment.

alternation   The correspondence between two or more allophones of a phoneme or allomorphs or a morpheme, for example, between [t] and [tʰ] in English.

alveolar   A speech sound produced by bringing the tip or blade of the tongue towards or against the alveolar ridge, for example, [t], [n].

alveolar ridge   The ridge on the hard palate just behind the upper front teeth.

alveopalatal   A sound produced with constriction in the region just behind the alveolar ridge, for example, the initial phone [ʃ] of *she*.

ambiguity, ambiguous   The term used to describe the situation in which a word, phrase or larger unit has multiple meanings. Ambiguity is not the same thing as *vagueness* (see that entry).

amelioriation   The process by which a word comes to acquire more positive connotations, for example, *fond* in Modern English comes from the past participle of *fonnen* 'to be silly, foolish' in Middle English.

American Sign Language (ASL)   The sign language used by the deaf community in the USA.

Amerind   The most contentious of the three groupings (stocks or phyla) of the languages of the Americas proposed by Joseph Greenberg.

analogical change   A process of change whereby an old form, usually irregular, is replaced by a new form constructed by extension of another pattern, usually the regular one. For example, the English plural *cows* was formed by analogical change, replacing the earlier plural *kine*.

animacy hierarchy   A scale of pronouns and nouns extending from the first and second persons pronouns (considered as the most animate) to the least animate entities (trees, stones, clouds, etc.). This hierarchy is used in the formulation of certain generalizations about languages, for example, if a language has accusative case-marking of inanimate nouns, it will have accusative case marking of pronouns.

anomic aphasia   A type of aphasia in which the patient shows inability to find words. See also *aphasia*.

anticipatory error   A speech error in which the speaker anticipates a subsequent word, morpheme or sound, and puts it earlier in their utterance, for example, *kindler and gentler* for *kinder and gentler*. See also *exchange error*.

antonymy   The relation of oppositeness in some component of the meaning of a pair of words, for example, *hot* and *cold* both concern temperature, but are opposite in terms of degree.

aphasia   A language loss or disorder following brain damage. This be a disorder of either production or comprehension; problems resulting from paralysis to the vocal organs due to brain damage are excluded.

applied linguistics   The branch of linguistics concerned with practical applications, for example, to second language learning, language maintenance, translation, machine generation of speech and so on.

approximant   A speech sound involving narrowing at some point in the vocal tract, but insufficient to produce fricative noise.

arbitrariness   The property of linguistic signs whereby there is no intrinsic or necessary relation between the signifier (form) and signified (meaning).

arculate fasciculus   The bundle of neurons connecting Broca's area with Wernicke's area.

articulatory phonetics   The study of how speech sounds are produced by the vocal apparatus.

ASL   American Sign Language

aspirated   A feature of a voiceless stop in which a puff of air follows its release, caused by a brief delay between the release of the stop and the beginning of voicing of a following vowel. See also *unaspirated*, *voice onset time*.

assimilation   The modification of a sound that makes it more like a nearby sound, for example, when the vowel in *pin* is nasalized due to the following nasal consonant. Assimilation can be progressive (when the sound becomes more like a preceding one) or regressive (when it becomes more like a following one). See also *dissimilation*.

auditory phonetics   The study of the perception of speech sounds by the ear.

Auslan   Australian Sign Language

Australian Sign Language (Auslan)   The sign language used by the deaf community in Australia.

Austronesian   Name of a large family of related languages spoken mainly on islands in the Indian and Pacific Oceans from Madagascar to Easter Island.

auxiliary   A verb that normally accompanies other verbs, and expresses purely grammatical information, like *was* in *He was going*.

babbling   An early stage of language acquisition that infants go through from about four to six months of age. Babbling may involve a wide range of speech sounds, though it typically consists of simple syllables (e.g. *ba*, *ma*); over time, the range of sounds tends towards the range in the language being acquired. Deaf children also babble with hand gestures.

backformation   Process whereby a new word is created by removing what is mistakenly analysed as affix from an old word, for example, *edit* from *editor*.

back vowel   A vowel produced by moving the body of the tongue towards the back of the mouth, so that its high point towards the back of the mouth, for example, [o], [ʊ].

basic vocabulary   The set of lexical items in a language expressing meanings of a basic type, that would be expected to be found in all languages, including lexemes for major parts of the body (e.g. 'head', 'hand'), fundamental human and animal categories (e.g. 'boy', 'girl', 'dog'), basic qualities (e.g. 'big', 'little'), common states (e.g. 'sit', 'stand') and events (e.g. 'hit', 'say'), etc.

bee dance   A set of bodily movements used by some species of honeybee to indicate the location of a nectar source.

bilabial   A sound made with both lips, for example, [m], [b].

bilingualism   The ability of a person to speak two or more languages. A range of types of bilingualism are distinguished depending on the time of acquisition of the languages, the person's competence in each, the contexts in which the languages are used and so on.

bird calls   Brief vocalizations by birds conveying information about the immediate environment, including danger, feeding and flocking.

bird-song   A complex pattern of vocalizations used for attracting mates and marking territory.

blade of tongue   The part of the tongue immediately behind the tip.

blend   A new word created by putting together parts of two existing lexical items, for example, *smog* is a blend of *smoke* and *fog*.

body of tongue   The main bulk of the tongue.

borrowing   The incorporation of a word or other item from one language into another, for example, English borrowed the words *government* and *science* from French.

bottom-up processing   The analysis of linguistic input beginning with the smallest units, the phones, and moving upwards step by step to larger and larger units such as words, phrases and clauses, until the complete utterance is interpreted. See *top-down processing*.

bound morpheme   A morpheme that cannot occur as a separate word by itself, but must be attached to another item, for example, the English morphemes *-ly* and *-ed*. See also *affix*, and *free morpheme*.

brain scanning   Technologies used for studying the human brain in operation, including Electroencephalography (EEG), Functional Magnetic Resonance Imaging (fMRI), Positron Emission Tomography (PET).

broadening   A process of semantic change whereby the meaning of a word becomes wider, for example, *bludger* in Australian English used to mean 'someone living off the earnings of a prostitute', but now means 'scrounger'. See also *narrowing*.

broad transcription   A transcription of a spoken utterance that indicates the major phonetic features, usually using a limited range of basic symbols. See also *narrow transcription*.

Broca's aphasia   A language disorder often resulting from damage to Broca's area, which is characterized by problems in speech production and the use of grammatical morphemes.

Broca's area   An area of the frontal lobe of the left hemisphere of the brain that is believed to play a role in language production. It is named after Paul Broca, a nineteenth century French scientist, who first observed its role in language.

calque   Also called a loan translation, this is a type of borrowing in which the morphemes making up the word in the source language are translated one by one into the borrowing language, for example, English *power politics* from German *Machtpolitik*.

caretaker speech   A special form of speech used by adults (especially mothers) and older children when talking to infants, that is characterized by exaggerated articulation and intonation. Also referred to as *baby talk*, *motherese* and *child directed speech*.

case   A morphological category of nouns and/or pronouns that indicates the grammatical role of a noun phrase in a clause or another noun phrase. For example, *us* is the accusative form of the first person plural pronoun, used when it serves in the object role, as in *they saw us*.

categorical perception   The perception of speech sounds in terms of phonemic categories, disregarding their physical differences.

central vowel   A vowel produced with the high point of the tongue in the centre of the mouth on the front-back axis.

cerebral cortex   The thin layer of neurons forming a outside covering of the two hemispheres.

chain shift   A series of two or more linked sound changes by which one sound changes to another sound, which in turn changes sound, and so on.

clause   A syntactic unit that is like a minimal or reduced sentence, typically consisting of one main verb and accompanying noun phrases and other items, for example, *the farmer kills the duckling with an axe.*

click   A speech sound produced by a velaric airstream mechanism. The back of the tongue makes a closure at the velum, and a second contact is made further forward in the oral cavity. The enclosed space is next enlarged so that the air within it is rarefied; the second closure is then released, and air flows inwards with a clicking noise. English *tut! tut!* is made up of clicks; clicks are part of the regular phonology of Khoisan and nearby Bantu language. See also *velaric airstream mechanism.*

clipping   The deletion of a part of a word resulting in a new and shorter word, for example, *fax* from *facsimile.*

clitic   A bound grammatical morpheme that behaves like an independent word, and at best loosely related to the word it is attached to: it does not a give rise to a new form of a lexical item (like an inflectional affix), or a new lexical item (like a derivational affix).

coarticulation   The simultaneous production of a speech sound at two places of articulation (e.g. the labio-velar /w/ of English) or with two manners of articulation (e.g. affricates).

code-switching   Switching from one language or dialect to another within a single speech interaction or even turn of speech.

cognate   Words in different languages that come from the same word in an ancestor language, for example, English *man* is cognate with Danish *mand* 'man'.

coinage   A lexical item that is a pure invention, and not created through use of any of the regular patterns of lexeme formation, for example, *nerd* and *barf.*

collocation   The relation between individual lexical items that often go together in sequences, for example, *pepper* collocates with *salt* in the common sequence *salt and pepper.*

comparative method   The method of comparing languages to determine if they have developed from a common ancestor. Lexical and grammatical items are compared in order to discover correspondences relating sounds in the languages; if these are sufficiently numerous and regular, the most reasonable hypothesis is that the languages have a common ancestor.

complementary distribution   When two speech sounds do not share any environments of occurrence they are said to be in complementary distribution, for example, in English [p] and [p^h] are in complementary distribution: [p] occurs following [s], [p^h] at the beginning of a word, and there is nowhere where both are normally found.

complex sentence   A sentence composed of more than one clause, for example, *When danger threatens your children, call the police.*

componential analysis   A semantic theory that analyses the semantics of lexical items into a small set of meaning components or 'semantic features' that take + and – values. For example, *boy* would have the features [+male] and [–adult], whereas *girl* would be [–male] and [–adult].

compounding   A process of forming new lexical items by putting together a pair of words, as in *wash basin*, and *handbook*.

conditioning factor   A circumstance that, when met, leads to the choice of one allophone or allomorph, for example, a conditioning factor for the unaspirated allophone [p] is that it follows a word initial [s], as in [spɪn].

conduction aphasia   A type of aphasia that may result from damage to the arculate fasciculus. Patients often experience difficulties in repeating words spoken to them, and in monitoring their own speech.

conjunction   A grammatical word whose primary function is to connect linguistic units, for example, *and*, *but* and *or*.

connotation   A term used in semantics in reference to emotional associations of a word or other linguistic unit.

consonant   A speech sound produced with a narrowing or closure at some point in the vocal tract.

constituent analysis   Hierarchical analysis of a syntactic construction into units. Two main types are Immediate Constituent Analysis and String Constituent Analysis.

contextual meaning   Part of the meaning of an utterance that is not encoded by the signs making it up, but which is engendered by the context in which the utterance is used.

contour tone system   A tone system in which the direction of tonal movement is significant; Mandarin Chinese has a contour tone system, with high level, high rising, low falling rising, and high falling.

contralateral control   This refers to the control of one side (left/right) of the body by the opposite hemisphere (right/left) of the brain. Many bodily sensations are also experienced contralaterally.

conventionality   The idea that the form and meaning of a sign are linked by agreed convention rather than by necessity.

conversation analysis   The field of linguistics that studies the structure of conversations, for example, the way turn-taking is organized.

cooing   A very early stage in language acquisition in which the infant produces cooing-sounds, typically made up of syllables consisting of velar consonants and back vowels.

cooperative principle   The principle formulated by H.P. Grice that speech interactants assume that they are each behaving rationally and cooperatively; this underlies the way people understand the intended meaning of an utterance.

corpus callossum   The bundle of nerve fibres connecting the left and right hemispheres of the brain.

creole   A language that began as a pidgin but eventually became the first language of a speech community. In the process of creolising, the earlier pidgin becomes more complex, and shares the major properties of other human languages. See also *pidgin* and *mixed language*.

critical period hypothesis   The idea that there is a biologically determined window of time, between infancy and puberty, for the acquisition of a first language. Outside of this period it is believed that it is impossible to achieve native fluency in a language.

dative case   The case of a noun or pronoun when it is an indirect object or recipient as in *she gave the book to me*. Dative case usually covers a range of meanings similar to the prepositions *to* and *for* in English. See also *case*.

deaf sign language   A language used by deaf people in which the lexical and grammatical units are represented by manual gestures and other body movements.

deictic, deixis   A means of establishing the reference of linguistic elements by situating them relative to speaker, hearer, and time and place of the speech interaction. Tense is deictic because it locates an event with respect to the time of speaking.

dental phone   A consonant with the teeth as the place of articulation.

derivational morpheme   A bound morpheme added to a root or stem to form a new stem, for example, the suffix *-er* in English. See also *inflectional morpheme*.

descriptive linguistics   The sort of linguistics that aims to describe the facts of a language as it is actually spoken as distinct from how speakers believe it ought to be spoken.

dialect   A variety of language characterized by a particular set of words, grammatical structures, and phonetic or phonological characteristics that is associated with a particular geographical region, as in the New Zealand dialect of English. The term dialect is sometimes used in reference to varieties associated with age, social class, gender, religion, etc.; thus we could talk of a middle class dialect. See also *accent*.

dichotic listening test   An experimental method used in neurolinguistics in which subjects hear different sounds in the left and right ears.

diglossia   A situation in which two very different varieties of a language are used throughout a speech community, that differ in terms of formality; thus one, the high variety, is associated with formal situations, the other, the low variety, with informal situations. The term is also used for bilingual situations in which the languages differ in terms of formality.

diphthong   A vowel sound involving significant movement of the tongue from one vowel position to another, for example, [aɪ], [æʊ].

direct speech act   A speech act in which the grammatical form directly indicates the type of act, for example, in English a question would be expressed as a direct speech act by use of a grammatical form like *Is she going?*

discourse analysis   The study of the structures and regularities in discourse.

displacement   A design features of language that refers to the fact that language can be used in reference to things that are not present in the immediate situation of the speaker.

dissimilation   The modification of a sound to make it less like a nearby sound, for example, the second rhotic of Latin *arbor* 'tree' was changed to a lateral in Spanish *arbol*. See also *assimilation*.

ditransitive clause   A clause that in its full form requires three noun phrases, for example, clauses of giving in English (*the farmer gave the duckling some bread*).

duality or duality of patterning   A design features of language referring to the simultaneous organization of language on both the level of form and the level of meaning.

dysphemism   An expression employing direct or harsh terms, usually with offensive overtones, for example, *shithouse* is a dysphemistic expression for *toilet* in Australian English. See also *euphemism*.

EEG   electroencephalogram

egressive airstream mechanism   An airstream produced by forcing air out of the vocal tract. Most sounds of most languages are produced on the egressive pulmonic airstream. See also *ingressive airstream mechanism*.

ejective   A speech sound produced on an egressive glottalic airstream. The air in a cavity above the larynx is compressed by raising the glottis, and the pent-up air is then released. See also *implosive* and *glottalic airstream mechanism*.

electroencephalogram (EEG)   A record of the electrical activity in the brain resulting from the firing of neurons as detected by electrodes placed on the scalp.

embedding   Inclusion of a unit in another of the same type, for instance of an NP in an NP.

enclitic   A type of clitic that is attached to the end of a word. See *clitic*.

epenthesis   See insertion.

ergative case   In some languages (e.g. Basque, West Greenlandic) nouns or pronouns are in one case when they are subject of a transitive clause but in a different case when they are subject of an intransitive clause or object of a transitive clause. In such systems the case of the subject of a transitive clause is called ergative. Ergative case has a meaning somewhat akin to the prepositions *by* in *the building was struck by lightning*. See also *accusative case, absolutive case, case, nominative case, intransitive, transitive*.

euphemism   An expression used instead of one thought to be offensive, for example, *pass away* instead of *die*. See also *dysphemism, taboo word*.

Event   Term for the grammatical role of a verb phrase in a clause, for example, this role of *kills* in *the farmer kills the duckling*.

evolutionary linguistics   An area of linguistics concerned with the origins and development of human language.

exchange error   A speech error in which two elements switch places in the utterance, as in *slicely thinned* for *thinly sliced*, where the two lexical items *thin* and *slice* have exchanged places. See also *metathesis*.

experiential meaning   The type of meaning relating to the construal and understanding of our world of experience; also called representational meaning.

experiential role   Grammatical roles that encode experiential or representational meaning.

extension   See *meaning extension*.

family   A set of languages that are genetically related to one another; that is, they derive from a common ancestor language.

family tree   A representation of the relations between languages of a family on a tree diagram.

felicity condition   A condition that an utterance must meet in order to be appropriate or successful as a speech act.

flap   A sound produced by a single rapid movement of one articulator against another. The most common flap is the apico-alveolar flap, [ɾ].

fMRI   functional magnetic resonance imaging

form   The perceivable aspect of the linguistic sign, for example, the form of a lexical sign is its representation in phonemes. See also *meaning, sign*.

formal grammar, formal linguistics   One of the two major divisions of linguistic theory, the formal approach places focus on language as an algebraic system made up of symbols manipulated according to rules. Formal theories tend to see meaning as peripheral, and do not normally recognize the linguistic sign as a fundamental unit. See also *functional grammar*.

free morpheme   A morpheme that can occur alone, as a separate word.

free variation Where one sound can replace another in a given environment without giving rise to a new word, for example, if [p˺] is replaced by [pʰ] at the end of the word *stop*.

fricative A consonant produced with a narrow but incomplete obstruction in the vocal tract, resulting in a friction sound as the airsteam passes through.

functional grammar, functional linguistics One of the two major divisions of linguistic theory, the functional approach focusses on language as it is used. Meaning occupies a central place in functional linguistics; in extreme varieties, form is marginalized or even may have no place. See also *formal grammar*.

functional magnetic resonance imaging (fMRI) A brain imaging technology in which brain activity is measured indirectly through changes in oxygen levels in the blood stream, as measured by different magnetic properties of oxygenated and deoxygenated blood. See also *positron emission tomography*.

fusional language A language in which words are typically morphologically complex, and it is difficult to determine where the boundaries between the morphemes lie. Latin and Sanskrit are examples of fusional languages. See also *agglutinating language, isolating language, polysynthetic language*.

garden path sentence A sentence the beginning of which suggests a particular analysis, but by the end this analysis cannot work. A well known example is *The horse raced past the barn fell*.

gender A grammatical category in which the nouns of a language are divided into groups according to the forms of syntactically related items such as verbs, demonstratives and adjectives. Standard Danish distinguishes two genders according to the form of the article (*en* or *et*) and agreement patterns of determiners and adjectives.

genetic relation The relation between languages that developed from a common earlier language, for example, there is a genetic relation between French and Spanish, both of which derive from Latin.

gesture Distinctive movement of a body part conveying meaning, for example, a manual gesture conveying the meaning OK, or shaking the head in denial.

glide A vowel-like consonant sound produced with minimal obstruction to the passage of air at its point of articulation. Also called a *semivowel*.

global aphasia A type of aphasia involving disturbance to all language functions. This is usually associated with damage to large parts of the left frontal and temporal lobes.

glottal A sound produced with constriction in the glottis, e.g with complete closure a glottal stop [ʔ] results.

glottalic airstream mechanism   An airstream produced by forming a cavity above the larynx, which is compressed or rarefied by raising or lowering the glottis; then the upper obstruction is released. See also *ejective*, *implosive*.

glottis   The opening between the vocal folds.

grammatical, grammaticality   A sequence of words that is formed according to the grammatical patterns of a language.

grammatical category   A category or concept distinguished in the grammar of a language, for example, tense, gender, case, number.

grammatical morpheme   A morpheme that provides information about the grammatical properties of a linguistic unit, and has little or no lexical meaning, for example, English *the* and *a*.

grammatical relation   Any function that a linguistic unit can serve in the syntax of a language, for example, a noun phrase can serve in grammatical relations such as Subject, Actor and Theme.

grammaticalization   The process by which grammatical morphemes in a language emerge over time, often from lexical items. The term is also used for the emergence of grammatical categories and other grammatical phenomena.

Gricean Maxims   Four maxims — principles governing the inferences conversational partners draw — that were formulated by H.P. Grice and make up the cooperative principle.

Grimm's Law   The description of a systematic sound change in consonants in an ancestor of the Germanic languages that was formulated by Jacob Grimm.

hierarchical structuring   The grouping and subgrouping of the units that make up a sentence, for example, the hierarchical structuring of *the duckling waddled* is [[[the] [[duck] [ling]]] [[waddle] [d]]], where square brackets enclose units. See also *tree*.

high vowel   A vowel with the high point of the tongue relatively high in the oral cavity, for example, [i], [u].

historical linguistics   The branch of linguistics that studies how languages change over time.

holophrastic stage   A stage in the acquisition of language typically reached around twelve to eighteen months in which the child produces one-word utterances that convey a complex message similar to what is conveyed by a phrase or clause in adult speech.

homophone, homophony, homonymy   Different words that share the same phonological form, for example, *threw* and *through*.

hyperbole   The process by which a word loses a strong aspect of meaning through overuse, as happened to intensifying adverbs like *terribly* and *awfully*.

hypernym   See *superordinate*.

hyperonym   See *superordinate*.

hyponym, hyponymy   A word with a more specific meaning than another, which it is an instance of, for example, *blue* and *green* are hyponyms of *colour*.

icon, iconic sign   A sign in which the form bears some resemblance to the meaning, for example, the manual gesture for 'two', ✌ .

idiom   An expression whose meaning is not predictable from the meaning of its component parts, for example, *kick the bucket* for 'die'.

illocutionary force   The speech act performed by a speaker in making an utterance, for example, promise, command, request, warning.

implicational universal   A generalization about human languages that is expressed in the form of an implication between two properties for example, if a language has voiceless nasals it also has voiced nasals. See also *non-implicational universal*.

implosive   A speech sound produced on an ingressive glottalic airstream. The air in a cavity above the larynx is rarefied by lowering the larynx, and closure in the oral cavity is released, allowing air to be sucked in. See also *ejective*.

inalienable possession   A grammatical category indicating a type of possession in which the possessor and possession are linked by close or intrinsic ties, for example, the possession of parts of the body (*my ear*, *her breasts*), and kindred (*your mother*, *my brother*). See also *alienable possession*.

indirect speech act   An utterance the linguistic form of which does not reflect its communicative purpose, for example, *I have no money* used as a request for a loan.

Indo-European   A well established family of languages spoken throughout most of Europe, across Iran, and into Central Asia and India; in more recent times Indo-European languages have expanded into the Americas, Australia, New Zealand and elsewhere. Branches of Indo-European include Germanic (German, Danish, Dutch, etc.), Romance (French, Spanish, Italian), Celtic (Breton, Welsh, Cornish), Balto-Slavic (Russian, Polish).

infix   An affix that is inserted within a root.

inflectional morpheme   A bound grammatical morpheme that gives rise to a form of a word expressing a certain grammatical category, such as past tense as in *walked*, or plural number as in *dogs*. See also *derivational morpheme*.

ingressive airstream mechanism   An airstream produced by drawing air into the oral or nasal cavity. Ingressive airstream may be used when speaking while taking a breath; it is also used with glottalic and velaric airstream in the formation of implosives and clicks. See also *egressive airstream mechanism*.

innateness   The idea that children are biologically predisposed to learn language, that they are born with knowledge of an abstract universal grammar that underlies the grammar of all human languages.

insertion   The addition of one or more phones into a word, as in the fairly frequent habit of speakers of English to add a schwa between the two final consonants of *film*.

intension   Defining properties of a lexical item, that must be met for it to be used appropriately.

interdental   A sound produced with the tip or blade of the tongue between the upper and lower teeth, for example, the initial segment of *the*.

interjection   A word that expresses an emotional attitude (e.g. *yuck!*, *erk!*) or is used as a warning or call for attention (e.g. *hey!*).

International Phonetic Alphabet (IPA)   The alphabet of the International Phonetic Association designed to represent the sounds of all of the world's languages.

interpersonal   A type of meaning that concerns the establishment and maintenance of social relations; also used of a grammatical relation that encodes this type of meaning.

interrogative   A grammatical construction that directly expresses a question, for example, *Are you going?*

intonation   The pitch contour of a phrase or sentence.

intransitive clause   A clause with one obligatory noun phrase, for example, clauses of state or motion in English (*the farmer slept, the duckling ran away*).

IPA   International Phonetic Alphabet

isogloss   A line drawn on a map to show the boundary of an area in which a linguistic feature is found.

isolating language   A language in which words tend to consist of a single morpheme. Mandarin Chinese and various other languages of South-East Asia are isolating; English is also fairly isolating. See also *agglutinating language*, *fusional language* and *polysynthetic language*.

L1   A person's first language or mother tongue.

L2   A language acquired by a person after their L1.

L2 acquisition   See *second language acquisition*.

labial   A sound articulated with the lips.

labiodental   A sound articulated with the bottom lip in contact with the upper teeth.

LAD   language acquisition device

language acquisition device (LAD)   The genetically encoded biological faculty enabling a person to learn and use a language. A controversial notion held by linguists who believe in the innateness of language.

language isolate   A language that forms a family on its own, having no known genetic relatives.

language death   The process whereby a language loses its community of speakers, and no (native) speakers remain.

language endangerment, language obsolescence   The process by which the community of speakers of a language reduces significantly, and fewer children acquire it.

language family   See *family*.

language maintenance, language revival   Strategies developed to maintain use of an endangered or dying language.

language shift   The process in which habits of using a language in a bilingual community changes over time in favour of one of the languages, and against the use of another or others. Language shift can result in language endangerment and ultimately death.

language universal   A property that holds of all or most human languages.

larynx   The part of the throat or windpipe lying behind the Adam's apple that holds the vocal folds.

lateral   A manner of articulation of a consonant whereby the air escapes via one or both sides of an obstruction in the oral cavity, for example, [l].

lateralization   The tendency for certain cognitive functions to be performed in one or the other hemisphere of the brain.

lexical item, lexeme   A linguistic sign of any size that expresses content meaning. A lexeme can be a morpheme, word or longer expression. See also *idiom*.

lexicon   A list of all lexical and grammatical items of a language. The full lexicon of a language will contain not just words but also idioms.

linguistic determinism   The notion that language determines the way people think about and perceive the world. See also *linguistic relativity*.

linguistic relativity   The idea that there is a correlation between the language you speak and the way you conceptualize the world. See also *linguistic determinism*.

linguistic typology   The branch of linguistics that is concerned with classifying linguistic phenomena. Linguistic typology is sometimes distinguished from language typology, which is concerned with classifying languages into structural types.

loanword   A word used in one language that has its origins in another language, for example, *kangaroo* is a loanword in many languages, deriving ultimately from a word in the Australian language Guugu Yimithirr. See also *borrowing*.

localization   The theory that different areas of the brain are responsible for different cognitive functions.

locative case   The case of a noun or pronoun that specifies it as a location for an object or event; the meaning is like that expressed by the preposition *at* in English. See also *case*.

logographic writing system   A system of writing in which each symbol represents a word or morpheme, for example, the system of Chinese characters.

loss, deletion   A fairly common type of sound change in which a segment is lost, for example, the final stop of *thumb* was lost at some point in the history of English.

low vowel   A vowel in the production of which the high point of the tongue is low in the mouth, and the body of the tongue is lowered from its neutral position.

magnetoencephalogram (MEG)   A record of brain activity by the measurement of magnetic fields. MEGs provide better spatial resolution than EEGs.

manner of articulation   The way the airstream is obstructed and modified as it passes through the constriction in the vocal tract in the production of a consonant. Manners of articulation include stop, nasal, fricative. See also *place of articulation*.

marked category   A category that is less natural than another it is in opposition to, for example, plurals of nouns in English are marked with respect to singulars. Marked categories tend to be expressed by larger forms, and tend to be less frequent than unmarked categories in language use, and across languages. See also *markedness, unmarked category*.

markedness   The notion that some grammatical categories are more natural or commonplace (less marked) than others. See also *marked category* and *unmarked category*.

mass comparison   A quick way of gaining an idea of the relatedness of a number of languages by comparing basic vocabulary items (excluding onomatopoeic words) in the languages.

Maxim of Manner   The maxim or convention formulated by H. P. Grice that a speaker's contribution to conversation should be orderly, and should avoid obscurity and ambiguity.

Maxim of Quality   The maxim or convention formulated by H.P. Grice that a speaker's contribution to conversation should be truthful and not make unsupported claims.

Maxim of Quantity   The maxim or convention formulated by H.P. Grice that a speaker's utterance should be no more nor less informative than required at that point in the conversation.

Maxim of Relevance   The maxim or convention formulated by H.P. Grice that a speaker's utterance should be relevant to the topic being discussed.

meaning   The idea that is conveyed by a sentence or utterance, it's content. See also *sense* and *reference*.

meaning extension   The process by which the meaning of a word is extended or broadened it to embrace new senses.

meaning narrowing   The process by which the meaning of a word is reduced so that it covers a smaller range of senses.

MEG   magnetoencephalogram

mental lexicon   The internal lexicon that speakers of a language have in their minds.

meronymy   The part-whole relation, for example, *hand* and *face* are meronyms of *clock*.

metaphor   Non-literal meaning in which an expression that means one thing is extended to another concept on the basis of similarity, for example, *grasp* is used metaphorically in *he grasped the idea*.

metathesis   The reordering of phonological segments, often transposition, for example, *bird* derives by metathesis from Old English *brid*.

metonymy   Broadening of meaning whereby the sense of an expression is extended to another concept it is typically or habitually associated with, for example, *crown* for 'king'.

mid vowel   A vowel in the production of which the high point of the tongue is in a relatively neutral position in the mouth, neither high nor low.

minimal pair   Two words that are identical except for a single phoneme in a certain position, for example, *pin* and *bin* in English.

mixed language   A language in which particular parts of the lexicon and grammatical system come predominantly from different sources. An example is Michif, whose nouns and nominal grammar come from French, while its verbs and verbal grammar are from Cree.

morph   Any minimal meaningful form in a language, including morphemes and allomorphs.

morpheme   The smallest linguistic sign, for example, *unlikely* consists of three morphemes, *un-*, *like* and *-ly*.

morphology   The branch of linguistics that studies the structure of words.

morphophonemic form   An abstract form postulated for phonological allomorphs that is operated on by morphophonemic rules to derive the phonological forms of the allomorphs.

morphophonemic rule   An explicit rule that accounts for the realization of a morpheme as phonological allomorphs.

motherese   See *caretaker speech*.

mutual intelligibility   The the main criterion used by linguists for recognising different forms of speech as dialects of a single language, this refers to the ability of speakers of one variety to understand speakers of the other without prior experience.

narrow transcription   A detailed phonetic transcription. See also *broad transcription*, *transcription*.

nasal   A sound produced when the velum is lowered, permitting air to pass into the nasal cavity, which acts as a resonating chamber.

nasal cavity   The chamber behind the nose through which air passes when the velum is lowered.

neurolinguistics   The study of the neurobiology of language. It is concerned with the brain functions underlying speech and the acquisition of language.

neuron   A nerve cell, the type of cell found in the brain and nervous system.

Niger-Congo   Perhaps the largest language family in the world with upwards of 1500 languages spoken over much of sub-Saharan Africa. The status of the grouping as a family widely accepted by Africanists, though its membership and division into branches is not uncontentious.

nominal   A term sometimes used as an alternative for, or replacement of, *noun* in languages that do not distinguish adjectives and nouns as distinct parts-of-speech.

nominative case   The case of a noun or pronoun when it is subject of either a transitive or intransitive clause, when this is different from its case as an object. For example, in English the nominative case of the first person singular pronoun is *I*. See also *accusative case*, *case*, *intransitive*, *transitive*.

non-absolute universal   A generalization that holds good for many (though not all) languages, a tendency, as in most languages have nasal phonemes. See also *absolute universal*.

non-implicational universal   A universal generalization that expresses a characteristic held by most or all languages, for example, all (spoken) languages have vowels. See also *implicational universal*.

noun   A part-of-speech made up of words that serve as the main lexical item in noun phrases, and in some languages show grammatical alternations for case, number and/or gender.

Nouns typically denote concrete or abstract things, for example, *dog*, *town*, *dishonesty*. See also *verb*, *part-of-speech*.

noun phrase (NP)   A syntagmatic grouping of words that typically functions as a referential expression, and serves in grammatical relations such as Subject, Object, Actor, Agent, etc.. Noun phrases are generally made up of a noun or pronoun, optionally together with modifying words such as adjectives and determiners, for example, *the moon*, *the ugly duckling*, *my pet pig*.

NP   noun phrase

Object   The grammatical relation traditionally associated with the Undergoer (or patent) of an action, as in *the farmer kills* **the duckling**.

onomatopoeia   Where the phonetic form of a word is suggestive of the meaning, for example, *meow*, *woof*.

oral cavity   The mouth.

overextension of meaning   Where a child acquiring a language generalizes the meaning of a word beyond the sense it has in adult language, for example, using *doggy* to refer to all four-legged hairy animals.

overgeneralization of regular forms   Where a child acquiring a language uses a regularly constructed form instead of the irregular form of the adult language, for example, *feets* instead of *feet* as the plural of *foot*.

palatal   A consonant produced with constriction in the region of the palate.

palate   The hard part of the roof of the mouth behind the alveolar ridge, and in front of the velum (sometimes called the *soft palate*).

Pama-Nyungan   Term used for a group of languages spoken over most of the Australian continent (except for the Kimberley and Arnhem Land) and generally believed to form a genetic family.

Papuan   A set of some 800 languages spoken on New Guinea and neighbouring islands that includes all languages that are not Austronesian.

paradigmatic relation   A relation between a linguistic unit and other units that can occur in the same position in a construction, for example, /p/ and /b/ are in paradigmatic opposition in English (though /p/ and /æ/ are not since they can't occur in the same position in a syllable). See also *syntagmatic relation*.

parsing   The process of dividing a sentence or smaller linguistic unit into its component units and assigning a structure to it.

part-of-speech A categorization of the morphemes of a language into types according to their grammatical behaviour. Parts-of-speech frequently identified include noun, verb, adjective, adverb and pronoun.

pejoration Where a word takes on negative connotations, for example, *abo* in Australian English is a clipping of *Aborigine*, and has acquired negative connotations that the full form does not have.

performative sentence A sentence that indicates its speech-act value explicitly, for example, *I resign*.

PET positron emission tomography

pharyngeal A consonant sound with the pharynx as its place of articulation, for example, the Danish rhotic is a pharyngeal approximant.

pharynx The tubular cavity in the vocal tract located above the larynx and oriented roughly at right angles to the oral cavity.

phonaesthesia The partially iconic association between certain sounds and meanings in a language, for example, between initial *sl* in English and uncontrolled sliding movements.

phone Smallest phonetic segment that can be isolated in a stream of speech, for example, /p/, /æ/.

phoneme A minimal unit in the phonology of a language that is capable of making the difference between words; a distinctive phone. See also *allophone*.

phonetic realization The realization of a phoneme as a material sound.

phonetics The scientific study of speech sounds. See *acoustic phonetics, articulatory phonetics, auditory phonetics*.

phonological rule An explicit rule that accounts for the allophonic realization of a phoneme as a phonetic segment.

phonology The sound system of a language, including the inventory of phonemes and their paradigmatic and syntagmatic patterning; also the study of the sound systems of languages.

phrase A group of words of smaller than a clause, such as an NP (e.g. *the dog*).

pidgin A reduced language with simple grammar, small lexicon and small stylistic range that is no one's the mother tongue. Pidgins arise in situations in which speakers of mutually unintelligible languages come into contact through economic activities such as trade and slavery.

pitch   The frequency of vibration of the vocal folds.

pitch accent system   A system in which pitch differences are used to distinguish between accented and unaccented syllables; Japanese has a pitch accent system.

place of articulation   The location in the vocal tract of the constriction of airflow in a consonant, for example, dental, palatal. See also *manner of articulation*.

polysemy   The situation in which a single lexical or grammatical item has a range of different though related meanings, for example, *foot* has polysemies including 'a part of the body at the extremity of a limb used for locomotion', 'lower part (e.g. of a hill)', 'part of an object that serves for support (e.g. of chair or building)'.

polysynthetic language   A language in which words are morphologically complex and typically made up of many morphemes, so that a single word may correspond to a full sentence in English. Many languages of North America are polysynthetic. See also *agglutinating language*, *fusional language*.

positron emission tomography (PET) scanning   A brain scanning technology used to detect the location of brain activity in which a radioactive isotope is injected in the bloodstream. See also *Functional Magnetic Resonance Imaging*.

possession   See *alienable possession*, *inalienable possession*.

postposition   A grammatical word or morpheme that follows a noun phrase and indicates its relation in a clause or another noun phrase. See also *preposition*.

postpositional phrase   A phase consisting of a noun phrase followed by a postposition.

poverty of the stimulus   The idea that the child acquiring a language is exposed to unstructured and noisy data, full of hesitations, incomplete utterances, slips of the tongue, and little good evidence on which to build a mental grammar.

PP   prepositional phrase or postpositional phrase

pragmatics   The study of meaning that is inferred from what is said rather than encoded.

prefix   An affix attached to the beginning of a root or stem, for example, *un-* of *unlike*.

preposition   A grammatical word or morpheme that precedes a noun phrase and specifies its relation in another noun phrase or clause, for example, *to*, *from*, *at*.

prepositional phrase   A phrase consisting of a noun phrase preceded by a preposition, for example, *to the woodshed*.

presupposition   Something that must be assumed true for a sentence to be appropriately uttered , for example, *Have some more tea* presupposes the addressee has already had some tea.

proclitic   A clitic that is attached to the beginning of a word. See also *clitic*, *enclitic*.

productivity   A design feature of language referring to the ability of speakers to make new meanings by putting together linguistic elements in new ways to form novel expressions.

pronoun   A grammatical morpheme that is used to index a referent in or external to the speech situation, for example, *I, him*.

proposition   That which is expressed by a clause and may be either true or false.

prosody   A phonetic quality that is spread over a sequence of phones, for example, stress, intonation, tone, loudness.

proto-language   The hypothetical language from which all languages of a family ultimately derive. Proto-Indo-European is the hypothetical language that was the parent of all Indo-European languages.

psycholinguistics   The branch of linguistics concerned with the mental processes involved in production and comprehension of speech, and in the acquisition of language.

pulmonic airstream mechanism   The airstream produced from the lungs, this is the most common airstream used in human languages.

reanalysis   A type of morphological change in which a word with a certain structure comes to be analysed differently.

reduplication   The morphological process involving repetition of whole or part of a morpheme to produce a new word, as in *wishy-washy, teeny-weeny*.

reference   The relation between a linguistic unit and something that it identifies, for example, between *the sun* and a certain celestial object.

reflexivity   A design feature of language referring to the property that it can be used to talk about itself.

register tone system   A tone system in which the relative height of the tone is crucial, not its direction of movement; such systems are found in many African languages, for example, Twi.

register, registerial variation   Speech varieties or variations in speech that are associated with different contexts of use, for example, scientific English, legalese, bureaucratese.

regularization   Any process by which irregular or partially regular constructions or patterns in a language are replaced by more regular forms, for example, the plural of *ox* is in the process of regularization to *oxes* in some varieties of English, replacing the irregular *oxen*. See *analogical change*.

respect variety   A speech register used to show respect to an interlocutor or someone being spoken about.

rhotic   An *r*-like speech sound.

root   The base form of a lexical item that cannot be further analysed morphologically, for example, *happy* in *unhappily*.

rounded vowel   A vowel accompanied by rounding of the lips, as with [u] and [y].

Sapir-Whorf hypothesis   A hypothesis about the relation between language and thought that was stated in its most explicit form by the American linguists Edward Sapir and Benjamin Whorf. It is sometimes referred to as simply the Whorfian hypothesis since Whorf adopted the most extreme version of the hypothesis. See also *linguistic relativity*, *linguistic determinism*.

second language acquisition   The acquisition of one or more languages after the first language has been fully or almost completely acquired. It is also called L2 acquisition.

secret variety   A speech register used by a subgroup of speakers of a language to exclude outsiders, and to underline the separate social identity of the members.

semantic change   A change in the semantics of a linguistic item over a period of time.

semantic compositionality   The idea that the semantics of a sentence (or any complex grammatical unit) can be accounted for by putting together the semantics of the components that make up the complex unit.

semantic bleaching   The process by which the lexical meaning of an item is lost or attenuated as it becomes more grammatical.

semantics   The study of the linguistic meanings of morphemes, words, phrases, sentences and grammatical relations. Semantic meaning is encoded in linguistic signs.

semivowel   See *glide*.

sense   The inherent meaning of a linguistic sign.

sentence   The largest unit of syntax; anything larger shows no grammatical structure (although it can be structured in other ways).

sentence comprehension   The mental and brain processes involved in understanding sentences.

sentence meaning   The linguistic meaning of a sentence, the meaning that remains constant throughout all instantiations of the sentence. See also *semantics*, *utterance meaning*.

sentence production   The psychological and neurological processes involved in production of sentences.

sign   A fundamental item made up of two inherent components, a form (sometimes called signifier) and a meaning (also called signified).

sign language   See *deaf sign language.*

Sino-Tibetan   A large genetic family of languages consisting of some 400 languages, that is second in size to the Indo-European family in terms of numbers of speakers. It is divided into two primary groups, Sinitic (fourteen languages, including Mandarin Chinese) and Tibeto-Burman (the remainder, including languages such as Tibetan).

SLI   Specific Language Impairment

slip of the tongue   An unintended divergence from the intended utterance, also called a *speech error.*

sociolinguistics   The field that studies language in its social context.

social variety and variation   Varieties of a language or variations in a language that are associated with different social groups, for example, ages, geographical regions, social classes, religions.

sound change   Changes in the sounds and sound system of a language over a period of time.

sound correspondence   Systematic correspondences between sounds in cognates across a set of genetically related languages, for example, the correspondence between /f/ and /p/ in English and French cognates.

Specific Language Impairment (SLI)   A cognitive disorder believed to be specific to language, which is characterized by difficulties in articulation and grammatical impairments.

speech act   The action a speaker accomplishes in using an utterance in a particular context, for example, *it's cold* could be used as a request for the hearer to turn on the heater.

speech community   A group of people who share a language or language variety and the norms for its use in social contexts.

split-brain patient   Someone whose corpus callosum has been surgically severed to separate the two hemispheres of the brain. This medical procedure used to be used in the treatment of epilepsy, but is no longer undertaken.

spoonerism   A type of speech error involving the exchange (metathesis) of initial segments of lexical words in a sequence, as in *our very queer dean* when *our very dear queen* was meant. Spoonerisms are named after the nineteenth century Oxford don Reverend William Spooner who is said to have regularly produced such errors.

standard dialect   A dialect of a language that is accepted by speakers as the most correct form, is promoted in schools, and used in public writing and speech.

stop   A speech sound in which the airflow is completely stopped for a brief time at some point in the vocal tract, for example, [ʔ], [g], [b].

stem   A word form (a root, root plus derivational affixes, or compound of roots) to which inflectional affixes are attached.

stress, stressed syllable   A syllable perceived as prominent due to greater length, loudness and/or higher pitch than other syllables in a word.

structuralism   Any approach to linguistics that focusses on the interrelatedness of linguistic units, the ways they form structures and systems of oppositions.

style (of speech)   A variety or manner of speech associated with certain interpersonal contexts, and usually differing from other styles in degree of formality. See also *register*.

Subject   The grammatical relation traditionally associated with the doer or performer of an action, as in ***The farmer*** *kills the duckling*. According to some linguists, subject is a meaningless category; others aver that it has a meaning relating to how the proposition is presented.

suffix   An affix attached at the end of a root or stem, for example, *-ed* of *finished*.

superordinate   A general term that is an inclusive term in a relation of hyponymy. For example, *colour* is a superordinate for *blue* and *green*.

suppletion, suppletive forms   Allomorphs of a morpheme that are not phonologically related, for example, the irregular past tense *went* of the verb *go* involves root suppletion.

suprasegmental   See *prosody*.

suspicious pair   A pair of phones that are sufficiently similar to be potentially allophones of a single phoneme, for example, [p] and [b] (both are bilabial stops).

syllable   A minimal unit of speech production, normally composed of a vowel or vowel-like consonant that is optionally preceded and/or followed by a consonant, for example, [ba] and [a] are syllables, though [b] is not.

symbol, symbolic sign   A sign in which the association between the form and the meaning is not motivated. See *icon*.

synecdoche   A type of meaning extension where the sense is extended from a part to a whole meaning, for example, the extension of *tit* 'nipple' to mean 'whole breast'.

synonymy   The relation of similarity of meaning, for example, *seat* and *chair* are synonyms.

syntactic bootstrapping   The use of syntactic knowledge by a language learner in order to determine the meaning of words; for example, experiments have shown that knowing a word is a verb (from its syntactic context) informs the child that it denotes an event.

syntactic change   A change in the syntactic patterns of a language, for example, change from SVO to SOV word order.

syntagmatic relation   A relation between linguistic items that are present in an utterance.

syntax   The study of the formation of sentences in a language.

taboo word   A word considered inappropriate in certain social contexts, for example, *fuck*, *cunt* and the like on formal occasions.

telegraphic speech   The stage in first language acquisition following the two word stage, that consists primarily of lexical items.

tense   A grammatical category, usually marked in verbs, that indicates the relative time of occurrence of an event, for example, past, present, future.

textural   The type of meaning that provides texture to an utterance, linking the component parts together; a grammatical relation that expresses this type of meaning.

Theme   A textural relation, the Theme of a clause anchors its message down, serving as a fixed point from which the message can be expanded. Usually the Theme indicates what the clause is about, or its starting point.

tone   The contrastive pitch on a syllable in a tone language, in which minimal pairs may exist that differ only in syllable tone, for example, in Cantonese the syllable [si] with high falling tone is the word for 'poem', but with mid level tone is the word for 'to try'.

tone language   A language in which tone is phonemic, as in many languages of Africa, America and South-East Asia.

top-down processing   Language processing that takes into account the larger linguistic environment, which generates expectations about what will be said. See also *bottom-up processing*.

transcription   The representation of a spoken or signed utterance in the written mode. See *broad transcription*, *phonemic transcription*, *narrow transcription*.

transfer, interference   The carrying over of grammatical patterns from a person's L1 to L2. The "foreign accent" of most second language learners results from transfer of the phonetic and phonemic systems of the first language. Transfer can also occur in the opposite direction.

transitive clause   A clause which, in full form, has two obligatory noun phrases, for example, clauses of caused states or movement (*the sergeant marched the soldier*), and many clauses of violence in English (*the farmer kills the duckling, the farmer chased the duckling*).

Trans-New Guinea   An uncertain genetic grouping of between three hundred and five hundred Papuan languages mostly spoken on the mountainous spine of the island of Papua New Guinea.

tree A diagrammatic representation of the hierarchical structure of a sentence. Trees can be labelled at nodes (indicating the type of unit) and branches (indicating the grammatical category). See also *family tree*.

trill A speech sound involving the vibration of one articulator, often the tip of the tongue, against another, usually an unmovable passive articulator. An example is the rhotic in the Spanish word *perro* 'dog'.

two-word stage A stage in the acquisition of a first language, usually beginning around eighteen months, in which words are put together to form two-word utterances.

unaspirated A voiceless stop which is not followed by a puff of air; in the production of an unaspirated stop the vocal folds begin vibrating at the same time as the stop is released. See also *aspirated*.

underextension Where the child assigns a narrower meaning to a word than it has in the adult language, for example, if *doggy* applies just to a pet dog.

Undergoer The grammatical role of a noun phrase the referent of which suffers the action designated by a transitive clause. For example, *the duckling* in *the farmer kills the duckling*. See also *Object*.

ungrammatical A syntactic form that does not conform to the grammatical patterns of a language.

unit Any stretch of language that behaves in some way as a single whole. Units range in complexity from the smallest indivisible units (e.g. morphemes, phonemes) to the largest (sentences).

universal See *language universal*.

unmarked A category that is more natural than another category it is in opposition to, for example, the singular category for nouns in English is unmarked with respect to the plural. Unmarked categories tend to be expressed by shorter forms, and tend to be more frequent than unmarked categories in language use, and across languages. See also *marked category*, *markedness*.

unrounded vowel A vowel produced with no rounding of the lips, for example, [ɪ], [e].

utterance A stretch of speech corresponding approximately to the sentence in grammar.

utterance meaning The meaning of an utterance in its context of occurrence, which may be different from its meaning in different context; pragmatics studies utterance meaning.

uvula The small appendage hanging down at the back of the soft palate or velum.

uvular phone A speech sound made with the tongue making contact or approximating to the uvula, as in [q].

vagueness Lack of specificity in the meaning of a linguistic sign, for example, *wrong* is vague between the senses 'immoral', 'inappropriate', 'incorrect'. See also *polysemy* and *homophone, homophony*.

velar A consonant produced with constriction in the region of the velum.

velaric airstream mechanism An airstream produced by placing the back of the tongue against the velum and making a second closure further forward in the oral cavity. The enclosed space is then enlarged, rarefying the air within; the second closure is next released, and air flows inwards. See *click*.

velum The soft part of the roof of the mouth behind the hard palate.

verb A part-of-speech containing words that serve as the main lexical item in a verb phrase, and in some languages display grammatical categories like tense, aspect, mood. Verbs typically denote events, states, processes, happenings and so on for example, *hit, sit, break*. See also *noun, part-of-speech*.

verb phrase (VP) A syntactic unit consisting of a verb together with syntagmatically related words (such as adverbials and auxiliary verbs) that typically serves in the grammatical relation Event. Examples are *was eating, might have been watching closely*. The term verb phrase in formal grammar is usually a larger unit containing also the object and other noun phrases and prepositional phrases with the exception of the subject.

vocal folds A set of muscles in the larynx resembling a pair of flaps that can be brought together more or less tightly to modify the stream of air passing through. Also called *vocal cords*.

vocal tract The body organs that are involved in the production of speech sounds, including the lungs, glottis, pharynx, and oral and nasal cavities.

vocalization Any sound produced by the vocal apparatus of an animal, for example, barking of a dog, bird songs.

voice onset time (VOT) The period between the release of a stop and the onset of voicing in a following vowel. Voice onset time can be negative, zero or positive.

voiced phone A speech sound produced with regular vibration of the vocal folds.

voiceless phone A speech sound produced with the glottis open, without vibration of the vocal folds.

VOT voice onset time

vowel A resonant speech sound that is produced without significant constriction in the oral cavity.

vowel height   The relative height of the highest point of the tongue in the mouth in the production of the vowel, for example, [i] is a high vowel because the highest point of the tongue is very high in the mouth (cf. [æ] where the high point is lower).

VP   verb phrase.

Wada test   A test for determining which hemisphere is dominant in language processing by injecting sodium amytal into the carotid arteries of neck. The ipsilateral hemisphere is deactivated, and if this is the language dominant one, speech is affected.

Wernicke's aphasia   The type of aphasia normally resulting from damage to Wernicke's area, and usually characterized by difficulties in comprehension of speech.

Wernicke's area   A classic language area of the brain located in the posterior (back) portion of the left hemisphere. This area is named after Carl Wernicke, the German neurologist who showed that damage to this area gives rise to certain language disorders.

word   A fundamental unit of grammar intuitively recognized by native speakers of a language. The term is difficult to define, and is used in a variety of different ways in linguistics. According to a famous definition by the American linguist Leonard Bloomfield, a word is a minimal free form.

zero morph, zero morpheme   A morpheme or allomorph of a morpheme that has no phonetic form. For example, in many languages the third person singular form of a bound pronominal is a zero.

References

Abley, M. (2003), *Spoken here: Travels among Threatened Languages*. London: William Heinemann.

Aitchison, J. (1981), *Language Change: Progress or Decay?* Fontana Linguistics. London: Fontana Press.

Aitchison, J. (1989), *The Articulate Mammal: An Introduction to Psycholinguistics*. London: Unwin Hyman.

Aitchison, J. (1996), *The Seeds of Speech: Language Origin and Evolution*. Cambridge: Cambridge University Press.

Aitchison, J. (1997), *The Language Web: The Power and Problem of Words*. Cambridge: Cambridge University Press.

Aitchison, J. (2003), *A Glossary of Language and Mind*. Edinburgh: Edinburgh University Press.

Allan, K. and Burridge, K. (1991), *Euphemism and Dysphemism: Language used as Shield and Weapon*. Oxford: Oxford University Press.

Allan, K. and Burridge, K. (2006), *Forbidden Words: Taboo and the Censoring of Language*. Cambridge: Cambridge University Press.

Anthony, D. W. (2007), *The Horse, the Wheel, and Language: How Bronze–age Riders from the Eurasian Steppes Shaped the Modern World*. Princeton, NJ and Oxford: Oxford University Press.

Anttila, R. (1972), *An Introduction to Historical and Comparative Linguistics*. New York: Macmillan.

Arbib, M. A. (2003), 'The evolving mirror system: a neural basis for language readiness', in M. H. Christiansen and S. Kirby (eds), *Language Evolution*. Oxford: Oxford University Press, pp. 182–200.

Arends, J., Muysken, P. and Smith, N. (eds), (1995), *Pidgins and Creoles: An Introduction*. Amsterdam: John Benjamins.

Aronoff, M. and Rees-Miller, J. (2001), *The Handbook of Linguistics*. Blackwell Handbooks in Linguistics. Oxford: Blackwell Publishers.

Ashcraft, M. H. (1993), 'A personal case history of transient anomia'. *Brain and Language*, 44, 47–57.

Ayto, J. (1990), *Dictionary of Word Origins*. New York: Arcade Publishing.

Baker, M. (2001), 'Syntax', in M. Aronoff and J. Rees-Miller (eds), *The Handbook of Linguistics*. Oxford: Blackwell Publishers, pp. 265–294.

Bakker, P. (1994), 'Michif, the Cree-French mixed language of the Métis buffalo hunters in Canada', in P. Bakker and M. Mous (eds), *Mixed Languages: 15 Case Studies in Language Intertwining*. Amsterdam: Institute for Functional Research into Language and Language Use (IFOTT), pp. 13–33.

Bakker, P. and Mous, M. (eds), (1994), *Mixed Languages: 15 Case Studies in Language Intertwining*. Studies in Language and Language Use, 13. Amsterdam: Institute for Functional Research into Language and Language Use (IFOTT).

Baron, I. and Herslund, M. (eds), (2001), *Dimensions of Possession*. Typological Studies in Language, 47. Amsterdam: John Benjamins.

Bauer, L. (1983), *English Word-formation*. Cambridge: Cambridge University Press.

Bauer, L. (2003), *Introducing Linguistic Morphology*. Edinburgh: Edinburgh University Press.

Bauer, L. (2004), *A Glossary of Morphology*. Edinburgh: Edinburgh University Press.

Bellwood, P. (2005), *First Farmers: The Origins of Agricultural Societies*. Malden, MA: Blackwell.

Berko, J. (1958), 'The child's learning of English morphology'. *Word*, 14, 150–177.

Berlin, B. and Kay, P. (1969), *Basic Color Terms: Their Universality and Evolution*. Berkeley, CA: University of California Press.

Bialystok, E. and Hakuta, K. (1994), *In Other Words: The Science and Psychology of Second Language Acquisition*. New York: Basic Books.

Biber, D. (1995), *Dimensions of Register Variation: A Cross-linguistic Comparison*. Cambridge: Cambridge University Press.

Biber, D., Conrad, S. and Reppen, R. (1998), *Corpus Linguistics: Investigating Language Structure and Use*. Cambridge Approaches to Linguistics. Cambridge: Cambridge University Press.

Birdsong, D. (ed.) (1999), *Second Language Acquisition and the Critical Period Hypothesis*. Mahwah, NJ: Lawrence Erlbaum Associates.

Blake, B. J. (2008), *All about Language*. Oxford: Oxford University Press.

Blakemore, D. (1992), *Understanding Utterances: An Introduction to Pragmatics*. Oxford: Blackwell.

Bloom, P. (ed.) (1996), *Language Acquisition: Core Readings*. Cambridge, MA: MIT Press.

Bolinger, D. (1975), *Aspects of Language*. New York: Harcourt Brace Jovanovich.

Bolinger, D. (1980), *Language –the Loaded Weapon: The Use and Abuse of Language Today*. London and New York: Longman.

Bond, Z. S. (1999), *Slips of the Ear: Errors in the Perception of Casual Conversation*. London: Academic Press.

Bowerman, M. and Levinson, S. C. (eds), (2001), *Language Acquisition and Conceptual Development*. Cambridge: Cambridge University Press.

Bradley, J. (1988), 'Yanyuwa: "Men speak one way, women speak another"'. *Aboriginal Linguistics*, 1, 126–134.

Bragg, M. (2003), *The Adventure of English: The Biography of a Language*. London: Hodder and Stoughton.

Breen, J. G. and Penselfini, R. (1999), 'Arrernte: a language with no syllable onsets'. *Linguistic Inquiry*, 30, 1–25.

Bright, M. (1984), *Animal Language*. Ithaca, NY: Cornell University Press.

Brown, R. (1957), 'Linguistic determinism and the part of speech'. *Journal of Abnormal and Social Psychology*, 55, 1–5.

Brown, R. (1973), *A First Language: The Early Stages*. Cambridge, MA: Harvard University Press.

Brown, C. H., Kolar, J., Torrey, B., Truong-Quang, T. and Volkman, P. (1976), 'Some general principles of biological and non-biological folk classification'. *American Ethnologist*, 3, 73–85.

Brown, R. and Berko, J. (1960), 'Psycholinguistic research methods', in P. H. Mussen (ed.) *Handbook of Research Methods in Child Development*. New York: John Wiley, pp. 517–617.

Burridge, K. (2004), *Blooming English: Observations on the Roots, Cultivation and Hybrids of the English Language*. Cambridge: Cambridge University Press.

Butler, C. S. (2003a), *Structure and Function – A Guide to Three Major Structural-Functional Theories. Part 1: Approaches to the Simplex Clause*. Amsterdam: John Benjamins.

Butler, C. S. (2003b), *Structure and Function – A Guide to Three Major Structural-Functional Theories. Part 2: From Clause to Discourse and Beyond*. Amsterdam: John Benjamins.

Bybee, J. (2003), 'Mechanisms of change in grammaticalization: the role of frequency', in B. D. Joseph and R. D. Janda (eds), *The Handbook of Historical Linguistics*. Oxford: Blackwell, pp. 602–623.

Bybee, J., Pagliuca, W. J. and Perkins, R. (1990), 'On the asymmetries in the affixation of grammatical material', in W. Croft, K. Denning and S. Kemmerer (eds), *Studies in Typology and Diachrony: Papers Presented to Joseph H. Greenberg on his 75th Birthday*. Amsterdam: John Benjamins, pp. 1–42.

Calvin, W. H. and Ojemann, G. A. (1994), *Conversations with Neil's Brain: The Neural Nature of Thought and Language*. Reading, MA: Perseus Books.

Campbell, L. (1998), *Historical Linguistics: An Introduction*. Edinburgh: Edinburgh University Press.

Capell, A. (1938), 'The structure of Australian languages', in A. P. Elkin (ed.) *Studies in Australian Linguistics*. Sydney: The Australian National Research Council, pp. 46–80.

Caplan, D. (2001), 'Neurolinguistics', in M. Aronoff and J. Rees-Miller (eds), *The Handbook of Linguistics*. Oxford: Blackwell Publishers, pp. 582–607.

Carr, P. (1993), *Phonology*. Modern Linguistics. Hampshire and London: Macmillan.

Carroll, L. (1899), *Through the Looking Glass and What Alice Found There*. London: MacMillan.

Carroll, L. (1927/1866), *Alice's Adventures in Wonderland*. New York: D. Appleton and Company.

Carstairs-McCarthy, A. (1992), *Current Morphology*. London and New York: Routledge.

Carstairs-McCarthy, A. (2001), 'Origins of language', in M. Aronoff and J. Rees-Miller (eds), *The Handbook of Linguistics*. Oxford: Blackwell Publishers, pp. 1–18.

Carter, R. (1998/2000), *Mapping the Mind*. London: Phoenix.

Cavalli-Sforza, L. L. (1991), 'Genes, people and languages'. *Scientific American*, November 1991, 72–78.

Cavalli-Sforza, L. L. (2001), *Genes, Peoples and Languages*. Translated by M. Seielstad. Harmondsworth: Penguin.

Chalmers, A. F. (1976), *What Is This Thing Called Science? An Assessment of the Nature and Status of Science and its Methods*. St Lucia: University of Queensland Press.

Chappell, H. and McGregor, W. B. (eds), (1995), *The Grammar of Inalienability: A Typological Perspective on Body Part Terms and the Part–Whole Relation*. Berlin: Mouton de Gruyter.

Charlesworth, B. and Charlesworth, D. (2003), *Evolution: A Very Short Introduction*. Oxford: Oxford University Press.

Cheney, D. and Seyfarth, R. (1990), *How Monkeys See the World: Inside the Mind of Another Species*. Chicago, IL: University of Chicago Press.

Childs, G. T. (2003), *An Introduction to African Languages*. Amsterdam and Philadelphia, PA: John Benjamins.

Chomsky, N. (1959), 'Review of B.F. Skinner *Verbal behavior*'. *Language*, 35, 26–58.

Chomsky, N. (1986), *Knowledge of Language: Its Nature, Origin and Use*. New York: Praeger.

Christiansen, M. H. and Kirby, S. (eds), (2003), *Language Evolution*. Oxford: Oxford University Press.

Clark, J. and Yallop, C. (1990), *An Introduction to Phonetics and Phonology*. Cambridge, MA: Basil Blackwell.

Cohn, A. (2001), 'Phonology', in M. Aronoff and J. Rees-Miller (eds), *The Handbook of Linguistics*. Oxford: Blackwell Publishers, pp. 180–212.

Collins, B. and Mees, I. M. (2003), *Practical Phonetics and Phonology: A Resource Book for Students*. London and New York: Routledge.

Comrie, B. (1981), *Language Universals and Linguistic Typology: Syntax and Morphology*. Oxford: Basil Blackwell.

Comrie, B. (2001), 'Languages of the world', in M. Aronoff and J. Rees-Miller (eds), *The Handbook of Linguistics*. Oxford: Blackwell Publishers, pp. 19–42.

Comrie, B. (2003), 'On explaining language universals', in M. Tomasello, (ed.) *The New Psychology of Language: Cognitive and Functional Approaches to Language Structure. Volume 2*. Mahwah, NJ and London: Lawrence Erlbaum, pp. 195–209.

Cook, V. (2001), 'Linguistics and second language acquisition: one person with two languages', in M. Aronoff and J. Rees-Miller (eds), *The Handbook of Linguistics*. Oxford: Blackwell Publishers, pp. 488–511.

Corballis, M. C. (2003), 'From hand to mouth: the gestural origins of language', in Christiansen, M. H. and Kirby, S. (eds), *Language Evolution*. Oxford: Oxford University Press, pp. 201–218.

Coulmas, F. (1996), *The Blackwell Encyclopedia of Writing Systems*. Oxford: Blackwell.

Coulmas, F. (2001), 'Sociolinguistics', in M. Aronoff and J. Rees-Miller (eds), *The Handbook of Linguistics*. Oxford: Blackwell Publishers, pp. 563–581.

Coulmas, F. (2003), *Writing Systems: An Introduction to their Linguistic Analysis*. Cambridge: Cambridge University Press.

Coulmas, F. (2005), *Sociolinguistics: The Study of Speakers' Choices*. Cambridge: Cambridge University Press.

Crain, S. and Lillo-Martin, D. (1998), *Language and Mind*. Oxford: Blackwell.

Croft, W. (1990), *Typology and Universals*. Cambridge: Cambridge University Press.

Croft, W. (2001), 'Typology', in M. Aronoff and J. Rees-Miller (eds), *The Handbook of Linguistics*. Oxford: Blackwell Publishers, pp. 337–368.

Crothers, J. (1978), 'Typology and universals of vowel systems', in J. Greenberg, C. A. Ferguson and E. A. Moravcsik (eds), *Universals of Human Language. Volume 2: Phonology*. Stanford, CA: Stanford University Press, pp. 93–152.

Crowley, T. (1992), *An Introduction to Historical Linguistics*. Auckland: Oxford University Press.

Crystal, D. (1980/2003), *A Dictionary of Linguistics and Phonetics*. 5th edn. Malden, MA: Blackwell.

Crystal, D. (1987), *The Cambridge Encyclopedia of Langauge*. Cambridge: Cambridge University Press.

Curtiss, S. (1977), *Genie. A Psycholinguistic Study of a Modern-day "Wild Child"*. New York: Academic Press.

Curtiss, S., Fromkin, V., Krashen, S., Rigler, D. and Rigler, M. (1974), 'The linguistic development of Genie'. *Language*, 50, 528–554.

Cutler, A. (ed.) (1982), *Slips of the Tongue and Language Production*. Berlin: Mouton.

Cutler, A., Hawkins, J. A. and Gilligan, G. (1985), 'The suffixing preference: a processing explanation.' *Linguistics*, 23, 723–758.

Dalton, L., Edwards, S., Farquarson, R., Oscar, S. and McConvell, P. (1995), 'Gurindji children's language and language maintenance'. *International Journal of the Sociology of Language*, 113, 83–98.

Daniels, P. T. (2001), 'Writing systems', in M. Aronoff and J. Rees-Miller (eds), *The Handbook of Linguistics*. Oxford: Blackwell Publishers, pp. 43–80.

Darwin, C. (1898), *The Expression of the Emotions in Man and Animals*. New York: D. Appleton and Company.

Davidoff, J. (1991), *Cognition through Color*. Cambridge, MA: MIT Press.

Denes, P. B. and Pinson, E. N. (1973), *The Speech Chain: The Physics and Biology of Spoken Language*. New York: Doubleday.

Denes, P. B. and Pinson, E. N. (1993), *The Speech Chain: The Physics and Biology of Spoken Language*. 2nd edn. New York: W.H. Freeman.

Dik, S. C. (1989), *The Theory of Functional Grammar. Part 1: The Structure of the Clause*. Dordrecht: Foris Publications.

Donald, M. (1991), *Origins of the Modern Mind: Three Stages in the Evolution of Culture and Cognition*. Cambridge, MA: Harvard University Press.

Donohue, M. (1997), 'Tone systems in New Guinea'. *Linguistic Typology*, 1, 347–386.

Dryer, M. S. (1997), 'Are grammatical relations universal?' in J. Bybee, J. Haiman and S. A. Thompson (eds), *Essays on Language Function and Language Type: Dedicated to T. Givón*. Amsterdam and Philadelphia, PA: John Benjamins, pp. 115–143.

Dunbar, R. (1996), *Grooming, Gossip and the Evolution of Language*. London: Faber and Faber.

Elman, J., Bates, E. A. and Johnson, M. H. (eds) (1997), *Rethinking Innateness: A Connectionist Perspective on Development*. Cambridge, MA: MIT Press.

Emmorey, K. (2002), *Language, Cognition, and the Brain: Insights from Sign Language Research*. Mahwah, NJ: Lawrence Erlbaum.

Enard, W., Przeworski, M., Fisher, S. E., Lai, C. S., Wiebe, V. Kitano, T., Monaco, A. P. and Pääbo, S. (2002), 'Molecular evolution of FOXP2, a gene involved in speech and language'. *Nature*, 418, 747–757.

Evans, N. (2000), 'Word classes in the world's languages', in G. Booij, C. Lehmann, J. Mugdan, W. Kesselheim and S. Skopeteas (eds), *Morphologie: ein internationales Handbuch zur Flexion und Wortbildung. Morphology: An International Handbook on Inflection and Word-Formation*. Berlin and New York: Mouton de Gruyter, pp. 708–732.

Evans, W. E. and Bastian, J. (1969), 'Marine mammal communication: social and ecological features', in H. T. Anderson, (ed.) *The Biology of Marine Mammals*. New York: Academic Press, pp. 425–475.

Fernald, A. (1985), 'Four-month-old infants prefer to listen to motherese'. *Infant Behaviour and Development*, 8, 181–195.

Fernando, C. (1996), *Idioms and Idiomaticity*. Oxford: Oxford University Press.

Finch, G. (2003), *How to Study Linguistics: A Guide to Understanding Language*. Basingstoke: Palgrave Macmillan.

Finlayson, R. (1995), 'Women's language of respect: isihlonipho sabafazi', in R. Mesthrie (ed.) *Language and Social History: Studies in South African Sociolinguistics*. Cape Town: David Philip, pp. 140–153.

Fitch, W. T. (2000), 'The evolution of speech: a comparative review'. *Trends in Cognitive Science*, 4, 258–267.

Fleischman, J. (2002), *Phineas Gage: A Gruesome but True Story about Brain Science*. Boston, MA: Houghton Mifflin.

Fletcher, P. and MacWhinney, B. (eds) (1996), *The Handbook of Child Language*. Oxford: Blackwell.

Foley, W. A. (1997), *Anthropological Linguistics: An Introduction*. Oxford: Blackwell.

Foley, W. A. (2000), 'The languages of New Guinea'. *Annual Review of Anthropology*, 29, 357–404.

Frawley, W. (ed.) (2003), *International Encyclopedia of Linguistics*. New York: Oxford.

Frisch, K. von. (1992/1973), 'Decoding the language of the bee', in J. Lindsten (ed.) *Nobel Lectures, Physiology or Medicine 1971–1980*. Singapore: World Scientific Publishing Co., pp. 76–87.

Fromkin, V. A. (1973a), 'Slips of the tongue'. *Scientific American*, 229, 110–117.

Fromkin, V. A. (ed.) (1973b), *Speech Errors as Linguistic Evidence*. The Hague: Mouton.

Fromkin, V. A. (ed.) (1980), *Errors in Linguistic Performance: Slips of the Tongue, Ear, Pen, and Hand*. San Diego, CA: Academic Press.

Fromkin, V. A. (1988), 'Grammatical aspects of speech errors', in F. Newmeyer (ed.) *Linguistics: the Cambridge Survey. Volume 2. Linguistic Theory: Extensions and Implications*. Cambridge: Cambridge University Press, pp. 117–138.

Fromkin, V. A. and Rodman, R. (1974), *An Introduction to Language*. New York: Holt, Rinehart and Winston.

Fromkin, V. A., Rodman, R., Hyams, N., Collins, P. and Amberber, M. (2005), *An Introduction to Language*. 5th edition. Melbourne: Thomson.

Gal, S. (1979), *Language Shift: Social Determinants of Linguistic Change in Bilingual Austria*. New York, San Francisco and London: Academic Press.

Gardner, B. and Gardner, A. (1971), 'Two-way communication with an infant chimpanzee', in A. Schrier and F. Stollnitz (eds), *Behavior of Non-human Primates*. Volume 4. New York: Academic Press, pp. 117–184.

Garrett, M. F. (1988), 'Processes in language production', in F. J. Newmeyer (ed.) *Linguistics: the Cambridge Survey, Volume 3. Language: Psychological and Biological Aspects*. Cambridge: Cambridge University Press, pp. 69–98.

Garrod, S. and Pickering, M. (eds) (1999), *Language Processing*. Hove: Psychology Press.

Garry, J. and Rubino, C. (eds), (2001), *Facts about the World's Languages: an Encyclopedia of the World's Major Languages, Past and Present*. New York and Dublin: The HW Wilson Company.

Gass, S. and Selinker, L. (1994), *Second Language Acquisition: An Introductory Course*. Hillsdale, NJ: Lawrence Erlbaum.

Gentner, D. and Goldin-Meadow, S. (eds), (2003), *Language in Mind: Advances in the Study of Language and Thought*. Cambridge, MA: The MIT Press.

Givón, T. and Malle, B. F. (eds), (2002), *The Evolution of Language out of Pre-language*. Amsterdam and Philadelphia, PA: John Benjamins.

Gleason, J. B. and Ratner, N. B. (eds), (1998), *Psycholinguistics*. Belmont: Wadsworth.

Goddard, C. (1998), *Semantic Analysis: A Practical Introduction*. Oxford: Oxford University Press.

Godffrey-Smith, P. (2003), *Theory and Reality: An Introduction to the Philosophy of Science*. Chicago, IL and London: The University of Chicago Press.

Golinkoff, R., Mervis, C. and Hirsh-Pasek, K. (1994), 'Early object labels: the case for a developmental lexical principles framework'. *Journal of Child Language*, 21, 125–155.

Goodall, J. (1986), *The Chimpanzees of Gombe: Patterns of Behaviour*. Cambridge, MA: Harvard University Press.

Gopnik, A., Meltzoff, A. N. and Kuhl, P. K. (2001), *The Scientist in the Crib: What Early Learning Tells us about the Mind*. New York: Perennial.

Gordon, R. G. and Grimes, B. F. (2005), *Ethnologue: Languages of the World*. 15th edn. Dallas, TX: SIL International.

Gray, R. D. and Jordan, F. M. (2000), 'Language trees support the express-train sequence of Austronesian expansion'. *Nature*, 405, 1052–1055.

Greenbaum, S. (1996), *The Oxford English grammar*. Oxford: Oxford University Press.

Greenbaum, S. and Quirk, R. (1990), *A Student's Grammar of the English Language*. Harlow: Longman.

Greenberg, J. H. (1987), *Language in the Americas*. Stanford, CA: Stanford University Press.

Greenberg, J. H., Ferguson, C. A. and Moravcsik, E. A. (1978), *Universals of Human Language*. Stanford, CA: Stanford University Press.

Greenfield, S. A. (2000), *Brain-story*. London: BBC.

Grenoble, L. A. and Whaley, L. J. (eds), (1998), *Endangered Languages: Language Loss and Community Response*. Cambridge: Cambridge University Press.

Grenoble, L. A. and Whaley, L. J. (eds), (2006), *Saving Languages: An Introduction to Language Revitalization*. Cambridge: Cambridge University Press.

Grice, H. P. (1975), 'Logic and conversation', in P. Cole and J. L. Morgan (eds), *Syntax and Semantics 3: Speech Acts*. New York: Academic Press, pp. 41–58.

Grice, H. P. (1989), *Studies in the Way of Words*. Cambridge, MA: Harvard University Press.

Gumperz, J. J. and Levinson, S. C. (eds), (1996), *Rethinking Linguistic Relativity*. Cambridge: Cambridge University Press.

Gussenhoven, C. and Jacobs, H. (1998/2003), *Understanding Phonology*. London: Arnold.

Haas, W. (1957), 'Zero in linguistic description'. *Studies in Linguistic Analysis*. Special Publication of the Philological Society. Oxford: Blackwell, pp. 33–53.

Hadamard, J. (1996/1945), *The Mathematician's Mind: The Psychology of Invention in the Mathematical Field*. Princeton, NJ: Princeton University Press.

Hale, K. L., Krauss, M., Watahomigie, L. J., Yamamoto, A. Y., Craig, C., Jeanne, La V. M. and England, N. C. (1992), 'Endangered languages'. *Language*, 68, 1–42.

Halliday, M. A. K. (1975/1977), *Learning how to Mean: Explorations in the Development of Language and Meaning*. London: Edward Arnold.

Halliday, M. A. K. (1978), *Language as Social Semiotic: The Social Interpretation of Language and Meaning*. London: Arnold.

Halliday, M. A. K. (1985), *An Introduction to Functional Grammar*. London: Edward Arnold.

Hammett, D. (1929/2003), *Red Harvest*. London: Orion Books.

Handke, J. (2000), The Mouton Interactive Introduction to Phonetics and Phonology. CD-ROM. Berlin: Mouton de Gruyter.

Haspelmath, M. (2002), *Understanding Morphology*. London: Arnold.

Haspelmath, M., Dryer, M. S., Gil, D. and Comrie, B. (2005), *The World Atlas of Language Structures*. Oxford: Oxford University Press.

Hawkins, J. A. and Cutler, A. (1988), 'Psycholinguistic factors in morphological asymmetry', in J. A. Hawkins (ed.) *Explaining Language Universals*. Oxford: Basil Blackwell, pp. 280–317.

Hayes, C. (1951), *The Ape in our House*. New York: Harper and Row.

Heath, J. (1978), *Linguistic Diffusion in Arnhem Land*. Canberra: Australian Institute of Aboriginal Studies.

Heider, E. R. (1972), 'Universals in color naming and memory'. *Journal of Experimental Psychology*, 93, 10–20.

Heine, B. (1997), *Possession: Cognitive Sources, Forces, and Grammaticalization*. Cambridge: Cambridge University Press.

Heine, B. (2003), 'Grammaticalization', in B. D. Joseph and R. D. Janda (eds), *The Handbook of Historical Linguistics*. Oxford: Blackwell, pp. 575–601.

Heine, B. and Kuteva, T. (2002), *World Lexicon of Grammaticalization*. Cambridge: Cambridge University Press.

Hengeveld, K., Rijkhoff, J. and Siewierska, A. (2004), 'Parts of speech systems and word order'. *Journal of Linguistics*, 40, 527–570.

Herman, L. M. (ed.) (1980), *Cetacean Behavior: Mechanism and Functions*. New York: John Wiley and Sons.

Herman, L. M., Richards, D. G. and Wolz, J. P. (1984), 'Comprehension of sentences by bottlenosed dolphins'. *Cognition*, 16, 129–219.

Hinton, L., Nichols, J. and Ohala, J. J. (eds), (1994), *Sound Symbolism*. Cambridge: Cambridge University Press.

Hock, H. H. (1991), *Principles of Historical Linguistics*. Berlin, New York and Amsterdam: Mouton de Gruyter.

Hockett, C. F. (1954), 'Two models of grammatical description'. *Word*, 10, 210–234.

Hockett, C. F. (1960), 'The origin of speech'. *Scientific American*, 203, 88–96.

Holm, J. (1988), *Pidgins and Creoles. Volume 1: Theory and Structure*. Cambridge: Cambridge University Press.

Holm, J. (1989), *Pidgins and Creoles. Volume 2: Reference Survey*. Cambridge: Cambridge University Press.

Holmes, J. (1992), *An Introduction to Sociolinguistics*. London: Longman.

Holmes, J. and Meyerhoff, M. (eds), (2003), *The Handbook of Language and Gender*. Oxford: Blackwell.

Hopper, P. and Traugott, E. (2003), *Grammaticalization*. Cambridge: Cambridge University Press.

Horgan, J. (1996), *The End of Science: Facing the Limits of Knowledge in the Twilight of the Scientific Age*. Reading, MA: Helix Books.

Huddleston, R. (1984), *Introduction to the Grammar of English*. Cambridge: Cambridge University Press.

Huddleston, R. and Pullum, G. K. (2002), *The Cambridge Grammar of the English Language*. Cambridge: Cambridge University Press.

Huddleston, R. and Pullum, G. K. (2005), *A Student's Introduction to English Grammar*. Cambridge: Cambridge University Press.

Hudson, G. (2000), *Essential Introductory Linguistics*. Malden, MA and Oxford: Blackwell.

Hudson, R. (1984), *Invitation to Linguistics*. Oxford: Blackwell.

Hughes, A., Trudgill, P. and Watt, D. (2005), *English Accents and Dialects: An Introduction to Social and Regional Varieties of English in the British Isles*. London: Hodder Arnold.

Hurford, J. R. and Heasley, B. (1983), *Semantics: A Coursebook*. Cambridge: Cambridge University Press.

Hurford, J. R., Studdert-Kennedy, M. and Knight, C. (eds), (1998), *Approaches to the Evolution of Language: Social and Cognitive Bases*. Cambridge: Cambridge University Press.

Ingram, J. C. L. (2007), *Neurolinguistics: An Introduction to Spoken Language Processing and its Disorders*. Cambridge: Cambridge University Press.

International Phonetic Association. (1999), *The Handbook of the International Phonetic Association*. Cambridge: Cambridge University Press.

Jakobson, R. (1978), *Six Lectures on Sound and Meaning*. Translated by J. Mepham. Sussex: Harvester Press.

Jakobson, R. and Waugh, L. R. (1979), *The Sound Shape of Language*. Bloomington, IN: Indiana University Press.

Jespersen, O. (1922), *Language: Its Nature, Development and Origin*. London: Allen and Unwin.

Johansson, S. (2005), *Origins of Language: Constraints on Hypotheses*. Amsterdam/Philadelphia, PA: John Benjamins.

Johnston, T. and Schembri, A. (eds), (2003), *The Survival Guide to Auslan: A Beginner's Pocket Dictionary of Australian Sign Language*. Sydney: North Rocks Press.

Joseph, B. D. and Janda, R. D. (eds), (2003), *The Handbook of Historical Linguistics*. Oxford: Blackwell.

Kaminski, J., Call, J. and Fischer, J. (2004), 'Word learning in a domestic dog: evidence for "fast mapping"'. *Science*, 304, 1682–1683.

Kaplan, R. B. (ed.) (2002), *The Oxford Handbook of Applied Linguistics*. Oxford: Oxford University Press.

Kay, P. and Kempson, W. (1984), 'What is the Sapir-Whorf hypothesis?'. *American Anthropologist*, 86, 65–79.

Kempson, R. (2001), 'Pragmatics: language and communication', in M. Aronoff and J. Rees-Miller (eds), *The Handbook of Linguistics*. Oxford: Blackwell Publishers, pp. 394–427.

Kennedy, G. (1998), *An Introduction to Corpus Linguistics*. London and New York: Longman.

Kirkpatrick, E. M. and Schwarz, C. M. (eds), (1995), *The Wordsworth Dictionary of Idioms*. Ware, Hertfordshire: Wordsworth.

Knight, C., Studdert-Kennedy, M. and Hurford, J. R. (eds), (2000), *The Evolutionary Emergence of Language: Social Function and the Origin of Linguistic Form*. Cambridge: Cambridge University Press.

Kolb, B. and Whishaw, I. Q. (1980/2003), *Fundamentals of Human Neuropsychology*. New York: Worth Publishers.

Kroodsma, D. E., Miller, E. H. and Ouellet , H. (eds), (1982), *Communication in Birds*. New York: Academic Press.

Kuhl, P. K. and Iverson, P. (1995), 'Linguistic experience and the "perceptual magnet effect"', in W. Strange (ed.) *Speech Perception and Linguistic Experience: Issues in Cross-language Research*. Baltimore, MD: York Press, pp. 121–154.

Labov, W. (1972), *Sociolinguistic Patterns*. Philadelphia, PA: University of Pennsylvania Press.

Ladefoged, P. (1992), 'Another view of endangered languages'. *Language*, 68, 809–811.

Ladefoged, P. (2001), *Vowels and Consonants: An Introduction to the Sounds of Languages*. Malden, MA: Blackwell.

Ladefoged, P. (2005), *Vowels and Consonants: An Introduction to the Sounds of Languages*. 2nd edn. Malden, MA: Blackwell.

Ladefoged, P. and Maddieson, I. (1996), *The Sounds of the World's Languages*. Oxford: Blackwell.

Langacker, R. W. (1990), *Concept, Image, and Symbol: The Cognitive Basis of Grammar*. Berlin and New York: Mouton de Gruyter.

Langacker, R. W. (1991), 'Cognitive grammar', in F. G. Droste and J. E. Joseph (eds), *Linguistic Theory and Grammatical Description*. Amsterdam: John Benjamins, pp. 275–306.

Langacker, R. W. (1999), *Grammar and Conceptualization*. Berlin and New York: Mouton de Gruyter.

Laver, J. (2001), 'Linguistic phonetics', in M. Aronoff and J. Rees-Miller (eds), *The Handbook of Linguistics*. Oxford: Blackwell Publishers, pp. 150–179.

Lee, P. (1996), *The Whorf Theory Complex: A Critical Reconstruction*. Amsterdam and Philadelphia, PA: John Benjamins.

Lenneberg, E. H. (1967), *Biological Foundations of Language*. New York: Wiley.

Lesser, R. and Milroy, L. (1993), *Linguistics and Aphasia: Psycholinguistic and Pragmatic Aspects of Intervention*. London: Longman.

Levinson, S. C. (1983/1992), *Pragmatics*. Cambridge: Cambridge University Press.

Levinson, S. C. (1995), 'Three levels of meaning', in F. R. Palmer (ed.) *Grammar and Meaning: Essays in Honour of Sir John Lyons*. Cambridge: Cambridge University Press, pp. 90–115.

Levinson, S. C. (1997), 'Language and cognition: the cognitive consequences of spatial description in Guugu Yimithirr'. *Journal of Linguistic Anthropology*, 7, 98–131.

Levinson, S. C. (1999), 'H.P. Grice on location on Rossel Island'. *Berkeley Linguistic Society*, 25, 210–224.

Lieberman, P. (2000), *Human Language and our Reptilian Brain: The Subcortical Bases of Speech, Syntax, and Thought*. Cambridge, MA and London: Harvard University Press.

Lieberman, P. (2003), 'Motor control, speech, and the evolution of human language', in M. H. Christiansen and S. Kirby (eds), *Language Evolution*. Oxford: Oxford University Press, pp. 255–271.

Löbner, S. (2002), *Understanding Semantics*. London: Arnold.

Lockwood, D. G. (2002), *Syntactic Analysis and Description: A Constructional Approach*. London and New York: Continuum.

Loring, D. W., Meador, K., Lee, G., Murro, A., Smith, J., Flanigan, H. and Gallagher, B. (1990), 'Cerebral language lateralization: evidence from intra-carotid amobarbital testing'. *Neuropsychologia*, 28, 831–838.

Lust, B. C. and Foley, C. (eds), (2004), *First Language Acquisition: The Essential Readings*. Malden, MA and Oxford: Blackwell Publishing.

Lyons, J. (1977), *Semantics. Volumes 1 and 2*. Cambridge: Cambridge University Press.

Lyovin, A. V. (1997), *An Introduction to the Languages of the World*. New York and Oxford: Oxford University Press.

MacWhinney, B. (2001), 'First language acquisition', in M. Aronoff and J. Rees-Miller (eds), *The Handbook of Linguistics*. Oxford: Blackwell Publishers, pp. 466–487.

Maddieson, I. (1978), 'Universals of tone', in J. Greenberg, C. A. Ferguson, and E. A. Moravcsik (eds), *Universals of Human Language. Volume 2: Phonology*. Stanford, CA: Stanford University Press, pp. 335–365.

Maddieson, I. (1997/1999), 'Phonetic universals', in W. J. Hardcastle and J. Laver (eds), *The Handbook of Phonetic Sciences*. Oxford: Blackwell, pp. 619–639.

Malinowski, B. (1923/1936), 'The problem of meaning in primitive languages', in C. K. Ogden and I. A. Richards (eds), *The Meaning of Meaning: A Study of the Influence of Language upon Thought and of the Science of Symbolism*. London: Kegan Paul, Trench, Trubner and Co., pp. 296–336.

Malotki, E. (1983), *Hopi Time: A Linguistic Analysis of the Temporal Concepts in the Hopi Language*. Berlin and New York: Mouton de Gruyter.

Marchand, H. (1969), *The Categories and Types of Present-day English Word Formation: A Synchronic-Diachronic Approach*. Munchen: C. H. Beck'sche Verlagsbuchhandlung.

Matras, Y. and Bakker, P. (eds), (2003), *The Mixed Language Debate: Theoretical and Empirical Advances*. Berlin and New York: Mouton de Gruyter.

Matthews, P. H. (1972), *Inflectional Morphology: A Theoretical Study Based on Aspects of Latin Verb Conjugation*. Cambridge: Cambridge University Press.

Matthews, P. H. (1974), *Morphology: An Introduction to the Theory of Word-Structure*. Cambridge: Cambridge University Press.

Matthews, P. H. (1995), 'Syntax, semantics, pragmatics', in F. R. Palmer (ed.) *Grammar and Meaning: Essays in Honour of Sir John Lyons*. Cambridge: Cambridge University Press, pp. 48–60.

Matthews, P. H. (2003), *Linguistics: A Very Short Introduction*. Oxford: Oxford University Press.

Matthews, P. H. (2007), *The Concise Oxford Dictionary of Linguistics*. Oxford: Oxford University Press.

McConvell, P. (1985), 'Domains and codeswitching among bilingual Aborigines', in M. Clyne (ed.) *Australia: Meeting Place of Languages*. Canberra: Pacific Linguistics, pp. 95–125.

McGregor, W. B. (2003), 'Language shift among the Nyulnyul of Dampier Land'. *Acta Linguistica Hafniensia* 35. 115–159.

McNeill, D. (1966), 'Developmental psycholinguistics', in F. Smith and G. Miller (eds), *The Genesis of Language: A Psycholinguistic Approach*. Cambridge, MA: MIT Press, pp. 15–84.

Meakins, F. and O'Shannessy, C. (2004), Shifting functions of ergative case-marking in Light Warlpiri and Gurindji Kriol. Paper presented at the Australian Linguistics Society Conference, Sydney.

Meier, R. and Newport, E. (1990), 'Out of the hands of babes: on a possible sign advantage in language acquisition'. *Language*, 66, 1–23.

Menzel, C. R. (1999), 'Unprompted recall and reporting of hidden objects by a chimpanzee (*Pan troglodytes*) after extended delays'. *Journal of Comparative Psychology*, 113, 426–434.

Mesthrie, R., Swann, J., Deumert, A. and Leap, W. L. (2000), *Introducing Sociolinguistics*. Edinburgh: Edinburgh University Press.

Mey, J. L. (1993), *Pragmatics: An Introduction*. Oxford: Blackwell.

Mithun, M. (1999), *The Languages of Native North America*. Cambridge: Cambridge University Press.

Morton, E. S. and Page, J. (1992), *Animal Talk: Science and the Voices of Nature*. New York: Random House.

Moskowitz, B. A. (1978), 'The acquisition of language'. *Scientific American*, 239, 92–108.

Mous, M. (1994), 'Ma'a or Mbugu', in P. Bakker and M. Mous (eds), *Mixed Languages: 15 Case Studies in Language Intertwining*. Amsterdam: Institute for Functional Research into Language and Language Use (IFOTT), pp. 175–200.

Mühlhäusler, P. (1986), *Pidgin and Creole Linguistics*. Oxford: Blackwell.

Mühlhäusler, P. (1997), *Pidgin and Creole Linguistics*. Westminster Creolistics Series. London: Battlebridge Publications.

Myers-Scotton, C. (1993), *Social Motivations for Codeswitching: Evidence from Africa*. Oxford: Clarendon Press.

Newport, E. and Meier, R. (1985), 'The acquisition of American Sign Language', in D. Slobin (ed.) *The Crosslinguistic Study of Language Acquisition. Volume 1: The Data*. Hillsdale, NJ: Lawrence Erlbaum Associates, pp. 881–938.

Oaks, D. D. (2001), *Linguistics at Work: A Reader of Applications*. Cambridge, MA: Heinle and Heinle (Thomson Learning).

Obler, L. K. and Gjerlow, K. (1999), *Language and the Brain*. Cambridge: Cambridge University Press.

Ochs, E. (1988), *Culture and Language Development: Language Acquisition and Language Socialization in a Samoan Village*. Cambridge: Cambridge University Press.

O'Grady, W., Dobrovolsky, M. and Aronoff, M. (1989), *Contemporary Linguistics: An Introduction*. New York: St Martin's Press.

Onions, C. T. (1966), *The Oxford Dictionary of English Etymology*. Oxford: Oxford University Press.

Parkvall, M. (2006), *Limits of Language*. London and Ahungalla: Battlebridge Publications.

Payne, D. L. and Barshi, I. (eds), (1999), *External Possession*. Amsterdam: John Benjamins.

Petersen, S. E. and Fiez, J. (1993), 'The processing of single words studied with positron emission tomography'. *Annual Review of Neuroscience*, 16, 509–530.

Petersen, S. E., Fox, P. T., Posner, M. I., Mintun, M. and Raichle, M. E. (1989), 'Positron emission tomographic studies of the processing of single words'. *Journal of Cognitive Neuroscience*, 1, 153–170.

Pierce, C. S. (1955), *Philosophical Writings of Pierce*. New York: Dover.

Pike, K. L. (1948), *Tone Languages: A Technique for Determining the Number and Type of Pitch Contrasts in a Language, with Studies in Tonemic Substitution and Fusion*. Ann Arbor, MI: University of Michigan Press.

Pinker, S. (1994), *The Language Instinct: The New Science of Language and Mind*. London: Penguin.

Premack, D. and Premack , A. J. (1993), *The Mind of an Ape*. New York: W.W. Norton.

Pyle, T. and Algeo, J. (1993), *The Origins and Development of the English Language*. Forth Worth, TX: Harcourt Brace Jovanovich.

Rankin, R. L. (2003), 'The comparative method', in B. D. Joseph and R. D. Janda (eds), *The Handbook of Historical Linguistics*. Oxford: Blackwell, pp. 183–212.

Rasmussen, T. and Milner, B. (1977), 'The role of early left-brain injury in determining lateralization of cerebral speech functions'. *Annals of the New York Academy of Sciences*, 299, 355–369.

Reid, N. (1999), Phonetics: An Interactive Introduction. CD-ROM. Armidale: University of New England.

Reid, N. J. (2003), 'Phrasal verb to synthetic verb: recorded morphosyntactic change in Ngan'gityemerri', in N. Evans (ed.) *The non-Pama-Nyungan Languages of Northern Australia: Comparative Studies of the Continent's Most Linguistically Complex Region*. Canberra: Pacific Linguistics, pp. 95–123.

Renfrew, C. (1987), *Archaeology and Language: The Puzzle of Indo-European Origins*. London: Jonathan Cape.

Renfrew, C. (1989), 'The origins of the Indo-European languages'. *Scientific American*, October, 1989, 82–90.

Renfrew, C. (1994), 'World linguistic diversity'. *Scientific American*, January 1994, 104–110.

Richards, D. G., Wolz, J. P. and Herman, L. M. (1984), 'Mimicry of computer-generated sounds and vocal labeling of objects by a bottlenosed dolphin'. *Journal of Comparateve Psychology*, 98, 10–28.

Riggs, P. J. (1992), *Whys and Ways of Science: Introducing Philosophical and Sociological Theories of Science*. Melbourne: Melbourne University Press.

Rijkhoff, J. (2007), 'Word classes'. *Language and Linguistics Compass*, 1, 709–726.

Roberson, D., Davidoff, J., Davies, I. R. L. and Shapiro, L. R. (2005), 'Color categories: evidence for the cultural relativity hypothesis'. *Cognitive Psychology*, 50, 378–411.

Robins, R. H. (1959), 'In defence of WP'. *Transactions of the Philological Society*, 1959, 116–144.

Robins, R. H. (1984), *A Short History of Linguistics*. London and New York: Longman.

Romaine, S. (1995), *Bilingualism*. Oxford: Blackwell.

Romaine, S. (2001), 'Multilingualism', in M. Aronoff and J. Rees-Miller (eds), *The Handbook of Linguistics*. Oxford: Blackwell Publishers, pp. 512–532.

Ross, M. D. (2005), 'Pronouns as a preliminary diagnostic for grouping Papuan languages', in A. Pawley, R. Attenborough, R. Hide and J. Golson (eds), *Papuan Pasts: Cultural, Linguistic and Biological Histories of Papuan-Speaking Peoples*. Canberra: Pacific Linguistics, pp. 15–66.

Ruhl, C. (1989), *On Monosemy: A Study in Linguistic Semantics*. Albany, NY: State University of New York Press.

Ruhlen, M. (1987), *A Guide to the World's Language. Volume 1: Classification*. London: Edward Arnold.

Ruhlen, M. (1991), *A Guide to the World's Language. Volume 1: Classification (with a postscript on recent developments)*. London: Edward Arnold.

Rymer, R. (1994), *Genie: a Scientific Tragedy*. London: HarperPerennial.

Saeed, J. I. (1997), *Semantics*. Oxford: Blackwell.

Sagart, L. (2005), 'Sino-Tibetan–Austronesian: an updated and improved argument', in L. Sagart, R. Blench and A. Sanchez-Mazas (eds), *The Peopling of East Asia: Putting together Archaeology, Linguistics and Genetics*. London: RoutledgeCurzon, pp. 161–176.

Sampson, G. (1997), *Educating Eve: The 'Language Instinct' Debate*. London: Cassell.

Sampson, G. (2005), *The 'Language Instinct' Debate*. London and New York: Continuum.

Sandler, W. and Lillo-Martin, D. (2001), 'Natural sign languages', in M. Aronoff and J. Rees-Miller (eds), *The Handbook of Linguistics*. Oxford: Blackwell Publishers, pp. 533–562.

Sapir, E. (1921), *Language: An Introduction to the Study of Speech*. New York: Harcourt, Brace and World.

Sapir, E. (1929), 'A study in phonetic symbolism'. *Journal of Experimental Psychology*, 12, 225–239.

Saussure, F. de. (1959/1974), *Course in General Linguistics*. Translated by W. Baskin. Glasgow: Collins.

Savage-Rumbaugh, S. and Lewin, R. (1994), *Kanzi: The Ape at the Brink of the Human Mind*. New York: John Wiley.

Saville-Troike, M. (1989), *The Ethnography of Communication: An Introduction*. Oxford: Basil Blackwell.

Schachter, P. and Shopen, T. (2007), 'Parts-of-speech systems', in T. Shopen (ed.) *Language Typology and Syntactic Description. Volume I: Clause Structure*. Cambridge: Cambridge University Press, pp. 1–60.

Seboek, T. A. and Rosenthal, R. (eds), (1980), *The Clever Hans Phenomenon: Communication with Horses, Whales, Apes, and People*. Annals of the New York Academy of Sciences, Volume 364. New York: The New York Academy of Sciences.

Seboek, T. A. and Umiker-Seboek, J. (eds), (1980), *Speaking of Apes: A Critical Anthology of Two-Way Communication with Man*. New York and London: Plenum Press.

Seiler, H. (1983), *Possession as an Operational Dimension of Language*. Tübingen: Narr.

Sheidlower, J. (1995), *The F Word*. New York: Random House.

Shopen, T. (ed.) (2007a), *Language Typology and Syntactic Description. Volume I: Clause Structure*. Cambridge: Cambridge University Press.

Shopen, T. (ed.) (2007b), *Language Typology and Syntactic Description. Volume II: Complex Constructions*. Cambridge: Cambridge University Press.

Shopen, T. (ed.) (2007c), *Language Typology and Syntactic Description. Volume III: Grammatical Categories and the Lexicon*. Cambridge: Cambridge University Press.

Silver, S. and Miller, W. R. (1997), *American Indian Languages: Cultural and Social Contexts*. Tucson, AZ: The University of Arizona Press.

Simpson, J. A. and Weiner, E. S. C. (eds), (1989), *The Oxford English Dictionary*. Oxford: Clarendon Press.

Sinclair, J. (ed.) (1990), *Collins COBUILD English Grammar*. London and Glasgow: Harper Collins.

Skinner, B. F. (1957), *Verbal Behavior*. Englewood Cliffs, NJ: Prentice-Hall.

Slobin, D. I. (ed.) (1985a), *The Crosslinguistic Study of Language Acquisition. Volume 1: The Data*. Hillsdale, NJ and London: Lawrence Erlbaum.

Slobin, D. I. (ed.) (1985b), *The Crosslinguistic Study of Language Acquisition. Volume 2: Theoretical Issues*. Hillsdale, NJ and London: Lawrence Erlbaum.

Slobin, D. I. (ed.) (1992), *The Crosslinguistic Study of Language Acquisition. Volume 3*. Hillsdale, NJ and London: Lawrence Erlbaum.

Slobin, D. I. (1996a), 'From "thought and language" to "thinking for speaking"', in J. J. Gumperz and S. C. Levinson (eds), *Rethinking Linguistic Relativity*. Cambridge: Cambridge University Press, pp. 70–96.

Slobin, D. I. (1996b), 'Two ways to travel: verbs of motion in English and Spanish', in M. Shibatani and S. Thompson (eds), *Grammatical Constructions: Their Form and Meaning*. Oxford: Clarendon Press, pp. 195–219.

Slobin, D. I. (ed.) (1997a), *The Crosslinguistic Study of Language Acquisition. Volume 4*. Hillsdale, NJ and London: Lawrence Erlbaum.

Slobin, D. I. (ed.) (1997b), *The Crosslinguistic Study of Language Acquisition. Volume 5: Expanding the Contexts*. Hillsdale, NJ and London: Lawrence Erlbaum.

Snow, C. E. (1995), 'Issues in the study of input: finetuning, universality, individual and developmental differences, and necessary causes', in P. Fletcher and B. MacWhinney (eds), *The Handbook of Child Language*. Oxford: Blackwell, pp. 180–193.

Song, J. J. (2001), *Linguistic Typology: Morphology and Syntax*. Harlow: Longman.

Speake, J. (2002), *The Oxford Dictionary of Idioms*. Oxford: Oxford University Press.

Spears, R. A. (ed.) (1990), *NTC's American Idioms Dictionary*. Lincolnwood, IL: National Textbook Company.

Spencer, A. (2001), 'Morphology', in M. Aronoff and J. Rees-Miller (eds), *The Handbook of Linguistics*. Oxford: Blackwell Publishers, pp. 213–237.

Spencer, A. and Zwicky, A. M. (eds), (1998/2001), *The Handbook of Morphology*. Oxford: Blackwell.

Stemmer, B. and Whitaker, H. (eds), (1998), *Handbook of Neurolinguistics*. New York: Academic Press.

Strozer, J. R. (1994), *Language Acquisition after Puberty*. Washington, DC: Georgetown University Press.

Talmy, L. (2003), 'Concept structuring systems in language', in M. Tomasello (ed.) *The New Psychology of Language: Cognitive and Functional Approaches to Language Structure. Volume 2*. Mahwah, NJ and London: Lawrence Erlbaum, pp. 15–46.

Talmy, L. (2007), 'Lexical typologies', in T. Shopen (ed.) *Language Typology and Syntactic Description. Volume III: Grammatical Categories and the Lexicon*. Cambridge: Cambridge University Press, pp. 66–168.

Terrace, H. S. (1979), *Nim: A Chimpanzee who Learned Sign Language*. New York: Knopf.

Terrace, H. S., Petitto, L. A., Sanders, R. J. and Bever, T. G. (1979), 'Can an ape create a sentence'. *Science*, 206, 891–902.

Thomas, J. (1995), *Meaning in Interaction: An Introduction to Pragmatics*. London and New York: Longman.

Thomason, S. G. and Kaufman, T. (1988), *Language Contact, Creolization, and Genetic Linguistics*. Berkeley and Los Angeles, CA and London: University of California Press.

Todd, L. (1990), *Pidgins and Creoles*. London: Routledge.

Tomasello, M. (1999), *The Cultural Origins of Human Cognition*. Cambridge, MA: Harvard University Press.

Tomasello, M. (2003a), *Constructing a Language: A Usage-Based Theory of Language Acquisition*. Cambridge, MA and London: Harvard University Press.

Tomasello, M. (2003b), 'The key is social cognition', in D. Gentner and S. Goldin-Meadow (eds), *Language in Mind: Advances in the Study of Language and Thought*. Cambridge, MA: The MIT Press, pp. 47–57.

Tomlin, R. (1986), *Basic Word Order: Functional Principles*. London: Croom Helm.

Trask, R. L. (1998), *Key Concepts in Language and Linguistics*. London: Routledge.

Trask, R. L. (1999), *Language: The Basics*. London and New York: Routledge.

Traugott, E. C. (2003), 'Constructions in grammaticalization', in B. D. Joseph and R. D. Janda (eds), *The Handbook of Historical Linguistics*. Oxford: Blackwell, pp. 624–647.

Traxler, M. J. and Gernsbacher, M. A. (eds), (2006), *Handbook of Psycholinguistics: Second Edition*. Amsterdam: Academic Press.

Trudgill, P. (1986), *Dialects in Contact*. Oxford: Basil Blackwell.

Tsunoda, T. (2005), *Language Endangerment and Language Revitalisation*. Berlin: Mouton de Gruyter.

Upfield, A. (1953/1958), *Murder must Wait*. London: Pan Books.

Vakhtin, N. (2002), 'Language death prognosis: a critique of judgement'. *SKY Journal of Linguistics*, 15, 239–250.

Van Valin, R. D. (2001a), 'Functional linguistics', in M. Aronoff and J. Rees-Miller (eds), *The Handbook of Linguistics*. Oxford: Blackwell Publishers, pp. 319–336.

Van Valin, R. D. (2001b), *An Introduction to Syntax*. Cambridge: Cambridge University Press.

Wasow, T. (2001), 'Generative grammar', in M. Aronoff and J. Rees-Miller (eds), *The Handbook of Linguistics*. Oxford: Blackwell Publishers, pp. 295–318.

Wescott, R. (1980), *Sound and Sense: Linguistic Essays on Phonosemic Subjects*. Lake Bluff, IL: Jupiter Press.

Whaley, L. J. (1997), *Introduction to Typology*. Thousand Oaks, CA: Sage.

Whitney, P. (1998), *The Psychology of Language*. Boston, MA: Houghton Mifflin.

Whorf, B. L. (1956), *Language, Thought and Reality: Selected Writings of Benjamin Lee Whorf*. Cambridge, MA: MIT Press.

Williams, J. M. (1975), *Origins of the English Language: A Social and Linguistic History*. New York: Free Press.

Wray, A. (ed.) (2002), *The Transition to Language*. Oxford: Oxford University Press.

Wurm, S. A. (ed.) (1975), *New Guinea Area Languages and Language Study. Volume 1: Papuan Languages and the New Guinea Linguistic Scene*. Canberra: Pacific Linguistics.

Yule, G. (1996), *Pragmatics*. Oxford: Oxford University Press.

Yule, G. (2006), *The Study of Language*. Cambridge: Cambridge University Press.

Zuckermann, G. (2006), 'Israeli as a semi-engineered Semito-European language: multiple causation, forms and patterns'. Unpublished manuscript.

Language Index

Name Index

Subject Index